AOL
IN A NUTSHELL

A Desktop Guide to America Online™

AOL
IN A NUTSHELL

A Desktop Guide to America Online™

Curt Degenhart & Jen Muehlbauer

O'REILLY™

Cambridge · Köln · Paris · Sebastopol · Tokyo

AOL in a Nutshell: A Desktop Guide to America Online™

by Curt Degenhart and Jen Muehlbauer

Copyright © 1998 O'Reilly & Associates, Inc. All rights reserved.
Printed in the United States of America.

Published by O'Reilly & Associates, Inc., 101 Morris Street, Sebastopol, CA 95472.

Editors: D.C. Denison and Tim O'Reilly

Production Editor: Jane Ellin

Printing History:

   June 1998:   First Edition.

This book is printed on acid-free paper with 85% recycled content, 15% post-consumer waste. O'Reilly & Associates is committed to using paper with the highest recycled content available consistent with high quality.

ISBN: 1-56592-424-X   [7/98]

Table of Contents

Part II: Communicating

Part III: Getting Information

Part IV: Getting Organized

Part V: Becoming an AOL Power User

Part VI: Configuration

Preface

Look closely at the book in your hands. You might notice that it's missing something: a blue AOL logo. You might call *AOL in a Nutshell* the "unauthorized biography" of AOL. It may not be objective at all times—as longtime AOL users, we have our biases—but it is always editorially independent. We teach you how to maximize AOL's potential, but we refuse to sugarcoat AOL's flaws in the process. As far as we know, this is the only AOL book that isn't a covert advertisement for the service.

Traditionally, AOL books target novices. This book, as part of the "In a Nutshell" series, has a wider audience. Nutshell books are geared towards users who know a little, but want to know more, and people who know a lot, but could use a reference for when they get stuck.

AOL in a Nutshell is designed to get under the skin of AOL. It's for the curious AOL user who wants to go deeper into a particular feature or get advice on how to carry out a specific task. We tell you everything, including the things that aren't obvious and the things that AOL hides from you. AOL, in its quest to be user-friendly, has buried some of its power under an easy interface. We help you unlock AOL's potential.

Who Should Use This Book?

If you're using AOL at a basic level, we show you how to get more out of AOL's service and its software; you can use *AOL in a Nutshell* to get some background about every feature AOL offers. On the other hand, if you feel you've outgrown AOL, we show you how to make it work as well as—or better than!—any other Internet service providers. This book takes you further inside the service and the software. It gives you the straight pros and cons of particular features and the in-depth information you need to know.

There are many types of AOL users: people who have been with AOL for years but use it only to send email; sophisticated beginners; computer experts with children who use AOL; experienced users who are bored with AOL; disgruntled users who can list at least five things about AOL that annoy them, but who aren't ready to quit. No matter what kind of user you are, we've got answers for you.

Contents

This book is organized around seven parts, including several appendices. In general, the earlier parts cover essential basics, and later parts include more advanced topics.

Part I, Getting Going

If you're just setting up AOL, we take you through the first steps. Included are chapters on installing the software, signing on, creating screen names and passwords, and touring the new 4.0 menubar and toolbar.

Part II, Communicating

Above all, people go online to communicate more quickly and effectively. We start this part out with email, the Internet's essential, most utilized service. Then, to make sure you've got all modes of online communication covered, we've got full chapters on Buddy Lists, Instant Messages, Chat, message boards, mailing lists, and newsgroups. We include netiquette, too, since everyone online could use a refresher in the dos and don'ts of online behavior. Miss Manners would be proud.

Part III, Getting Information

There's so much out there, who wouldn't need a little help finding it all? This part will help you search for and find information on AOL and the Web, and we include a directory to AOL's main content areas and landmark web sites.

Part IV, Getting Organized

AOL gives you a couple of ways to help you get organized, features that are often overlooked or under-utilized. We explain how to make Favorite Places and the Personal Filing Cabinet more useful, even indispensable.

Part V, Becoming an AOL Power User

You don't have to know it all or be a geek to want to learn how to speed up your online experience or get more out of AOL. This part helps you optimize how you use AOL and all its features. Chapter 23, *Web Publishing and FTP*, covers how to get your stuff up on the Web. The chapter on keyboard shortcuts helps save time and wear and tear on your wrists. We also cover the benefits (and the drawbacks) of downloading files, using Automatic AOL, billing, and Telnet. In addition, we direct you to vendors of third-party software that help you modify or extend AOL's standard ways of doing things.

Part VI, Configuration

The chapters in this part detail all the ways to get AOL to work the way you want. This part covers the basics of setting up your account, as well as the details you need to know about hardware, modems, access numbers, parental controls, account preferences, and canceling and suspending your AOL membership. Many of you might be especially interested in the chapter about online privacy: we strive to help you stay clear-headed and aware of how you use and distribute your personal information online.

Part VII, Appendixes

Here's the bonus information that serves as a reference when you really need it or just because you're curious. Included is some help comparing AOL to other ISPs. There's a comprehensive list of file extensions—those three-letter codes that make up filenames, such as *.zip*, *.exe*, and *.doc*. We list scores of top-level domain names, which are the parts of Internet addresses such as *.com*, *.org*, and *.net*. Finally, we provide a synopsis of AOL's own Terms of Service (TOS) so you can easily refer to the rules of the road AOL has for its subscribers.

How to Use This Book

AOL in a Nutshell may be a technical reference, but we've tried to make it easy to use. In the Contents section above, we showed you a bit about the book's seven parts, each part a collection of related chapters on specific aspects of AOL. While related chapters are grouped together, you need not read each part in its entirety. You can skip from chapter to chapter, depending on what you need to learn.

Using the Chapters

Most of this book uses a familiar narrative structure. In Part I, the chapters are intended to be read sequentially (although you can certainly skim material you already know or that isn't immediately relevant).

Some of the chapters in Part I and select chapters throughout the rest of the book use a more unusual reference format consisting of a brief overview, followed by a set of alphabetically organized reference entries.

Each chapter's introduction serves as a compass and guide to all of the information therein. We point out important information for beginners and essential tips for everyone. If you want to explore an unfamiliar topic, or dig deeper into a topic you already know something about, we encourage you to read an entire chapter, from start to finish.

Once you've noted the information for both beginners and advanced users in each chapter's introduction, you can move on to the inner working of the chapters. Here's where *AOL in a Nutshell* acts as a reference. The main contents of each chapter are often organized like an almanac or encyclopedia: specific points are listed alphabetically, or listed so that easier material comes first, followed by more advanced entries.

When you have a particular problem or question, you should go to the proper chapter, perhaps read the introductory material, and then skip directly to the information you need in the reference section. Once you've found the entry that addresses your concern, you'll find a navigational path of action and explanatory material. The navigational path tells what you need to do in AOL to get to the feature described.

It is also a good idea to refer to the index when you have a particular problem. That way, you can follow up on a topic in chapters where you may not have thought to look initially.

The Choice Is Yours

Use *AOL in a Nutshell* as a tutorial, as a refresher course, or as an encyclopedic reference. Of course, another way to use this book is to read it from cover to cover. While this probably isn't what experienced users want, we certainly won't stop you! In using it this way, you'll probably learn ways to do things you never thought possible on AOL.

About Platforms and Versions

We've been through more than a few AOL software upgrades, on more than a few platforms, and we've applied that hard-earned experience to this book. We decided to write the book using the latest version of AOL, AOL 4.0 for Windows 95/98.

We want to emphasize, however, that there's plenty of valuable information in this book for AOLers who use a Macintosh or earlier versions of the AOL software. Many of the features we discuss, like Buddy Lists, newsgroups, and Favorite Places, apply equally to all platforms and versions. Problems such as privacy and spam exist across the board (though newer versions sometimes have better tools to combat these problems). AOL is essentially the same service no matter how you enter it. As long as you aren't trying to access AOL via your car radio, we promise you'll find plenty of insight and information between these covers.

Fortunately, keywords are the great equalizer. Every keyword we mention works whether you're using, say, AOL 4.0 for Windows 95/98, AOL 3.0 for Windows 3.x, or AOL 2.7, 3.0, or 4.0 for Macintosh. If a keyword doesn't work, it's almost certainly because AOL has changed it recently, not because your software is too old.

If You're Using a Mac

Why did we focus on the Windows 95/98 version of AOL? It's not because we're partial to Emperor Gates (we are staunchly platform-neutral), but because we've seen how AOL has recently been focusing its development efforts on Windows-compatible versions of its software. There's no mystery here: although AOL began with a distinct Apple orientation, the percentage of Windows-compatible AOL members has grown steadily. Currently, Windows users are a strong, almost overwhelming, majority, and AOL wants to make them happy first. That means that every new AOL version arrives first for the Windows crowd. The Mac version is always promised (and sometimes delivered) a few months down the road.

AOL is developing AOL 4.0 for the Macintosh. The interface is similar to the Windows version of 4.0. We've used Windows screenshots, but AOL 4.0 for the Mac will probably look the same. Throughout the book, you'll have to substitute the `Command` key whenever we tell you to use the `Control` (`CTRL`) key—no big deal. But until AOL rolls out 4.0 for Macs, follow our advice for users of older software.

If You're Using Older Software

We know that many members still use AOL 3.0, and that some members will be reluctant to upgrade to 4.0. However, our experience has shown that most people eventually convert from old to new software. We suspect that if you're not using AOL 4.0 now, you will be soon (and if you're not using 3.0 yet, what are you waiting for?). If you're on a PC, and your computer can handle an upgrade (see also Chapter 26, *System Requirements*), we urge you to try AOL 4.0. Its new features actually do help you get more out of your AOL experience.

Members using AOL 3.0 will notice one big inconsistency in this book: our *paths of action* (the series of clicks that take you to a destination) don't usually apply to your version of AOL. Since the AOL 4.0 toolbar is completely new, many of our paths start with icons (such as `My AOL`) that don't exist in older versions of the software. However, as we mentioned earlier, keywords work the same on all platforms. Use keywords whenever possible to get where you're going faster, and with less confusion.

There are some similarities between the AOL 4.0 and 3.0 interfaces. The 3.0 `Members` menu contains some of the same items as the 4.0 `My AOL` toolbar icon and `People` toolbar icon. The `Mail` menu in 3.0 is roughly equivalent to the `Mail Center` toolbar icon in 4.0. The `File`, `Edit`, `Window`, `Sign Off`, and `Help` menus have many of the same features in both 3.0 and 4.0. If a feature (such as `Switch Screen Name`) is missing from your AOL, it's because the feature is 4.0-specific.

Conventions Used in This Book

`Constant Width`
: is used to denote items found onscreen, such as clickable buttons, checkboxes, tabs, window titles, menus, and drop-down lists. It is also used for commands, code fragments and examples, and keyboard keys.

`Constant italic`
: is used for replaceable text you fill in yourself, such as `filename`. Using this convention will be obvious when you're actually following the path on AOL.

Italic
: is used for filenames, newsgroups, Internet addresses, URLs, email addresses, and terms being used for the first time.

Bold italic

>is used to refer you to reference the alphabetical sections in Chapters 6, 8, 14, and 20 of the book, such as ***keyword help*** or ***Members Helping Members***.

Indented paths of action

>Special indented paths are used when we lay out the steps of an action to take you to a particular feature within AOL. Arrows (→) are placed between steps in the path you should follow; when you're done with one step, follow the arrow to the next step. Again, items that you see onscreen or that are clickable are in `Constant Width`. For example:
>
>`My AOL toolbar icon` → `Preferences` → `General` → check the box `Display Channels at Sign On`
>
>This path is shorthand for "Click the `My AOL` toolbar icon. Select `Preferences` from the drop-down menu. Click the `General` icon that appears. Check the `Display Channels at Sign On` box." See how much shorter the path is than explaining exactly when to click and check something?

Request for Comments

AOL, like most of the online universe, changes its look-and-feel fairly frequently. We've made every attempt to publish the most up-to-date book possible, but errors happen. Please help us to improve future editions of this book by reporting any such errors, inaccuracies, misleading or confusing statements, and plain old typos that you find anywhere in this book. Email your comments to us at:

>*bookquestions@ora.com.*

Please also let us know what we can do to make this book more useful to you (we're sorry, we can't actually change AOL). We joke around a lot in this book, but we take your comments seriously. We will try to incorporate reasonable suggestions into future editions.

You can write us at:

>O'Reilly & Associates, Inc.
>101 Morris Street
>Sebastapol, CA 95472

Telephone:

>800-998-9938 (in the U.S. or Canada)
>707-829-0515 (international/local)
>707-829-0104 (Fax)

To be put on the mailing list or request a catalog, send email to:

>*nuts@ora.com.*

Acknowledgments

We offer our thanks to the many people who were instrumental in making this book happen. Thanks to our sidekick and managing editor at Songline, D.C. Denison, who guided us and kept our spirits up as we slowly circled with new ideas and revisions. Thanks to our editor Tim O'Reilly for his sagacity and even-handed assistance with large issues of organization and perspective. Dale Dougherty deserves special mention for allowing us the many months to write.

Thanks to Mike Sierra for providing us with the necessary templates and much needed formatting wisdom, even though it was beyond his call of duty.

Thanks to Edie Freedman for designing the cover (roar!) and winning points for coming up with the book's subtitle. Nancy Priest deserves a merit badge for helping to overcome obstacles with internal formatting. Robert Romano created the figures and put up with us when they all had to be moved around in the book.

Jane Ellin was the Production Editor, who navigated around bulleted lists, poor handwriting, and frighteningly long figure captions; we hope her fingers survived. Nancy Wolfe Kotary and Clairemarie Fisher O'Leary did valuable quality control. Seth Maislin and Marie Rizzo wrote the index, giving a new meaning to the term "detailed."

Thanks also to our fearless freelancers, Sebastian Banker, Susan Reinbold, Will Plummer, and Kimo Carter, who helped turn mounds of marked-up pages into the book you are holding.

Thanks to Sheryl Avruch for her patience, understanding, and flexibility as the deadlines came and went.

Jennifer Alexander answered all our nudgnik computer questions, and kept our puny 486s up and running.

Our tech reviewers offered indispensable advice and helped us clarify a lot of items in the chapters. Our sincerest thanks to: Cathy Miner, Robert Denn, Frank Willison, Kim Brown, Cathy Pate, and Jan Gardner.

In addition, Michael Pureka lent his MU* expertise to the Telnet chapter, and Jesse Vincent made sure we had our top-level domain names straight in Appendix C.

PART I

Getting Going

Part I of this book gets you on AOL and helps you understand what you'll see when you get there. We tell you the practical things, like how to install your AOL software, sign on, choose your screen name and password, and navigate the service. We'll also explain how to translate "net speak" into English, and where to find help when you need it. Some of this information is particularly important for beginners, but a lot of it will help anyone who has just upgraded to AOL 4.0.

No matter how long you've been on AOL, don't miss Chapter 7, *Essential AOL Survival Tips*. You might be surprised how easy it is to break AOL of its annoying habits. Now if only it were that easy with roommates and family.

Chapter 1, *Introduction*: A brief history of AOL, and what every beginner needs to know.

Chapter 2, *Installing and Upgrading*: Get it right the first time with our step-by-step guide.

Chapter 3, *Screen Names, Passwords, and Signing On*: Your screen name establishes your AOL identity. Your password protects it.

Chapter 4, *Getting Around AOL: Toolbars and Menus*: AOL's toolbar and menu options in a nutshell.

Chapter 5, *Online Shorthand*: LOL, BRB, :-D, AFK...WTH? Figure it out here.

Chapter 6, *Help from AOL*: AOL's online help is quick and dirty, but sometimes it's necessary.

Chapter 7, *Essential AOL Survival Tips*: How to keep AOL from driving you crazy.

CHAPTER 1

Introduction

If you haven't heard of AOL, we wonder what cave you've been living in (and can we spend our vacations there?). AOL is ubiquitous. Like Microsoft and the President, AOL is a powerful entity that everyone has an opinion about: people love AOL, hate AOL, or both.

AOL began its road to omnipresence in 1985, when the Web didn't even exist. CEO Steve Case's goal was to make the online world accessible to everyone, even those who found computers intimidating. AOL was the first online service to be graphical instead of text-based, and people responded with enthusiasm.

Case has stuck with his philosophy that getting online should be a piece of cake, and 11 million members later (at last count), it looks like he was right. We're not sure why AOL beat out the other major online services, Prodigy and CompuServe, which also developed graphical interfaces and were easy to use. Maybe it's because AOL's graphical interface was the first one out of the gate, or because they mailed out so many free disks, people thought, "Why not give the little guy a try?"

Whatever the reason, we can safely say that AOL beat its competition. Since adding Internet access to its service, AOL has been struggling to beat the Internet service provider (ISP) competition, too. AOL is now the largest single provider of Internet access in the United States, and it is steadily expanding into the international market. To many people's surprise, AOL is winning the ISP war, and it doesn't look like anyone is going to catch up any time soon.

That's why AOL is important. Whether we like it or not, everybody knows somebody who's on AOL. For many people, AOL is synonymous with "the Internet" and "the Web." AOL is the only way many people have experienced email, chat, newsgroups, and mailing lists. It deserves a closer look than most AOL guidebooks give it.

Like anything popular, AOL has a lot of hype to cut through before you get to the truth. AOL itself constantly says how great it is: "It's so easy to use, no wonder it's number one!" What AOL doesn't tell you is that the simplicity its members love often comes at the expense of the latest features and the best technology. On the other hand, AOL's foes insist that it's "not a real ISP," and can't stop talking about how much AOL stinks. The anti-AOL camp isn't telling the whole story either; there are some powerful features hidden under that user-friendly interface—you just have to know where to look. We think that after you've used this book for a while, you'll know what's truly good about AOL and what isn't.

If you've used AOL before, you can skip the rest of this introduction and dive right into the chapters that interest you. If you need to brush up on the basics, read the rest of this chapter first.

Getting Familiar with the AOL Interface

There are many facets of the AOL interface that aren't intuitive, even to long-time Internet aficionados who are using AOL for the first time. AOL's interface is graphical, which means you get around by pointing, clicking, and dragging with your mouse—not by typing with your keyboard. The only time you type a navigational task on AOL is when you type a word into a keyword box (see the section "What Are These Things Called Keywords?").

If you've used Windows or a Mac before, you've used a graphical interface. In this book, we focus on AOL 4.0 for Windows 95/98. You'll recognize a lot of standard elements that are present in all Windows programs, including drop-down menus and graphical icons (File, Edit, and some AOL-specific ones). Just as with Windows programs, you can minimize and maximize AOL windows, cut and paste text, and use an offline help directory.

The sections that follow take you step by step through AOL 4.0's graphical interface.

What Can You Click?

Though AOL is riddled with clickable icons, buttons, and text, you won't see the words "click here" very often. The cardinal rule is: if your cursor arrow turns into a hand when you move the mouse over something, you can click it and it does something. In general, when you click something, you'll go to another area on AOL, or you'll open a web page. An example of mild-mannered text that passes what we call the "Hand Test" is shown in Figure 1-1.

There are some exceptions to the Hand Test, such as the Favorite Places heart (see also Chapter 17, *Favorite Places*) and the tiny Windows maximize and minimize buttons in the upper-right of most windows. You can click these items even though they fail the Hand Test.

Almost every graphical image with a border around it is clickable, such as the icons on the right in Figure 1-1. Text is often clickable; if text is blue and underlined, you *know* it's clickable. Clickable icons can be circular, square, rectangular—when in doubt, click! If you have no idea what to click on at first, just click on something and see what happens—it's not going to kill you! With a

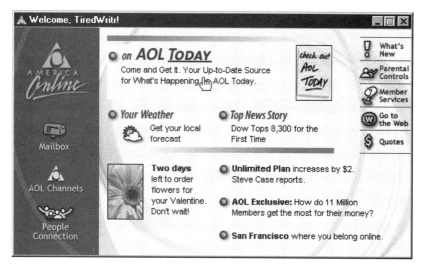

Figure 1-1: If it turns your mouse pointer into a hand, you can click it

little experimentation and experience, you'll soon "just know" when something is clickable.

What Are These Things Called Keywords?

Keywords are the fastest, easiest way to navigate AOL. Type in a word or a phrase, and you're taken directly to the area. Keywords are shortcuts: you needn't follow an endless trail of clickable icons. It's like being "beamed up" in *Star Trek*: there's no travel time.

In this book, we usually supply a keyword if there is one. This is your best route to a feature. In addition, we provide a navigational path of action as a way of getting around. Use navigational paths if you've forgotten the keyword.

Getting a keyword box

To use a keyword, type it into any keyword box. In AOL 4.0, there are three different ways to get a keyword box:

- The best way is to call up a keyword box using your keyboard. You need to do what's called a CTRL-k: that is, hold down the CTRL key on your key-board and type the letter k. Figure 1-2 is an example of a keyword box that's been called up using CTRL-k.

- Click the Keyword icon on the lower part of the AOL navigational bar (see Figure 1-5). This will bring up a Keyword box.

- Type the keyword directly into the large white box on the navigational bar (see Figure 1-5). This is the box that says Type Keyword or Web address here and click Go.

Figure 1-2: Using a keyword to go directly to an AOL area

Using keywords versus following paths: an example

Just to make sure you understand the difference between using a path to get somewhere and using a keyword, here's a real-world example:

- *Following a path*: Let's say you need some information about running. Because AOL is so hierarchical, you could go to the Channels menu, click Sports, then click More Sports, then scroll down until you see Running/ Track & Field, then double-click it. It's fairly easy to find what you wanted, but it could be easier.

- *Using a Keyword*: To go directly to the Running area, enter the word *running* in any Keyword box, hit Enter, and you're there!

Welcome!

The first thing you'll see when you sign on to AOL is the Welcome screen. In AOL 4.0, the Welcome screen looks something like Figure 1-3.

Some of the features of the Welcome screen change daily, but some are a permanent part of AOL's interface—as permanent as any online entity is, anyway. Some of the features of the Welcome screen, as numbered in Figure 1-3, are:

1. The AOL logo itself: Click it to see a postcard, your horoscope, and other random diversions (also found at Keyword: Delights).

2. Your Weather icon: Click it to get your local forecast. Your location is determined by your access numbers, so Your Weather won't work if you're connecting via TCP/IP (see also Chapter 27, *Connecting*).

3. Mailbox icon: Click it to open your new mail (also found by using CTRL-r).

4. AOL Channels icon: Click it to bring up the Channels screen (see the next section, "The Channels Screen") (also found at Keyword: Channels).

5. People Connection icon: Click it to go to the main area for AOL chat rooms (also found at Keyword: People) (see also Chapter 10, *Chatting*).

6. Special Feature: This icon and its text change, depending on what AOL chooses to feature.

7. Top News Story icon: Click it to visit AOL's News Channel (also found at Keyword: News).

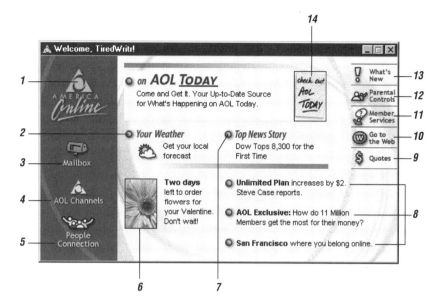

Figure 1-3: AOL's Welcome screen

8. Potpourri: These three buttons and their text change depending on what AOL wants to highlight. Count on one of them to be a link to the area for your nearest city.

9. Quotes icon: Click it to get stock quotes or view your online portfolio (also found at Keyword: Quotes).

10. Go to the Web icon: Click it to open a web browser (also found at Keyword: Web).

11. Member Services icon: Click it to visit AOL's main help area (also found at Keyword: Help).

12. Parental Controls icon: Click it to learn about and adjust Parental Controls (also found at Keyword: Parental Controls) (see also Chapter 28, *Parental Controls*).

13. What's New icon: Click it for a list of new content and features (also found at Keyword: New).

14. Check out AOL Today: Link to news and special features that vary as the day progresses (also at Keyword: Today).

The Channels Screen

The Channels screen pops up automatically when you sign on to AOL. It shows you AOL's Channels, which are AOL's way of dividing and organizing its content. For our take on AOL Channels and the content they contain, see Chapter 15, *AOL Content Reference*.

There is also a Find icon on the Channels screen; clicking it takes you to Find Central (Keyword: Find Central). Find Central contains a Channel guide; tools for searching AOL and the Web; and help finding software, online events, and people.

Your Channels screen will look like Figure 1-4. If you get tired of having the Channels screen pop up every time you sign on, see how to turn it off in the section "General" in Chapter 29, *Preferences*.

Figure 1-4: AOL's Channels screen

Toolbars and Menus

Throughout this book, we refer to *toolbar icons* and *menus*. These are options on the new AOL 4.0 toolbar, which is shown in Figure 1-5.

Figure 1-5: AOL 4.0's toolbar

1. *Menus* are the text options at the top of the toolbar: File, Edit, Window, Sign Off (or Sign On, if you're already signed off), and Help. If you click on any of these menus, such as File, a list of menu items drops down. To

select a menu item, move your mouse pointer over it and click. When we refer to menus and menu items in this book, it may look something like this:

`File` menu → `Save As`

That means you should click `File`, move your mouse down to `Save As`, and click.

2. *Toolbar icons* are the graphical buttons on the toolbar: `Read`, `Write`, `Mail Center`, `Print`, `My Files`, `My AOL`, `Favorites`, `Internet`, `Channels`, `People`, `Quotes`, `Perks`, and `Weather`. Some of the toolbar icons (`Read`, `Write`, `Print`, `Quotes`, `Perks`, and `Weather`) are just buttons you can click to open a window or go to an AOL area. The rest of the toolbar icons (`Mail Center`, `My Files`, `My AOL`, `Favorites`, `Internet`, `Channels`, and `People`) have arrows on them. Toolbar icons with arrows on them function like menus: when you click one, it drops down a list of options. To select an option, move your mouse over the option and click it. When we refer to toolbar icons in this book, it may look something like this:

`My Files` toolbar icon → `Personal Filing Cabinet`

That means you should click the button that says `My Files` on it, move your mouse down to `Personal Filing Cabinet`, and click.

If you have no idea what a toolbar icon does, hold your mouse pointer over it. A box with a short explanation will appear. For a fuller explanation, see Chapter 4, *Getting Around AOL: Toolbars and Menus,* for detailed explanations of every menu item and toolbar icon.

Is It AOL? Or Is It the Web?

It might be easier to tell if it's live or if it's Memorex. AOL used to clearly label web links as such, but they don't do that much anymore. As a result, it's not always clear whether you're on AOL or on the Web. Some areas look like web pages and have web browser interfaces, but don't have a web address and are actually proprietary AOL areas. Some areas have proprietary AOL front screens, but following any of that area's links takes you to the Web. Some areas are touted as part of AOL's content but are actually entirely web-based.

This blending of AOL content with web content can be convenient as well as confusing. For instance, you can enter a URL (web address), such as *http:// www.songline.com,* in a keyword box and go right to that web page.

AOL 4.0 adds a dual-purpose keyword box and URL window in the third row of the toolbar. In this special box, you can type both keywords and URLs. To go to the Web, you don't have to type *http://* into the dual-purpose keyword box, as you would if you typed a URL into the `CTRL-k` keyword box. For more on this new feature, see Chapter 4.

It usually doesn't matter whether you're on AOL or on the Web. The situations when it would matter are:

• You have children whose web access you've blocked, or are a child whose web access has been blocked (see also Chapter 28).

- You rely on AOL's Terms of Service (TOS) to provide you with an inoffensive/homogenized online experience. The Web isn't regulated by TOS (see also Appendix D, *Terms of Service*).

- You prefer to use a web browser other than AOL's (see also the section "Using Alternate Browsers" in Chapter 16, *The Web*).

Finding What You Need

If you don't know the right keyword and you don't feel like browsing through the Channels, remember that you can always search AOL content at `Keyword: AOL Find`. For a more extensive look at searching for information online, see Chapter 14, *Finding & Searching*.

All About Netiquette

Before you plunge into the world of online communication, you should understand the concept of *netiquette*. Netiquette, a conjunction formed from the words network and etiquette, is the system of voluntary rules and practices that most people on the Internet use to get along. Basically, netiquette keeps us from killing each other. And it's a good thing, too, that so many people understand the common practices that keep the Internet running pretty smoothly. We say pretty smoothly because there's always someone out there who, through oversight, neglect, stupidity, and/or sheer evil, seeks to erode the smooth paths the Internet community has built up over the better part of a generation. But such is the destiny of any systems of rule in society; they're constantly being reinvented; and although cracks increasingly do appear, the overall system is still holding up.

Netiquette applies to everyone on the Internet, from the Silicon Valley programmer to the junior high school student to the university professor; we're all part of the same community and therefore we're all expected to play by the same set of rules. AOL users in particular have the onus of being labeled newbies; that is, people who are new to the Net. Whether you're clueless or not, the fact that *@aol.com* appears as part of your email address still leaves some Internet die-hards to wonder about your position in the Internet caste system. That said, this perception is waning as AOL continues to grow in popularity. We're not trying to encourage the practice of labeling AOL users. We subscribe to the school that says "pay attention to deeds, not to the letters of one's domain name." But we think it is your duty, as an AOL user and as a member of the Internet community, to be particularly aware of netiquette.

General Netiquette Guidelines

No matter where you are online, you should keep these basic guidelines in mind. They might seem condescending now, but just wait until you find yourself in a discussion war of nasty messages in which it's clear the participants have little or no respect for one another (by the way, a slew of nasty messages, flying back and forth between newsgroup, mailing list, or chat participants is called a *flame war*). But on to the tips:

- When you're feeling superior, nasty, or angry, remember you're talking to other human beings. Behave online as you would behave in person.

- Assume that the people you're talking to are at least as smart as you. That way, you won't treat them like they're idiots.

- Assume that anyone, at any time now or in the future, will read what you've posted in a newsgroup, mailing list, or web site. Archives can and have been used before by job recruiters—and potential mates, too—to investigate what your interests are, your grammar, and your way of conducting yourself in public.

- Understand that emotion is not easily expressed in email. If you read something that seems harsh, critical, or downright mean, wonder whether the sender really intended it that way. Assume he or she wrote it with points 1 and 2 (see above) in mind.

- Get to the point. We're all busy, so try to save bandwidth and readers' time by posting only what's necessary for your message. This is especially important in newsgroup and mailing-list posts.

- Go easy on people who don't pay attention to netiquette. Be polite in showing them how they could improve.

For specific tips about email, Instant Message, chat, message board, mailing-list and newsgroup etiquette, see the "Netiquette" sections of those chapters.

More Help for First-Time Users

Now that you've finished the Introduction, other chapters we strongly recommend for beginners are:

- Chapter 6, *Help from AOL*: Where to go if you need more step-by-step help than is offered in this book.

- Chapter 7, *Essential AOL Survival Tips*: What you need to know to keep AOL from driving you crazy.

- Chapter 8, *Email*: Email continues to be the most popular activity on the Internet.

- Chapter 14, *Finding & Searching*: Tips on where to locate what you need on AOL and the Web.

CHAPTER 2

Installing and Upgrading

AOL makes it easy to install its software. If you've ever installed a program before, you'll have no problem. In our opinion, where things get just a bit cloudy is when you're upgrading from an existing account: you're given the option to save your preferences, transfer downloaded files, and move the contents of your Personal Filing Cabinet. It's a nice move on AOL's part, since you get to pick and choose which parts of your old account you want to transfer to your new version, but it can be dizzying. If you want the upgraded version—in this case, Version 4.0—to retain the preferences you've spent a lot of time customizing, you'll want to pay special attention when you're upgrading.

What we do in this chapter, to a more extreme degree than in most other places in the book, is walk you through setting up AOL 4.0. You have several options available, and we take you step-by-step through each. When the paths diverge, we branch off into subsections.

Getting the Software

There are three ways to get AOL:

- On a CD-ROM

- Via a download either from within AOL itself (in this case you're probably upgrading from Version 3.0 or earlier) or from AOL's web site, *AOL.Com*, at *http://www.aol.com*

- Preinstalled on a new computer

Before you do anything, you should know that the AOL installation file is huge—over 15 megabytes—and takes at least two hours to download with a 28.8Kbps modem.

Get the Disk

By far, the best way to get AOL is on CD-ROM. Why? It makes life much easier. You won't risk a lengthy or botched download. By having the CD-ROM handy, you can always reinstall it without too much hassle. You'll also get extra online art—the more you install on your hard drive, the faster AOL will run. The only bad thing about getting AOL software on disk is that any slight updates released since the disk was pressed will have to be patched in to your software once you sign on. For instance, if the software goes from 4.0 to 4.1, the added files may have to be added to AOL later. Thankfully, these small updates are automatic, and take only a few minutes.

AOL makes it difficult to successfully request a disk from them. Call 1-888-265-8006 and talk to a live customer service representative. Or sign on to AOL (borrow a friend's account) and mail one to yourself from **Keyword: Upgrade Order.** In addition, you can request one be mailed to you via AOL's web site at *http://www.aol.com.* Once you're at the site, look for the link to their free software. We don't feel that either of these options is great: we've heard reports that the disk takes forever or never arrives.

Save time: get one from a magazine

You'll save time and frustration if you find an AOL disk on your own. It shouldn't be too much trouble: open any popular computing magazine and, bam, there's an AOL disk. It used to be that AOL distributed so many free disks that people made tree ornaments and other *objets d'art* with them.

If You Can't Get the Disk

If you're not already an AOL member, and you can't find the software on disk despite our advice above, go to AOL's web site, *AOL.Com,* at *http://www.aol.com,* and look for a link to their free software. You can download it right away and/or request that they mail you a disk. If you choose to download it, you could be in for a two-hour ride, even at fast modem speeds.

For those of you with an older version of AOL already installed, go to **Keyword: Upgrade** where you can download AOL's latest release. Download times still apply, but as long as you're on the default Standard Unlimited pricing plan, it won't cost you extra. There are two ways to upgrade via download, but not all methods are available to all users. The first method is to download one huge executable file onto your local drive, which you then run. The other method, the one that AOL tends to prefer, is via an automated upgrade. In the automated installation, AOL downloads, unzips, and installs a series of update tool files or UTFs. We, however, prefer the large executable file, because you can keep it on your hard drive and run it later if you ever want, or need, to reinstall. If you go the automated installation/UTF route and you ever need to reinstall, you have to start from scratch.

Installing the Software

Locate the executable file, *setup95.exe*, on the installation disk or on your hard drive. You should see a bright blue AOL symbol with an open box in front of it.

AOL recommends a Pentium-based machine for best performance: this is probably true, but it still works with a 486. (We've installed 4.0 on a 486 66-Mhz with 32MB RAM. With this configuration, starting AOL is a bit slow for our tastes, but otherwise it functions.) For more on hardware concerns, see Chapter 26, *System Requirements*.

Decide Who You Are

Nicely, AOL gives you a number of installation options so you're covered whether you already have an AOL account and are upgrading to a newer version of the software, or are signing on as a new member. We explain your four options below. Choose which one applies to you. The section headings below correspond to the onscreen prompts shown in Figure 2-1.

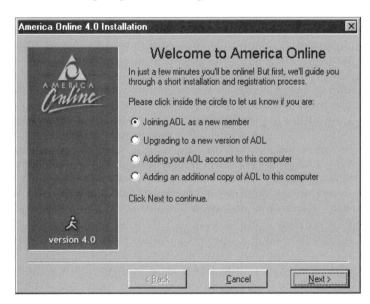

Figure 2-1: Deciding how you want to install AOL

Joining AOL as a new member

You know who you are! You'll follow every single one of the steps we cover in the rest of this chapter.

Upgrading to a new version of AOL

You've already got an account on the current machine, and you want the newest version of AOL. When you choose this option, you'll be allowed to transfer preferences or move downloaded files into the new version. Once you've noted what

AOL does when it upgrades you (below), move on to the section, "Checking for Older Versions," below. Work your way from there through all the steps, in order, until you get to the section titled "If You Haven't Upgraded (i.e., You Didn't Transfer Old Preferences or You're New)." Then stop. You're done. Because you already have an account, all of the steps starting with "If You Haven't Upgraded (i.e., You Didn't Transfer Old Preferences or You're New)" (including setting up your modem) will have already been taken care of in the upgrade.

Here's what's involved in upgrading:

- *Transferring preferences:* this means moving your old screen names, stored passwords, My AOL settings, Personal Filing Cabinet, Favorite Places, email preferences, and any other preference to your upgraded version. Nothing is removed from your old copy of AOL, unless you put your new version into the same directory, which essentially overwrites it.

   You're prompted to choose a copy of the AOL software already on your machine from which to upgrade. The software will recommend the copy you've used most recently (if you have more than one copy of AOL on your computer). You can choose any copy of AOL that you want the preferences transferred from.

- *Transferring downloaded files:* do you want your downloaded files from the old copy's \download\ folder? You're usually asked whether you want to Move them from your other AOL version, Copy them, or Do Not Move the files. If you've got downloaded files you want to keep track of, we recommend you Move or Copy them. If you choose Copy, you'll have two sets of identical downloads, one in your new AOL and one in your old copy. If you don't like duplicates of all those copied files, you can go back later and delete the old \download\ folder once you know the transfer was successful.

   Note that sometimes when upgrading, you won't be asked what to do with the downloaded files in your \download\ folder. We've found that in this case, AOL automatically moves the files to the new version.

Adding your AOL account to this computer

You already have an account, but not on this machine. Say you want to take AOL to work with you, to check your email during the day. Or you just got a new laptop or desktop, and you want to install an existing account there. In any of these cases, AOL won't look for preferences to carry over to this installation. After you complete all the steps to install the software, you'll have to input your existing screen name, but that's later down the line, in the section "If You Haven't Upgraded (i.e., You Didn't Transfer Old Preferences or You're New)."

Adding an additional copy of AOL to this computer

This option doesn't check for other copies of AOL on your machine. No preferences are imported. Use this option if you've got more than one account, and you want both on the same machine. Or, if you're having problems with your AOL software, you could install AOL again without the old settings, and run the new one until you're sure it works properly. If things are satisfactory, you can go back to uninstall the older version.

Checking for Older Versions

AOL looks to see if you have another copy of AOL in the machine (if you choose New Member, it goes through the motions of checking for other versions, but won't use this information).

Choose a Directory

You decide where the AOL software will reside. AOL recommends the location *C:\ America Online 4.0*, but you can change this by typing in another valid location of your choice, or using Browse to locate a place to put it.

Select Launch Options

You have two options, both of which are shown in Figure 2-2:

1. Start AOL when you start your computer. This option is not enabled as a default (i.e., the box next to it isn't checked). We recommend you leave the default alone, since booting AOL at the same time you boot your operating system causes huge delays. The OS boot is already long enough without AOL booting up, too.

2. Add AOL to the Microsoft Office toolbar. If you have MS Office installed, and you have the toolbar running when you install AOL, this option is enabled as a default (i.e., the box next to it is checked). We don't like this because it makes for too many AOL icons on your desktop. You already have an AOL icon in your Start menu, in your tray (near the clock in Windows 95/98), and on your desktop. You probably don't need another one. On the other hand, adding it to the MS Office toolbar doesn't hurt anything. (If this option is grayed out, it's because you don't have the MS Office toolbar running.)

Disk Space

AOL examines how much free disk space you have on the drive you install it on. If there's enough, you can continue the installation. If not, you have to remove some unwanted files or programs, or you can compress one of your drives. We recommend removing unwanted files first; compressing a drive slows it down somewhat.

AOL Installs the Files

Installation of the files typically takes about three minutes, depending on the speed of your system. On our Pentium 166 with 48MB of RAM, file installation took less than one minute. On our 486 machines, it took more like five minutes, but it seemed like hours.

Ready to Sign On Now?

Choose to sign on immediately or return later. If you've chosen Upgrading to a new version of AOL in the earlier section "Decide Who You Are," you're done with installation and also with this chapter.

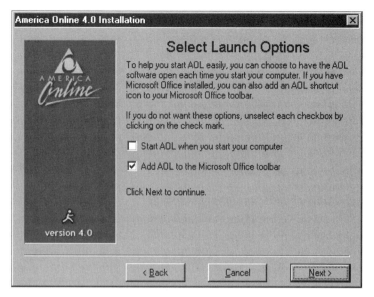

Figure 2-2: Selecting launch options

If You Haven't Upgraded (i.e., You Didn't Transfer Old Preferences or You're New)

Unless your preferences were transferred from another version of AOL, you'll have to complete several steps the first time you use your newly installed software.

You'll be asked to `Begin automatic setup` or `Go to custom setup` (see Figure 2-3). Automatic setup works well, with the software recognizing whether you have a modem connction or a TCP/IP connection. But if you want total control over the setup, choose `Custom`. Don't use `Custom` if you're going to connect using TCP/IP, since you'll just repeat the steps AOL automatically would have performed for you more quickly.

A note about custom setup

The only benefit we can see to choosing a custom modem setup is that you can set the modem speaker volume right away. If you don't want to hear AOL dialing in, then set it to off. Even so, we recommend you wait on this, since you can always choose to change the default modem volume later on.

If you choose custom, you'll have to choose the Com port for your modem, which you can locate in the control panels of Windows 95, under the system settings (to get there in Windows 95/98, follow this path from the taskbar: `Start → Settings → Control Panel → System → Device Manager` tab → `Modem`). You'll also need to know the speed of your modem. If you don't know it, check your computer documentation. If you had chosen `Automatic`, AOL would have done all these things for you. Don't say we didn't warn you.

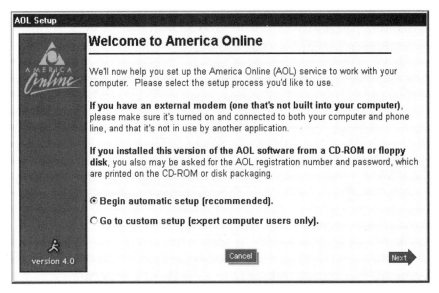

AOL Setup

Welcome to America Online

We'll now help you set up the America Online (AOL) service to work with your computer. Please select the setup process you'd like to use.

If you have an external modem (one that's not built into your computer), please make sure it's turned on and connected to both your computer and phone line, and that it's not in use by another application.

If you installed this version of the AOL software from a CD-ROM or floppy disk, you also may be asked for the AOL registration number and password, which are printed on the CD-ROM or disk packaging.

⦿ Begin automatic setup [recommended].

○ Go to custom setup [expert computer users only].

version 4.0

Cancel   Next▶

Figure 2-3: Choosing automatic or custom installation

Automatic modem setup

If you're connecting via a modem, AOL tests it and tries to determine its brand and type. Often AOL screws up and chooses a generic modem. This generic is probably fine for signing on the first time, and maybe you'll get reliable connections forever. But if you want to maximize the reliability of your phone connections with AOL, we strongly recommend making sure that AOL has the correct modem type selected. See Chapter 27, *Connecting*, for instructions on how to set up the modem, especially if AOL gets it wrong.

Access Numbers

Once the modem is selected, you'll be walked through an automated search of local access numbers. First, AOL asks if you need to dial a prefix, such as 9, to get an outside line, or *70 to disable call waiting (these are just common examples; your local phone service may require other prefixes). These are important setup steps; be sure to give the correct line information when prompted. We go over finding your town and choosing access numbers that match your modem capacity in the next section. In addition, see Chapter 27 for more detailed information.

Find your town

Next, you're presented with local numbers and the modem speeds those numbers serve. To start, look for your town. In almost all cases, your town or one near it will be listed. It is a pretty safe bet those numbers are in your local calling area. However, you may find that some of the numbers are outside what your local phone company considers your local calling area—even if it is in the same area code. It is your responsibility to make sure that any number(s) AOL dials are local.

For example, if you live in a large urban area, you might find that your telephone plan has a "free" calling area as well as additional areas—nearby villages, towns, or even adjacent neighborhoods—that are not really long-distance calls, but for which the phone company charges a small fee. What happens when the AOL number you choose is outside your calling area? Your local phone company—not AOL—may charge you an added toll to call these numbers.

Check the numbers with your phone company to confirm if you're unsure. Or look in your local phone book to see which local exchanges are included in your monthy telephone plan.

If you can't find a number that's a local, nontoll call for you, it's often possible to get a larger local area from your local phone company. (We go into more detail in Chapter 27.)

Choose your modem speed

Once you've found some local numbers, you must be sure the modem capacity attached to those numbers is appropriate for the type of modem you have on your computer. Note that in choosing the access number's modem capacity you can always choose a modem capacity higher than the one you have on your computer. Don't choose an access number with modem capacity that's lower than your modem, since you'll just be losing the added ability of your modem. For instance, if your modem is 28.8, look for a local access number with a capacity of at least 28.3, 33.6, or 56K/x2. Don't choose 2400, 9600, or 14.4, because you'd be wasting your modem capacity. When you choose a higher capacity modem on AOL's end, their modem recognizes the capacity of your modem and adjusts itself accordingly.

Sign On

There are only two sign-on options after you've installed the new software, creating a new account or using an existing one (see Figure 2-4).

If you're joining as a new member or creating an additional, new account

Check the `You want to create a new account or additional AOL account` radio button. Enter the code and password from your AOL software; this number usually appears on the packaging that came with the disk. If you don't have a number, you can call AOL at 1-800-827-6364 and request one. Continue to the next section, "New Members Only: Creating a New Member Account."

If you already have an AOL account

Click the `You already have an AOL account you'd like to use` radio button. Rather than asking for a "registration number" the interface changes so that you're asked for your primary ("master") screen name and your password. Note that you must use a master screen name, not one of the subordinate screen names. Click `Next` and you'll be done; you can skip the rest of this chapter.

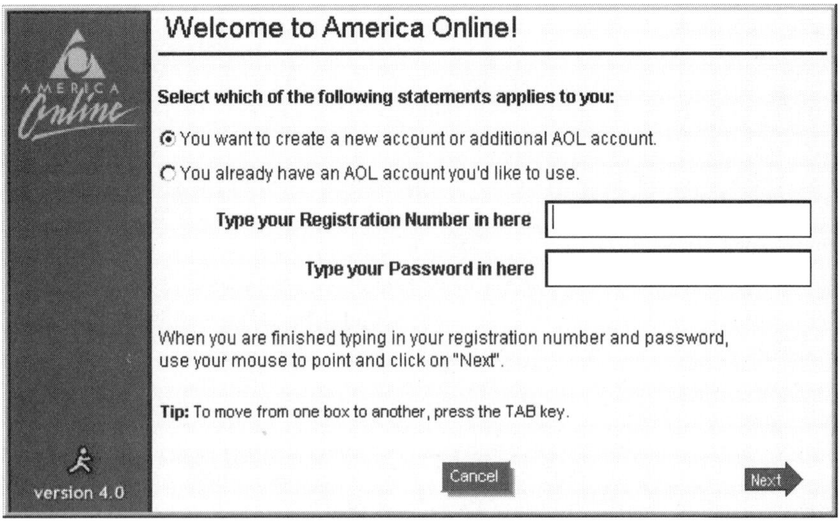

Figure 2-4: Choosing the setup method for your first login with new software

New Members Only: Creating a New Member Account

If you're joining as a new member or are adding an additonal primary account, you now come to a screen where you're asked to enter your name and home address (both are used for billing purposes; be sure this is the same address that's on the Visa, Master Card, or AmEx card you used to sign on).

Read the Conditions of Membership

You can choose to read the conditions immediately online or agree to them and continue the sign on. They are full of legalese. If you'd like our take on TOS and the Rules of the Road as well as a synopsis of the most salient points there, see Appendix D, *Terms of Service.*

Choose Your Screen Name

This can have important repercussions for as long as you own your AOL account. The screen names you choose become your email account. You can never change the first screen name you create, called the *master screen name*, although you can later create up to four other screen names. What you do with your screen names once you're signed on can determine how much junk email you receive, what kind of reception you get in chat rooms and message boards, and how easily other members, including friends and family, remember your identity online. We suggest you read Chapter 3, *Screen Names, Passwords, and Signing On*, for information on how to select one.

Currently, screen names must be 3–10 characters long (this will be expanded to up to 14 characters in the near future, but we don't know when that'll be). Before moving on, AOL asks you to confirm or change your screen name if you don't like it or if it is taken by another member.

Choose a Password

The current restrictions apply as of this writing: 4–8 characters only; alphanumerics only. Be sure you write it down, since you'll have to call AOL if you forget. Once you've created your initial password and signed on for the first time, be sure to go to Chapter 3 to read our tips for keeping your account as secure as possible.

You're Almost Done

AOL recommends reviewing Quick Start, setting up your Marketing Preferences, and checking out The America Online Tour Guide. If you're totally new, check Quick Start for highlights of what you can do with AOL.

Set up your marketing preferences

We highly recommend you go right in and set up your Marketing Preferences, since they give you some control over how or even if AOL markets other products to you. In our experience, most members hate AOL's tactics for marketing products, sending marketing email, or using invasive pop-up screens—advertisments that appear each time you sign on to AOL. Shutting off marketing mail and popups lets you avoid the ubiquitous marketeers (to adjust Marketing Preferences at any time, go to **Keyword: Marketing Prefs**).

Call to verify your account information

Remember, you can only sign on as a new member between 8 a.m. and 2 a.m. EST when phone operators are available. It seems that AOL wants to reconfirm via the phone all of the information you've entered online. Get ready to repeat your phone numbers and account information.

After you've signed on for the first time

At this point, you get offered several books. When writing this book, we were offered the *Official AOL Tour Guide* and its companion, the *All-New Official America Online Internet Guide*. We're not sure what books will be offered in the future. Here's our little caution: AOL often makes special deals with publishers to produce tutorials and guides to AOL. Before you buy, consider whether you want a book about AOL that AOL itself may have had editorial control over, or at the very least, editorial input on. (To be fair, other large software companies, such as Microsoft Corp., have publishing branches that produce books about their own products.) Is the book more about what AOL wants you to hear, and less about how things really work?

Now you're free to use AOL. If you've never been inside AOL before, you might want to consult Chapter 1, *Introduction*, for some general orientation and navigational tips.

CHAPTER 3

Screen Names, Passwords, and Signing On

You wouldn't think that things as simple as screen names would be of much importance. But they are. They're your email address, followed by *@aol.com*. They're what other people see of you in the Buddy View window and in chat rooms. Your screen names can speak volumes about you to other people online, even if you don't intend them to. Choose them carefully.

Likewise, passwords should also be chosen with care. They help prevent others from gaining access to your account and to your personal correspondence, such as email. In this chapter, we cover how to choose your screen names and passwords, how to modify them, and how to maintain your privacy and the integrity of your account.

The screen names you choose and what you do with them once you're signed on can determine how much junk email you receive, what kind of reception you get in chat rooms and message boards, and how easily other members, including friends and family, remember your identity online. In this chapter, we show you how to add new names, delete ones you don't want, and make the best use of each one.

The only screen name you're stuck with is the master screen name, even if it is CD314159. If you're an online newbie—that means new user in computerspeak— you can be forgiven for choosing a first screen name that's a little awkward.

Even if your master moniker is ugly and has a bunch of numbers in it, you needn't worry; you can create up to four additional screen names, and delete them at any time if you don't like them. This ability to have up to five different screen names (really five different email addresses) for just one AOL account is one feature in which AOL has outdone its competition. Most other ISPs and online access companies allow only one username per account, or they charge you more money for additional names.

Master Versus Additional Screen Names

AOL makes a distinction between the screen name you originally set up and any subsequent screen names you create. The master screen name is the one you choose when you first create your AOL account. You can never change your master screen name. Only through your master screen name can you add or delete additional screen names, or implement or modify Parental Controls. The master screen name is always the uppermost screen name in the sign-on screen drop-down menu. For as long as you have your account, you will have—or be stuck with—this screen name.

The holder of the master screen name is billed for online time, including time in areas that carry a surcharge. Any purchases made through the AOL store are typically charged to the master screen name. Note that purchases made on the Web, even if you're using AOL, are not billed via AOL but through whatever process is used by the web site. If you're worried about buying something by accident, you should know that such a feat is rather impossible since you have to give out credit card information—an act that isn't accidental.

The master screen name is ultimately responsible for the actions and activities of all subordinate screen names. AOL will cancel a master account due to the rogue activity (mass emailing, harassment, and other violations of its Terms of Service) carried out by children or other users of the account.

By default, only the master screen name can access premium areas. All others are blocked until unlocked via the master screen name. To find out more about premium services, see also the section "Premium Services" in Chapter 28, *Parental Controls*.

Once you've got your master screen name, you can begin to create up to four alternate screen names. Have fun with these. Pass them out to your kids and to your spouse. We discuss how to create and delete additional screen names further on in this chapter.

Signing On Requires a Screen Name

Every time you want to access AOL, whether from your own computer, your computer at work, or from a friend's computer, you'll have to sign on using one of your screen names. Go to the Sign On screen. Once there, you might notice the drop-down menu that includes each of your currently active screen names and one at the bottom labeled Guest. To sign on, you simply select from the drop-down menu the screen name you want to use for that online session.

Once you've chosen the screen name, a password is also required. Unless you've elected to store your password on your computer, you'll have to type your password into the box just below the screen name. If you're signing on as a guest, you'll have to dial up AOL, connect, and then type in both the screen name you want to sign on with and its corresponding password. We explain more about passwords later in this chapter.

If You're Not at Your Computer, Use Guest

Guest is one of the options in the drop-down menu on the Sign On screen. Use it to access your account from any computer in the world where the AOL software is installed. It is easy to use when you're visiting friends and family—everyone knows a few people who are AOL members!

When you're a guest, you'll be able to read and respond to email, you'll see your Buddy View window, and you'll be able to access all of AOL's content and the Web. However, your Personal Filing Cabinet, your Favorite Places, the download manager, Automatic AOL, and your Email Address Book won't be available, since those items are stored on your local computer.

Remember, charges you rack up while signed on as a guest (if you don't have the Unlimited billing plan or if you enter Premium areas) are billed to your account, not the account of the person whose computer you're using.

To sign on as a guest, simply choose Guest from the drop-down menu. Note: if you just want to check your AOL email, you can do that with any Internet Explorer browser, which we cover in detail in the entry *web-based email* in Chapter 8, *Email.*

When AOL Says Your Account Is Signed On

Sometimes, when you try to sign on, AOL will say you can't, because your account is already signed on. That could mean that another screen name on your account is signed on. For instance, you won't be able to sign on at work if your child (whose screen name is on your account) is signed on at home.

AOL also may think your account is signed on if you've just suddenly lost your connection, like if someone picks up the phone while you're signed on via modem. It sometimes takes AOL a few minutes to realize that you've been abruptly disconnected. Our only advice in this case is: try, try again.

Your Screen Name = Your Email Address and Web Address

Whenever you're on AOL and you spot a screen name, whether it is in your Buddy View window, in a chat room, or on a message board, you are also seeing that AOL member's email address. You could send him or her email from within AOL simply by addressing the message to that screen name. No additional characters are needed. Although we go on and on about email in Chapter 8, we include information here to help you get your bearings since your screen name forms the basis for your email address.

Follow the guidelines below when sending email messages to various types of addresses, such as within AOL and out to the Internet.

Mail Sent Between AOL Accounts Only

Internal AOL email is faster than email AOL receives from the Internet, which is sometimes delayed from minutes to hours to days in extreme cases. If you're sending email to another AOL account, it's best to use only the screen name. Just type the AOL member's screen name into the To: box.

Mail Sent To or From the Internet

Non-AOL members and those people sending mail from the Internet to AOL need to add a few characters to your screen name, if they want the mail to arrive in your email box, rather than return an error message to them. If you're outside of AOL and want to send mail to your AOL screen name or to another AOL screen name, you'll also have to add the extra characters.

Making your AOL screen name into a valid Internet email address is easy: simply take your screen name and append the domain name *@aol.com.* For example, if my screen name is *WristAche* on AOL, my Internet email address would then be *wristache@aol.com.* Your Internet email address will be *Your_Screen_Name@aol.com.*

Many AOL members actually forget to add the *@domainname* part to AOL addresses, but are soon reminded when the mail can't be successfully sent from anywhere other than within AOL itself. After all, if you're sending an email to a CompuServe user, you'd type the domain *@compuserve.com,* although from within the service, CompuServe's members don't have to use *@compuserve.com.*

When in doubt, give out the full Internet address to friends and colleagues. Experienced AOL users know to drop the *@aol.com* from your address when sending internal AOL mail.

Your AOL Web Address

If you choose to utilize your AOL server space, your screen name will also be part of your web or FTP address. We explain how to set up and use your AOL server space in Chapter 23, *Web Publishing and FTP,* but here are the URLs for quick reference: *http://members.aol.com/Your_Screen_Name* or *ftp://members.aol.com/Your_Screen_Name.*

Creating and Managing Screen Names

Creating your additional (or subordinate) screen names is easy. Just go to Keyword: Names or follow this path:

> My AOL toolbar icon → Screen Names → Create a Screen Name

Follow the onscreen instructions. The center of attention for carrying out all of your screen name duties is shown in Figure 3-1. AOL has a number of restrictions on the length and tone of screen names, so you might want to read the paragraphs below before you try to create an illegal one.

You can't sign up for a name that is in use by another member. In addition, screen names that other members have had in the past six months aren't available to you, since AOL keeps them available to their old creators in the event that they want to recreate them.

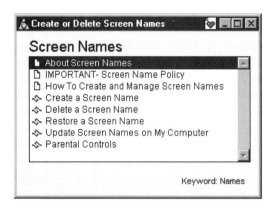

Figure 3-1: Create, delete, restore, or update screen names

AOL restricts you from creating screen names that include letter combinations that denote AOL staff or volunteers. You don't know in advance what these are, but when you happen upon one, you'll get a message stating that you should try again. Obviously, *AOLman* or *SteveCase* won't be allowed.

Screen names and passwords are not case-sensitive. Only letters A–Z and numbers are permitted. Screen-name length is limited to between 3 and 10 characters, while password length must be between 4 and 8 characters (longer screen names and passwords are coming but have not arrived yet).

AOL says "vulgar or sexually explicit screen names can offend the sensibilities of many members, and it is only common courtesy to remember this when you are adding screen names." AOL reserves the right to delete or ask that you delete screen names it deems offensive. You can create some rather racy screen names, but beware that if AOL gets a complaint about it, they can remove it under their Terms of Service. For more about anything naughty or possibly offensive on AOL, see Appendix D.

The Benefits of Multiple Screen Names

By now, you've probably already signed onto AOL for the first time, thereby having created your master screen name. But you've got four more to go! We laud AOL's five-screen-name policy—it's a nice account perk—and encourage you to make many. The benefits include:

- Giving you the options to have a screen name for each member of your household or for separate tasks that you'd like to do online (such as one each to use when corresponding with friends, carrying out business, chatting, or posting to newsgroups).

- Setting up different parental controls for each screen name so that you can do everything on AOL and the Internet, while your kids have access only to the areas you deem appropriate for them (see Chapter 28).

- Using screen names to filter email that comes into your account. By separating (or segregating) screen names based on the types of activities you use them for, you can reduce clutter (see the entry *Mail Controls* in Chapter 8, *Email*, and the section "Reading Your Mailing Lists" in Chapter 12, *Mailing Lists*).

• The ability to set aside a particular screen name for chat, for posting to news-groups, or for registering email addresses at some web sites. Reserving a screen name for any or all of these activities helps to avoid unsolicited email that gets sent by people who have pulled your screen name from your return address (for more on this, see the section "Discussion Groups" in Chapter 30, *Privacy*). Using a chat-only screen name helps you avoid random Instant Mes-sages. Any screen names that we've used to enter the Town Square Lobby begins the flood of unsolicited email. And when you're tired of one chat screen name, you can ditch it and create another (just remember to tell your chat friends about your new name). For more, see Chapter 10, *Chatting*.

Deleting Screen Names

You might find that you'd like to delete particular screen names. At any time and for any reason, you can delete any but the master screen name. Perhaps you've grown tired with a particular name and want to create another, or maybe your chat or newsgroup screen name receives too much spam or too much notoriety. Go to `Keyword: Names` or follow the path:

My AOL toolbar icon → `Screen Names` → `Delete a Screen Name`

Once you delete a screen name it is not gone forever! Unless you're at the maximum of five screen names, you can get the deleted screen name back if you want it back. Bringing a deleted screen name back from the dead is called recre-ating a screen name. There are only two catches: only you can bring the name back, and you must do so within the six-month period that immediately follows its deletion. After six months, you cannot recreate the deleted screen name and AOL releases the name from its database, making it available to anyone.

Restoring a deleted screen name

When you invoke this option, you'll see a list of screen names deleted by your account in the past six months. The Personal Filing Cabinet for that screen name may still be available on your hard drive: look for it when you sign on with the restored screen name. To restore a delete screen name, go to `Keyword: Names` → `Restore a Screen Name` or follow this path:

My AOL toolbar icon → `Screen Names` → `Restore a Screen Name`

Switching Screen Names Without Disconnecting

A new, much needed, and potentially time-saving feature allows 4.0 users to switch screen names without disconnecting from AOL. You needn't dial in to the AOL modem a second (or third or fourth or fifth) time to switch screen names. Now, you stay connected to AOL, but just switch the screen name you're using.

To switch without disconnecting simply go to the `Sign Off` menu from within AOL, then choose `Switch Screen Name`. You'll see a new window with all of your screen names listed, as in Figure 3-2. Click the screen name you want to switch to, and click `Switch` or hit `Enter` on your keyboard. You may be prompted to give a password for the account.

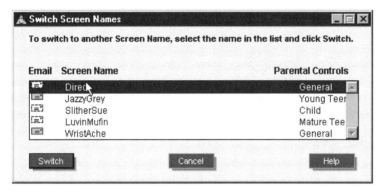

Figure 3-2: Switching screen names without signing off

Benefits of switching without signing off

- You can see whether another of your screen names on the current account has mail without actually signing on. A yellow envelope signals new mail; white signals no new mail.

- Use it to quickly sign on to any of your five screen names.

- It is especially helpful during busy times on the network.

Drawback

- The Switch Screen Names feature is sometimes unavailable during peak hours.

If You Have an Account on More Than One Computer

If you move around a lot, you might have multiple installations of AOL on various computers in your life; you may have a copy at home, one on your laptop, and one on your computer at work. If you ever create or delete a screen name for your account on one of these computers, you will find that the screen name deletions or additions aren't automatically reflected in the drop-down box on the Sign On screen on the other computers. Say you decide to add a new screen name, `CasbahMA`, while you're at work. You go home and want to sign on to `CasbahMA`, but the screen name isn't there! This happens because that information is stored on your local computer, not on AOL's.

But you want all the accounts to look the same. Sounds like a reasonable request. AOL has a remedy for this; it's called *updating*. You have to manually update the list of screen names on all computers that have AOL software for your account. To update the screen names on a given computer, go to **Keyword: Screen Names → Update Screen Names**. You'll have to repeat this update procedure on each of the computers on which you have the account installed.

Screen Names and Privacy

Screen names are your main means of presenting yourself publicly on AOL. Unless you post a picture, no one can see your face online. But they can see your screen name. There are a number of ways people can get information about you via your screen name, many of which we outline here. In addition, you'll want to consult Chapter 30, *Privacy*, for other discussions about ways to protect your personal information.

When You're in a Chat Room

As you chat, your screen name appears in the **People Here:** window for all the world to see. Mysteriously, the amount of unwanted email you get correlates highly with how much time you spend in a chat room with that screen name. You can't prevent the other chatters in the room from seeing you as a chat participant. In addition, each of these chatters can click on your screen name and immediately pull up your Member Profile, if you've created one. Of course, if you've created a special chat screen name (or two), and you've designed your member profile with chatting in mind, you should be prepared for the attention it gets.

Anyone, including chatters, who sees your screen name can add it to his Buddy List. Effectively, when a person adds you to her Buddy List, she can see when you're logged on, and she can find out the chat room you're in, as well as follow you there! If you're concerned about being on someone's Buddy List, you can block him (likewise, you can do this to other people, like friends, enemies, or ex-lovers). For more information on protecting your screen name from appearing on strangers' Buddy Lists, see the section "Privacy" in Chapter 9, *Instant Messages and Buddy Lists*.

The Member Directory and Your Member Profile

It used to be that everyone on AOL had at least the rudiments of a profile, often with their real names and their cities or states in them. Members who were new to AOL could use the Member Directory to search through the member profiles for the names of long lost friends and family members. You might get the name and then send email saying, "Hey, you're online too!" Profiles were our way of telling others, "I'm here! Email me!"

But times have changed. As more people flock online, privacy issues become more important to some of us. Gone are the days when people online represented a small, rather elite minority. Today, we might still call ourselves a minority group, and we might still feel pretty privileged to be part of this new way of communicating, but the sheer numbers of people online throughout the U.S. and the world point out that our chances of being plagued online by the ills of our offline society are great.

You aren't listed in the Member Directory unless you
put up a profile

The Member Directory on AOL still serves as a way to help people find and communicate more effectively with one another. If you choose, you can put in your name, your nickname, your city, hobbies, interests, hopes, and fears. You can link to your web page. You can also be anonymous, allowing you to list things in your member profile that would make your mother blush. The member profile is a place where AOL members can tell about themselves or their alter-egos.

Every screen name you create can have its own member profile and is searchable in the member directory. You choose what to include in your profile. If you don't create one, no one can search the Member Directory and find you (and you may like that!). Here's our take on the benefits and drawbacks of having an online member profile:

Benefits

• Long lost friends can look you up if you have your real name stored.

• Other members can search the directory and match to yours based on your interests, last name, geographic location, and just about anything else you can think to put in your profile.

• You can advertise yourself quickly. If you chat, fellow chatters can see with one click what you've put into your profile. And often the profile can say quite a lot! (See also the section "People in Chat Rooms" in Chapter 10, *Chatting.*)

Drawbacks

• Spammers can search the AOL member-profile database and add you to their spam lists.

• Other AOL members may know more about you than you'd like; be sure to include only what you want the whole world to see. Our advice is, protect your privacy: don't include your exact street address or your phone number.

Create, Edit, or Delete Your Member Profile

You don't start out with a profile; you have to create one. Go to **Keyword: Profile** → **My Profile** or follow this path:

> **My AOL** toolbar icon → **My Member Profile**

If at any time you want to change the contents of your profile, you can return to this screen (shown in Figure 3-3) to modify the information. To delete the profile, click **Delete** when you're viewing it. You'll get a screen saying that "profiles may take a while to update," but actually we've found that the information is updated immediately.

Figure 3-4 shows the Main Member directory screen at **Keyword: Directory** or follow the path:

> **People** toolbar icon → **Search AOL Member Directory**

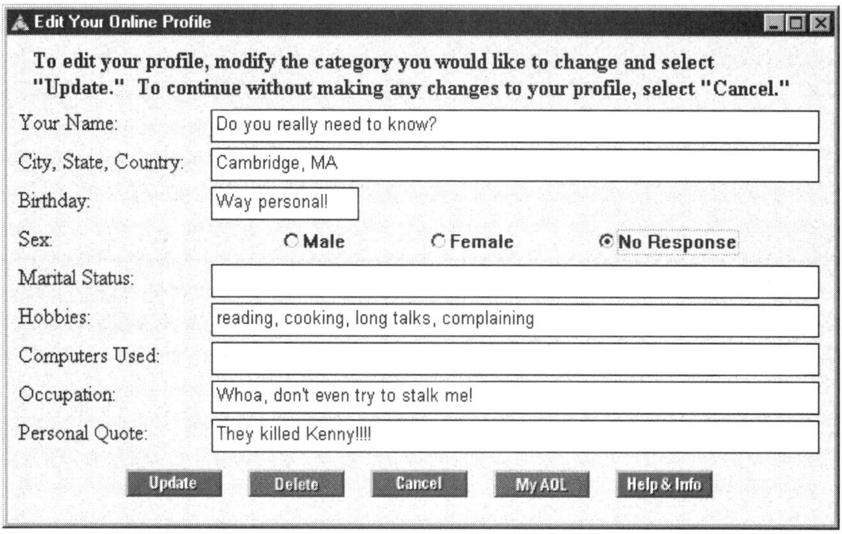

Edit Your Online Profile

To edit your profile, modify the category you would like to change and select "Update." To continue without making any changes to your profile, select "Cancel."

Your Name:	Do you really need to know?
City, State, Country:	Cambridge, MA
Birthday:	Way personal!
Sex:	○ Male ○ Female ● No Response
Marital Status:	
Hobbies:	reading, cooking, long talks, complaining
Computers Used:	
Occupation:	Whoa, don't even try to stalk me!
Personal Quote:	They killed Kenny!!!!

[Update] [Delete] [Cancel] [My AOL] [Help & Info]

Figure 3-3: Creating your member profile (limited imformation)

Note that you can type in search words and phrases, limit the search based on geographic location, or even type the member name directly. You might try typing in your last name (if it's not too common) to see what the directory finds!

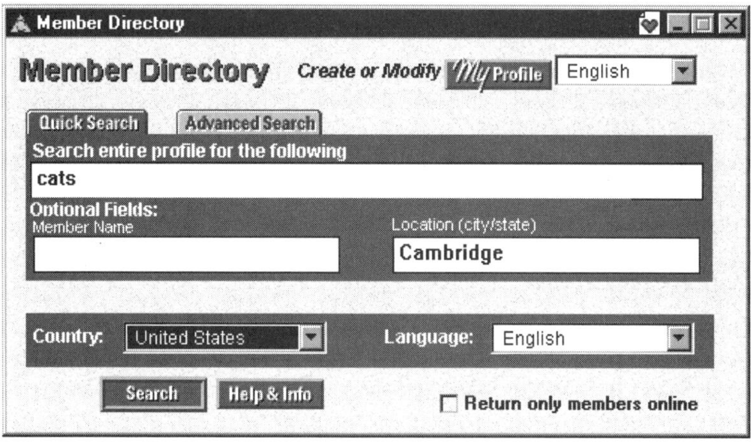

Member Directory

Member Directory   *Create or Modify* My Profile   English

[Quick Search]   [Advanced Search]

Search entire profile for the following

cats

Optional Fields:

Member Name

Location (city/state)

Cambridge

Country: United States   Language: English

[Search] [Help & Info]   ☐ Return only members online

Figure 3-4: Locating screen names using the Member Directory

Passwords

Passwords are pretty simple, but pretty important. They help you protect the integrity of your entire AOL account. If someone gets your password, there's no telling what he or she could do with it: send spam to tens of thousands of people from your email address, harass others in your name, and purchase merchandise throughout AOL with your credit card number. There's actually a cadre of these password scammers on AOL who will try just about any means to trick you into telling them what yours is, including impersonating AOL staff. We give tips below on how not to fall for their tactics.

But first, you'll find tips on creating your passwords, changing them, and what to do if you forget one (duh!). We also cover the new 4.0 feature that allows you to password your Personal Filing Cabinet (PFC).

Creating and Changing Your Passwords

Don't use your name, screen name, home address, or anything else that your evil coworkers or nosy children would be able to guess. Length is currently limited to between 4 and 8 characters, although AOL has plans for longer ones in the future. Don't use any normal English words, like anything that you can find in the dictionary, since there are many password-deciphering programs that can crack these passwords. Don't use a password that you also use for something else (such as a web site or a LAN).

The best password is one with a combination of numbers and letters. For even better security, change your password occasionally, and never tell anyone what it is, no matter how nicely they ask.

To change your password go to `Keyword: Password` or follow this path:

> `MY AOL` toolbar icon → `Passwords`

Forgotten Passwords

Oops! You forgot your password. Now that you've smacked yourself in the forehead, what do you do? You call 1-888-265-8004 and ask AOL to reset your password for you. Be prepared to supply your screen name, billing address, and billing information (credit card or checking account number). Sign on with your new password and change it. This time, choose something a bit more memorable, and/or write it down and hide it.

Storing Your Password

AOL gives you the option of storing your password so you don't have to type it every time you sign on, and you don't have to remember it, either. The default is to not to store your password; that is, you have to enter your password manually every time you sign on.

AOL 4.0 users are constantly nagged to store their passwords, and given explicit instructions on how to do so. If you decide to store your password at a time when you aren't being nagged, or if you want to unstore your password, this is the path to follow:

> `MY AOL` toolbar icon → `Preferences` → `Passwords` → `Sign On` checkbox corresponding to your screen name

You'll then have to type in your valid password.

- If you don't store your password, you'll have to manually sign on to AOL to activate Automatic AOL, which defeats the purpose if you're using Automatic AOL to avoid connectivity problems or save time (see also the section "Scheduling" in Chapter 21, *Automatic AOL*).

- If AOL's graphical point-and-click interface is a pain in the wrists, storing your password saves valuable keystrokes (see also Chapter 19, *Keyboard Shortcuts*). Just click `Sign On` (or hit `Enter` on your keyboard), and you're in.

Drawbacks

- If you do store your password, anyone who can turn on your computer can sign on to your AOL account. So don't do it unless you trust your family/roommate/coworkers not to abuse your account.

- Storing the password to your account defeats the purpose of passwording your Personal Filing Cabinet (see the next section, "Password Protecting the Personal Filing Cabinet" in this chapter) since anyone can sign on to your account and then unpassword your PFC.

Password Protecting the Personal Filing Cabinet

New to 4.0 is the ability to password your Personal Filing Cabinet (see "Password Protection" in Chapter 18, *Personal Filing Cabinet*). This is theoretically a way to keep your saved email, newsgroup posts, and download history from prying eyes, but we've found that it can be breached by anyone who signs on to your account. However, if no one can gain access to your account, your PFC is safe.

To get there, follow this path:

> `MY AOL` toolbar icon → `Preferences` → `Passwords`

Once there, check the `Personal Filing Cabinet` checkboxes corresponding to those screen names you want to password protect.

Drawbacks

- Anyone who signs on to your account with your computer (where your PFC files are located) can still gain access by signing on in your name and turning off passwording the same way you turned it on.

- If you store both your PFC password and your sign-on password, they will be the same (if you store only your PFC password, enter a new password of your choice).

Beware Evil Password Solicitations

It is almost certain that during your tenure on AOL, at least one random stranger will ask you for your password and expect you to email it or send it in an Instant Message (IM). Often these password solicitors are called *phishers*, since they fish for your private information. The most common phisher sends IMs asking you for your credit card number or password, as in Figure 3-5. Perhaps you're in a chat room or lobby, innocently going about your business. They'll often impersonate

AOL employees, use a lot of technical terminology (usually incorrectly), and may have screen names full of numbers.

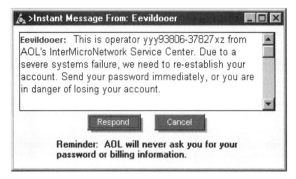

Figure 3-5: A password-phishing Instant Message

What's surprising is that despite warnings, many AOL members actually fall for these schemes. On every single IM window, it clearly states that AOL will never ask you for your password or billing information. Don't be a sucker. Instead, we recommend responding to the IM and telling the phisher what a loser he is. Then report it. Password and credit card solicitations are clear violations of AOL's Terms of Service (for more on TOS, see Chapter 4).

Report phishers: you'll do the world good

If you're solicited, don't just sit there, report it. Go to Keyword: Notify AOL → Instant Message™ Notes (see Figure 3-6). Once you're there, you'll need to copy and paste the Instant Message text, so don't close that IM window.

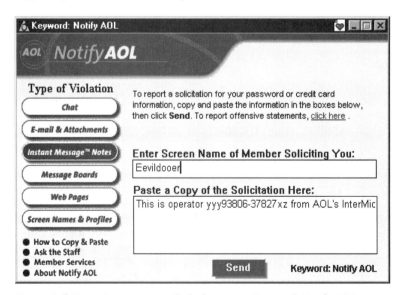

Figure 3-6: Reporting a password phisher using Keyword: Notify AOL

CHAPTER 4

Getting Around AOL: Toolbars and Menus

If you close all your AOL windows, you will be left with one of AOL's most important features: the toolbar, shown in Figure 4-1. The toolbar is the backbone of AOL, with three main elements: menus, toolbar icons, and a navigation bar. You can use the toolbar to do just about anything you want to do on AOL. It helps you get your bearings, staying constant even when text and images on the screen are appearing, changing, and disappearing.

Figure 4-1: The default state of the toolbar and menus

The toolbar is the centerpiece of what's known as a graphical user interface, or GUI—an environment in which you click, double-click, drag, and drop items in order to get things done. Before the days of the GUI, you had to know a string of commands to get around a computer, typing in required words in exactly the right place at the right time. Now, things are done with pictures—you can look and see what to do, relying on the GUI to provide clues as to what lies inside.

If you see an icon that looks like a filing cabinet, you can start to guess what's inside, such as files, or folders, or important, saved information! When you move something around on your screen by dragging and dropping, you're literally moving it around, as if you had moved a stack of papers from your desk and put them in a drawer for later retrieval. In the same way, when you click an icon, it's like opening a door, or sliding open a drawer: you want to go in there and see what's on the other side.

This chapter gives you a tour of AOL's toolbar and all its component parts. You can read through this chapter to familiarize yourself with AOL 4.0's interface or to find out which features are new. Another way to approach this chapter is as a reference: if you don't know what a certain toolbar or menu item does, you can look it up here.

In each menu and toolbar icon's introduction, we tell you which of its features are new (or improved) in AOL 4.0. We do this so AOL 3.0 users can know which sections to ignore and because members who have recently upgraded may want to skip directly to the new information. We've also supplied keywords whenever possible, in part because they make life easier for everyone, including members using older software and/or Macintoshes.

Since this chapter is so specific to AOL's menus, toolbar icons, and navigation bar, it may not answer all your questions about getting around the service. For more of an overview of AOL's look and feel, see the section "Getting Familiar with the AOL Interface" in Chapter 1, *Introduction.*

What's in This Chapter?

Since there are three parts of the AOL menu and toolbar, we detail each of these in three sections, as follows:

- "Menu Item Inventory": These are the topmost drop-down menus in the default window. The most basic navigational and functional abilities are here, similar to most other Windows programs.

- "Toolbar Icon Inventory": The toolbar icons are located in the middle row of the toolbar, and are brightly colored icons that span the entire length of the AOL window. While previous versions of AOL have had clickable toolbar icons, 4.0 adds even more. When clicked, most toolbar icons drop down to reveal related functions or links to AOL areas. If you've got your screen resolution set to greater than 800×600, you'll also see three extra icons, Quotes, Perks, and Weather, which you can remove and replace with favorite AOL areas of your choice.

- "AOL and Web Navigation Bar": This navigation bar is wholly new to 4.0. With it, AOL attempts to let its members seamlessly navigate to both AOL areas and web sites in the same manner, by typing the address into a dual-purpose box. You can use the dual-purpose box as a keyword window, for inputting keywords, and you can use it as a URL box, for inputting web addresses such as *www.oreilly.com*, the O'Reilly web site. There's also a new history-trail drop-down window that allows you to view and quickly navigate back to the last 25 places you've been.

After the toolbar tour, we've provided three sections about using toolbar preferences and customizing the toolbar:

- "Toolbar Preferences": We think it is a good idea to take a look at the toolbar preferences, especially the new history trail preferences, which opens up a potential privacy issue: other users of your account will by default be able to see a history of your travels on AOL and the Web.

- "Adding and Removing Toolbar Icons": How to place links to your favorite web sites or AOL areas on the toolbar.

- "Using the Toolbar Versus Keyboard Shortcuts": A brief discussion of why we love shortcuts.

Menu Item Inventory

Menus are the text options at the top of the toolbar: File, Edit, Window, Sign Off (or Sign On, if you're already signed off), and Help. If you click on any of these menus, such as File, a list of menu items drops down. To select a menu item, move your mouse pointer over it and click. None of these menus is new with 4.0, though some of their features are new. AOL 3.0 users will discover that the old Go To, Mail, and Members menus are gone.

The System Menu

The menu represented by a small blue AOL triangle in the upper left of the window is called the System menu. It is a Windows 95/98 application menu identical to the menus found in Microsoft Word, Netscape Navigator, and every other Windows 95/98 program. The System menu is shown in Figure 4-2.

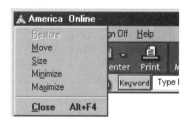

Figure 4-2: The System menu

Throughout this chapter, we'll show you a picture of a menu or a toolbar with explanations of it below. If necessary, items in the figure will be numbered, with the numbers corresponding to the numbers in the text explanation.

- Restore: Returns a moved or resized AOL application window to its previous size and position.

- Move: Alters the cursor so you can easily move the AOL application window around.

- Size: Alters the cursor so you can easily make the AOL application window larger or smaller.

- Minimize: Minimizes the entire AOL application window, so that it is only visible on your Windows taskbar.

- Maximize: Returns the AOL application window to a full-screen size after it has been partially minimized.

- Close: Signs off your account, disconnects you from AOL, and exits the AOL application.

File Menu

The File menu should look familiar, since both Windows computers and Macs have them in almost every application. Most File menu items affect documents such as pictures and text documents. The items Open Picture Gallery and Save to Personal Filing Cabinet are new in 4.0. The File menu is shown in Figure 4-3.

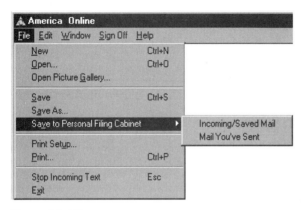

Figure 4-3: File menu

- **New**: Opens a new, untitled text document within AOL.

- **Open**: Choose any file on your computer to open and click OK to open it within AOL.

- **Open Picture Gallery**: Choose a folder on your computer that contains image files and click OK. This opens an AOL Picture Gallery of the images, with six images per page.

- **Save**: Saves the current, topmost text or image file. The first time you save, you'll be asked to name the file and choose a location to save it to. Subsequent Saves have the same name and location.

- **Save As**: Saves the current, topmost text or image file. When you Save As, you're asked to name the file and choose a location to save it to.

- **Save to Personal Filing Cabinet**: Saves new, old, or sent email messages to the Incoming/Saved Mail or Mail You've Sent folder in your Personal Filing Cabinet. To configure AOL to automatically save your email to your personal filing cabinet, see the entry *saving* in Chapter 8, *Email*.

- **Print Setup**: Choose your printer settings, paper size, and orientation (portrait or landscape), and click OK.

- **Print**: Serves the same function as the Print toolbar icon. Select print range, print quality, and number of copies. Click OK to print.

- **Stop Incoming Text**: Stops incoming text and graphics in AOL areas from loading.

- **Exit**: Signs off your account, disconnects you from AOL, and exits the AOL application.

Edit Menu

If you've ever word-processed, you'll recognize the `Edit` menu as the place to alter text. Likewise, many items in AOL's `Edit` menu (`Undo`, `Cut`, `Copy`, `Paste`, `Select All`, `Spell Check`) apply only when you are working with text, such as an outgoing email or instant message. The items `Spell Check` and `Capture Picture` are new in 4.0. `Dictionary` and `Thesaurus` are new menu items, but their features existed in 3.0. The `Edit` menu is shown in Figure 4-4.

Figure 4-4: Edit menu

- `Undo`: Erases the last word typed, or last formatting (such as bolding or pasting) applied to the text.

- `Cut`: Removes highlighted text from the current document and holds it for pasting.

- `Copy`: Stores highlighted text for pasting but doesn't remove it from the document.

- `Paste`: Inserts the most recently cut or copied text at the point in the document where your cursor is located.

- `Select All`: Highlights an entire document to prepare it for cutting, copying, or other formatting (e.g., bolding, color change, font change), but doesn't actually cut, copy, or format.

- `Find in Top Window`: Searches for a word or phrase in a text window such as an email message or a list of message board topics (doesn't work for web pages or graphical AOL areas).

- `Spell Check`: Spell checks text documents, outgoing email messages, instant messages, and chat room comments. See also the section "Spelling" in Chapter 29, *Preferences*.

- `Dictionary`: The searchable *Merriam-Webster Collegiate Dictionary*, also at `Keyword: Dictionary`.

- **Thesaurus**: The searchable *Merriam-Webster Thesaurus*, also at `Keyword: Thesaurus`.

- **Capture Picture**: Intended for use with a digital camera. Sends graphics files through email and instant messages.

Window Menu

The `Window` menu helps you organize the AOL area windows, Instant Message windows, web windows, and any other open window on your screen. The `Window` menu is shown in Figure 4-5.

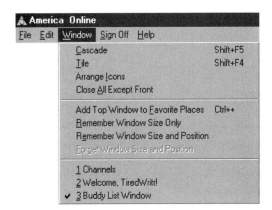

Figure 4-5: Window menu

- **Cascade**: Displays all open AOL windows, staggering them like a down staircase, so that their title bars are visible.

- **Tile**: Displays all open AOL windows; we prefer `Cascade`.

- **Arrange Icons**: Neatly lines up minimized AOL windows along the bottom of your screen.

- **Close All Except Front**: Closes all open AOL windows except the topmost one. The exception is that the Welcome screen and front Channel screens (e.g., News, Personal Finance, Sports) can't close, so they are minimized.

- **Add Top Window to Favorite Places**: Selects the topmost open window as a Favorite Place (if it has a Favorite Place-able red heart icon in the upper-right corner of the window). Add it to your Favorite Places, add it to an email message, or add it to an Instant Message.

- **Remember Window Size Only**: Configures the topmost window to always appear as the same size. For instance, use it to make your Buddy List six inches tall so you can see all the screen names.

- **Remember Window Size and Position**: Configures the topmost window to always appear in the same location and at the same size on your screen.

- **Forget Window Size and Position**: Undoes `Remember Window Size Only` or `Remember Window Size and Position` command for the topmost window.

- The numbered items (Channels; Welcome, TiredWritr!; Buddy List Window) represent any open (or minimized) windows, either AOL or web sites. This list holds up to 25 open windows, though the Window menu only displays the first nine. (If you've got more than nine windows open, you'll see a **More Windows** option. Click it for a complete list.) Select an item to make it the top window.

Sign Off Menu

You use the Sign Off menu to sign off, obviously. When you are signed off, but the AOL application is open, it's called the Sign On window, and you use it to bring up the Sign On screen (if it's not already visible). The item Switch Screen Name is new in 4.0—and extremely useful if you have more than one screen name. The Sign Off menu is shown in Figure 4-6.

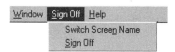

Figure 4-6: Sign Off menu

- **Switch Screen Name**: Opens a window with all your account's screen names listed. A yellow envelope next to a screen name means that screen name has new email. Highlight a screen name and click Switch to sign off from your current screen name and on to the new one, without disconnecting from AOL. For more on switching screen names without signing off, see the section "Switching Screen Names Without Disconnecting" in Chapter 3, *Screen Names, Passwords, and Signing On*.
- Sign Off: Signs off your screen name and disconnects you from AOL.

Help Menu

The Help menu is just what it sounds like: a list of places where you can learn more about AOL. Many of these items don't appear in 3.0 menus, but do appear elsewhere in 3.0. The Help menu is shown in Figure 4-7.

Figure 4-7: Help menu

- **Member Services Online Help:** AOL's main member help area, Keyword: Help.

- **Offline Help:** Offline help directory that works like all other Windows-compatible help directories.

- **Parental Controls:** The Parental Controls main screen, where you can restrict your child's access to parts of the online world. Also at Keyword: Parental Controls. See also Chapter 28, *Parental Controls*.

- **Help With Keywords:** If you don't understand how keywords work, you can find out here (or see the section "Getting Familiar with the AOL Interface" in Chapter 1, *Introduction*).

- **Accounts and Billing:** AOL's main billing area, also at Keyword: Billing. See also Chapter 22, *Billing*.

- **AOL Access Phone Numbers:** AOL's main access numbers area, also at Keyword: Access. See also Chapter 27, *Connecting*.

- **What's New in AOL 4.0:** An interactive demo of new content and 4.0 features, Keyword: Click & Go 4.0.

- **About America Online:** Tells you what version of AOL you're currently using. In addition, you can use key commands to view error messages (Ctrl-e); to view connection devices, locations, and access numbers (Ctrl-i); and to view your computer's specs (Ctrl-r).

Toolbar Icon Inventory

Toolbar icons are the graphical buttons on the toolbar: Read, Write, Mail Center, Print, My Files, My AOL, Favorites, Internet, Channels, People, Quotes, Perks, and Weather. Some of the toolbar icons (Read, Write, Print, Quotes, Perks, and Weather) are buttons you simply click to open a window or go to an AOL area. The rest of the toolbar icons (Mail Center, My Files, My AOL, Favorites, Internet, Channels, and People) have arrows on them. These types function like drop-down menus: when you click one, it drops down a list of options. To select an option, move your mouse over the option and click it. All these toolbar icons are new in AOL 4.0 except for Read, Write, and Print, which exist (but look different) in earlier versions.

Read and Write Toolbar Icons

The Read and Write toolbar icons are just redesigned versions of the mailbox and paper-and-pencil icons in AOL 3.0. (We can't resist telling you to try Ctrl-r for Read and Ctrl-m for Write. See also Chapter 19, *Keyboard Shortcuts*.) The Read and Write toolbar icons are shown in Figure 4-8.

1. **Read:** Opens your email box and shows you the contents of the New Mail folder. From there, click the Old Mail or Sent Mail tab to view those folders.

2. **Write:** Opens a Write Mail window where you can compose a new, outgoing email message.

Figure 4-8: Read and Write toolbar icons

Mail Center Toolbar Icon

AOL defines the `Mail Center` toolbar icon as "everything about email," and we are inclined to agree. It also includes `Automatic AOL` items, which can be used for more than just email (see also Chapter 21, *Automatic AOL*). It contains many of the same items as AOL 3.0's `Mail` menu. `Mail Preferences` and `Mail Controls` exist in earlier versions, but they are new to the toolbar. The `Mail Center` toolbar icon and its related drop-down list are shown in Figure 4-9.

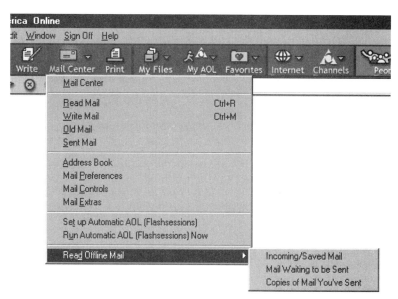

Figure 4-9: Mail Center toolbar icon

- `Mail Center`: AOL's main email area. Good tips and how-tos for beginners.

- **Read Mail**: Like the **Read** toolbar icon, opens your email box and shows you the contents of the **New Mail** folder. Click the **Old Mail** or **Sent Mail** tab to view those folders.

- **Write Mail**: Like the **Write** toolbar icon, opens a **Write Mail** window where you can compose a new, outgoing email message.

- **Old Mail**: Opens the **Old Mail** folder of your email box, which contains mail you've read.

- **Sent Mail**: Opens the **Sent Mail** folder of your email box, which contains mail you've written and sent.

- **Address Book**: Opens your email address book. See also the entry *Address Book* in Chapter 8, *Email*.

- **Mail Preferences**: Opens the Mail Preferences screen, where you can adjust email settings. See also the entry *preferences* in Chapter 8, *Email*.

- **Mail Controls**: An area where you can block unwanted email, **Keyword: Mail Controls**. See also the entry *Mail Controls* in Chapter 8, *Email*.

- **Mail Extras**: An explanation of AOL email enhancements, **Keyword: Mail Extras**. See also *Mail Extras* in Chapter 8.

- **Set Up Automatic AOL (Flashsessions)**: Walks you through setting up Automatic AOL for the first time. See also Chapter 21.

- **Run Automatic AOL (Flashsessions) Now**: Click **Begin** to start an Automatic AOL session; click **Set Session** to adjust your settings or schedule a session. If you've never run Automatic AOL before, you're walked through setting it up as if you'd chosen **Set Up Automatic AOL Now**. After setting it up, you'll have to rechoose **Run Automatic AOL Now**.

- **Read Offline Mail**: Read, online or offline, mail that you've sent or received during an Automatic AOL session, and/or mail that you've saved. You can also review copies of mail that you've cued up to be sent later, during an Automatic AOL session. See also *saving* in Chapter 8, *Email* and "Email" in Chapter 21, *Automatic AOL*.

Print Toolbar Icon

The **Print** toolbar icon actually doesn't print your document with one click, but it's easier than selecting **Print** from the **File** menu, which is another option. It's a redesigned version of AOL 3.0's printer icon. The **Print** toolbar icon is shown in Figure 4-10.

1. **Print**: Select print range, print quality, and number of copies. Click **OK** to print.

My Files Toolbar Icon

The **My Files** toolbar icon includes several organizational features such as the **Personal Filing Cabinet**, **Download Manager**, and **Log Manager**. **Save To Personal Filing Cabinet** and **My Web Page** are new to the 4.0 toolbar, but exist in AOL 3.0. The **My Files** toolbar icon is shown in Figure 4-11.

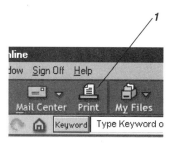

Figure 4-10: Print toolbar icon

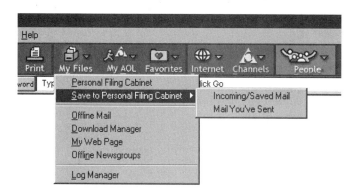

Figure 4-11: My Files toolbar icon

- **Personal Filing Cabinet**: Opens your PFC, where you can store old email, message board and newsgroup posts, and downloaded files. See also Chapter 18, *Personal Filing Cabinet.*

- **Save to Personal Filing Cabinet**: Saves any open new, old, or sent email messages to the **Incoming/Saved Mail** or **Mail You've Sent** folder in your Personal Filing Cabinet. So you won't have to do this manually, you can configure AOL to automatically save your email to your PFC; see the entry *saving* in Chapter 8, *Email.* You can't save message board or newsgroup postings to your PFC this way.

- **Offline Mail**: Displays the three **Mail** folders in your Personal Filing Cabinet. From these folders, whether you're signed on or not, you can read mail that you've saved in your personal filing cabinet or mail that you've sent or received during an Automatic AOL session. See also *saving* in Chapter 8, *Email* and "Email" in Chapter 21, *Automatic AOL.*

- **Download Manager**: Opens your **Download Manager**, a tool so useful we can't cover all the features right here; see the entry *Download Manager* in Chapter 20, *Downloading.*

- **My Web Page**: AOL's Personal Publisher, a tool for creating a personal web page.

- **Offline Newsgroups**: Displays the three Newsgroups folders in your PFC. From these folders, whether you're signed on or not, you can read message board and newsgroup postings you've sent or received during an Automatic AOL session. See also the sections "Message Boards" and "Newsgroups" in Chapter 21, *Automatic AOL*.

- **Log Manager**: Opens the **Log Manager**, used for saving records of online activity such as chats and instant messages. See also the sections "Saving Chats and Chat Rooms" in Chapter 10, *Chatting*, and "IM Tricks and Treats" in Chapter 9, *Instant Messages and Buddy Lists*.

My AOL Toolbar Icon

The **My AOL** toolbar icon contains many of the features that allow you to customize AOL, such as your account's preferences, Parental Controls, screen names, Buddy List, and stock portfolios. This toolbar icon is new to AOL 4.0, but all of its features appear in AOL 3.0 (though not on the 3.0 toolbar). The **My AOL** toolbar icon is shown in Figure 4-12.

Figure 4-12: My AOL toolbar icon

- **My AOL**: A beginners' explanation of AOL's customizable features, such as **Parental Controls** and **Preferences**; Keyword: **My AOL**.

- **Set Up AOL**: Walks you through setting up your screen names, member profile, Buddy List, parental controls, news profiles, and stock portfolios.

- **Preferences**: The main AOL Preferences screen, where you can adjust your settings to make your AOL experience more pleasant. See also Chapter 29.

- **My Member Profile**: Where to create, edit, or delete your member profile.

- **Screen Names**: The place to create, update, restore, or delete screen names, Keyword: **Names**. See also the section "Creating and Managing Screen Names" in Chapter 3, *Screen Names, Passwords, and Signing On*.

- **Passwords**: The place to change your password, `Keyword: Password`. See also the section "Passwords" in Chapter 3.

- `Parental Controls`: The `Parental Controls` main screen, where you can block your child's access to parts of the online world, `Keyword: Parental Controls`. See also Chapter 28.

- `Online Clock`: Tells you the date, the time, and how long you've been online, `Keyword: Online Clock`.

- `Buddy List`: The `Buddy List` settings screen, `Keyword: Buddy`. See also the section "Setting Up Your First Buddy List" in Chapter 9, *Instant Messages and Buddy Lists*.

- `Personal Publisher`: AOL's Personal Publisher, a tool for creating a personal web page.

- `Stock Portfolios`: Looks up stock quotes and manages your online profile, `Keyword: Portfolio`.

- `Reminder Service`: An AOL service that reminds you, via email, of important events, `Keyword: Reminder`. See also the entry *reminder service* in Chapter 8, *Email*.

- `News Profiles`: An AOL service that emails you news briefs tailored to your interests, `Keyword: News Profiles`. See also the entry *News Profiles* in Chapter 8, *Email*.

Favorites Toolbar Icon

The `Favorites` toolbar icon contains a list of your Favorite Places (both the defaults and the favorites you add) and special numerical shortcut keys you can `Edit` to go to areas of your choice. All these features exist in AOL 3.0. The `Favorites` toolbar icon is shown in Figure 4-13.

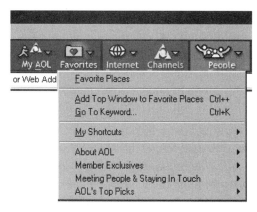

Figure 4-13: Favorites toolbar icon

- `Favorite Places`: Opens a separate window that contains your Favorite Places; you can modify your Favorite Places from here. See also Chapter 17, *Favorite Places*.

- **Add Top Window to Favorite Places**: Selects the topmost open window as a Favorite Place (if it has a red heart icon in the upper right). Add it to your Favorite Places, add it to an email message, or add it to an Instant Message.

- **Go To Keyword**: Opens a Keyword box. If you don't understand keywords, see the section "Getting Familiar with the AOL Interface" in Chapter 1, *Introduction*.

- **My Shortcuts**: Contains a listing of default keyboard shortcuts to certain areas. Select **Edit Shortcuts** to delete these and make your own. For details on making your own keyboard shortcuts, see Chapter 19.

- **About AOL, Member Exclusives, Meeting People & Staying In Touch,** and **AOL's Top Picks** are the default **Favorite Places** folders that house the default Favorite Places. Edit or delete these folders and Favorite Places, or add your own, by selecting **Favorite Places** from the **Favorites** menu. In addition, any Favorite Places you add appear here among the defaults. An item with an arrow to the right of it indicates a folder with more Favorite Places inside; move your mouse over the folder to view its contents. An item without an arrow is an individual Favorite Place.

Internet Toolbar Icon

The **Internet** toolbar icon houses many of AOL's Internet features: the Web, newsgroups, FTP, and several web pages. Remember that when you're on the Internet, AOL's Terms of Service don't generally apply (see also Appendix D, *Terms of Service*). You can use all of these features on AOL 3.0 (though they aren't located in the same places, if at all, on the 3.0 toolbar). The **Internet** toolbar icon is shown in Figure 4-14.

Figure 4-14: Internet toolbar icon

- **Internet Connection**: AOL's main area for Internet (Web, newsgroup, FTP) activity. Good for Internet beginners, **Keyword: Internet**.

- **Go to the Web**: Launches a web browser and opens your default start page.

- **AOL Netfind**: A web page, *http://www.aol.com/netfind/*, that can help you find people, places, and things on the Web.

- **Newsgroups**: AOL's main newsgroups area, **Keyword: Newsgroups**. See also Chapter 13, *Newsgroups*.

- FTP (File Transfer): AOL's main page for FTP'ing, **Keyword: FTP**. See also Chapter 23, *Web Publishing and FTP*.

- Internet White Pages: Finds people and businesses on the Web via a web page called Switchboard at *http://www.switchboard.com*.

- Internet Yellow Pages: Searches for businesses by name and city via Switchboard's business-specific search engine at *http://www.switchboard.com*.

Channels Toolbar Icon

The Channels toolbar icon lists AOL Channels: content about a certain topic, such as sports or news, gathered in one place. We don't explain what each of these drop-down menu choices are in this chapter. Instead, we go into more detail about the channels and their subareas in Chapter 15, *AOL Content Reference*. The Channels toolbar icon is shown in Figure 4-15.

Figure 4-15: Channels toolbar icon

People Toolbar Icon

The People toolbar icon connects you to other AOL members through chat rooms, your Buddy List, Instant Messages, and the AOL Member Directory. It also links to a web site where you can search for non-AOL members' email and street addresses, and phone numbers. This toolbar icon doesn't exist in AOL 3.0, but all its features are accessible via 3.0. The People toolbar icon is shown in Figure 4-16.

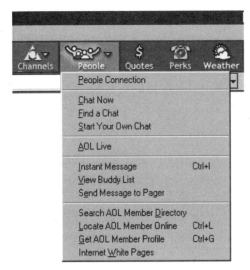

Figure 4-16: People toolbar icon

- **People Connection**: The entrance to AOL's main chat area, **Keyword: People**. See also Chapter 10, *Chatting*.

- **Chat Now**: Takes you directly into a chat lobby, **Keyword: Lobby**. See also the section "Featured and Member Rooms" in Chapter 10.

- **Find a Chat**: Browse **Featured** and **Member** chat rooms for ones you'd like to enter. See also the section "Featured and Member Rooms" in Chapter 10.

- **Start Your Own Chat**: This feature has three options: create a new Member room that other members will be able to see and join; create a new Private room that only others who know the exact name will be able to join; enter an existing Private room, if you know its name. See also the sections "Private Rooms and Buddy Chat" and "Featured and Member Rooms" in Chapter 10.

- **AOL Live**: AOL's main area for celebrity and event chats, **Keyword: Live**. See also the section "Auditorium Chats" in Chapter 10.

- **Instant Message**: Opens an **Instant Message** window, as does **Ctrl-i**. To initiate an Instant Message, type a screen name and a message and click **Send**. See also the section "Sending Instant Messages" in Chapter 9, *Instant Messages and Buddy Lists*.

- **View Buddy List**: Displays your Buddy List, also at **Keyword: Buddy-View**. See also the section "Buddy Lists: Where Your Friends Are" in Chapter 9.

- **Send Message to Pager**: Page someone through AOL, if you know her pager number and paging company. Also at **Keyword: SendPage**.

- **Search AOL Member Directory**: Searches the directory of profiles that contain any word or phrase. Also at **Keyword: Directory**.

- **Locate AOL Member Online**: Type a screen name and click OK to see if that member is in a chat room (and, if so, which one). You can also use **Ctrl-l**.

- **Get AOL Member Profile**: Type a screen name and click OK to view that member's profile (if she has one). You can also use **Ctrl-g**.

- **Internet White Pages**: Find people and businesses on the Web via this link to a web page called Switchboard, *http://www.switchboard.com.*

Quotes, Perks, and Weather Toolbar Icons

You can see the **Quotes**, **Perks**, and **Weather** toolbar icons if you have a monitor resolution of 800×600 or better. They are all new to AOL 4.0 (but available in 3.0 via keywords), and they can all be removed from your toolbar if you either don't like them, or want to replace them with icons of your own (for information on how to add your own toolbar icons in 4.0, see the section "Adding and Removing Toolbar Icons" later in this chapter). The **Quotes**, **Perks**, and **Weather** toolbar icons are shown in Figure 4-17.

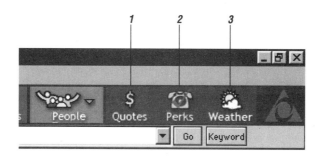

Figure 4-17: Quotes, Perks, and Weather toolbar icons

1. **Quotes**: Look up stock quotes and manage your online profile. Also at **Keyword: Quotes**.

2. **Perks**: An area that promotes offers like the AOL Visa and the AOL long-distance plan. Also at **Keyword: Perks**.

3. **Weather**: AOL's main weather area, searchable by zip code or city.

AOL and Web Navigation Bar

The AOL and Web navigation bar is a result of AOL's desire to integrate its own content with web content and make it easier for you to get around both AOL and the Web. The navigation arrows on the left (which symbolize moving back or forward through pages you've viewed) work for both AOL areas and web pages.

To get around, you can type either a keyword or a URL (web address) in the navigation bar's large white box, and go directly to that area.

Our favorite part of the navigation bar is a history trail drop-down window that allows you to view and quickly navigate back to the last 25 places you've been. All these features are new in AOL 4.0. The history trail and the rest of the navigation bar are shown in Figure 4-18.

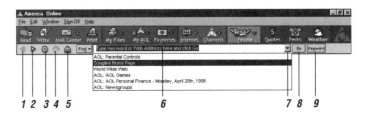

Figure 4-18: AOL and Web navigation bar

1. The left arrow takes you to the previous AOL area or web page in the history trail.

2. The forward arrow takes you to the next AOL area or web page, if any, in the history trail.

3. The circle with the X in it stops the current AOL area or web page from loading.

4. The circular arrow reloads the current web page.

5. The house icon takes you to your "home" page. The default is *http://www.aol.com*. To change it, see the section "WWW" in Chapter 29, *Preferences*.

6. The box that says **Type Keyword or Web Address here and click Go** is a dual-purpose keyword box and URL window. Follow those instructions to go directly to an AOL area or web page; no need to type *http://*. You can hit the **Enter** or **Return** key on your keyboard rather than clicking Go.

7. When you click on the arrow to the right of the keyword box/URL window, you open what's called a history trail. This is a list of the last 25 AOL areas and web pages you've been to. You can return to any history trail location by clicking it. In its default state, the history trail does not clear itself after each **Sign Off** or **Switch Screen Name**. To adjust this, see the later section "Toolbar Preferences."

8. The Go button is used with the keyword box.

9. The **Keyword** button opens a window where you can type a keyword in a box. You can also use **Ctrl-k** or type the keyword in the keyword box (see the next section, "Using the Toolbar Versus Keyboard Shortcuts").

Find Icon

Like the name says, use the Find icon to find things online: AOL content, web content, and access numbers. This Find icon is new in AOL 4.0 (there is a Find icon in 3.0 that links to Keyword: Find Central), but you can find most of its individual features in 3.0 through keywords or web pages. The Find icon is shown in Figure 4-19.

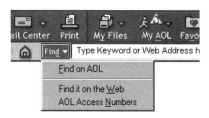

Figure 4-19: Find menu

- Find on AOL: An AOL area, Keyword: Find Central, that gathers all the options of the Find menu onto one screen.

- Find it on the Web: Searches for people, places, and things on the Web at *http://www.aol.com/netfind/.* Also at Keyword: NetFind.

- AOL Access Numbers: Type in an area code to find local access numbers. See also Chapter 27.

Toolbars & Menus

Using the Toolbar Versus Keyboard Shortcuts

There are really two camps when it comes to getting around: either you use keyboard shortcuts or you stick almost exclusively to the menus and toolbar. We know people who use only the toolbar to get around AOL, preferring the ease of the graphical interface and the mouse to having to remember a series of keystrokes. On the other hand, keyboard shortcuts are easy to learn and can save a lot of time and wrist strain. For the shortcut-inclined, we list them all in Chapter 19. In addition, keyboard shortcuts for menu items are often printed on the menus themselves; look for them as you use AOL's menus and toolbar.

Toolbar Preferences

Now here's a vast improvement in AOL 4.0: the ability to alter your toolbar's settings didn't exist in earlier versions. We especially like being able to clear the history trail upon sign off to protect our privacy.

To adjust your toolbar preferences:

MY AOL toolbar icon → Preferences → Toolbar

The toolbar preferences screen is shown in Figure 4-20.

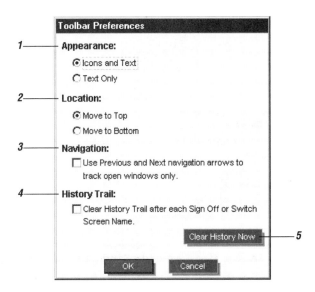

Figure 4-20: Toolbar preferences screen

Your options include:

1. **Appearance: Icons and Text or Text Only**: The default is to use toolbar icons with text and pictures. Changing to text only makes the buttons take up less vertical space but slightly more horizontal space on your monitor.

2. **Location: Move to Top or Move to Bottom**: The default toolbar location is the top of your screen, but you can move it to the bottom.

3. **Navigation: Use Previous and Next navigation arrows to track open windows only**: The arrow icons on the toolbar let you navigate backwards and forwards through your History Trail (the record of the last 25 AOL areas or web sites you've visited). The default is to have this option disabled, so you can use the arrows to navigate to windows you've closed. If you enable this option by checking the checkbox, you'll use the arrows only to navigate within open windows (though you'll be able to revisit closed windows with the History Trail drop-down menu).

4. **History Trail: Clear History Trail after each Sign Off or Switch Screen Name**: The History Trail is located in the drop-down toolbar menu between the Keyword button and the Go button. It lists the last 25 places you've been on AOL or the Web. The default is to keep the last 25 places at all times—but by enabling this preference, you can clear the history trail every time you sign off or switch screen names. This is a good way to keep other screen names on your account from seeing where you've been.

5. **Clear History Now**: This button clears the history trail, but you'll have to enable the Clear History Trail After Each Sign Off or Switch Screen Name preference to have it cleared regularly and by default.

Adding and Removing Toolbar Icons

With AOL 4.0, it is possible to customize your toolbar with icons that link directly to your favorite areas or web sites, as long as your screen resolution is set at 800×600 or better. If you prefer using the toolbar to navigating with keywords or keyboard shortcuts, this is an ideal feature for you.

Creating New Toolbar Icons

With AOL 4.0, you can add your own favorite places to the toolbar. When you add your own icons, you'll have one-click access to any areas you choose, including web sites, AOL areas, newsgroups, and chat rooms.

Here's how to set up your new toolbar icons. Drag and drop any heart icon onto AOL's main toolbar. When you release the mouse, you'll see a window that allows you to choose your own icon for your link. Click an icon to select it, type a name for the icon in the `Label` box, and click `OK`. Figure 4-21 shows some choices you have in creating your own toolbar icons.

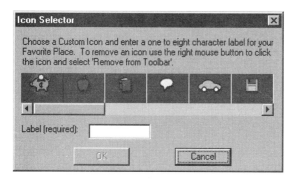

Figure 4-21: Selecting a name and a picture for your new toolbar icon

Your new icon appears in the toolbar alongside AOL's default icons. It has a slightly different font than the other icons, but otherwise it blends right in. Figure 4-22 shows our custom icon, `Cat Care`, in the toolbar.

Figure 4-22: A sample customized icon, "Cat Care"

Benefits

- You can customize your toolbar with your favorite areas.

- One-click access to AOL areas and web sites from within AOL.

- Only people signed on to your account with your PC see these favorites; they're not for public viewing like desktop icons.

Drawback

- Your monitor resolution must be at least 800×600 or there's no room for your own icons. At 800×600 resolution, you'll have to remove at least one of the default icons before there's room for yours; we removed the Weather toolbar icon. At resolutions of 1024×768 or more, you have plenty of extra room for the default icons plus your own toolbar icons.

Removing Toolbar Icons

If you've added icons to the toolbar—or if you don't use or like the Quotes, Perks, and Weather toolbar icons—it's easy to remove them. Just right-mouse-click on the icon and select Remove from Toolbar. We're removing the Perks icon in Figure 4-23.

Figure 4-23: Right-clicking on a toolbar icon to remove it

CHAPTER 5

Online Shorthand

Online communication is speedy and informal—just like the way we talk to each other on the phone, over the tops of our office cubicles, or in line at the super-market. Yet online communication is also dramatically different. For one, most of us can talk faster than we can type. We rely on body language, voice inflection, and facial expressions to get our point across. And, for some reason, most of us take more care when writing letters on paper than we do when writing letters in email. Online communication, for all its speed and informality, can become muddled by unclear writing, slow typing, and the lack of visual or audio clues.

Fortunately, some conventions have evolved to help make online communication (almost) as easy to understand as any other kind, while at the same time retaining the speed and informality that characterizes spoken language. Such conventions include the use of types of online shorthand called *smileys* and acronyms.

Smileys, also called *emoticons*, are symbols that make online conversation (including email, chat, and Instant Messages) clearer and more entertaining. They're keyboard characters that look like sideways smiley-faces and are meant to convey emotion. For example, it's hard to convey sarcasm in a medium where no one can hear your tone of voice, and you've only got one sentence to express yourself. In this chapter, we explain smileys and other ways of showing emotion or physical actions online.

Acronyms are abbreviations that make online communication faster, just as they make offline communication faster. You probably already know some common acronyms: Typing "ASAP" is faster than typing "as soon as possible," and most of us already know that AKA stands for "also known as." We use acronyms whether we're chatting on AOL or typing a memo at work. This chapter offers a short guide to acronyms and phrase abbreviations you might see in online conversations. The next time you see a jumble of alphabet soup in a chat room, in email, or on a message board, you can look it up in this chapter.

Before we get right into the smileys and acronyms, we'd like to point out that they're no substitute for good writing. Always think before you type!

Smileys

Smileys, or emoticons, as they're often called, are easy to understand as long as you realize that variations on :) mean something positive and variations on :(mean something negative.

>:) = smile
>
>:(= frown
>
>;) = wink
>
>:* = kiss
>
>:P = sticking your tongue out
>
>:D = laughing or grinning
>
>:/ = feeling ambivalent

The above emoticons, and variations on them, are the emoticons that actually get used in online conversations. You can start using emoticons like this:

>:-)===

just for fun, but no one will know what you're talking about. If you really want to get creative, it's best to label your creations, like this:

>:-)===   (a giraffe)

If you can't get enough smileys, there's an O'Reilly & Associates book appropriately titled *Smileys* that documents more than 600 of them: the catalog in which to find it is at the URL *http://www.oreilly.com/catalog/smileys*.

Other Emoticons

It doesn't end with smileys. Other ways to express actions and emotions online include:

Grinning

>\<g> = person is grinning
>
>\<eg> = person is wearing an evil grin
>
>\<vbg> = person is wearing a very big grin

Grinning is very much like typing a happy or winking smiley. Just like in real life, grinning might signify that you're happy, or that you're kidding. For example:

>But I LOVE the Spice Girls! \<g>

Emoting

Brackets, asterisks, or colons around an action indicate what a person is doing. For example:

```
<emote> or *emote* or ::emote::
```

Just replace "emote" with any action, like:

```
<looks around>
*ponders last night's X-Files*
::runs away from inane chat room::
```

Hugging

{{{Screen_Name}}} means someone is giving member Screen_Name a big hug. As in real life, it's probably wise to refrain from hugging random people. {Hug} your friends, if you don't think they'll take it the wrong way. The exception to this rule is online support groups, where strangers {hug} each other all the time.

For example:

```
Sorry your day has been so bad. {{RSIouch}}
```

Pointing

When in a chat room, type an arrow pointing to the left,

```
<-----
```

followed by an action or emotion. In chat, the arrow will appear pointing to your screen name, like this:

```
TiredWritr: <----- hoping you'll like this book
```

That means member TiredWritr hopes you'll like this book.

Poofing

When someone types poof, that means the person is leaving the chat room. It will look something like this:

```
TiredWritr: Oh jeez, look at the time.
TiredWritr: poof
```

Acronyms

Some acronyms on this list are more common than others; as long as you know what LOL and IMHO mean, you'll probably be okay. But netizens are acronym-happy, so it can't hurt to be familiar with a bunch of them so you'll be able to decode chat-room conversations and message-board posts. Use sparingly: we think that once you start using acronyms like ROTFLMAOWTIME (Rolling On The Floor Laughing My Ass Off With Tears In My Eyes), it's time to sign off for a while and read a book.

Some common online acronyms are:

AFAIK = As Far As I Know

AFK = Away From Keyboard

AKA = Also Known As

ASAP = As Soon As Possible

BAK = Back At Keyboard

BBL = Be Back Later

BF = Boyfriend

BRB = Be Right Back

BTW = By The Way

BWL = Busting With Laughter

CNP... = Continued Next Post

CYA = See Ya

EG = Evil Grin

FWIW = For What It's Worth

FYI = For Your Information

GF = Girlfriend

GFN = Gone For Now

GMTA = Great Minds Think Alike

GTSY = Glad To See You

H&K = Hug and Kiss

HTH = Hope This Helps

IC = I See

IMHO = In My Humble Opinion

IMNSHO = In My Not-So-Humble Opinion

IMO = In My Opinion

IRL = In Real Life

JK = Just Kidding

JMO = Just My Opinion

JTLYK = Just To Let You Know

k = Okay

KIT = Keep In Touch

KOC = Kiss On Cheek

KOL = Kiss On Lips

L8R = Later

LDR = Long Distance Relationship

LOL = Laughing Out Loud

LTNS = Long Time No See

OIC = Oh, I See

OTTOMH = Off The Top of My Head

PMFJI = Pardon Me For Jumping In

POAHF = Put On A Happy Face

ROFL or ROTFL = Rolling On The Floor Laughing

RTFM = Read The F***ing Manual

SO = Significant Other

SWAK = Sealed With A Kiss

SYS = See You Soon

TCOB = Taking Care Of Business

thx = Thanks

TLA = Three Letter Acronym

TTFN = Ta-Ta for Now

TTYL = Talk To You Later

TTYS = Talk To You Soon

WB = Welcome Back

WTF? = What The F***?

WTG = Way To Go

WTH? = What The Hell/Heck?

WYSIWYG = What You See Is What You Get

YMMV = Your Mileage May Vary

Acronym Humor

And now, just for fun, some computer acronyms. This file has been floating around the Internet for a while and we can't find the author, but we think it's too hilarious not to include. Warning: computer geek humor ahead.

AMIGA = A Merely Insignificant Game Addiction

APPLE = Arrogance Produces Profit Losing Entity

BASIC = Bill's Attempt to Seize Industry Control

CD-ROM = Consumer Device, Rendered Obsolete in Months

COBOL = Completely Obsolete Business Oriented Language

DEC = Do Expect Cuts

DOS = Defunct Operating System

IBM = I Blame Microsoft

ISDN = It Still Does Nothing

LISP = Lots of Infuriating and Silly Parentheses

MACINTOSH = Most Applications Crash; If Not, The Operating System Hangs

MICROSOFT = Most Intelligent Customers Realize Our Software Only Fools Teenagers

MIPS = Meaningless Indication of Processor Speed

OS/2 = Obsolete Soon, Too

PCMCIA = People Can't Memorize Computer Industry Acronyms

PENTIUM = Produces Erroneous Numbers Through Incorrect Understanding of Mathematics

RISC = Reduced Into Silly Code

SCSI = System Can't See It

WINDOWS = Will Install Needless Data On Whole System

WWW = World Wide Wait

CHAPTER 6

Help from AOL

When you're signed on to AOL, you'll sometimes find that you need additional help. AOL, like most other programs that strive to be as user-friendly as possible, has its own collection of online help resources. While it's usually not exhaustive, and is often difficult to know how to find, AOL's online help often contains the most up-to-date information on a particular topic. When AOL changes its software or adds a new feature, you might need to consult the online help. AOL's online help can be great if you're really confused and need to be walked step by step through a feature or you hit a snag in an area that's new to you.

When you use AOL online help, keep one caveat in mind: their job is to make you happy, not point out the limitations in the way AOL does things. Online help is a quick and dirty "how to." You'll get the job done, but online help often won't explain all of the ramifications of modifying your AOL setup or software. Also, it usually doesn't help you understand the exact benefits and drawbacks of what you'll do.

The main place for AOL help is found at `Keyword: Help`. Go there for all your general woes. We like what's at `Keyword: Help`, for the most part, but we have trouble tracking down a few items as readily as we'd like. That's where this chapter comes in. We've found it and now give it directly to you in this alphabetically organized chapter. We especially refer you to the following entries: ***accounts and billing***, ***canceling***, and ***Live Help***. For some reason, these are the things many people have difficulty finding on AOL.

Use the entries below as a reference to point you in the right direction. You can read all of the entries or go right to the area that covers your problem in the alphabetical list.

access phone numbers

AOL is constantly adding new local-access numbers throughout the world. If you're going on a trip and plan to take your laptop with you, you can get a list of numbers in that area, usually numbers that are local calls. While we recommend AOL's new, automatic method of finding access numbers, which we discuss in Chapter 27, *Connecting*, you can also go to Keyword: Access to get lists of new numbers throughout the world.

Help menu → AOL Access Phone Numbers

accounts and billing

Check your account activity (including master and secondary screen names). Learn what you're spending in premium areas, how much your current bill comes to, or, if you have the hourly plan, what your usage has been. Go to Keyword: Billing or follow this path:

Help menu → Accounts and Billing

If you have billing questions that can't be answered via the online help text, you can go into a special chat to talk to a representative at Billing Help Interactive.

See also Chapter 22, *Billing*, for detailed information on managing your account and understanding billing intricacies.

canceling

At Keyword: Cancel you'll find out how to cancel your AOL account, but you won't actually be able to cancel online! Imagine that, an online service which doesn't allow you to sever your ties with it without picking up the telephone, sending a fax, or writing a letter!

Call us opinionated, but we're not happy with AOL's decision to disallow online cancellations. Since the advantage to having an online account with a service like AOL is the immediacy with which you can do things, shouldn't canceling also be immediate? Until online cancellation is possible, you have the following three options:

- *Telephone*: Toll free at 1-800-827-6364 or 1-888-265-8008

  AOL Representatives are waiting to convince you not to cancel. They get paid to get you to stay on AOL. Be strong if you want to cancel. To make the process a bit quicker and less painful, be ready to give your name, address, day and evening phone numbers, and payment method (credit card or checking-account debit information). Alternatives to the dreaded phone reps are fax and mail.

- *Fax*: 1-801-622-7969

  Include in the fax your full name, address, phone number, and master account screen name.

- *Mail*:

  America Online
  P.O. Box 1600
  Ogden, UT 84401

Whether you mail or fax, be sure to include your full name, address, phone number, and master screen name. If you mail it in, give it some time to arrive, since you don't want to be charged for an extra month because you sent it in the day before a new billing period.

See also Chapter 31, *Canceling and Suspending Service*.

---

computing

For help with computers in general, not AOL, go to Keyword: Help Desk. You'll find support forums, Frequently Asked Questions, newsletters, and virus and hardware information.

GPF (General Protection Fault)

Keyword: GPF is where to go when AOL keeps crashing. You'll get help deciphering the error messages, understanding the cause of the problem(s), and preventing recurrences by following AOL's solution (Windows only).

---

keyword help

We think keywords are pretty basic stuff. But some people don't use keywords, or don't even know how to use them. Some haven't even heard of them! Keyword: Learn Keywords is the place for some hand-holding, or go to Help menu → Help with Keywords.

---

learn AOL

Keyword: Learn AOL is mainly for beginners. Take tours and learn lessons about mail, message boards, navigating AOL, chat, the Internet, and family use.

---

live help

You've got two options, neither of which is optimal because you usually have to wait for anywhere from a few minutes to a half an hour before getting a warm body to assist you. Member Services online help—covered in the next section—is better because it is quicker. In any case, all live help is free. The sections below give your live options.

Member Help Interactive

You chat with a live technical representative by typing in your problem, just like in a chat room. The wait usually isn't too bad, and you can do other things online while you wait your turn as a timer shows the estimated amount of time until a live person shows up. It's available seven days a week, from 7 a.m. to 2:45 a.m. There's a small Catch-22 which is that you must be able to connect to AOL via your modem.

Getting there isn't easy (AOL buries its live help, presumably so that you'll use other online help first). Go to `Keyword: Help`. Choose any one of the topics listed under `Pick a help topic`, then click `Ask The Staff`. You'll see a screen with a number of help options listed. Follow the link for "online" help.

Telephone Help

Below, we list the places to call when you want to talk to a live person. Waits can be long (we've heard reports of 30-minute waits for technical support help), so you're better off using this book to answer your questions, or going online for some text-based help. If you're looking for access numbers, see the entry *access phone numbers* in this chapter. Again, each of these telephone numbers is toll-free.

*   Screen name or password problems: 1-888-265-8004

*   General questions/problems: 1-888-265-8006

*   Billing: 1-888-265-8003

*   Access numbers: 1-888-265-8005

*   Another customer service number we throw in, just for completeness, is this one for technical support: 1-800-827-3338 or, if you're outside the U.S. and Canada, 1-703-264-1184.

See also *canceling* for a special number to call if you want to cancel, *Members Helping Members* to read other members' suggestions to your problem, and *Member Services Online Help* to try a quicker fix to your problem than live help.

Member Services Online Help

Member Service Online Help houses the main body of AOL help. You must be signed on to AOL to access this help. You can pick a help topic and read the sub-entries that pertain to your problem. Or, you can search a good-sized database that explains the rudiments of carrying out any activity or changing any preference on AOL.

The simplest way to get there is `Keyword: Help` or follow this path:

> Help menu → `Member Services Online Help`

In the case where you can't find the information you need from online help, you can get help from a live technical assistant. Live help comes in two forms, over the telephone or in online chat (we cover this information in the entry *live help* in this chapter).

Members Helping Members

At `Keyword: MHM` members help one another by posting questions and answers on AOL. We wouldn't waste too much time here, since there are more questions than answers.

modem help

When you're having modem troubles, go to `Keyword: Modem` for assistance with the diagnoses and cure.

For more in-depth information, see also Chapter 27, *Connecting*.

net help

`Keyword: nethelp` is a database of help with browsing the Web, FTP, email, newsgroups, mailing lists, and gopher. If you're experiencing an error message, you can find out what it means here.

new member

Take a tour and get some information on the details of your general and mail preferences, passwords, and screen names at `Keyword: My AOL`.

See also Chapter 8, *Email*; Chapter 29, *Preferences*; and Chapter 3, *Screen Names, Passwords, and Signing On.*

offline help

Offline help works like all other Windows-compatible help directories. You can browse the directory, get a list of topics to choose from, or search by typing in a phrase or sentence that describes what you're looking for. Be warned that it's not exactly comprehensive. Get there at:

`Help` menu → `Offline help`

Parental Controls

While there's online information for parents at `Keyword: Parental Controls`, we think our more detailed analysis in Chapter 28, *Parental Controls*, gives you more of the big picture.

Quickstart

Help on the basics, as well as an interactive system called Match Your Interests that delivers lists of AOL content areas that suit your interests at Keyword: Quickstart.

system response

If you consistently get the dreaded system-response message from AOL, which states that AOL can't access the information you requested, go to Keyword: System Response. From there, you can get help determining whether you need to make some changes to your AOL software or to your own computer's configuration. Usually, however, the problem is AOL's: their servers are experiencing delays or bogging down.

tips for using AOL, expert and beginner

Written by a fictional character (based on a real person, but currently represented by a cartoon), Meg dispenses some helpful advice and workarounds at Keyword: AOL Insider.

CHAPTER 7

Essential AOL Survival Tips

We know that not everyone has time to read this entire book. Reading technical books cover-to-cover isn't our idea of fun, either. With that in mind, we've gathered the most important advice in this book into one short chapter, to make sure you don't miss any of it. If you read only one chapter in this book—horrors! ;)— make it this one.

Each of these survival tips is a crucial, don't-leave-home-without-it piece of advice that you need to live with AOL. AOL's quirks can be annoying, but AOL itself often gives you to tools you need to make the annoyances go away. Too bad that they don't try harder to publicize ways to get rid of the ubiquitous marketing advertisements, unfreeze the frozen hourglass, or block more of your unwanted email.

We use these to keep our sanity and patience intact, and we hope you'll use them, too. Don't be tempted to skip this chapter because you think you already know all of AOL's ins and outs: even if you've been online for a while, you might not know all these tips.

Annihilating Spam

Junk email, a.k.a. spam: we hate it. True, it doesn't waste any paper, but it does waste time and bandwidth. Fortunately, spam can be avoided.

The most important thing you can do to avoid spam is use multiple screen names. You can have one screen name that only your friends and family know about and another screen name for everything else—including spam. There is a long list of activities that can attract spam, and which you should never do with a screen name you want to keep spam-free. For example:

- Chatting: spammers collect screen names from chat rooms.

- Posting to AOL message boards, Usenet newsgroups, and mailing lists: Spammers use automated tools to troll discussion forums for email addresses.

Survival Tips

- Registering at web sites that request an email address: Some, though certainly not all, web sites have no moral qualms about selling your email address to spammers.

To learn how to create an alternate screen name you can use for spam-attracting activities, see the section "Creating and Managing Screen Names" in Chapter 3, *Screen Names, Passwords, and Signing On.*

If you'd like to combat spam that's already coming, take advantage of AOL's mail controls to block specific email addresses and domain names from sending you email. See the entry **mail controls** in Chapter 8, *Email.*

One final tip: consider deleting your member profile. Spammers search profiles and send spam tailored to what you've stated are your areas of interest, your location, and other information. See the section "Screen Names and Privacy" in Chapter 3, *Screen Names, Passwords, and Signing On.*

What To Do When Your Screen Freezes

You know the scene: all you wanted to do was go to a simple keyword, and now you're staring at an hourglass, waiting. If, like us, you're too impatient to stare at the hourglass for long, you should know how to get rid of it.

Click the bright blue AOL logo in the upper-left corner of your screen. Highlight the Restore option. See Figure 7-1.

Figure 7-1: Breaking out of a frozen hourglass

Continuing to hold the mouse button down, slide your mouse to the right, off of the menu, and onto the Help menu. Click to drop down the menus. Now highlight any menu option, such as About America Online, release the mouse button, and watch the hourglass disappear. Now you can go about your AOL business as usual.

Turning Off Advertisements

We have yet to find someone who truly enjoys those ads for the AOL Visa and AOL Long Distance Plan that greet you when you sign on. To make matters worse, you can now get pop-up ads when you visit AOL content areas, not just when you first sign on. There is, however, an easy way to get rid of those annoying pop-up ads:

Go to Keyword: Marketing Prefs, and double-click Tell us what your pop-up preferences are. You're on your way, but AOL makes you jump through some hoops here. Make sure you carefully watch the screen and complete all the steps, or you won't turn off the pop ups.

First, click the box next to `If you prefer not to receive any special member benefit pop-up offers, click here...` (it's hidden among a lot of other text and boxes). Once you've done that, another box will pop up. Check the box next to `I prefer not to receive special member pop-up offers from AOL`. Click OK. If all went well, the pop-up advertisements will now be turned off. What you'll see onscreen is shown in Figure 7-2.

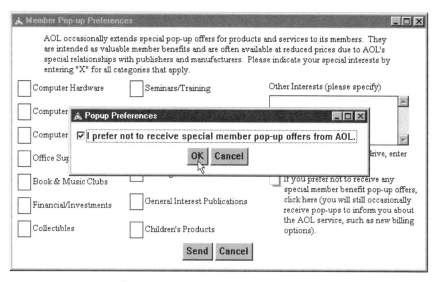

Figure 7-2: Turning off pop-up ads

See also "Marketing" in Chapter 29, *Preferences*.

Making Email Work Better

The first thing most people want to know about AOL email is how to get rid of spam (unwanted email). We've given spam its own section of this chapter under the heading "Annihilating Spam."

There are a few other important points to know about AOL email—points AOL should make clearer to its members.

When Email Gets Deleted by the System

The default is for old email to remain on AOL in the `Old Mail` folder for three days after you read it. Sometimes you want it to stick around longer, so that you can refer to it. To change the length of time old email stays on the system from one to seven days, follow this path:

```
My AOL toolbar icon → Preferences → Mail → Keep my old mail
online [number] days after I read it → OK
```

See also the entry *reading* in Chapter 8, *Email*.

You should also be aware that unread mail stays on AOL's servers for 27 days, so check your email regularly. After 27 days, you'll probably still see the mail listed in your mailbox (or `Read Mail` folder), but you won't be able to read it. You'll have to get the person who sent you the email to resend it.

See also the entry *undeliverable* in Chapter 8, *Email*.

Saving Your Email in Your PFC

We like having a running record of incoming and outgoing mail, so we enable archiving in the Personal Filing Cabinet. That way, if mail gets lost, or you want to go back and read old letters from colleagues and friends, you won't be told "Sorry, that mail is no longer available." The default on AOL is not to put any mail in your PFC.

To keep a permanent record of all the mail you read:

> `MY AOL` toolbar icon → `Preferences` → `Mail` → check `Retain All Mail I Receive in My Personal Filing Cabinet` → `OK`

To keep a permanent record of all the mail you send:

> `MY AOL` toolbar icon → `Preferences` → `Mail` → check `Retain All Mail I Send in My Personal Filing Cabinet` → `OK`

See also the entry *saving* in Chapter 8, *Email*.

Replying

To include part of the original message in your reply, you need to highlight the part of the message you want to copy, then click `Reply` or `Reply All`.

See also entry *replying* in Chapter 8, *Email*.

Recovering from Interrupted Downloads

The single best feature of AOL's downloading setup is this: when your download from somewhere on the AOL service gets interrupted, you can pick up where it left off. This doesn't count for downloads from web or FTP sites, however. To resume an AOL download, follow this path:

> `My Files` toolbar icon → `Download Manager` → highlight the interrupted file → `Download`

Don't delete the already downloaded portion of the file, or you won't be able to resume downloading where you left off.

See also *interruptions* in Chapter 20, *Downloading*.

You should also know about AOL's Download Manager, a useful tool for keeping track of files. We explain the Download Manager in detail in the section *Download Manager* in Chapter 20, *Downloading*.

Favorite Places: Getting Back To Where You've Been

Ever come across a web site or a handy tool on AOL, but then forgotten how to return later? Favorite Places is a tool you can use to help you return to the places you visit frequently or places you want to go back to at any point in the future. Primarily, Favorite Places help you get back to where you've been, functioning nearly exactly like the Bookmarks feature in Netscape Navigator, or the Favorites in MS Internet Explorer. When you're viewing an AOL area or web page you want to note for later, just click the heart icon in the upper right of the open window, and you've got a permanent record you can come back to at any time.

See also Chapter 17, *Favorite Places.*

Curtailing Harassment

Sometimes, someone just won't leave you alone. Whether a member is flooding your email box, deluging you with Instant Messages, or following you into chat rooms, you can make it stop.

Email

Unwanted email can come from individuals as well as advertisers (see also *spam* in Chapter 8, *Email*). AOL lets you specify the people from whom you want to block email:

> Keyword: Mail Controls → Set Up Mail Controls → select a screen name → Edit → Block mail from the addresses listed

Once you get to the right place in Mail Controls, you'll have to type the offending screen name or Internet email address in the **Type mail address here** box, and click **Add**. Then click **OK** to complete the block. When this person tries to send you email, he receives a message that says you're not accepting email from his account.

See also *mail controls* in Chapter 8, *Email.*

Buddy List

If someone can add you to her Buddy List, it's much easier for her to follow you to chat rooms, Instant Message you, and generally track your every online move. When you block someone from adding you to her Buddy List, she also can't use the **Locate** feature to locate you; she'll be told that you're not online, even if you are. To block someone from adding you to her Buddy List:

> Keyword: Buddy → Privacy Preferences → Block only those people whose screen names I list

Once you get to the right place in the Buddy List Privacy Preferences, type the offending screen name in the **Type screen name here** box, and click **Add**.

Repeat the step for as many screen names as you'd like to block. Click **Save** to lock in your changes when you're all done.

See also Chapter 9, *Instant Messages and Buddy Lists.*

Instant Message

Blocking Instant Messages from someone is just like blocking someone from adding you to his Buddy List. After entering the offending screen name and clicking **Add**, look for the section of the screen that says **Apply Preferences to the Following Features**. Click the **Buddy List and Instant Message** radio button. Click **Save**.

We think AOL should make it easier to block Instant Messages from somebody. For instance, if someone IM'ed you something that was immediately offensive or stupid, wouldn't it be nice to check a "Block" box right on the IM screen and never hear from him again? This feature exists in AOL's standalone Instant Messenger and other Internet messaging clients, and AOL would be doing its members a service to add it to Instant Messages.

See also Chapter 9.

Reporting Harassment

AOL wants to hear about the following trespasses: password or credit-card solicitations, offensive language, and suspicious email attachments. You can report harassment at **Keyword: Notify AOL**.

See also Appendix D, *Terms of Service.*

The AOL Tray Icon

The Windows Tray is the little gray box on the lower right of your screen, to the right of the toolbar. When you install AOL 4.0, you'll notice a turquoise AOL logo appears there, unbidden by you. You can start AOL by double-clicking it (or clicking it once and selecting **Launch**), which some people find useful. If you'd rather have the intrusive turquoise thing out of your tray, you can quit the application or remove the icon altogether.

To make the AOL tray icon temporarily disappear, click the icon, select **Exit**, and answer **Yes** to the window that pops up. The AOL tray icon goes away, but it will be back the next time you start up or reboot your computer.

To make the AOL tray icon permanently disappear, click the icon, select **Exit**, and answer **No** to the window that pops up. The icon still remains in your Windows StartUp menu, even though you'll never again see it in your tray. It only takes up 1KB of space, but anal-retentive types like us remove it anyway. To delete the AOL tray icon from your StartUp menu:

> Windows **Start** menu → **Programs** → **Windows Explorer** → Double-click **Windows** → Double-click **Start Menu** → Double-click **Programs** → Double-click **StartUp** → Highlight **America Online Tray Icon** → **File** menu → **Delete** → **Yes**

Disabling Call Waiting

If you don't disable call waiting when you're online, the signals from incoming calls cause interference in the line, and you'll probably lose your connection to AOL. Call waiting is restored when you sign off of AOL. Follow the path below to ask AOL to disable call waiting:

> From the Sign On screen, click Setup → Expert Setup → Locations tab → Highlight the number (connection) for which you want to disable call waiting → Edit → check the box Dial *70 to disable call waiting

Note: type a new number into the default box if *70 is not the way to disable call waiting in your area. Be sure that there's a comma after the dialing prefix (e.g., *70,).

You also have to edit each number in this location, otherwise, you'll still get bumped by incoming calls when you use other access numbers.

See also Chapter 27, *Connecting*.

Escaping Long Email and Big Graphics

The File menu says the Escape key on your keyboard will "Stop incoming text." That means you can use it to stop a long piece of unwanted email from downloading fully. If you've erroneously opened a huge chain letter, for instance, you can hit Esc and all those forwarded headers will stop loading.

The Escape key is also useful for stopping incoming pictures. If you're in an AOL area that's taking forever to load a huge graphic, hit Esc and it will stop. AOL's large graphics can be frustrating, so remember this tip if your computer has a slow modem and/or a slow processor.

PART II

Communicating

AOL and the Internet may be powered by machines, but you'll probably spend a lot of your online time talking to other human beings. Part II of this book details the many ways to meet new people, keep in touch with friends and family, and discuss specific topics on AOL. You'll find six different forms of communication in this section:

Chapter 8, *Email*: end electronic letters to friends, family, coworkers, and anyone else you can think of.

Chapter 9, *Instant Messages and Buddy Lists*: Keep track of your friends and exchange quick messages with them.

Chapter 10, *Chatting*: "Live" way to talk to lots of AOL members at once.

Chapter 11, *Message Boards*: Discussions of specific topics with AOL members.

Chapter 12, *Mailing Lists*: Talk about a subject via email with other interested people from all over the Internet.

Chapter 13, *Newsgroups*: They're like AOL message boards, except that anything goes!

CHAPTER 8

Email

Electronic mail (email) is, on the most basic level, like sending letters or postcards through the Internet. However, instead of arriving days later, email letters can arrive almost instantaneously—even on Sundays and holidays. Email is the most popular activity on the Internet (though we suspect chat might be the most popular activity on AOL, specifically). These days, not having an email address is like not having a TV: you may be happier without one, but some people wonder how you survive.

Personally, we would find it easier to live without TV. We love email for many reasons. For one, it's cheaper than long-distance phone calls (and an email message never makes you leap out of the shower to answer it). Email keeps you in touch: often people who never write letters on paper have no trouble dashing off an email during their morning coffee break or between classes. Unlike Instant Messages and chat, email can happen anytime; you don't have to catch someone online to email him.

Email has also changed the way people work. We send and receive scores of work-related email messages every day, including web links, HTML pages, Microsoft Word documents, and spreadsheets. Plenty of people have their email up and running for at least forty hours a week, and they wouldn't want it any other way.

Maybe not having email isn't quite like not having a television. But someday, we suspect that not having email will be like not having a phone.

So if you're wondering why this chapter is so huge, it's because email is such an expansive and important topic. It's changing the way people communicate, and email technology is getting better all the time. This introduction contains three sections that help you break email into manageable chunks:

- "If You're New to Email": listen up, beginners. This section tells you which parts of this chapter teach the absolute basics.

- "Email Essentials": the most important facts to know about AOL email and which parts of this chapter you can use to find out more.

Email

- "Benefits and Drawbacks": like the "Force" in *Star Wars*, AOL email has a good side and a dark side.

After you've read the introduction, use the alphabetical reference that comprises the rest of the chapter to look up specific email topics, just like in an encyclopedia. We've organized it alphabetically because email has so many small, specific subtopics. We wouldn't want you to have to read 20 pages just to find out how to send an electronic postcard or use rich text!

If You're New to Email

See the following sections of this chapter before you do anything else:

- To read the email you receive, see *reading*.
- It's easy to write email. If you don't believe us, see *writing*.
- After you've written email, see *sending* to send it on its way.

Once you understand the mechanics of reading and writing email, there are other entries in this chapter beginners shouldn't miss:

- *addressing* helps your email get where it's going.
- *carbon copy* and *blind carbon copy* are different ways to send one piece of email to many people at once.
- *replying* allows you to answer an email, and *forwarding* lets you pass it on.
- Learn the rules of *netiquette*, and you're unlikely to offend with your email.
- You should know what *acronyms* and *smileys* are.
- *password solicitations* are evil, but they happen. Protect yourself.

Email Essentials

- There's been a lot of talk about junk email (a.k.a. spam), but there are ways around it. See *Mail Controls* and *spam* for our suggestions.
- Don't get too paranoid, but there are a few things you should know about the potential dangers of email. If you read *Trojan horses* and *viruses*, you'll learn how to email with impunity.
- Have you ever lost an important piece of email? See *saving* to learn how to keep your email around as long as you want.
- There's more to email than text. See *attachments* to find out how much more.
- Email may be a casual medium, but it's always nice to see words spelled correctly. See *spellchecking*.
- We know some people are fond of the "you've got mail" sound, but if you're not one of them, you can change it. See *sound*.

- If you have a lot of friends and family online, you'll need to organize all those email addresses. See *address book*.

- What are AOL's future plans for email? See *clients* and *web-based email* to find out.

Benefits and Drawbacks

AOL email has a lot of pros and cons, so we decided to spell them out here. Since AOL email has special properties other email programs don't, these benefits and drawbacks refer specifically to AOL's email tools and features.

Benefits

- You can format your mail by adding rich text (see *rich text*), background color (see *background color*), embedded graphics (see *images*), and hyperlinks (see *hyperlinks*).

- AOL lets you see if AOL recipients have read your email (see *status of email*), or receive an email confirmation of receipt (see *sending*).

- With AOL 4.0, PC users can now send multiple file attachments (see *attachments*). Mac users have been able to for a while, and they still can.

- You can set up Automatic AOL to download your email at a scheduled time, and/or to read and write email offline (see *Automatic AOL*).

- Many members don't know how, but you can send carbon copies (email to multiple recipients) and blind carbon copies (email to multiple recipients who are hidden from each other) (see *blind carbon copy* and *carbon copy*).

- There is an easy way to spellcheck your outgoing email (see *spellchecking*).

- You can save important email permanently in your Personal Filing Cabinet or Favorite Places (see *saving*).

- Mail Controls let you block mail from annoying people or spammers (see *Mail Controls*).

- AOL email is MIME-compliant (see *MIME*).

- AOL allows you to see if your other screen names have new email without signing off or even switching screen names (see *screen names*).

- You can unsend email (to AOL members only) if the recipient hasn't read the email yet (see *unsend*).

Drawbacks

- Internet users can't see AOL email formatting (rich text, background images, etc.). Most Internet users can't see hyperlinks, though they can see, in plain text, the URL the hyperlink points to.

- You can't redirect your AOL email to another email account. That is, you can't have your AOL email automatically forwarded to your work email account (some mail programs allow this).

Email

- As of this writing, you can't telnet to your AOL email (see Chapter 24, *Telnet*), or use Eudora or some other client to read it. See **clients**.

- The AOL mail client can't send messages longer than 31K (unless you send an attached text file (see **attachments**).

- If you receive an incoming email message from an Internet user that is larger than 25K, the first 2K of the message is displayed and the rest is contained in an attachment you have to download (see **attachments**).

- You can't automatically attach a signature file to outgoing email. For our solution, see **signatures**.

- AOL-to-Internet or Internet-to-AOL email is sometimes delayed, from a few minutes to (in extreme, rare cases) several days.

acronyms

People sometimes use acronyms like TTYL (Talk To You Later) in their email messages to save time.

See also Chapter 5, *Online Shorthand.*

Address Book

The Address Book is, like the name implies, a place to store email addresses. A sample address book is shown in Figure 8-1. The two-person icon next to "Friends" and "Writer's Group" represents an address book "group" (one entry for more than one email address). The one-person icon next to the rest of the screen names represents an address book entry for a single person.

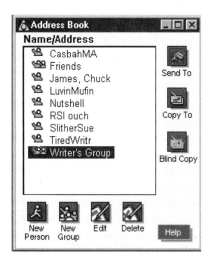

Figure 8-1: A sample email address book

There are three ways to get to the Address Book:

- `Mail Center` toolbar icon → `Address Book`
- `Write` toolbar icon → `Address Book`
- `CTRL-m` → `Address Book`

For the sake of brevity and clarity, all the address-book entries below use the `Mail Center` toolbar icon path, but be aware that two other options exist. Memo to Steve Case: may we humbly suggest `Keyword: Address Book`?

Benefits

- The ability to set up AOL mailing lists (i.e., groups) is convenient. Send the same piece of email to 20 people without typing 20 addresses!
- Helps you remember unmemorable screen names.
- Addresses in AOL 4.0 are sorted alphabetically; in earlier versions, they weren't.

Drawback

- It's not as good as the "alias" or "nickname" functions on other email systems. That is, you can't simply type **bob** in the `Send To:` field and have it go to Bob's screen name. You need to go to the address book, click **bob**, then click `Send To`.

Adding Entries to the Address Book

`Mail Center` toolbar icon → `Address Book` → `New Person`

Remember, Internet addresses have to be in the format of *name@domain.com*, while AOL screen names can be just the one-word screen name.

To add the address of someone you've just received email from:

From any email message, highlight the address in the `From:` field → `Add Address`

Drawback

- If you add more than one address at a time, they'll be added to the address book as separate entries, not as a group.

To add a group (mailing list) of addresses

`Mail Center` toolbar icon → `Address Book` → `New Group`

Make sure you separate the email addresses with commas, like so:

`Wristache, TiredWritr`

Changing Address Book Entries

To change an individual person or group's address book information:

`Mail Center` toolbar icon → `Address Book` → highlight the entry you want to edit → `Edit`

You can change an individual person's first name, last name, and email address, and add some comments and a picture. You can also change a group's (mailing list's) name and email addresses.

Deleting Address Book Entries

To delete an address book entry:

Mail Center toolbar icon → Address Book → highlight the entry you want to delete → Delete

Adding Images to Address Book Entries

To add a picture to an individual person's address book entry:

Mail Center toolbar icon → Address Book → highlight an entry → Edit → Picture → Select Picture

Of course, a picture must be on your hard drive to be added. It can be an *.art*, *.jpg*, *.bmp*, or *.gif* file.

Addressing Mail with the Address Book

To use the address book to address your email:

Write toolbar icon → Address Book → highlight name or group → click Send To, Copy To, or Blind Copy

You can address to as many names or groups as you want. You'll see them appear in the Send To: or Copy To: fields of your Write Mail window.

Another method of addressing mail with the address book:

Mail Center toolbar icon → Address Book → highlight name or group → click Send To, Copy To, or Blind Copy

This automatically generates an addressed piece of email.

Blind Carbon Copy

Mail Center toolbar icon → Address Book → highlight person or group → Blind Copy

When you're done, just close the Address Book window. There's no OK or Exit to prompt you.

Benefit
- This method can be quicker than having to manually put BCC'd recipients in parentheses. See also *blind carbon copy* in this chapter.

Drawback
- If you want to BCC all your recipients, you'll have to put your own screen name in the Send To: field, or paste all the BCC'd addresses into the Send To: field. AOL won't send the mail unless there's at least one address in the Send To: field.

Carbon Copy

> Mail Center toolbar icon → Address Book → highlight person or group → Copy To

This puts the person or group in the Copy To: field of an outgoing piece of email. Again, remember that AOL won't send email without at least one address in the Send To: field as well.

When you're done, just close the Address Book window. There's no OK or Exit to prompt you. See also *carbon copy* in this chapter.

Transferring Your Address Book to a New Copy of AOL

When you upgrade from 3.0 to 4.0, you can take your 3.0 address book with you. Just make sure you choose Upgrading to a new version of AOL when installing, and that you choose to Move or Copy your old files.

Make sure you upgrade the version of AOL that has your current address book.

All 3.0 address book entries appear as "groups" in your new 4.0 address book.

---

addressing

Sending email to an AOL member is different from sending email to an Internet user, which is different from sending to three Internet users, which is different from sending to an AOL member and secretly sending the same email to another AOL member. This sounds confusing, but it doesn't have to be. Here are your addressing options:

AOL-to-AOL

Address outgoing email to *Screen_Name*. If you're sending email to another AOL account, it's best to use only the screen name, not *Screen_Name@aol.com*.

AOL-to-CompuServe

If the CompuServe member has a number for a username, replace the comma in the number with a period, and add *@compuserve.com*. So member 3,141596 becomes *3.141596@compuserve.com*. If the username is a word, not a number, just add *@compuserve.com* to the username; for instance, *compuserve_member@compuserve.com*.

AOL-to-Internet

Make sure you include the username and domain, like: *internet_user@domain.com* or *internet_student@school.edu*. Make sure you don't use any capital letters unless you're specifically told to, since improper capitalization may prevent your email from reaching its destination.

AOL-to-Prodigy

Use the recipient's Prodigy username, followed by *@prodigy.com*: *prodigy_member@prodigy.com*.

Internet, CompuServe, Prodigy-to-AOL

> *Your_Screen_Name@aol.com* is the address non-AOL members should use. When in doubt, give out the full Internet address. Experienced AOL users know to drop the *@aol.com* from your address when sending internal AOL mail.

Now that you know how to correctly address email to fellow AOL, Prodigy, and CompuServe members, and Internet users, here are some more addressing notes:

Multiple recipients

> To send email to more than one person, make sure you put a comma and one space between each screen name.

Repeated

> If you repeat an email address, such as addressing email to *other_screen_ name* and *other_screen_name@aol.com,* the recipient receives the email only once.

See also **Address Book, blind carbon copy,** and **carbon copy** in this chapter

---

alignment

See *justification* in this chapter.

---

attachments

An attachment is a file that arrives along with an email message, but is not part of the email message itself. People use attachments to send pictures, word processing files, programs, sounds, and many other files that can't be included in the body of the email message. You can also use attachments to send text files larger than AOL's outgoing mail limit of 31K.

You should know that if you're sending only to other AOL members, you can send pictures without using attachments (see *images* in this chapter). We also can't tell you enough times: beware of attachments from strangers. They could be offensive at best, and virus-carrying at worst (see also **Trojan horses** in this chapter).

Sending Attachments

To attach a document to your email message:

> Write toolbar icon → Attachments → Attach → highlight file on hard drive → Open → OK

To send more than one attachment without sending more than one email message:

> Write toolbar icon → Attachments → Attach → highlight file on hard drive → Open

Continue the Attach → highlight file → Open process until you've attached all the files you want to attach. Then click OK.

Please note that when you send multiple files in one email message, the multiple attachments are automatically compressed (zipped) into one *.zip* file for the recipient.

Benefits

• In AOL 3.0 for Windows, you would have had to send five individual email messages in order to send five attachments.

• Zipping speeds the delivery of the email and the time the recipient spends downloading.

Drawbacks

• AOL recipients have to unzip the files by hand, or sign off to unzip, meaning that the files aren't immediately available to the recipient (see also the entry *decompressing* in Chapter 20, *Downloading*).

• Recipients who use other email programs than AOL's have to unzip the files also, causing headaches for many users who'd rather just have the individual files, even if that means they come one at a time in separate emails. The unzipping headaches are larger for Windows users trying to decompress Mac files, and vice versa. If you don't want to inconvenience non-AOL recipients, send one attachment per piece of email.

Detaching

If, after attaching a file to an outgoing email, you change your mind, you can detach the attachment:

Write Mail window → Attachments → Detach

If you don't change your mind until after you've sent the email, see *unsend* in this chapter.

Viewing What You've Attached

Once you've attached files to an email message, you can view them. From your outgoing (but unsent) email message, click the Attachments button to view a list of attached files.

You can also set up AOL to show you thumbnail versions of images before you attach them to outgoing mail. This is convenient because you won't have to open up every picture file in a directory to make sure you have the right one. To set up AOL to preview image files:

Write toolbar icon → Attachments → Attach → Preview picture checkbox

From then on, whenever you highlight an *.art*, *.bmp*, *.gif*, or *.jpg* file to attach it, you'll see a small thumbnail version of it, as in Figure 8-2.

Email

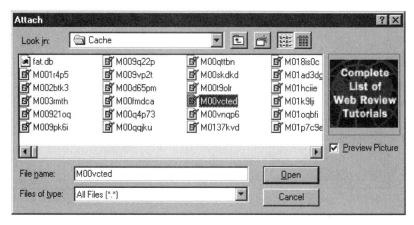

Figure 8-2: Check the Preview Picture box to view attachments before sending

Receiving Attachments

To download an email file attachment you've received, click `Download Now` from any open email with a file attachment.

In the headers of the email, you see the name of the file, its size, and approximately how long it takes to download. When downloading very large attachments, you might want to click `Download Later`, so you can download them with Automatic AOL at the end of the session or some other time (see also Chapter 21, *Automatic AOL*).

If you receive an email attachment with the suffix *.mme*, it's in what's called *MIME* format. This happens when the AOL email reader can't decode an attached file. You'll have to download the file and decode it yourself. There is a Windows decoder called *Wincode* at *http://www.members.global2000.net/snappy/software.html*. Macintosh users can download a MIME-capable decoder at *http://www.concentric.net/~Columbin/*.

See also the *MIME* and *Trojan horses* entries in this chapter.

Automatic AOL

With Automatic AOL, you can write email offline and send it at a low-traffic time (like the next morning). You can download incoming email at a low-traffic time (like the middle of the night) and read it offline after work. Automatic AOL helps you circumvent busy-signal problems and keeps your phone line as free as possible.

For a detailed guide to using Automatic AOL to send and receive your email, see the section "Email" in Chapter 21, *Automatic AOL*.

background color

To change your default page background color for email (and chat and IMs) from white to something else:

> My AOL toolbar icon → Preferences → Font → the button with the blue background → choose a color from the palette → OK → OK

The Font Preferences screen is shown in Figure 8-3.

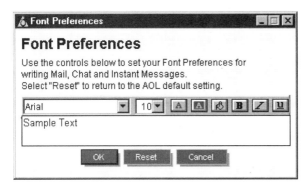

Figure 8-3: Changing the background color in email

To change the page background color of your current email:

> Write toolbar icon → the button with the blue background → choose a color from the palette → OK

or:

> Write toolbar icon → right-mouse-click the body of the email message → Background Color → choose a color from the palette → OK

Make sure you choose a font color that shows up in the background. Remember that Internet users can't see rich text in your AOL email.

Text Background Color

Don't confuse Page Background Color with Text Background Color. Text Background Color turns the background behind any line or paragraph of text a certain color. Page Background Color, if used with Text Background Color, applies to the parts of the email with no text in them. Text Background Color just highlights text in colored strips. Text Background Color isn't usually very attractive, though it can be effective if you're trying to create borders with text inside them.

To change your text background color, do one of the following:

- Write toolbar icon → highlight the text you want to change → the button with the blue background → choose a color from the palette → OK

- Write toolbar icon → highlight the text you want to change → right-mouse-click the body of the email message → Background Color → choose a color from the palette → OK

Restoring Defaults

Hate your new color scheme? To restore the default page background and font settings:

My AOL toolbar icon → Preferences → Font → Reset → OK

See also the *images* and *font* entries in this chapter.

---

blind carbon copy

When you send email to more than one person, you can say that the multiple recipients were "copied" (or CC'd) on the mail. When you "blind carbon copy" (or BCC) email to someone, one or more recipients is hidden. The BCC'd recipients see the CC'd and primary recipients, but they don't see each other. No one sees BCC'd recipients.

To blind carbon copy:

Write toolbar icon → put the addresses you want to hide in parentheses in the Send To: or Copy To: field

For instance, if you wanted to send your child and your wife the same email message, but you didn't want your kid to know that Mom was reading it too, you would put your wife's screen name in parentheses.

Multiple BCC'd addresses can be in the same set of parentheses, like (*Screen_ Name, internet_user@domain.com, Other_Screen_Name*).

Benefit

- Many users don't know that you can BCC on AOL. You can.

Drawbacks

- AOL won't send email without at least one address in the Send To: field. If you want to BCC all of your recipients, you have to use parentheses in the Send To: field. Or, you can put your own screen name in the Send To: field.

- AOL would be doing its members a service if it put a BCC: window in the Write Mail window. However, we're glad to have a Blind Copy button on our address book (see *Address Book* in this chapter).

---

blocking

You can make sure email from certain people or companies never reaches your email box. See *Mail Controls* in this chapter.

---

capitalization

AOL email isn't case-sensitive, so it doesn't matter if you address your email to *Screen_Name* or *screen_name*. When sending to the Internet, however, capitalization does matter sometimes; make sure you address your email with exactly the address you were given.

See also *addressing* in this chapter.

carbon copy

Sends a copy of an email to someone other than the primary recipient(s). All recipients will be able to see each other. As a side note, AOL calls cc's *courtesy copies*, but most people still call them carbon copies or cc's.

> Write toolbar icon → enter addresses in Copy To field

If you receive a carbon copy, you can check to see if the other recipients have read it. See *status of email* in this chapter.

chain letters

Our personal pet peeve. Chain letters clog the Internet's bandwidth and can clog servers (especially letters to young children who are tragically struck by a fatal disease and whose dying wish is to receive the most email). The general rule is not to participate in or forward chain letters. Besides, most people you'll send the chain letter to will have seen it already anyway, and you'll just annoy them.

See also *forwarding* in this chapter.

checking

See *reading* in this chapter.

children

See *Mail Controls* in this chapter.

clients, installing and using other

A client is basically a program that requests and gathers information. Your web browser is a client (see also Chapter 16, *The Web*), and so is the software that allows you to read Usenet newsgroups (see also Chapter 13, *Newsgroups*). Likewise, your AOL email is made possible by a client.

At the moment, AOL only allows you to use its own clients: the one that's built into your AOL application and their new web-based email system, Netmail (see *web-based email* in this chapter for more information about NetMail).

Email

Using an outside email client such as Eudora isn't yet possible. AOL plans to integrate Microsoft Outlook Express technology into their email system, but no one knows when this will happen. If and when MS Outlook Express is integrated, AOL email will be able to send and receive HTML content, filter incoming email, and use other Outlook Express features.

close email after sending

The default is for an email message to close after the email has been sent, but some people prefer to keep the email open on the desktop after sending.

> Mail Center toolbar icon → Mail Preferences → clear the box next to Close mail after it has been sent → OK

color

See the **background color** and **rich text** entries in this chapter.

compose email

See **writing** in this chapter.

confirmation

The default is to have this option enabled, which gives you a message on screen that says Your mail has been sent. If you're tired of the message and/or are tired of clicking OK, you can disable it. To disable confirmation (or enable it again):

> Mail Center toolbar icon → Mail Preferences → check (enable) or clear (disable) Confirm mail after it has been sent → OK

See the Mail Preferences window in Figure 8-4.

You can also disable confirmation for email marked to send later (see also "Email" in Chapter 21, *Automatic AOL*):

> Mail Center toolbar icon → Mail Preferences → clear Confirm when mail is marked to send later → OK

The Send Later confirmation box says:

> Your mail has been placed in the "Mail Waiting to be Sent" folder of your Personal Filing Cabinet. To see your outgoing mail, click "Mail Waiting to Be Sent". To schedule a time to automatically send your Mail Waiting To Be Sent, click "Auto AOL."

It's probably not a bad idea to keep confirmation around the first few times you use Automatic AOL, but after that, you might find it easier to ditch it.

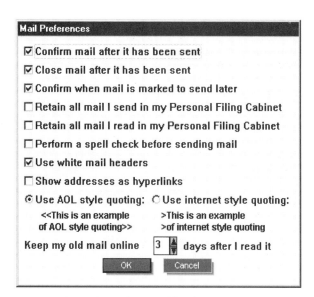

Figure 8-4: Confirm when mail has been sent

customizing

See *preferences* in this chapter.

delays

Internal AOL email is faster than email that AOL receives from the Internet, which is sometimes delayed from minutes to hours to days in extreme cases. Also note that internal AOL email is extremely reliable and nearly instantaneous.

deleting

When you read an email, you don't have to delete it when you're done reading it. AOL deletes it for you after three days (by default) or after the number of days you set in your mail preferences. You can also save all your mail in your PFC so it doesn't get deleted unless you do it manually (to do either of these things, see *saving* in this chapter).

If you don't want to read the email (for instance, if it is spam, or some mailing-list message you don't have time for) you can quickly delete multiple items at the same time. No more hitting the Delete key for each message. You can also use these tricks to delete email from your PFC.

To Delete a Range of Email Messages in a Row

Read toolbar icon → while holding down the Shift key, click on the first then click the last email in the series that you want to delete (they'll be highlighted) → Delete

To Delete Multiple Email Messages Not in a Row

Read toolbar icon → while holding down the CTRL key, click on each message you want to delete (they'll be highlighted) → Delete

---

dictating

Voice E-Mail allows you to send audio messages (instead of text email) via AOL. To find out more about this software, see this web site: *http://www.bonzi.com/america-online/e-mail.htm.*

On a slightly different note, some voice-recognition software allows you to dictate to your computer instead of typing. This works for all computing tasks that involve typing, not just AOL email. To find out more about two voice-recognition software packages, see these web sites:

- Dragon Systems: *http://www.dragonsystems.com*
- IBM: *http://www.sgoftware.ibm.com/is/voicetype/*

---

electronic postcards

These are graphical messages (like a postcard) you can send others as an attachment for a fee. There are three ways to get to them:

- Mail Center toolbar icon → Mail Extras → Online Postcards
- Write toolbar icon → Mail Extras → Online Postcards
- Keyword: Online Greetings

This is the easy, proprietary way to send electronic postcards, but there are a multitude of web sites that do it for free. Most of these electronic postcards are retrieved at a web address, not attached to the email itself. To browse electronic postcard offerings on the Web, check the ubiquitous *Yahoo: http://www.yahoo.com/Entertainment/Humor__Jokes__and_Fun/Greeting_Cards_on_WWW/*

---

error messages

To decode email error messages, see the following entries in this chapter: *host unknown, unavailable, unrecoverable error,* and *user unknown.*

---

favorite placing

See *saving* in this chapter.

---

faxes, receiving and sending

AOL has partnered with JFAX, a personal telecommunications company, and is currently implementing fax and voice mail services. Members will be able to receive faxes and voice mail through their AOL email boxes. This fax/voice email service costs $12.50 per month for up to 200 messages, plus a one-time $15 registration fee. As of this writing, JFAX was offering a 30-day free trial, but you still have to give them your credit card number.

For the latest information on this service, see **Keyword: JFax**.

Sending Faxes

We've heard rumors that, for a fee, you can send faxes from your AOL account. We know for a fact that this was possible once, but we can't find any evidence of this service in AOL's current documentation. The good news is, you can send faxes via the Internet. To find out all about it, see the web page *http://www.faqs.org/faqs/internet-services/fax-faq/*.

font

The default font for email is black Arial 10 on a white background. We think this looks fine. In fact, we think most of the other fonts AOL offers are hard to read. However, if you want to use a different font, we'll tell you how.

To Change the Font Size, Font Face, or Font Color

> My AOL toolbar icon → **Preferences** → **Font**

Select the default font, size, and color to use in your outgoing email, including background color. Click **OK** when you're done. Be sure to send email to yourself first to see what the new font looks like on the receiving end.

To Go Back to the Default Font

> My AOL toolbar icon → **Preferences** → **Font** → **Reset** → **OK**

Remember, non-AOL recipients won't be able to see your rich text, including font sizes, font faces, and colors. They'll see your email in whatever the default font is on their email reader.

To See Examples of Fonts Before You Start Using Them

> **Write** toolbar icon → right-mouse-click the body of the email message → **Font**

As with changing your default font, we recommend sending newly fonted email to yourself before sending it to anyone else. It often looks different on the sending and receiving ends. Remember that larger fonts are easier to read.

See also *rich text* in this chapter.

formatting

See the following entries in this chapter: *background images, hyperlinks, images, inserting,* and *rich text.*

forwarding

To send an email message along to others, click `Forward` from any open email message.

Drawback

- When you forward on AOL, you send the whole email; you can't edit forwarded text. That's right, the AOL mail client is partially responsible for those long forwarded email messages that consist mostly of other people's headers. What you can do to get around that is:

  From any open email message, highlight the text you want to forward → `Reply` → delete the address in the `Send To:` field → add the appropriate email address(es) to the `Send To:` field

The ability to forward email to others is a useful feature, but also a great annoyance. These are our personal rules about forwarding email, which you might want to follow to keep your friends and colleagues happy:

- Don't send chain letters, ever (see *chain letters* in this chapter).

- Consider whether the people to whom you're about to forward a piece of email will be interested. If you father hates science fiction, don't send him the *Star Trek* jokes you just received, no matter how hilarious they are to you.

- Consider having a separate mailing list for forwarded humor, so you can send it only to friends who want it. To create a mailing list, see *Address Book* in this chapter.

- Respect the wishes of anyone who tells you not to send them forwarded mass-email, such as humor and petitions.

- Don't forward personal email without permission from the author. Everyone we know breaks this rule, including us, but it could get someone angry at you. You never know when a message is for your eyes only.

- Don't forward anything that you'd be embarrassed to have your name on. Always assume that your ethnic jokes or lewd ASCII art could eventually be sent to your boss or your mother, with your name still on it.

- Don't send out virus warnings (see *viruses* in this chapter).

See also *quoting* in this chapter.

grammar checking

The default is to have grammar checking enabled when you spellcheck your email. To disable it (or enable it again):

My AOL toolbar icon → Preferences → Spelling → Advanced → Ungrammatical Expressions → click On or Off radio button → OK

The grammar checking option is shown in Figure 8-5.

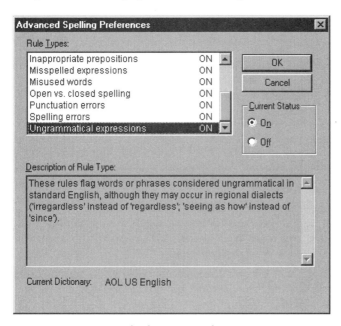

Figure 8-5: Grammar checking in email

The default is to check for grammar, but you can turn it off. You'll probably want to disable it, since AOL doesn't actually check for true grammatical errors. It checks for commonly misused words instead of actual grammatical errors such as run-on sentences.

headers

When you receive email, there is a bunch of text before the main message that tells you more about the message: the subject (if the sender provides one), the date and time it was sent, who sent it, and who else received it (unless the message has been blind copied. See also *blind carbon copy* in this chapter). If the message is from another AOL member, you will see which version of the software they're using. A header will look something like this:

Subj:I need a nap!
Date:2/12/98 2:14:41 PM Eastern Standard Time

```
From:TiredWritr
To:Wristache, Oreillyfan
Sent on:AOL 3.0 for Windows 95 sub 64
```

By default, headers are black text on a white background. You can change this:

> `Mail Center` toolbar icon → `Mail Preferences` → check or clear `Use white headers` → `OK`

However, the alternative to white headers is black text over a headache-inducing landscape of tiny gray dots, so we recommend you leave your headers alone.

host unknown

If your email bounces back to you with this error message, double-check your spelling. Or try experimenting with the addressing: maybe email sent to *student@insomnia.finals.school.edu* will arrive while email sent to *student@school.edu* bounces. On some systems, it's the other way around: the shortest domain name is the one most likely to work. Your best bet may be to ask the person you're sending mail to.

hyperlinks

A hyperlink is an image or text that is clickable. You can add text hyperlinks to your email to direct your friends and family to other places online. There are several ways to do this, which we explain later. First, we want to explain what various recipients see if you send them a hyperlink.

- AOL members using AOL 3.0 or 4.0 see a blue, underlined hyperlink. They will be able to click on the hyperlink and be taken to the AOL area or web site the hyperlink leads to.

- AOL members using software older than 3.0 see a jumble of code. The part of the code starting with *aol://* or *http://* indicates an address. They have to key-word to that address (`CTRL-k`, enter the address in the box), or paste it into their web browser. This can be confusing, especially for hyperlinks that lead to AOL-only areas. Consider sending a straightforward keyword or URL (web address) instead of, or in addition to, your hyperlink.

- Most non-AOL Internet recipients see just code, not an active hyperlink. Depending on their email reader, an Internet recipient may be able to click on the link and follow it. Otherwise, he'll have to cut and paste the link into his web browser. Internet users can use hyperlinks that lead to web pages, but not hyperlinks that lead to AOL-only areas

Many Ways to Add Hyperlinks

To add a hyperlink to an outgoing email message, drag any area's red-heart icon into the body of the open email message. Dragging and dropping the heart icon onto highlighted text causes that text to become hyperlinked. Dragging and dropping a heart icon into the body of a message in which no text is highlighted results in a hyperlink whose text is the default title of the AOL area or web page.

Dragging a heart icon from an AOL area to an email message is shown in Figure 8-6.

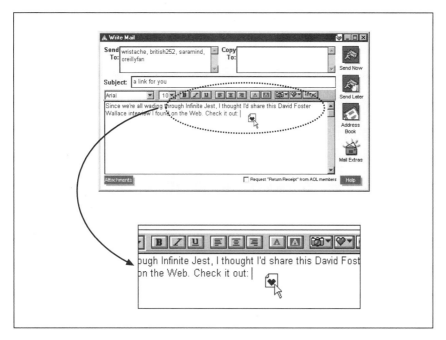

Figure 8-6: Dragging a "heart" into an open email

To use a Favorite Place as a link, click the blue-heart icon in the same window as any open piece of email. Choose any Favorite Place from the list. This results in a hyperlink whose text is the same as the title of the Favorite Place.

You needn't be composing an email to send a link. If you're browsing the Web or AOL, and you find a site you want to email, you can click the heart icon and choose **Insert in Mail** from the set of options. A **Write Mail** window opens with the link inside. You can then format and send your mail in the usual manner.

To manually add the URL and descriptive text of your choice to your hyperlink, click the **Write** toolbar icon to start an email message. Right-mouse-click the body of the email message and select **Create Hyperlink**. Enter the URL and descriptive text in the boxes.

Hyperlinked Screen Names in the Headers of Incoming Mail

There is one other hyperlink topic involved in email, and it has nothing to do with sending one to someone else. You can configure AOL to turn all email addresses in mail you receive into hyperlinks:

Mail Center toolbar icon → Mail Preferences → check Show addresses as hyperlinks → OK

The default is to have this option disabled, and we're not sure why you'd want to enable it. Clicking a name starts an email message to that screen name, but it's just as easy to use the Reply or Reply To All button.

images

New in AOL 4.0 is the ability to embed graphic files in the body of your email. It is easy and convenient, since you don't have to attach files. However, only other AOL members can see embedded images.

To send a graphic file as an attachment (not in the body of your outgoing message), see *attachments* in this chapter.

Embedding a Graphic File in the Body of Your Outgoing Email Message

> Write toolbar icon → camera icon → Insert a Picture

This is shown in Figure 8-7. Then highlight an *.art*, *.bmp*, *.gif*, or *.jpg* file on your hard drive and click Open.

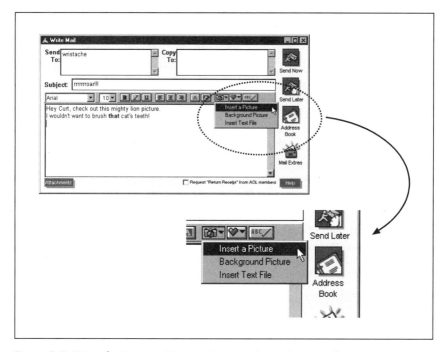

Figure 8-7: Using the "camera" icon to insert a picture into email.

Windows 95/98 users can also embed an image this way:

> Write toolbar icon → right-mouse-click the body of the email message → Insert a Picture...

Again, you'll have to choose an image from your hard drive and click **Open**.

Benefits

- You won't have to mess around with attachments to send graphics to AOL members.

- It's possible to resize large pictures to fit your email message. See "Graphics" in Chapter 29, *Preferences*.

Drawbacks

- Internet recipients won't see the images. To send images to Internet users, you have to attach them (see ***attachments*** in this chapter).

- Artistic types won't be able to do any layout this way, such as wrapping text around pictures.

- If you embed a large image, it could take the recipient a long time to open the email. 50K is too big!

Inserting an Image into the Background of Your Outgoing Email

Write toolbar icon → camera icon → Background Picture

or:

Write toolbar icon → right-mouse-click the body of the email message → Background Image

Choose an *.art*, *.bmp*, *.gif*, or *.jpg* file from your hard drive. The image will be repeated throughout your email; that is, placed under the text so as to fill the entire window.

Make sure you use a font color that's legible on the background you've chosen (see ***rich text*** in this chapter). Remember that Internet recipients can't see the background images.

To Disable Warnings When Receiving Images

Whether it's an embedded image or a tiled background image, you (and most users) get a warning when you receive email with a picture in it. The warning is shown in Figure 8-8.

To disable this warning, you can check the Don't show me this warning again box on the warning screen. Or you could disable the warning before you ever see it:

My AOL toolbar icon → Preferences → Graphics → clear the box next to Notify before opening mail containing pictures → OK

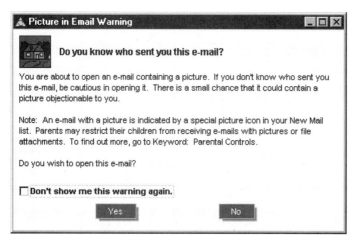

Figure 8-8: The Picture in an Email Warning

When you receive email that contains pictures, it has a special icon next to it. In Figure 8-9, the email from LuvinMufin contains an embedded picture. If you pay attention to the icons, you won't need a warning.

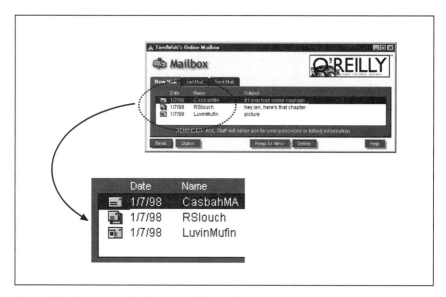

Figure 8-9: Three emails: plain text, file attachment, and embedded picture

junk email

See *spam* in this chapter.

justification

To align text to the left (default), right, or center, there are three buttons in the style toolbar above the body of outgoing email messages (to begin writing an email message, click the `Write` toolbar icon). Use either the style toolbar buttons, shown in Figure 8-10, or right mouse click and select `Justification`.

The alignment buttons shown in Figure 8-10 are:

1. The `Align Left` button
2. The `Align Center` button
3. The `Align Right` button

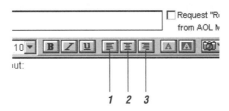

Figure 8-10: Left, center, and right justification icons in email

Full justification is available only via right mouse-clicking and choosing `Justification`. Full justification makes text flush to both the left and the right margins, stretching the whitespace between words as necessary.

Whether you're using the onscreen button or you're right mouse clicking, the changes apply to the paragraph where the cursor currently resides. To align specific text (like several paragraphs at once, or the entire email message), click and drag to highlight the text.

Remember that Internet recipients see the text as left-justified, no matter what you see in your AOL email window.

keep as new

To keep incoming email in your `New Mail` mailbox:

> `Read` toolbar icon → `New Mail` or `Old Mail` mailbox → click an email message → `Keep As New`

The mail remains in your `New Mail` mailbox for about 27 days or until you read it again.

To save mail permanently, see *saving* in this chapter.

keep open after sending

See *close email after sending* in this chapter.

keyboard shortcuts

If you write a lot of email, these keyboard shortcuts can save you some time:

- `CTRL-m` opens a new, blank, outgoing email.
- `CTRL-r` opens your `New Mail` folder, with easy access to `Old Mail` and `Sent Mail`.
- `CTRL-Enter` sends outgoing email. No more `Send Now` button!

Mail Controls

You must be signed on with your master screen name (see "Master Versus Additional Screen Names" in Chapter 3, *Screen Names, Passwords, and Signing On*) to use Mail Controls. Mail Controls help you restrict the email received by any screen name in your account, whether that's spam, other AOL users, email from any domain (such as *songline.com*), or specific accounts (such as *crazywriter@songline.com*).

To block unwanted email, do any of these:

- `Keyword: Mail Controls → Set Up Mail Controls →` choose screen name `→ Edit`
- `Mail Center` toolbar icon `→ Mail Controls → Set Up Mail Controls → ` choose screen name `→ Edit`
- `Keyword: Parental Controls → Fine Tune with Custom Controls → Mail → Mail Controls →` choose screen name `→ Edit`

No matter what Mail Controls preferences you set, you won't receive email from any address on AOL's list of known spammers. Figure 8-11 details your options, which are described in the list below.

1. `Allow all mail`: You receive email from anyone who sends it to you. The default setting for all screen names (18+, Mature Teen, Young Teen, and Kids Only).

2. `Allow mail from AOL Members and addresses listed`: You can receive email from any AOL member, plus any Internet addresses you specifically enable.

3. `Allow mail from AOL Members only`: You can't receive email from the Internet, but you can receive email from any AOL member. If you think this option prevents spam, you're wrong: many spammers have AOL accounts.

4. `Allow mail from the addresses listed only`: You choose the addresses (AOL and/or Internet) you want to receive email from. All other email is blocked. You can use this to limit your child's incoming email to a set list of friends and relatives.

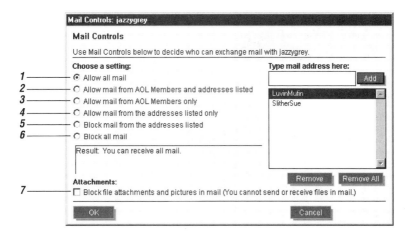

Figure 8-11: Mail Controls main screen

5. **Block mail from the addresses listed**: You choose the addresses (AOL and/or Internet) that you never want to get email from, ever. This is a good option if someone has been harassing you, or if you get spam from an address that isn't automatically blocked by AOL's list of known spammers.

6. **Block all mail**: Like it says, nobody can send you email. This is a good option for screen names you're sending into chat rooms and other spam-attracting places (see also "Annihilating Spam" in Chapter 7, *Essential AOL Survival Tips*).

7. **Block file attachments and pictures in mail**: This is the default for Young Teen and Kids Only screen names. Use it if you're afraid your children will be emailed pornography or computer viruses. For adults, we recommend ignoring this option and simply never downloading files from strangers.

When you've chosen your Mail Controls settings, click OK.

Mail Extras

There are three ways to get to AOL's Mail Extras, shown in Figure 8-12:

- Keyword: Mail Extras
- Mail Center toolbar icon → Mail Extras
- Click the Mail Extras icon in any open Write Mail window

AOL's email extras are really automatic ways to use jazzy font styles, colors, and rich-text "stationery" to pretty-up your correspondence. We're not thrilled with them, mainly because Internet recipients and users of older versions of AOL (pre-3.0) can't see your extras, except for Online Postcards. Our recommendation is that you send AOL rich text and extras only to other AOL members whom you know have the proper software to make reading the message a pleasure, not a chore.

Figure 8-12: Mail extras

Here is a summary of each of these extras:

- **Colors & Style**: ASCII art spiced up with colors, such as "It's a Boy" building blocks and a "Happy Birthday" cake. To use them, double-click the art of your choice and then click **Add to New Mail**. Warning: to Internet recipients and AOL members using older software, your happy green Xmas tree looks like this:

```
*

#*#

*. *.-

~.~. ~

-._ . _.*

~~~~~~~

| |

Have a Very

Happy Holiday!
```

   If you like the idea of ASCII art, you can do it yourself, if you have the time.

   See also ***rich text*** in this chapter.

- **Smileys**: Simply a guide to smileys, complete with helpful tips like "To view this smiley, tilt your head to the left." We humbly suggest that you see Chapter 5 for our take on smileys.

- **Photos**: Some photos, like daisies and teddy bears, that AOL thinks your loved ones would enjoy receiving in email. This would be a better feature if it actually embedded photos into your email, but instead, it creates a hyperlink to AOL's copy of the photo. To actually embed photos in your email, see ***images*** in this chapter.

- **Hyperlinks**: A hand-holding tutorial to inserting hyperlinks in email. See *hyperlinks* in this chapter.

- **Online Postcards**: Simply a link to **Keyword: Online Greetings**. See *electronic postcards* in this chapter.

- **Stationery**: Header templates meant to give email a personalized look. This would be a better feature if you could create a default header instead of having to go back to Mail Extras and create a new header for every new piece of email. To use this feature, double-click an option (such as **Blue Striped Border**) to view it, click **Create** to personalize it, fill out the form you're given, and click **Create** to insert it in email. Again, Internet users (and AOL members using software older than Version 3.0) see only the plain text of your "stationery," not the color and style font, or justification.

  Like **Colors & Style**, you can create the same effect yourself with a bit of effort. See also *rich text* in this chapter.

mail flag, fixing

To fix a broken mail icon (called a *mail flag* by AOL), send email to your screen name with the subject, **set mail flag**. Type at least one character in the body of the email and send it.

You would need to use this in two situations:

- Your email flag is not up, even though you have email.

- Your email flag is up, but when you click it, you get a message that you have no unread email.

mailing lists

See *address book* in this chapter and Chapter 12, *Mailing Lists*.

maximum email messages

The total number of unread messages your AOL mailbox can hold is 550 items, including mail you have read and sent. However, you should be concerned primarily with unread mail, since AOL makes room for incoming mail up to the 550-item limit by deleting mail you have sent and read from its mail server.

If your mailbox is full at 550 messages, AOL bounces back (returns) incoming mail to the sender.

See also "Reading Your Mailing Lists" in Chapter 12, *Mailing Lists*.

MIME

MIME stands for Multipurpose Internet Mail Extensions. It's a system of encoding binary (nontext) email attachments.

Email

How MIME Affects Email You Receive

Often, AOL's mail reader is able to decode MIME-encoded attachments automatically. You receive the attachment in its original, binary format, not as text. If AOL is unable to decode the attachment, it will have a *.mme* extension. You have to download the file and decode it yourself. There is a Windows MIME-capable decoder at *http://www.members.global2000.net/snappy/software.html*. Macintosh users can download a MIME-capable decoder at *http://www.concentric.net/~Columbin/*.

How MIME Affects Email You Send

When you send a binary attachment to an Internet address, AOL converts it into a MIME-encoded text document. The recipient needs to decode the attachment. Many email programs (such as Eudora) can automatically decode the attachment; a few won't and the recipient has to use a decoding application.

---

netiquette

Netiquette is the system of online etiquette that allows us to (somewhat) peacefully coexist online. There are so many ways to offend using email that we've just listed the big ones. Remember, first and foremost, just be decent and follow the general guidelines outlined in the "General Netiquette Guidelines" section in Chapter 1, *Introduction*.

- We've said it before, and we'll say it again: Don't send chain letters, virus alerts, Neiman-Marcus cookie recipes, or notes to dying children who supposedly want to receive a lot of email. Such email clogs the system and overwhelms people's mailboxes. We've seen these messages, or derivations of them, a million times. Your best bet is to not forward junk, no matter how cute or useful it seems. See also *forwarding* in this chapter.

- When replying, quote only the material necessary to give your responses enough context to make them understood. Quoting a two-page memo when you only want to clarify one of the sentences wastes the readers' time and hogs bandwidth. See also *replying* in this chapter.

- Try to keep your signature to four lines or fewer and keep rich-text enhancements to a minimum. Long *.sigs* (signature files at the end of your message), such as the multicolored 20-line ones we've seen occasionally, clog bandwidth. If your *.sig* is longer than your email message, there's a problem.

- Understand that your "private" email correspondence could go public if the recipient resends it or makes it public in some other way (like going into your company's server, taking your mail from the archives there, and using it against you in a harassment suit). Write only what you'd not be ashamed to see in public 10 years from now.

News Profiles

News Profiles is an AOL service that emails you news articles in your areas of interest from national news services. You choose the words and phrases, and News Profiles scours the news reports, sending full-text articles to your email in-box. To start receiving news features of your choice via email, sign up at Keyword: News Profiles.

newsletters, subscribing

Many AOL channels and content areas produce email newsletters on a variety of subjects. It can't hurt to try one, since they're free, and they let you in on content that might be useful or timely.

To subscribe

Keyword: Newsletter → double-click a category folder → double-click a newsletter name → Subscribe

To unsubscribe

Most newsletters, with rare exceptions (shame on you, *Insomniac's Asylum*), have unsubscription information at the bottom of each issue.

For other forms of news and discussion that come to your email box, see also Chapter 12.

offline

Reading mail offline is a good way to save hourly changes, or to read messages when you're on the road. For a how-to, see "Email" in Chapter 21, *Automatic AOL.*

Parental Controls

See *Mail Controls* in this chapter.

password solicitations

Some unscrupulous sorts like to send email to people asking them for their passwords. They'll often impersonate AOL employees, use (usually incorrectly) a lot of technical terminology, and have screen names full of numbers. These people are never AOL employees: it's a scam. Forward the mail to screen name *TOSEmail1*.

A sample password solicitation is shown in Figure 8-13.

Here's another potential hazard: an email attachment. You may receive mail claiming to be an AOL software update. Beware: AOL never sends updates via an email attachment; for that matter, AOL never sends email attachments. If you download a bad attachment and run it, there is a chance the file could contain viruses, or a small program that locates your AOL password and sends it to a third

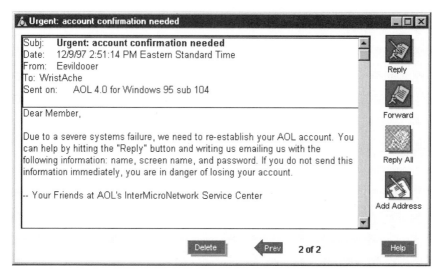

Figure 8-13: A password phisher

party. The best protection is not to download file attachments from people you don't know. You can tell a file attachment by the icon next to the piece of email. The first piece of email in Figure 8-14 has an attachment; the second email doesn't.

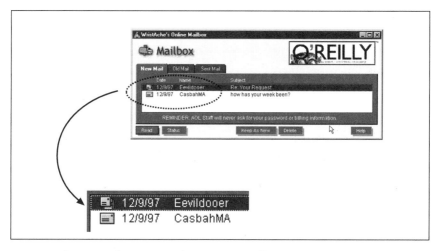

Figure 8-14: An email message with a mysterious file attachment

See also the section "Beware Evil Password Solicitations" in Chapter 3.

personal filing cabinet

See *saving* in this chapter and Chapter 18, *Personal Filing Cabinet*.

pictures, inserting

See *images* in this chapter.

preferences

To adjust your email preferences—the settings that affect how your AOL email works—do one of the following:

- My AOL toolbar icon → Preferences → Mail
- Mail Center toolbar icon → Mail Preferences

See the following sections of this chapter to adjust individual preferences: *close email after sending, confirmation, headers, quoting, reading, saving,* and *spell checking.*

Preferred Mail

AOL has a list of known spammers' email addresses. If someone sends you email from one of those addresses, you'll never get it. They call this feature *Preferred Mail.* This could be construed as censorship, but we think we get enough 900-number announcements in our email boxes already, so we don't mind.

AOL used to let you look at their list of spammers, and even elect to get email from all the spammers. It looks like they've taken that feature away.

privacy

For our thoughts on keeping your email correspondences private, see "Email" in Chapter 30, *Privacy.*

quoting

To choose your quoting style (when replying to or forwarding email):

- My AOL toolbar icon → Preferences → Mail
- Mail Center toolbar icon → Mail Preferences

Choose between AOL-style and Internet-style quoting, click the appropriate radio button, then click OK.

```
><<AOL-style quoting puts two brackets at the beginning and end
of the forwarded message.>>

>Internet style quoting puts one bracket at the beginning of
>each line. When mail has been repeatedly replied to or
>forwarded,
>>>>>>>>>>>Internet-style quoting starts to look like
>>>>>>>>>>>this.
```

Email

reading

You'll be alerted to new email by the "you've got mail" sound (or some alternate sound: see *sound* in this chapter). If you don't have a sound card or you have sound disabled, you can still see that you've got mail: the Read toolbar icon changes from a closed mailbox to an open mailbox with a yellow envelope sticking out.

To read new email while signed on:

* Read toolbar icon

* Mail Center toolbar icon → Read Mail

To download automatically and read new mail offline, see Chapter 21.

To reread old email:

* Mail Center toolbar icon → Old Mail

* Write toolbar icon → Old Mail

To reread email you've sent:

* Mail Center toolbar icon → Sent Mail

* Write toolbar icon → Sent Mail

See also the *saving* and *status of email* entries in this chapter.

reminder service

To receive email reminders of important dates, sign up at Keyword: Reminder. This can be a useful service. Enter dates (or holidays) you want to remember, and you'll receive an email reminder 14 days before the event (just in time to shop for that birthday gift). You can also opt for a second reminder four days before the event (just in time to get that birthday gift in the mail).

Benefit

* Can help you save face if you're the type that always forgets your own anniversary.

Drawbacks

* AOL forces you to include your name and gender, plus the age group (adult, teen, or child), name, and gender of the "gift recipient" whose birthday or anniversary you want to remember. They claim all the information in their database is confidential.

* This service is rife with marketing. They want you to buy your gifts in AOL's Shopping Channel, but you don't have to, of course.

* It's hard to customize the reminder service for nongift occasions like "Book Deadline."

You can find a web reminder service at *http://www.infobeat.com*.

replying

To reply to the author of an email message, click Reply from within any open email message (new or old).

You can also reply to the author of the email message and everyone who received the original message (except BCC'd recipients. See also *blind carbon copy* in this chapter). From within any open email message (new or old), click Reply to All, and everyone who received the original message will receive your reply.

To include (or "quote") part of the original message in your reply, you need to highlight the part of the message you want to copy. A netiquette tip: when replying, quote only the material necessary to give your responses enough context to make them understood.

See also the *quoting* and *netiquette* entries in this chapter.

return receipt

See *sending* in this chapter.

rich text

When you're composing email, you can add new fonts, text styles, colors, and justification to your email messages, which AOL calls *rich text*. Remember that only AOL members using Version 3.0 or better can see your rich text. We suggest using rich text sparingly; it can become an eyesore to the people reading your email.

To add rich text, use the features in the style toolbar, which you'll see above the body of the message in any open Write Mail window (see Figure 8-15).

The following list details the rich text options:

1. The large drop-down menu selects the font. There are some completely unreadable ones, so we don't recommend bothering much with font changes (we stick with the default ourselves). See also *font* in this chapter to learn how to preview fonts.

2. The smaller drop-down menu selects the font size.

3. The black B button bolds the text. Keyboard shortcut: CTRL-b.

4. The slanted I button italicizes the text. Keyboard shortcut: CTRL-t.

5. The underlined U button underlines the text. Keyboard shortcut: CTRL-u.

6. The blue A button brings up a font color palette. Select a color and click OK.

7. The A with blue shading brings up a background color palette. Select a color and click OK (see *background color* in this chapter for ways to use this feature).

See also the *font*, *hyperlinks*, and *justification* entries in this chapter.

Email

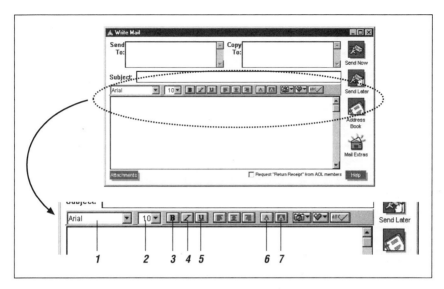

Figure 8-15: Options for rich text in email

saving

There are three ways to keep your email around longer than the three days AOL leaves it on the system. You can change your account settings so that AOL keeps your mail for up to seven days. To save your mail permanently, you can add it to your list of Favorite Places or save it in your PFC.

Keeping Mail on the Server for a Few More Days

The default is for old email to remain on AOL in the Old Mail folder for three days after you read it. To change the length of time old email stays on the system (one to seven days):

> My AOL toolbar icon → Preferences → Mail → Keep my old mail online [*number*] days after I read it → OK

If you choose this method, mail still disappears forever after the number of days you specify.

Favorite Places

To add an email message to your Favorite Places:

> From any open email message (new, old, or sent), click the heart icon in the upper right of the open window → Add To Favorites

Benefit

- When you save email in your Favorite Places, it stays there permanently, unless you manually delete it. It remains intact even after AOL deletes that piece of email from the system after three days.

Personal Filing Cabinet

We like having a running record of the mail that comes in and goes out of our email box, so we enable archiving in the Personal Filing Cabinet. That way, if mail gets lost, or you want to go back and read old letters from colleagues and friends, you won't be told "Sorry, that mail is no longer available."

To keep a permanent record of all the mail you read:

My AOL toolbar icon → Preferences → Mail → check Retain All Mail I Receive in My Personal Filing Cabinet → OK

To keep a permanent record of all the mail you send:

My AOL toolbar icon → Preferences → Mail → check Retain All Mail I Send in My Personal Filing Cabinet → OK

The screen where you check these boxes is shown in Figure 8-16.

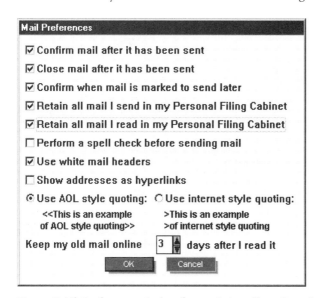

Figure 8-16: Preference window for retaining all mail read and sent in the PFC

If you want to save only individual pieces of email to your PFC, you can do that, too. Just open the piece of email (new, old, or sent) you want to save. Click the My Files toolbar icon, select Save to Personal Filing Cabinet, and choose the Incoming/Saved Mail or Mail You've Sent folder. The open piece of email is saved in that folder.

The PFC is also used for storing incoming and outgoing Automatic AOL email. For an explanation of Automatic AOL and how it is used, see the section "Email" in Chapter 21, *Automatic AOL.*

screen names, checking email

To see if any of your other screen names have new email:

> Sign Off menu → Switch screen names → highlight the screen name of your choice → Switch

The Switch Screen Names screen is shown in Figure 8-17.

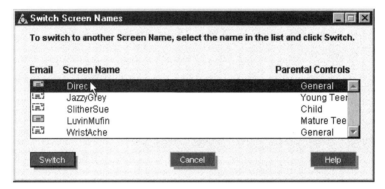

Figure 8-17: Checking email by switching screen names

A screen name with new email has a yellow envelope icon. If there is no new email, the envelope icon is white.

See also section "Switching Screen Names Without Disconnecting" in Chapter 3, *Screen Names, Passwords, and Signing On.*

send later

Use Send Later if you want to send off all your messages at once, or even when you're away from your computer. For details, see "Email" in Chapter 21, *Automatic AOL.*

sending

To send your email:

> Write toolbar icon → write email → Send Now

or:

> Write toolbar icon → write email → CTRL-Enter

To receive an email confirmation when a recipient has read the email you've sent:

> Write toolbar icon → compose your email as usual → check Request 'Return Receipt' from AOL Members → Send Now

You'll get a piece of email with the subject line Receipt for [subject line of previous message] that tells you when the email was read.

Benefit

- Getting an email receipt saves you from having to check the status (see **status of email** in this chapter) to see if your email has been read.

Drawbacks

- Only works for email you send to AOL members.

- If you send a lot of email, all the return receipts quickly get annoying.

To write mail offline and send it later see "Email" in Chapter 21, *Automatic AOL*.

To reread email you've sent:

> Mail Center toolbar icon → Sent Mail

or:

> Write toolbar icon → Sent Mail

AOL leaves your sent mail on the system for three days, as a default. For a permanent record of mail sent, see **saving** in this chapter.

To check and see if AOL members have received the email you sent, see **status of email** in this chapter.

---

signatures

Some people like to use signature files in their email. Signature files ensure that the people to whom you send email know whatever contact information you want to give them (and they also often include a quotation; we're not sure how that got started). An example signature file that might be used in an informal business or between friends:

```
Jen Muehlbauer
tiredwritr@aol.com
(617) 555-1234
"Spooooooooon!"    -The Tick
```

We don't advocate putting your phone number in your signature file unless you'll be sending it only to people you trust, like friends and coworkers.

Try to keep your signature to four lines or fewer and limit your use of rich-text enhancements (see also **netiquette** in this chapter).

As of this writing, there is no way to automatically attach a signature file (*.sig*) to your outgoing email. The fastest way we can figure out is this:

To create a *.sig* file (you'll have to do this only once):

> CTRL-n → write the text you want to appear as your signature file → save as *sig.txt* file on your hard drive

To attach the *.sig* file to outgoing email (you'll have to do this every time), do one of the following:

- Position the cursor where you want to insert the *.sig* file in the body of any open email → camera icon on the style toolbar → Insert Text File → locate sig.txt on your hard drive and highlight it → OK

- Position the cursor where you want to insert the *.sig* file in the body of any open email → right-mouse-click the body of the email message → Insert Text file → locate sig.txt on your hard drive and highlight it → OK

Figure 8-18 shows you someone choosing clicking the camera icon and selecting Insert Text File.

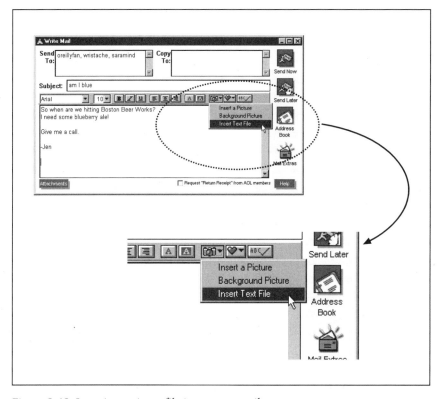

Figure 8-18: Inserting a sig.txt file into your email

smileys

Smileys such as :) are used to convey emotion in email. See also Chapter 5.

sound

If you get tired of the ubiquitous "you've got mail" voice, you can change it to any *.wav* file on your hard drive. Our suggestion is that you choose a sound that isn't long, since you'll have to wait for the file to play before you can get to your mail.

Windows 95/98 users can replace the sound this way:

> Windows Start menu → Settings → Control Panel → Sounds → scroll down to You've Got Mail and click once to highlight it → Browse → locate file on your hard drive and highlight it → OK

To find new *.wav* files, you can use AOL's huge collection of sounds that staff and members have uploaded:

> Keyword: PC Music → Software Libraries

You can also try one of many web sites, like the ones at *http://www.yahoo.com/ Computers_and_Internet/Multimedia/Sound/*.

spam

Spam, a.k.a. unwanted email, is evil. AOL seems to get hit hard by it, particularly since they have millions of subscribers, which makes it easy and profitable to collect and resell email addresses.

AOL has aggressively fought spam recently, including suing several known spammers, and forcing them to cease blanketing the service with email. But tons of spam still gets through, so AOL has provided a few methods aimed at reducing the spam that you receive. See *Mail Controls* in this chapter for information on how to block domains and users from whom you wish not to receive email. See *Preferred Mail* in this chapter to understand how AOL, by default, automatically filters out email from spammers on its hit list.

Besides AOL's remedies, we have other suggestions about the best ways to prevent spam:

* Never enter a chat room with any screen name you don't want spammed. Spammers collect screen names from chat rooms.

* Never post to an AOL message board, Usenet newsgroup, or mailing list with any screen name you don't want spammed. Spammers use automated tools to troll discussion forums for email addresses.

* Consider deleting your profile. Spammers search profiles and send spam tailored to what you've stated are your areas of interest, your location, etc.

We give more antispam advice in Chapter 7.

spellchecking

It's a new feature for AOL 4.0 for Windows and a welcome one. However, we think that AOL goes a bit overboard on checking the spacing between words and

Email

after periods, but you can customize all the settings and turn off the ones that annoy you.

Checking Outgoing Email for Spelling Errors

> Write toolbar icon → write an email message → ABC icon on the style toolbar

Once you've written an email, click the ABC icon to spellcheck. It's self-explanatory from there, and similar to Word or WordPerfect spellcheckers.

Automatically Checking Spelling (and Grammar) Before Email Is Sent

- My AOL toolbar icon → Preferences → Mail → check Perform a spell check before sending mail → OK

- Mail Center toolbar icon → Mail Preferences → check Perform a spell check before sending mail → OK

The screen showing this checkbox in Figure 8-19.

Benefit

- You won't have to think about spellchecking, and if you're a poor speller, it could save some embarrassment.

Drawback

- As we said, it can get annoying. To get the most out of automatic spellchecking, customize the spellchecker to ignore things that aren't worth checking. See the next section.

Figure 8-19: Setting up automatic spellchecking

Customizing Spellchecker Settings

My AOL toolbar icon → `Preferences` → `Spelling`

The default is to have every spellchecking option enabled. Most people are much happier with the spellchecker after they adjust the its settings. We urge you to see the section "Spelling" in Chapter 29, *Preferences*, where we explain every spellchecker setting in detail.

status of email, checking

You can check to see what an AOL recipient (not an Internet recipient, though) has done with the email you've sent. AOL even allows you to check mail another user has sent you and other people; for instance, you can see whether your mother read your grandmother's email. We love this feature, even if it does toy with invading someone's privacy. But we don't mind too much since it can often be useful when you're coordinating a meeting or a party.

To check the status of mail you've sent:

- `Mail Center` toolbar icon → `Sent Mail` → `Status`
- `Write` toolbar icon → `Sent Mail` → `Status`

To check the status of mail you've received:

- `Mail Center` toolbar icon → `Old Mail` → `Status`
- `Write` toolbar icon → `Old Mail` → `Status`

By each screen name, there will be one of several comments, such as the ones shown in Figure 8-20.

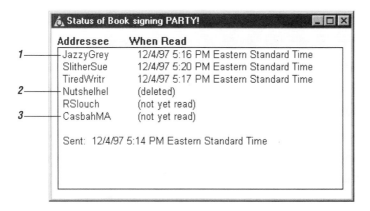

Figure 8-20: Checking the status of sent mail.

1. `12/4/97 5:16 PM Eastern Standard Time`: The recipient read the email on the date and time indicated.

2. `(deleted)`: The recipient deleted the email without reading it.

3. **(not yet read)**: Like it says, the recipient hasn't read the email yet.

You'll also see when the email was sent:

`Sent: 12/4/97 5:14 PM Eastern Standard Time`

Benefits

- You can satisfy your curiosity, figure out when you're being ignored, and catch excuses like "Oh, it must have gotten lost in the mail."

- As a recipient, see who's read an important email: for example, "I wonder if the CEO read the VP's email yet."

Drawbacks

- You can't check for Internet recipients.

- This can be considered an invasion of privacy.

See also *unsend* in this chapter.

---

subject headings

It used to be that you needed to fill in the `Subject` field when sending email. With AOL 4.0, you can leave it blank. We like this new feature, since some mailing lists ask you to leave the subject line blank when you subscribe (see also the section "Finding and Subscribing" in Chapter 12, *Mailing Lists*). In general, however, it's nice to include a subject line so the recipient has an idea what she's getting (we usually skip to important-looking email first).

---

text file, inserting

To insert a text file into the body of an outgoing email message:

`Write` toolbar icon → camera icon → `Insert Text File`

or:

`Write` toolbar icon → right-mouse-click the body of the email message → `Insert Text File`

Locate the file on your hard drive, highlight it, and click `OK`.

Benefit

- This sure beats the usual cut-and-paste method; no more opening the document in a separate window or application then pasting it into your email.

See also *signatures* in this chapter.

Trojan horses

Trojan horses are rogue programs that get onto your machine and do some damage. They often come disguised in pretty packages; we've heard of hoaxes such as "free software," "fun games," or even "AOL updates." None of these are true (AOL never sends updates via email). But they can contain viruses, or code that gets your screen name and password from your hard drive and mail it to a third party. Clearly, no one wants to get a Trojan horse.

On AOL, the only way you can get a virus or a Trojan horse is from an attached file. Even then, you'll have to play a somewhat active role, since it can't get into your machine unless you do two things to let it in: download an *.exe*, *.zip*, or *.sit* file and then run it.

Simply downloading one of these won't be a problem. You have to run an *.exe* for it to do damage. *.zip* files are more complicated: as compressed files, they're actually small executable files that are run in order to decompress the contents. Here's where things get tricky: the default is that AOL automatically decompresses a *.zip* file when you sign off. To help you prevent accidents, you can change the preferences, which we describe later in this entry.

Here are the basic rules of attachment safety:

- Don't download *.zip* files unless you are expecting them and are certain you trust the sender.

- Don't run *.exe* files unless you trust the sender.

- Also think twice before downloading anything that comes from a screen name or username you don't recognize, even when accompanied by a chummy "remember me?" message or a "Re: Your Request" subject header—those messages are usually spam (see *spam* in this chapter).

- There is a school of thought that says you shouldn't trust anyone when it comes to downloading attached files. That may sound paranoid (or inspired by the *X-Files*), but it may be a valid point. We know someone who received an email attachment with the well-intentioned message "Don't download this file if you get it. It's a virus." Also, an attachment may be infected with a virus the sender doesn't even realize is there. It's up to you how cautious you want to be.

- If you do download an attachment, be prepared to check it for viruses. There are plenty of good shareware virus eradicators out there. You can download virus software at `Keyword: Virus`.

AOL helps you remember to check the source of the attachment with a `Download Warning` dialog box (see Figure 8-21).

If you aren't worried about rogue downloads (for instance, if you use your virus software regularly), you can check the `Don't show me this warning again` box.

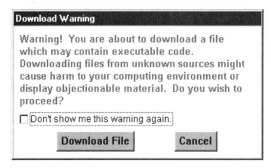

Figure 8-21: The download warning

By default, AOL decompresses *.zip* files for you when you sign off. To turn off automatic decompression of *.zip* files:

> My AOL toolbar icon → Preferences → Download → clear the box next to Automatically Decompress Files at Sign-off → OK

Benefit

• You reduce the risk of inadvertent execution of a rogue *.zip* file.

Drawback

• You'll have to manually locate the file and decompress it at a later time (for more on *.zip* files, see **decompressing** in Chapter 20, *Downloading*).

See also **viruses** in this chapter and the entry **attachments** in Chapter 20.

---

unavailable

The error message That mail is no longer available or is not accessible to this account can mean one of two things:

• The mail has expired. By default, read mail remains on the system for three days. You have two ways around expired mail: saving and/or extending AOL's default expiration a few days. See *saving* in this chapter to explore both those options. You should also be aware that unread mail stays on AOL's servers for 27 days, so check your email regularly. After 27 days, you'll probably still see the mail listed in your mailbox (or Read Mail folder), but you won't be able to read it. You'll have to get the person who sent you the email to resend it.

• If you know you haven't missed the expiration date on the mail, it's possible that AOL's email system is burping. Try again later.

undeliverable

See the following entries in this chapter: *host unknown, unrecoverable error,* and *user unknown.*

undo

When writing email, you can undo the last bit of typing or formatting you did by choosing any one of the following:

- `Edit` menu → `Undo`

- `CTRL-z`

- Right-mouse-click the body of the email message → `Undo`

unrecoverable error

When your email bounces back to you with this error message, it's not AOL's fault (believe it or not). There's a problem with the system to which you're sending the email.

unsend

In some cases, you can recall email you've already sent to other AOL email addresses (not Internet addresses):

> `Mail Center` toolbar icon → `Sent Mail` → highlight a piece of mail → `Unsend`

Benefit

- If you change your mind about sending the email, forget to attach an attachment, or reread the email and find a heinous grammatical error, you can literally remove it from their in-box.

Drawback

- This works only if the email was sent solely to AOL screen names and if not a single one of the recipients has opened the email. If you want to take back mail you've sent to a non-AOL Internet user, you're out of luck. See also *status of email* in this chapter.

Here's an interesting note: if the open mailbox on your `Read` toolbar icon ever automatically turns to an empty mailbox icon under its own accord, it might be that someone has just unsent email to you. Or your mail flag could just be broken (see also *mail flag* in this chapter).

user unknown

If your email bounces back to you with this error message, check the spelling and capitalization of the username (the part that comes before the @ sign). AOL member names are not case-sensitive, but usernames on many other systems are: capitalization matters.

viruses

You can't get a virus simply by reading email. It is possible, however, to get a virus by downloading an infected email attachment. You'll be safest if you follow these tips:

- Don't download files from strangers.

- Don't download files ending in *.exe* or *.zip* unless you know specifically what the file is and completely trust the person who sent it to you (see *Trojan horses* in this chapter).

- Don't configure Automatic AOL to download email attachments automatically (see also the section "Downloading" in Chapter 21, *Automatic AOL*).

- Do scan all downloaded email attachments (even attachments sent by friends and family) for viruses. Virus-scanning software is available at Keyword: Virus. We use McAfee VirusScan, which you can find at *http://www.nai.com/ download/downloads/*.

Another word about viruses: relax. Remember, it's attachments, attachments, attachments. There is no Good Times virus, or Penpal Greetings virus, or any other similar email virus. No simple piece of email can damage your system, erase your hard drive, or send your boss dirty Instant Messages from your screen name. Be extremely skeptical of any forwarded email warning that tells about such viruses. These warnings are hoaxes. Don't spread virus warnings, and don't let them scare you.

The only time it's appropriate to send a virus warning is if you know you've given someone a virus. If you send a friend a diseased email attachment, for instance, it's your duty to tell him about it as soon as you realize your error.

web-based email

AOL NetMail is a new service that allows AOL members to send and receive email from the Web, without being signed on to AOL. You would want to use NetMail if you wanted to check your AOL email, didn't have access to AOL, but did have access to the Web.

To use AOL NetMail, you need to have a 32-bit version of Microsoft Internet Explorer 3.0 or 4.0 for Windows 95 and an Internet connection other than the one you get from AOL. You don't need AOL software. If you don't have Internet Explorer, see the section "Using Alternate Browsers" in Chapter 16, *The Web*, for instructions on downloading and installing it.

To try AOL NetMail:

- Connect to the Internet through a non-AOL connection, like an ISP or a LAN. You can't be signed on to AOL while using NetMail.

- Start Internet Explorer, and visit *http://www.aol.com/netmail/home.html* (or follow the NetMail link from *http://www.aol.com*). Click the Read Your Mail icon and prepare to wait a while. You're waiting for the web page to install an Active X control, a small piece of software you download once, which runs from your computer—not from the Web. You need to have Active X controls enabled in your browser:

  - Enabling Active X for Internet Explorer 3 (follow the paths below from within IE3):

    View menu bar → Options → Security tab → in the Active Content section, make sure all boxes are checked → Safety Level button → Medium radio button → OK

  - Enabling Active X for Internet Explorer 4 (follow the paths below from within IE4):

    View menu bar → Internet Options → Security tab → in the Active Content section, make sure the Medium radio button is checked → OK

After the first Active X download, using NetMail is simple. The NetMail interface looks just like AOL's email interface, and the features are basically the same. If you're familiar with AOL email, you can easily figure out NetMail.

Some things you should know about NetMail:

- To check for new email while using NetMail, click the Old Mail or Sent Mail tab, then click the New Mail tab.

- You won't appear on AOL members' Buddy Lists while signed on to NetMail.

- You can use NetMail with any of your screen names.

- You can't unsend mail sent to AOL from within NetMail, but you can unsend mail sent to NetMail from within AOL (see also *unsend* in this chapter).

- As of this writing, rich text and hyperlinks aren't supported in NetMail.

- If you are on the Light Usage or Limited billing plan, regular connect time charges apply.

- To sign off, click Sign Off. You'll also be automatically signed off if you leave the NetMail web page.

As of this writing, AOL NetMail was still being beta tested—in other words, the software hadn't been officially released yet—but you can find the latest details at *http://www.aol.com/netmail/home.html*.

There are other free, Web-based email services which we discuss in the section "Email" in Chapter 30, *Privacy*.

Email

writing

To compose outgoing email:

> Write toolbar icon

To learn about your options when sending email, see *sending* in this chapter.

To write email when you're not signed on to AOL, see the section "Email" in Chapter 21, *Automatic AOL.*

"your mail has been sent" confirmation, removing

See *confirmation* in this chapter.

"you've got mail" sound, changing

See *sound* in this chapter.

CHAPTER 9

Instant Messages and Buddy Lists

Instantaneous communication with other members is one of AOL's real strengths. With AOL's own Instant Messages (IMs) and the Buddy List feature, you can see which of your friends and colleagues are online, and have immediate, private conversations with them in real time. These features are spur-of-the-moment, time-saving, and as private as talking on the phone.

We must admit, we love IMs and Buddy Lists. Other people agree; in fact, some members consider Buddy Lists the *best* feature on AOL. You can use these features any time you're online to make quick dinner plans, ask a colleague a question, or just send a funny hyperlink. They're great for sending a few quick words, or even for holding entire conversations; some people use them to cut back on long-distance phone calls to friends across the country, or even on another continent. Figure 9-1 shows an instant message between two AOL members.

AOL was the first place in the online universe in which Internet messaging and Buddy Lists really got a foothold. AOL members and non-AOL members who have access to the Internet can send IMs to one another, and they do, as millions of IMs get passed back and forth every day

The Instant Message feature and its very close friend, Buddy Lists, are features that, combined, give you serious communicating potential. IMs and Buddy Lists are separate features, but they really show their potential as a pair. You use Buddy Lists to see who's online to talk to, while you use Instant Messages to actually send the notes back and forth. You don't need to have your Buddy List set up to send Instant Messages, but it sure helps, and we recommend it.

The first part of this chapter takes you through the basics of using Instant Messages, like sending a message, inserting a hyperlink or picture, or formatting your text. In the second part of the chapter, we uncover Buddy Lists, walking you through how to set yours up with all your friends' and colleagues' names. The third and final part of this chapter covers AOL's Instant Messenger, the free way

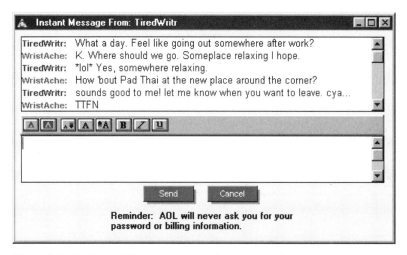

Figure 9-1: An Instant Message conversation

that non-AOL members can see friends online and send IMs. All they need is an Internet connection, and you'll be able to talk, talk, talk.

Sending Instant Messages

The first thing you should know about IMs is that they're easy. There's no setup necessary; IMs are enabled by default on every AOL account except for Kids Only accounts (see also Chapter 28, *Parental Controls*).

Now all you have to do is start sending your IMs. There are two ways to send an IM: directly or via the Buddy View window. We prefer using the Buddy View window to send messages to people we know, but when you just want to send a quick IM, to someone in a chat room, for instance, direct IMs are clearly the quickest way to go.

Sending a Direct IM

Just hit two keys, CTRL-i. In addition, you can go to the People toolbar icon, then choose Send an Instant Message. Once you've got the IM screen, type in the member's screen name and click Send. CTRL-Enter also sends the message, as a keyboard shortcut for clicking the Send box (very handy, especially if you don't want to use the mouse). Note that you can't send an IM if the recipient isn't signed on. If the recipient isn't online, you'll get a message saying so. The IM dies out and is not passed on to the person the next time they sign on.

Sending via the Buddy View Window

You must first have the screen name in your Buddy List. Once it's in there, you'll have to wait until you see your buddy online. You'll know a buddy is online if her screen name is visible in the Buddy View window. Double-click on the buddy's name, and the IM window appears, already filled in with the proper screen name. Type your message and click Send (or use CTRL-Enter). We'll go into more detail regarding Buddy Lists and sending IMs in the second part of this chapter, "Buddy Lists: Where Your Friends Are."

Checking to See if a Recipient Is Available

Before you send an IM, check to see if the intended recipient is online and able to receive IMs. If you have a Buddy List set up (which is covered in the next part of this chapter) you never have to use the Available feature, since you can glance at your Buddy View to see immediately whether a friend is online and available.

If you still want to use the Available feature, open an IM window in the usual way (see "Sending a Direct IM" above), type the recipient's screen name into the To: box, then click Available?

IM Netiquette

The following pertains to AOL's Instant Messages and to Internet messaging clients such as ICQ, Internet Messenger, web-based chat rooms, and the like. In addition, follow these guidelines if you're sending private messages to a fellow IRC chatter or to an AOL chat room participant:

- If you send unsolicited IMs to someone you don't know (for instance, to chat-room participants) don't expect or demand an answer. Respect the silence and don't continue to resend.

- Once engaged in conversation, keep each message short. Break up long paragraphs into sentences or even phrases so that the person on the other end has something to read and respond to.

- Some people think you should use online abbreviations to keep conversation flowing more smoothly; for example, *u* for "you", *c* for "see", *4* for "for". "c u later" is a common example. If someone really busts you up, you can use LOL for "laugh out loud," etc. Use your own judgment: one of us likes them, another doesn't. What it comes down to is that people need to understand what you're saying. If you can't type fast enough to keep someone's interest, the abbreviations will probably help. On the other hand, if you use so much shorthand that others can't understand you, you're probably going overboard with the ROTFL and IMNSHO. For more abbreviations, see Chapter 5, *Online Shorthand.*

Password Scams

Occasionally you receive an IM from someone you don't know who claims to be an AOL employee. Often these scammers or "phishers" send a clever IM telling you that the AOL software went down, and that they need your password to determine the validity of your account or to restore functionality.

To protect the security of your account, never give out your password online, in email, or over the phone—even if someone claims to be an AOL employee.

You can help prevent phishers by reporting the screen name that sent the offending message. Go to:

Keyword: Notify AOL → Instant Message™ Notes

You will be instructed to provide the body of the IM, which you should cut from the IM window (don't close the offending IM window until you have reported the solicitation).

For more on all forms of privacy violations and how to protect yourself, see also Chapter 30, *Privacy.*

Disabling IMs

If you totally hate interruptions, you can disable IMs either temporarily or permanently. There are several ways to stop IMs, some that block them only during your current session, others that block them for days or months (until you return to reenable them). In addition, if you've got your Buddy List set up, you can block or allow IMs from specific users of your choice. For instance, you might want to block all of your child's IMs except for those coming from your family or certain friends.

Using Parental Controls to Block IMs

By default, Kids Only accounts can't send or receive Instant Messages. Using Parental Controls on IMs completely blocks them, with no selection of "safe" senders. As with all Parental Controls, you must be logged on from the master screen name to set them up (see "Master Versus Additional Screen Names" in Chapter 3, *Screen Names, Passwords, and Signing On*). Follow the path below:

Keyword: Parental Controls → Fine Tune with Custom Controls
→ Instant Messages → IM Controls

Check off the features that you want to block; clear the boxes next to the features you want to enable. You'll notice that for certain screen names, some features are already blocked by default.

For information about other Parental Controls, see also Chapter 28, *Parental Controls.*

Once you block using this feature, there's typically a delay before the blocking takes effect.

Selective Blocking Using the Buddy List Preferences

You can also apply your Buddy List preferences to Instant Messages, such that any selective blocking or allowing you've applied to Buddies will also apply to IMs. Follow the path below to set it up:

Keyword: Buddy → Privacy Preferences → click Buddy List and
Instant Messages in the section labeled Apply Preferences to the
Following Features

Block Messages for the Current Session Only

In one of the strangest little quirks we've seen on AOL, you can actually type a string of letters and symbols into the IM window to block all IMs until the next time you sign on.

Use CTRL-i to bring up an IM window. Type $im_off into the To: box, type at least one character into the Message field, and click Send (see Figure 9-2). You will receive the confirmation You are now ignoring Instant Messages. If you want to reenable your IMs before you sign off from the current session, repeat the steps to disable IMs but type ,$im_on into the To: box.

Figure 9-2: Disabling all IMs for the current session using the manual method

Benefits to blocking IMs with $im_off

- No IMs will get through, no matter which screen names you've blocked or allowed in your preferences.

- You get left alone.

Drawbacks

- IMs you actually want might not get through.

- IM blocking only lasts until you sign off.

IM Tricks and Treats

Besides sending just plain text in IMs, you can add things like hyperlinks and jazzy rich text. In addition, you can use AOL's logging feature to keep a record of your IM conversations. As an added feature, AOL also plans to allow you to send pictures in IMs, although this feature hasn't yet been implemented. In the sections that follow, we show you the available IM extras.

Send Your Favorite Places

Send an IM that includes a hyperlinked Favorite Place. If you've got a web site or an AOL area in your Favorite Places, you can send it in an IM. Click on the Favorite Place heart icon in any open window (see Figure 9-3). From the new screen that appears (see Figure 9-4), click `Insert in Instant Message`. Type the recipient's screen name, a message if you wish, and click `Send` (see Figure 9-5).

Figure 9-3: Clicking the red heart icon for use in an Instant Message

Figure 9-4: Inserting a Favorite Place into an Instant Message

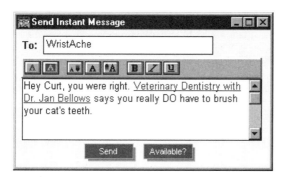

Figure 9-5: An Instant Message with a Favorite Places hyperlink

Benefit

- Send someone immediately to any area, without typing out the link or cutting and pasting from a browser window.

Drawback

- The links you receive could contain anything, and perhaps offend your sensibilities. You can't turn off hyperlinks in IMs, but, as we covered in the section above, you can turn off IMs. More importantly, you don't have to follow any link you receive.

Formatting with Fonts and Colors

In an active IM window, you can format the text with font sizes, styles, and colors. Select the text in the `Message` field you want to apply formatting to, then select the button that corresponds to the type of formatting that you want to apply. Figure 9-6 shows the formatting buttons in the open IM window.

Figure 9-6: The Instant Message style toolbar

Saving Your IMs for Posterity

Keep a record of your IMs as a text file. There are two ways to do this, the hard way and the easy way. We cover the easy way first.

Save using `File` → `Save`. When you're done with an IM conversation you want to save, don't close the window right away. Instead, go to the `File` menu item, then select `Save`. You're then prompted to name the IM and choose a location on your hard drive. When you want to refer to the IM again, choose `File` → `Open` and select the file you want to read or open it with any word-processing program.

Using the Logging feature is a little more difficult: First, create what AOL calls *session logs*, which essentially collect and save information about any online session. When you save IMs, you've got the option of creating a wholly new session log or appending an IM to an already existing log file.

To create a new log, go to the `My Files` toolbar icon → `Log Manager`. Click `Open Log` under the `Session Log` section, name your log (the default is *session.log*) and click `Save`, then click the `Log Instant Message conversations` checkbox (see Figure 9-7). Click the `Close Log` window to stop logging. If you close the `Logging` window, that will also stop the logging (you can minimize it, however, to get it out of your way). As with the `File` → `Save` method, open the file in AOL or a word processor (see Figure 9-8).

Note: When you use IM logging, the text from all open standard text windows is logged, in addition to your IM conversation. What this means is that if, while you're recording your IM, you enter any other windows, you'll have huge amounts of other textual information that has been logged as well. All this extra text can get annoying, and the only ways around it are (1) don't open any other windows when you're logging IMs or, (2) open the log later and cut out the log material you don't want (i.e., edit the log file by hand).

For other tips on logging chats, see also "Saving Chats and Chat Rooms" in Chapter 10, *Chatting*.

Buddy Lists: Where Your Friends Are

Buddy Lists might have a funny name, but they're useful, and the advantages to setting up and using yours are many. What is a Buddy List? Essentially it's a collection of screen names of people you know that appears in the upper-right corner of

Figure 9-7: Preparing to log your Instant Message conversation

Figure 9-8: Reading an Instant Message log file

your AOL window. Whenever one of your friends, family members, or coworkers is signed on to AOL, you'll see her name in the `Buddy View` window. By clicking on the screen name in the `Buddy View` window, you can begin to instantly communicate via Instant Messages.

We like the Buddy List feature because we can see which of our colleagues and friends are available online. It makes it easy to fire off a missive, rather than picking up the phone or sending email. When we want a question answered right away, the Buddy List and an IM are the best way to go. Like we've said before, Buddy Lists can save you money on long-distance phone calls, if you can sacrifice hearing someone's voice.

So, who uses Buddy Lists? Almost everybody, that's who. AOL reports that over 80% of their members have active Buddy Lists. What's even better is that your non-AOL friends and colleagues don't have to be on AOL in order to use Buddy Lists and IMs. All you have to do—or have your non-AOL friends do—is download and install AOL's special standalone Buddy List, called the *AOL Instant Messenger*. We cover the Instant Messenger in the final part of this chapter.

While AOL's Buddy List isn't as full-featured as some messenger clients, it has the distinct advantage of allowing you instant contact with nearly all of AOL's millions of members. We say nearly all, since you can block others from contacting you if you want peace and quiet, or if you just don't want others to see when you're signed on. We cover these features later in the section "Privacy."

Setting Up Your First Buddy List

Before you do anything else, you'll have to set up your Buddy List. It's easy, especially since AOL often prompts you to set up your new Buddy List if you've just joined AOL as a new member, or if you've created a new screen name. When you sign on with this new screen name, a special box appears asking you to create your list. Simply follow the onscreen instructions for inputting each of your buddies' screen names, and placing them into categories, such as *Buddies, Family*, and *Co-Workers.*

Getting to the Setup Screen

If AOL doesn't automatically prompt you to set up your first Buddy List, or you want to go back later and change some of the settings, you'll have to maneuver to it by yourself.

Go to Keyword: Buddy. Alternately, if the Buddy View window is already visible on your screen, click the tiny Setup icon in the bottom right of the Buddy View window. No matter which method you choose, you'll be taken to the Buddy List setup screen shown in Figure 9-9.

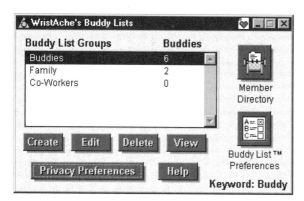

Figure 9-9: Setting up your Buddy List

In general, you can get to the Buddy List setup screen in two ways: the long way and the short way, as follows:

- The long way: My AOL toolbar icon → Buddy List

- The short way: Keyword: Buddy

We're going to use the short version throughout this chapter, but feel free to use the menu if that's easier for you.

Getting Your Buddies into the Buddy List

Once you get to the setup screen, configuring your Buddy List involves two steps: creating the list and adding new names to your list. Add as many buddies as you'd like to your Buddy List. Some online instructions we've seen say there's a maximum of approximately 100 screen names. We've gone over this limit, believe us. You're not limited to AOL members, either: you can add anyone who uses AOL Internet Messenger, too.

After you're done with this section, you might want to read the later section "Privacy" to see how to prevent other people from adding *your name* to *their* Buddy Lists. Perhaps you don't want some people to know when you're signed on.

Adding new names

If you simply want to insert your buddies' names into the predefined categories of Buddies, Family, and Co-workers, just add names to that group. To get to the group, highlight the one you want to add the names to, then click Edit. Figure 9-9 shows the group "Buddies" highlighted.

You'll be taken to the Edit List screen, where you can type in your buddies' names, one at a time, into the Enter a Screen Name box. Once the name is in there, click Add Buddy. Keep putting each name into the box, until you're done, then be sure to click Save. Your buddies' names are stored on AOL's computers, so they'll show up whenever you use your account, even if you're logged on as a guest.

Creating additional groups

What happens if you don't like the pre-defined groups of Buddies, Family, and Co-workers, or you want to create your own, more creative ones? You can invent your own. We suggest you create additional groups within the list since they'll help you stay organized. To create a group, go to the main Buddy List setup screen at Keyword: Buddy. From there click Create, then type your Buddy List Group Name into the box provided. You can then begin to add buddies' names to this new group, if you wish, in the manner described above in "Adding new names." When you're done, be sure to click Save.

We prefer to have many small groups, rather than just the three default groups. With smaller groups, we can know at a glance who's online, and we can more easily invite our buddies into a private chat room or send them off to our favorite web sites or AOL areas. We describe both features later in "Chatting with Your Buddy List."

Removing Buddies

So what do you do when someone is no longer your buddy? Just remove them from your Buddy List. You can delete a single screen name, or you can wipe out an entire group, like Buddies, Family, or Co-workers. Note however that, once removed, you can't automatically restore any lost screen names; you'll have to restore them by hand.

Deleting just one screen name

Go to the main Buddy List setup area at `Keyword: Buddy`. Highlight the group that contains the screen name you want to remove, then click `Edit`. Find the name you want to remove, highlight it, and click `Delete`.

Deleting an entire group

From the main setup area at `Keyword: Buddy`, highlight the group to be deleted and click `Delete`.

Viewing and Using Your Buddy List

Once you've got your Buddy List set up, it always appears in the upper-right corner of the AOL window. If you don't want it to appear automatically when you sign on, you can change the default settings. Go to `Keyword: Buddy → Buddy List Preferences →` then clear the box `Show me my Buddy List(s)` imme-diately after I sign onto AOL.

If at any time you want to see your `Buddy View` screen, you can call it up by following one of these paths: `Keyword: Buddy View` or `People` toolbar icon → `View Buddy List`.

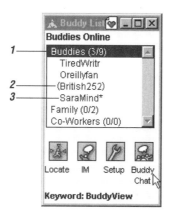

Figure 9-10: A Buddy View window with three buddies online

Who's Online?

You can tell which of your buddies are online, because their names appear in your Buddy View window. If you look at Figure 9-10, you can see that in the group Buddies, there are several people online. You'll see some names enclosed in ( ) or marked with an *; here's what these mean when you see them in the Buddy View window:

1. People online are visible under the group you've placed them in. The (3/9) after the group name Buddies means that three of nine people in that cate-gory are online.

2. Screen names enclosed by parentheses ( ) have very recently signed off.

3. An asterisk (*) after a screen name signals that the person is the most recent buddy to sign on.

Want to hear your buddies come and go?

If the visual cues aren't enough for you, AOL can play a sound whenever your buddies come and go. We think the sounds can get pretty distracting and down-right annoying, so if you've got a lot of buddies, we'd recommend no sounds. Thankfully, the sounds aren't enabled by default so you're safe if you like peace and quiet.

But if you want sounds, you'll have to complete two steps: enabling sounds, then downloading the sound installer. The default is the sound of a door opening or slamming shut when anyone from your Buddy List signs on or off. We've included a third step if you want to change your buddy sounds. The following describes the needed steps:

1. To enable the sounds, go to `Keyword: Buddy`, click `Buddy List Prefer-ences`, then check the boxes next to `Play sound when buddies sign on` and `Play sound when buddies sign off`. Click `Save` when you're done. Figure 9-11 shows what you'll see at the `Buddy List Preferences` window.

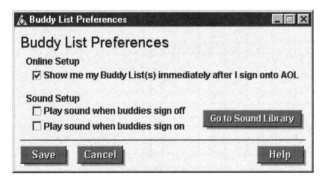

Figure 9-11: Enabling Buddy List sounds

2. Once you have the preferences set up in Step 1, download a special sound installer. From the `Buddy List Preferences` screen above, click `Go to Sound Library`, then click `Download Buddy List Sound Installer`.

   You're all done. The installer automatically places two files on your machine, plus two small default *.wav* files (one of a door opening, the other of a door closing). If you want to change the default sounds, use Step 3.

3. To make your Buddy-In and Buddy-Out sounds more personal, you can choose any *.wav* file on your local drive in the `Sound` section of your `Windows Control Panel`. Download the files of your choice, note their

location on your hard drive, and point to the *.wav* file in the control panel in Windows 95. Here's the path to follow:

Windows Start menu → Settings → Control Panel → Sounds → BuddyIn or BuddyOut

AOL also has a file library of sounds that you can substitute for the sounds you initially install: most are more fun than the originals. Get them at:

Keyword: Buddy → Sound Preferences → Go to Sound Library → Buddy List Sound Library

Send an IM to a Buddy

Helping to facilitate Instant Messages is what the Buddy List is all about. Sending IMs to buddies online is easy; just double-click the member's screen name in the Buddy View window. Alternately, you can highlight the name, then click the small IM icon. The IMs that you send via the Buddy View window are exactly the same as those you send using CTRL-i, as we describe in the first part of this chapter. See the first part of this chapter for more on sending and formatting Instant Messages.

Chatting with Your Buddy List

If you want to talk simultaneously to more than one of your buddies, you can, using the Buddy Chat feature. Or you can just invite one person into a private chat, which makes long conversations easier than sending a series of IMs back and forth. Buddy Chat is a truly amazing feature and one of AOL's strengths. Essentially it enables you to instantly invite up to 15 friends to a private chat room that you create. Others can't join you unless they are personally invited.

Just follow the instructions below. In addition, AOL lets you send a short message to your invitees, so they'll know why you're inviting them. Just put your special message in the Message to Send box that appears, such as "Let's plan our family reunion" or "Let's talk dirty" (we hope not at the same time).

Inviting just one person

Click the screen name in the visible Buddy View window, then click Buddy Chat. Type you Message to Send if you'd like and click Send.

Inviting everyone in a particular Buddy List group (like Buddies, Family, Co-Workers, etc.)

Highlight the group title, then click Buddy Chat (see Figure 9-12). A screen appears with all of the group names in it (see Figure 9-13). From this screen, you can add or delete names from the list of Buddies to invite; you'll save time because you won't have to type each person's screen name. Type you Message to Send if you'd like and click Send.

Figure 9-12: Inviting a group to a Buddy Chat with the Buddy List

Figure 9-13: Typing screen names into a Buddy chat invitation

Locating a Buddy in an Online Chat Room

Here's where spies can have a field day. Using the `Locate` feature, you can find a friend in a chat room, send an IM, or follow him to the room. You can then choose to `Send IM` or, if the person is in a chat room, you can join him there by clicking `Go`. Figure 9-14 shows that we've located our friend TiredWritr in the chat room called "lonelyHousewives."

You've got three options for locating a member:

- `Keyword: BuddyView` → highlight the name you want to locate → click the `Locate` button

- `People` toolbar icon → `Locate AOL Member Online`

- `CTRL-1` → type the member's screen name

Figure 9-14: The results of using the Locate feature to find someone in a chat room

Benefits

- You can locate chatting friends and join them.

- You can follow someone from chat room to chat room.

- You can catch your friends in embarrassing chat rooms ("Is that my best friend's mother in 'lonelyHousewives'?!").

Drawbacks

- You can't find people if they are not in a chat room.

- Someone else can locate and follow you.

To prevent others from locating and following you, see the following section, "Privacy."

Privacy

While the potential for instantaneous and worthwhile communications via the Buddy List is great, there may be people out there who will use their lists to monitor your online activity or to harass you. You may find, especially if you spend any amount of time in a chat room, that you get IMs from people you don't want to hear from, or you get followed around from chat room to chat room. Perhaps friends or even your mother will have the uncanny ability to find out where you're chatting—even when you want privacy.

If want to keep others from knowing when you're signed on or from following you into online chats, use the Buddy List's privacy preferences. The privacy preferences let you block others from spotting you, and let you give only certain members the privilege of seeing when you're signed on. In addition, you can choose to apply blocks to just Buddy Lists or to both Buddy Lists and Instant Messages, which should reinforce the privacy that you establish for yourself.

When your Buddy List preferences are set to block screen names, you effectively prevent those people from using any method to find out where you are online. In fact, blocked users get a message saying you're not even online, whether you are logged in or not. In addition, you can allow a select number of people to see and locate you, while blocking out the rest. That way, you prevent your mom from changing her screen name and *still* coming after you!

We cover each of your privacy options in the entries below. To start, you'll have to go to Keyword: Buddy → Privacy Preferences. Use the entries below to help you decide what sort of preferences to set up for yourself. When you're done, be sure to click Send to save your changes, otherwise all your work will be lost.

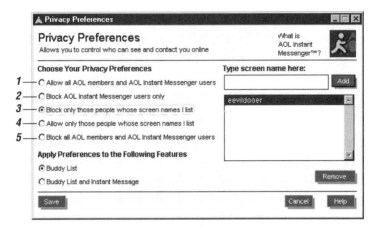

Figure 9-15: Privacy Preferences for Buddy Lists (and IMs)

Figure 9-15 shows Buddy List and IM privacy options, and the following list details them:

1. **Allow all AOL members and AOL Instant Messenger users**: This is the default when you first set up and use your Buddy List. All members can look you up in the member directory and add you to their lists. Typically, however, only people you know and correspond with will add you to their lists.

2. **Block AOL Instant Messenger users only**: All AOL members can add you to their lists, but nonmembers can't see when you're online.

3. **Block only those people whose screen names I list**: The people you choose to list won't be able to see you in their Buddy Lists. All others can add you to their lists and can use the Locate feature to find out what chat room you're in. Type foes' names into the box labeled Type screen name here.

   If you want to know how they (or you) can use Locate, see the section earlier in the chapter, "Locating a Buddy in an Online Chat Room."

Benefits

- Stalkers/former friends/surly chat-room participants can't find you online, even if you are online.

- New members and friends are allowed to add you to their list.

Drawback

- Stalkers/former friends/surly chat-room participants can use other, non-blocked screen names to find out where you are.

4. `Allow only those people whose screen names I list`: When you specify who can add you, no other member can see you in his or her Buddy List. Your friends can find you, foes can't. Type the friends' names into the box labeled `Type screen name here`.

Benefit

- You know precisely who's watching, since you allow them to watch.

Drawback

- Friends who join AOL, or who are trying to locate you, won't ever see you when you're logged on unless you manually add them to your list of enabled members.

5. `Block all AOL members and Instant Messenger users`: People can't see you in their Buddy Lists. If they try to locate you using `CTRL-1` or the `People` toolbar icon → `Locate a Member Online`, they get a message stating you are not currently signed on, even if you are. There's no need to type any names to block.

Benefit

- Stalkers/former friends/nemeses can't find you, even if they change their screen names

Drawbacks

- You'll never receive an IM from anyone, unless you originate the message.

- You're blocked from view of friends and relatives who might want to contact you.

For information on how to keep your identity private by using various screen names or deleting your member profile, see also Chapter 3, *Screen Names, Passwords, and Signing On.*

Instant Messenger for Non-AOL Members

Instant Messaging and buddy lists aren't just for AOL members anymore. If you know people you'd like to send IMs to, but who don't have AOL, don't fret. Anybody can keep track of buddies on the Net and AOL. It's all done using AOL's free Internet Messenger, available in three flavors: PC, Mac, and Java. Anyone with an Internet connection can exchange IMs with others both on the Internet and on AOL—provided they have the Instant Messenger *or* an AOL account. Below, we provide information on where to get the free download and how to set it up.

As we've said before, the singular advantage to using either Instant Messages on AOL or the Instant Messenger for the Internet is in the numbers: AOL's millions combined with scores of Instant Messenger users equals a vast communication network. Competing messaging products, like ICQ and PAL, claim only three million users at most. Another big plus with AOL's Instant Messenger: we understand that it's being integrated into Netscape and Microsoft's web browsers, and Qualcomm's Eudora email client, so ever greater numbers of people will be able to use it.

There are some drawbacks to AOL's implementation of messaging. Unlike ICQ, Instant Messenger won't save up messages and deliver them the next time the recipient is logged on. That means your recipient must be logged on and connected live to the Internet for a message to get through.

Benefits for the non-AOL person

- Send short notes to colleagues and friends whenever they're logged on with Instant Messenger or AOL. AOL members can see you, too.

- Use it over any Internet connection; no AOL subscription is required.

- Allow or block the users of your choice. Privacy preferences work just like those for AOL's own Buddy Lists. See the section "Privacy" in the main section on Buddy Lists above for information on how to use privacy protection.

- Send hyperlinks in messages to guide people to places you want them to see.

- You've got privacy from the moment you sign up. Once you set up your alias, only people who already know your email address can find your Instant Messenger screen name. That reduces your chances that random strangers or marketers can add you to their Buddy Lists. Just remember to tell friends who you are online.

- Warn users who send unwanted IMs. If you're being annoyed or harassed, you can hit a **Warn** button that temporarily slows or halts that person's ability to send IMs. The more warnings they receive, the fewer IMs they can send. More about this under "Special Features" below.

Drawback

- Unlike ICQ, Instant Messenger doesn't store messages for you and deliver them the next time the recipient signs in.

Setting Up Instant Messenger

Basically, all your friends or colleagues have to do is to download and install the Instant Messenger, and set up an alias (or screen name). If they don't already have it attached to their web browser or to Eudora, you have to tell them where to get the application.

The free client is on AOL's web site, *AOL.Com*. You should find a link from the main page which is located at *http://www.aol.com*. Installation is as easy as locating the 1.4-MB file on your friend's local drive and double-clicking it to run the setup program.

The program walks you through setting up a new alias or screen name. Before you start up the Instant Messenger, make sure you have a live connection to the Internet, either through work or via an Internet service provider at home. The online instructions on the web site are surprisingly complete. We'll detail just a few features that differ significantly from AOL's own Buddy List. If you need more on setting up Buddy Lists, see the second part of this chapter, "Buddy Lists: Where Your Friends Are," since Instant Messenger is similar.

Once everything is set up, a user must sign on with her alias, using a password (see Figure 9-16). Once the Instant Messenger is running, the user can see which-ever AOL members and Instant Messenger users she's added to her list (see Figure 9-17).

Figure 9-16: Signing on with AOL's Instant Messenger for the Internet

Special Features

Even though Instant Messenger looks and acts a lot like AOL's own Buddy List, there are some differences. Mainly AOL has added features to the Instant Messenger that make it even better than Buddy Lists. Here are the most striking added features:

- `Registration`: Non-AOL members can register any unused name and a password, just like a regular AOL account (see Chapter 3 for advice on choos-ing a name and password). It's this screen name that the new user should give to all his friends and AOL users, to be added to their own Buddy Lists.

- `Warning users`: If you're receiving harassing or unwanted IMs, you can send a warning that marks that account (call it a Scarlet Letter for the Inter-net). In particular, the warnings a person has received affect his ability to send IMs: the more warnings he gets, the more slowly he'll be able to send messages. If a person goes for an extended period without a warning, the

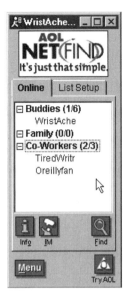

Figure 9-17: The Instant Messenger window (similar to the Buddy View window)

restrictions fade out. It's all very similar to driver's license points; violations have less strength over time.

- **Instant blocking**: If you don't want someone to IM you, you can instantly block them using the special **Block** button. This is a feature unfortunately not found on AOL's internal Buddy List, where you must modify the blocked screen names by hand.

- **Auto responding**: When you're away or idle, you can have messages sent out; for instance, you can automatically let someone know when you'll be back. If you're idle, but not away, you can also send a message. In addition, other users of the Internet version can see whether you've been idle before they decide to IM you, since your name is dimmed.

CHAPTER 10

Chatting

Chatting is talking live (or "in real time") to other AOL members by typing your comments. When you type something and send it to a chat room, people see it immediately. The only limitation to how fast a chat conversation flows is how fast the participants can type and read. People love chat because it's the closest the online world comes to live, face-to-face conversation.

Chat is big on the Internet (see also "Internet Chat" in Chapter 24, *Telnet*), but it is biggest on AOL. We hear unverified reports that 30% to 50% percent of all time spent by members on AOL is spent in chat rooms. To its credit, AOL is the undisputed king of online chat: MSN, CompuServe, Prodigy, and all the web-based chat centers can't compare to the sheer number of packed chat rooms on AOL. Any time of day, you're bound to find a room with at least ten people in it, chatting.

Personally, we never really jumped on the chat bandwagon. When we want interesting, enlightening online discussion, we avoid chat rooms altogether and head straight for message boards, mailing lists, and newsgroup discussions (see also Chapter 11, *Message Boards*, Chapter 12, *Mailing Lists*, and Chapter 13, *Newsgroups*). But that's our bias. If you enjoy chatting, we hope you'll use this chapter to make it easier and more fun. However, we feel it's our duty to remind you that potentially unwanted things can happen when you chat. For our tips on avoiding the unwanted side effects of chat, see "Chat Essentials" in this chapter.

In this chapter, we sometimes give instructions that start from the `People Connection` front screen, the main area for AOL chat. Navigate there with any of the following three paths:

* `People` toolbar icon → `People Connection`
* `Keyword: People`
* The `People Connection` icon on the `Welcome` screen

We use `Keyword: People` in the paths in this chapter because it's fast, and because everyone (Mac or PC, 3.0 or 4.0) can use keywords. But if you'd rather use the toolbar or the Welcome screen, go ahead. All these paths go to the same place.

If You're New to Chat

- You need to know the difference between AOL's four different kinds of chat rooms. To familiarize yourself with each, see "Four Types of Chat" in this chapter.

- Before you chat, you'll have to find a chat room. See "Find a Chat" in this chapter.

- To participate in a chat, type your comment into the box at the bottom of the window and click Send. See "Chatting" in this chapter.

- Familiarize yourself with netiquette, the unofficial (but crucial) rules of online conduct. See also "Chatting" in this chapter.

- Acronyms such as LOL (Laughing Out Loud) are popular in chat rooms. They speed up the flow of chat conversation, but they can be confusing for newcomers. Additionally, smileys such as :) are used to show feelings and actions when talking online. Be prepared: see also Chapter 5, *Online Shorthand*.

Chat Essentials

- Many parents are concerned about the language and ideas their children might be exposed to in chat rooms. We suggest spending some time in chat rooms to see how founded your fears are. If your 10-year-old wants to talk about Fido in a Pet Care conference room, you'll see that it's pretty tame. But if your 10-year-old is begging for access to a People Connection lobby, you might be justified in saying "no way!" Once you decide what's appropriate, you can set Parental Controls to allow or block certain kinds of chat rooms. This chapter is long enough already, so we didn't go into Parental Controls here; see the section "Chat" in Chapter 28, *Parental Controls* for all the details.

- The biggest hazard of chatting is spam (a.k.a. unwanted email). Many spammers collect names for their distribution lists by hanging out in AOL chat rooms. They then sell these names to many groups, and voila! you start getting unwanted email from marketers of all kinds, including people peddling HOT HOT LIVE GIRLS. Even if your screen name only enters a chat room for a second, it may be recorded by a screen name-grabbing computer program. Always, always, always chat with a screen name that you don't expect real email to (to learn how to create new screen names, see Chapter 3, *Screen Names, Passwords, and Signing On*). You'll get all your spam at one account, and you can ignore it.

- If spam isn't enough reason to create a chat-only screen name, we also suggest you use an alternate screen name for chat to maintain the anonymity you want. Do you really want to use your professional screen name to join the chat "LonelySoccerMoms?" You might also want to create a chat-only screen name so that you don't get badgered by chat buddies when you're online for other reasons, such as work.

- Avoid People Connection lobbies like the plague (see the section later in this chapter, "The Lobby"). The conversation is insipid, and hanging out in lobbies will ensure that you get a ton of unwanted email. AOL has massively improved People Connection so that you no longer have to go through a lobby to get to a Private Room; take advantage of this. You can also get to Featured (a.k.a. Public) and Member rooms without entering the lobby.

- There will always be some clueless people who IM you persistently, no matter how much you ignore them. There is also a chance that overzealous chatters may put you on their Buddy Lists and follow your every move. Fortunately, you can keep those IMs from getting through and stay off those Buddy Lists. See also "Bothersome Chat Room Participants" in this chapter.

- Don't miss the "Private Rooms and Buddy Chat" section of this chapter. The ability to create invitation-only chat rooms is a big benefit of AOL's chat setup.

Four Types of Chat

While all chat rooms on AOL look fairly similar, they serve different purposes. They range from the sometimes highbrow conference rooms to the more pop cultural auditoriums where you'll meet celebrities. Below, we detail what you typically find in each type of chat room:

- *Auditorium Chats*: These are special events chats, typically with a celebrity, less frequently with someone who is a newsmaker, author, artist, or politician. You get to listen in on the conversation, and ask questions, as if on a call-in radio show. You can also chat freely with the other AOL members in your "row."

- *Featured and Member (a.k.a. People Connection) Rooms*: These rooms are listed and open to the AOL community. This is where most of AOL's chatting takes place. Featured rooms are always open, and they have standard room names that have been given by AOL itself; the names loosely correspond to the theme of a room. Member rooms are created by members on any topic they choose; they may cease to exist if all people leave the room. Member rooms are often randy, with names to match. Featured rooms are supposed to be cleaner than Member rooms, but are often equally naughty.

- *Private Rooms and Buddy Chat*: Private rooms are rooms that only you—and the people you tell—know about. They're not publicly listed. You invite your friends, and they show up. AOL's Terms of Service (*see* Appendix D, *Terms of Service*) are not in effect in Private rooms, so you can say anything you want with impunity.

- *Conference Rooms*: Basically, conference rooms are chat rooms inside AOL content areas. Usually chatting is more formal in conference rooms, possibly moderated, and run on a schedule. Sometimes the room is closed when conferences are not in session. You can learn something from a conference.

Find a Chat

Before you can chat, you'll have to find a chat room. The easiest way to get to a public AOL chat room is the relatively new feature called, conveniently, Find a Chat, found via one of the following paths:

- Keyword: People → Find a Chat
- People toolbar icon → Find a Chat

Benefit

- You'll avoid the lobby if you use Find a Chat to get to the room you want.

Drawback

- You'll only find Featured and Member chats this way. See the "Auditorium Chats" and "Conference Rooms" sections of this chapter for instructions on finding a wide selection of celebrity events and subject-oriented chats.

Click the Member Chats button for a list of Member rooms.

To search for a Featured chat room about a certain subject:

Keyword: People → Find a Chat → Search Featured Chats

Enter search words, and you'll theoretically find a list of chats about that subject, complete with cheesy descriptions that make Featured rooms sound a lot more structured and cerebral than they are. Searching for "sex" yields no results; we know better.

For chats about a certain subject, you're better off with chats hosted by AOL content areas (see the "Conference Rooms" section in this chapter).

To search for particular Member room:

Keyword: People → Find a chat → Member Chats button → Search Member Chats

You have to search by exact room name, not by subject. If you don't type the exact title of the room name, you get no matches. You might as well just scroll through the list and choose a chat that appeals to you.

Chatting

When you first enter a chat room, you'll see a window on your screen with text running across it. Each comment is preceded by the screen name of the member that made the comment. Chat room conversation may fly by too fast for you to absorb, at first, but most people get used to the rapid pace.

To make a comment the entire chat room can read, type what you want to say in the box shown in Figure 10-1, then click Send or hit Enter. You can send up to 92 characters at a time—that's about two lines on the chat screen. Sending a comment to a chat room is the same for all kinds of chat rooms on AOL.

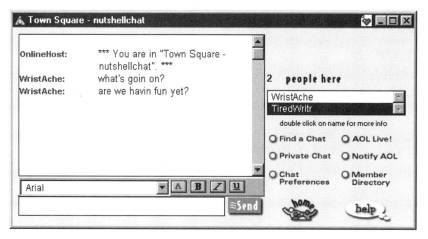

Figure 10-1: Sending a comment to a chat room

Most chat rooms have the same buttons and icons on the lower right of the chat window (see Figure 10-1). Here, we describe the icons and tell you which parts of this chapter to read for further explanation:

- **Find a Chat**: Takes you to **Keyword: People** → **Find a Chat**, where you can enter a Featured or Member room. All rooms except Conference Rooms have this button. See also "Find a Chat" in this chapter.

- **AOL Live**: Takes you to **Keyword: Live**, the home of AOL's Auditorium chats. All rooms except Conference Rooms have this button. See also "Auditorium Chats" in this chapter.

- **Private Chat**: Takes you to a screen where you can enter or create a private chat room. See also "Buddy Chat" and "Private Rooms" in this chapter.

- **Notify AOL**: Click this button to report Terms of Service violations. All rooms except Private Rooms (like the one shown in Figure 10-1) have this button. See also "Reporting Terms of Service Violations" in this chapter

- **Chat Preferences**: Goes to the **Chat Preferences** screen, where you can adjust certain settings. See also "Chat Preferences" in this chapter.

- **Member Directory**: Takes you to **Keyword: Member Directory**, where you can search AOL's database of member profiles. See also "Profiles" in this chapter.

- **Home**: Takes you out of the chat room you're in and goes to **Keyword: People**, AOL's main chat area.

- **Help**: Some rudimentary chat help from AOL

Before you say a word in a chat room, you should brush up on netiquette. Whether you're in AOL's own very popular chat rooms, a web-based chat, or a conference room, these guidelines help keep conversation interesting and flowing, not banal and halting.

- Don't greet everyone in the room individually. One "Hello" is plenty.

- Listen for a bit before piping up. There may be a conversation already in progress you know nothing about.

- Refrain from using ALL CAPS. In chat, it is the equivalent of SCREAMING AT EVERYONE.

- Don't assume that people want to talk to you. If you send a message (to the whole room or as an Instant Message (IM) or personal message in IRC) and receive no response, respect that silence and don't continue to resend.

People in Chat Rooms

This section will help you keep track of members you want to chat with. Find out how to track down a friend in a chat room and follow him there. Change how your People Here list looks. Get notified when someone enters or leaves the room. Profile someone in your chat room or send her an Instant Message. This section applies to all kinds of chat rooms on AOL except auditoriums (some don't apply to Private Rooms/buddy chats either, and we've indicated those).

Locating a Member in a Chat Room

There are two easy ways to find out which chat rooms your friends are in:

- CTRL-1 → type member name → OK
- Click name in Buddy List window → Locate button → Go

You either find out which chat room the member is in, shown in Figure 10-2, or you get this message:

> Screen_Name is online, but not in a chat area.

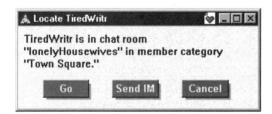

Figure 10-2: Locating a member in a chat room

If a member you're trying to locate—or spy on—is in a chat room, you can follow him there. You can't follow a member into a private chat room.

Benefit

- Makes it easy to find your friends and join them in chat rooms.

Drawback

- Makes it easy to stalk or be stalked. If you don't want someone following you to a chat room, block him from adding you to his Buddy List (see Chapter 9, *Instant Messages and Buddy Lists*).

Who's Chatting?

Looking for someone? More importantly, are you trying to avoid someone? Keep an eye on who's in the chat room of your choice, either before or after you enter it.

View members before entering the room

Before you ever set foot in a chat room, you can view a list of the members who are already there:

> Keyword: People → Find a Chat → highlight a chat room from the list → Who's Chatting button

Benefits

- Helps you avoid any online nemeses you might have (other tips for online nemeses are in the "Bothersome Chat Room Participants" section of this chapter).

- Helps you check people out before chatting with them, by clicking the Get Profile button and reading their profiles.

Text notification

The default is to have the "Notify me when members arrive" preference disabled. To enable it (or disable it again):

> MY AOL toolbar icon → Preferences → Chat → Notify me when members arrive

Whenever someone enters the room, a line like this appears amidst your usual chat-room conversation:

> OnlineHost: *Screen_Name* has entered the room.

The default is to have "Notify me when members leave" preference disabled, too. To enable it (or disable it again):

> MY AOL toolbar icon → Preferences → Chat → Notify me when members leave

Whenever someone leaves the room, a line like this appears amidst your usual chat-room conversation:

> OnlineHost: *Screen_Name* has left the room.

Benefit to text notification

- Keeps you aware of who's in the room.

Drawback to text notification

- When lots of people enter or leave, all the notifications makes the chat dialogue hard to read.

Alphabetize the member list

The default is not to alphabetize chat room member lists. As a result, the screen names of chat room participants are displayed in random order in the `People Here` box. To switch between alphabetized or random member lists:

> `MY AOL` toolbar icon → `Preferences` → `Chat` → `Alphabetize the member list`

Benefit

- Makes it easier to locate specific members in chat rooms.

Drawback

- You must reenter the room or switch rooms to have this take effect.

Profiles

Both your own member profile and the profiles of other members can affect your chat experience. If someone thinks your profile is interesting, he might be more eager to talk to you. Reading other members' profiles can help you find the people in a chat room with whom you have the most in common. These profile instructions don't apply to Auditoriums; see also "Rows and the People in Them."

Your profile

To view or edit your member profile:

> `Keyword: Profile` → `My Profile`

or:

> `People` toolbar icon → `Search AOL Member Directory` → `My Profile`

Put descriptive information about yourself (or your alter ego) here. When you're done, click `Update`. Our advice is, protect your privacy: don't include your exact street address or your phone number. See the drawbacks below if you're worried about spam.

Benefit

- Allows fellow chatters to know more about you and compare their interests and location to yours.

Drawbacks

- Allows fellow chatters to find out too much about you; watch what you say. If you want to include deeply personal information, you probably shouldn't include your real name. With millions of members on AOL, you never know who might read it (see the section "Member Profile" in Chapter 30, *Privacy*).

- Spammers can search the AOL member profile database and add you to their spam lists.

Profiles of other members

To view the profile of any member in a chat room with you:

> From any chat room click the `People Here` list → double-click screen name → `Get Profile`

To view the profile of any member:

> `CTRL-g` → type screen name → `OK` (or hit `Enter`)

To view the profile of someone chatting in a People Connection room that you're not currently in:

> From any list of rooms, highlight the room of your choice → `Who's Chatting` → highlight any screen name → `Get Profile`

Benefit

- See what people have to say about themselves.

Drawback

- It's easy to lie about your identity online. The 19-year-old freelance artist you just profiled might actually be a 45-year-old AOL marketing rep.

Instant Messages

In response to a member's profile, or based on what he says in a chat room, you might want to send a chat-room participant an Instant Message. We discuss Instant Messages in detail in Chapter 9, but there are particular ways to send IMs from within chat rooms. (These directions apply to all chat rooms except Auditoriums. See "Rows and the People in Them" in this chapter for Auditorium-specific IM instructions.)

To send an Instant Message to someone in your chat room:

> From any chat room, double-click member's name in the `People Here` box → `Send Message` → type message → `Send` (or hit `CTRL-Enter`)

To send an Instant Message to anyone, anytime:

> `CTRL-i` → enter member's name in the `To:` box → type message → `Send` (or hit `CTRL-Enter`)

Bothersome Chat Room Participants

One of the disadvantages of hanging out in chat rooms is that not every chat room denizen is as intelligent and charming as you are. This section covers three situations: someone is babbling foolishly in a chat room, someone is pestering you with Instant Messages, and someone is being so irritating that it's worth reporting to AOL.

Ignoring a Chat Room Participant

If someone in a chat room isn't saying anything worth hearing, you can block his comments:

> From the `People Here` box in any chat room, double-click a screen name → `Ignore Member` checkbox

Figure 10-3 shows the final step in blocking a member's chat comments.

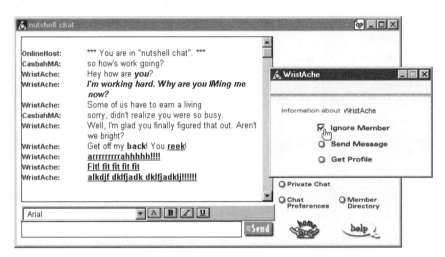

Figure 10-3: Ignoring a chat room participant

This doesn't work in Auditoriums; you'll have to turn off row chat. See also "Rows and the People in Them" in this chapter.

Benefit

- An annoying chatter's inane babble goes away. While you're in the current room, you won't see what that person says.

Drawback

- This won't keep annoying people from IM'ing you.

Blocking People's Instant Messages

Follow these instructions to keep specific people from Instant Messaging you, and from adding you to their Buddy Lists:

> `Keyword: Buddy` → `Privacy Preferences` → `Block only those people whose screen names I list` → enter screen name in box → click `Buddy List` and `Instant Messages` in the section labeled `Apply Preferences to the Following Features` → `Save`

When your Buddy List and Instant Messages preferences are set to block screen names, you effectively block those people from using any method to find out where you are online. In fact, blocked users get a message saying you're not even online, whether you are logged in or not.

Reporting Terms of Service Violations

We consider this a last resort. Usually, blocking IMs from a person is enough to keep him quiet, but if he still finds ways to bother you (like using alternate screen names, or sending you harassing email) you might have to take stronger measures. If someone is threatening you or deluging your email box with obscenities, you can report him to the AOL Terms of Service police.

AOL's TOS also apply in both Featured and Member rooms, since both are open to the public, but again, we feel that blocking someone's chat room comments (which we explain above) is usually satisfying enough.

To report a TOS violation, go to Keyword: Notify AOL and fill out the form there.

You may find this method easier:

From any People Connection Room → Notify AOL button

You'll need to paste the offending chat text (or IM) into your complaint, so don't close that window.

For more about TOS, see also Appendix D, *Terms of Service.*

Saving Chats and Chat Rooms

Chats can be slippery: once you leave a chat room, you no longer have a record of the conversation. And once you leave a chat room, who knows if you'll be able to find it again? This section explains how to save chat room conversations and remember where chat rooms are. These features work for all kinds of AOL chats.

Logging a Chat

To save a chat room conversation, you could cut and paste the chat window into a new document, then save the new document to your hard drive. We prefer to log our chats, which is automatic and effortless once you start. Logging a chat is like tape recording a spoken conversation; you'll have a record of everything that was said. To begin logging a chat:

Enter the chat room you want to log → My Files toolbar icon → Log Manager → Chat Log section of dialog box → Open Log → Save

See Figure 10-4 for a beginning chat log screen.

The default name of this file is *chat_room_name.log*, and its default location is your *C:\America Online 4.0\download folder.* You can name it whatever you want and put it wherever you like after clicking Open Log.

To finish logging, close the Logging window, click the Close Log button, or exit the chat room.

Figure 10-4: Starting to log a chat

To read the log, open it like you would open any other file: Go to the `File` menu and choose `Open`.

Benefits

- You can do something else while Log Manager records the chat and read it at a later, more convenient time.

- Allows you to save important chats.

Drawbacks

- If the log file is larger than 64K, you won't be able to read it in AOL. Use a word-processing application instead.

- You have to be in a chat room before you can start logging it, so the log might miss the beginning of your chat conversation.

- In the case of multiple screen name accounts, any chat log is available to any of your screen names. You can circumvent this little privacy problem by mailing the chat log to yourself, storing it in your PFC, making sure your PFC is passworded (to password your PFC, see Chapter 18, *Personal Filing Cabinet*), then deleting the original log.

Favorite Placing a Chat Room

To add a chat room to your list of Favorite Places:

From any chat room, click the heart icon in the upper-right of the open window → Add To Favorites

This is an easy way to save the location of any chat room.

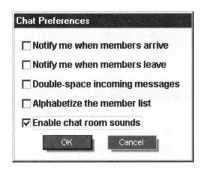

Benefits

- Saves time entering often-visited chat rooms.

- Helps you remember the names of Private Rooms, which don't appear on any chat list.

You can also use Favorite Places to alert your friends to good chat rooms. Just click Insert in Instant Message or Insert in Email instead of Add to Favorites. You can also tell your friends by dragging a chat room's red Favorite Places heart into an email or an Instant Message.

See also Chapter 17, *Favorite Places.*

Chat Preferences

Chat preferences are the settings that affect how chat rooms look and sound. To adjust your preferences:

> My AOL toolbar icon → Preferences → Chat

or:

> From any chat room (except an auditorium), click Chat Preferences

These preferences apply to every chat room on AOL. The Chat Preferences screen is shown in Figure 10-5.

Figure 10-5: Chat Preferences

We cover the Notify me when members arrive, Notify me when members leave, and Alphabetize the member list preferences in the "Who's Chatting?" section of this chapter. Enable chat room sounds is discussed in the "Playing and Hearing Chat Sounds" section of this chapter. The only preference we haven't explained elsewhere is:

Double-space incoming messages: The default is to have this preference disabled, which means that your chat text is single-spaced.

Benefit

- Can make chatting easier on the eyes.

Drawback

- Can make fast-paced chat unreadable

Stylizing Chats with Rich Text

The style toolbar, shown in Figure 10-6, has a drop-down menu and four buttons that can format your chat text. It's fairly easy: if you can use any of the popular word processors, including MS Word, you will find it easy to format your chat text. You can't stylize text in Auditorium chats.

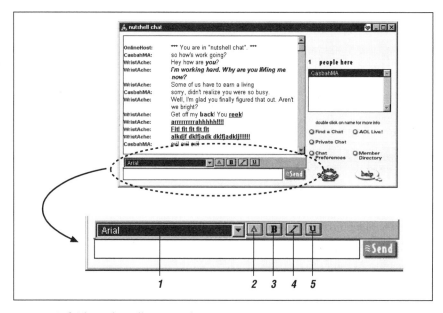

Figure 10-6: The style toolbar in a chat room

1. The drop-down menu selects the font (it defaults to Arial). There are some completely unreadable ones, and readability varies depending on each member's screen resolution and monitor size, so we don't recommend bothering much with font changes.

2. The blue **A** button brings up a color palette. Click a color and click OK.

3. The black **B** button bolds the text. Keyboard shortcut: CTRL-b

4. The slanty *I* button italicizes the text. Keyboard shortcut: CTRL-t

5. The underlined <u>U</u> button underlines the text. Keyboard shortcut: CTRL-u

Playing and Hearing Chat Sounds

Some members find that sounds enhance their chat experience. Others find them annoying. We have advice for both camps.

The default is to have member *.wavs* enabled, which means you can hear the sounds that members play in chat rooms. To disable member *.wavs* (or enable them again):

> MY AOL toolbar icon → Preferences → Chat → Enable chat room sounds

This only applies to member *.wavs*.

To play *.wav* files during your chat room conversations:

> From any chat room, type {S followed by the name of a *.wav* in your AOL directory → Send

For instance, you could type {S goodbye and the chat room hears the AOL "goodbye" sound. You don't need to type goodbye.wav, though you can.

Benefit

* Could potentially make chats more entertaining.

Drawbacks

* Only members with the same sound on their computers (with chat sounds enabled and speakers turned on) will hear it.

* Overuse of member *.wavs* won't endear you to fellow chatters.

Hyperlinks

In this section we tell you how to configure your account to receive hyperlinks in chat rooms, and how to send hyperlinks in chat rooms. Hyperlinks can lead to AOL areas, web sites, chat rooms, message boards, and anything else with a red Favorite-Place icon. This section applies to all chat rooms on AOL.

Receiving

Blocking hyperlinks in chat is the default, even for 18+ (general access) screen names. To allow your screen name to receive hyperlinks in chat:

> Keyword: Parental Controls → Fine Tune With Custom Controls → Chat → Chat Controls → clear the box next to Block Hyperlinks in Chat → OK

When a hyperlink is blocked, you don't see a blue and underlined phrase, but you do see the URL in plain text. An example of a blocked hyperlink is shown in Figure 10-7. You can keyword to the URL or enter it in a web browser.

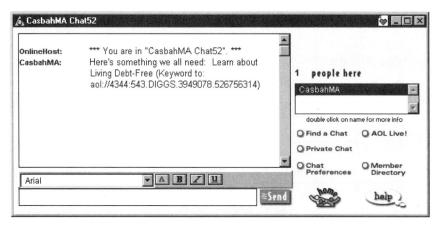

Figure 10-7: An example of a default, blocked hyperlink

When a hyperlink is unblocked, words appear as blue underlined text. If you click the phrase Learn About Living Debt Free in Figure 10-8, you'll go directly to the area it links to.

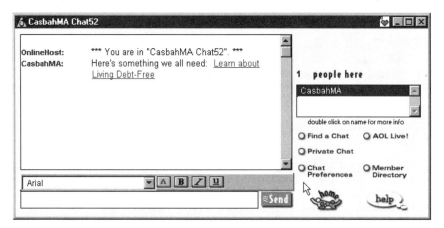

Figure 10-8: An example of an unblocked hyperlink

Benefit to unblocking

• It's faster and easier to visit chat-recommended URLs.

Drawback to unblocking

• A child (or any sensitive type) could follow a link to something they don't want to view. The phrase "happy day" could be linked to Bianca's Smut Shack for all you know. Your best bet to avoid what some may consider offensive material is to not follow a link from someone you don't know.

Sending

You can send a hyperlink to any AOL area, web site, chat room, message board, or anything else with a red Favorite-Place icon. Only members with hyperlinks unblocked can see the hyperlink; everyone else sees the URL they can manually keyword to (with CTRL-k, for instance).

To send a hyperlink, drag the area's red Favorite Place heart icon into the Send window of your chat room. The title of the area appears as a blue, underlined hyperlink. Figure 10-9 shows a Favorite Place heart being dragged into a chat.

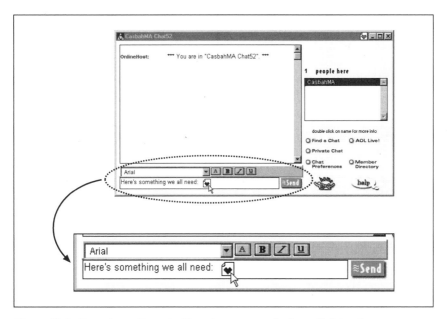

Figure 10-9: Dragging a Favorite Place heart to send a hyperlink in chat

Featured and Member Rooms

People Connection Featured (formerly known as "Public") and Member Rooms are free-for-all chat rooms open to anyone on AOL. We've seen them hold up to 27 people, though AOL tells you they only hold 23.

The previous sections of this chapter all apply to Featured and Member Rooms, so we only talk about three unique Featured/Member Room features here: the lobby, creating a Member Room, and how to leave a room.

The Lobby

We've said it before, and we'll say it again: we can't stand People Connection lobbies. We think the conversations in lobbies are stupid, and whenever we set foot in one, we're deluged with unwanted Instant Messages and commercial spam. Of course, some people love them, or they wouldn't be so crowded all the time. We'll tell you all the ways to enter chat lobbies and all the ways to avoid them.

Entering a People Connection lobby

- People toolbar icon → Chat Now
- Welcome screen → People Connection → Chat Now
- Keyword: People → Chat Now

Benefit

- This is theoretically where you should start, so it's good to know how to get there.

Drawback

- Spam-o-rama.

Avoiding lobbies

It used to be that to enter any People Connection or Private room, one would have to go through a lobby. The only way to avoid it was terribly convoluted: invite your own screen name to a Buddy Chat, enter that Private Room, and proceed to a different chat room from there. Kudos to AOL for making lobby avoidance easy; all you have to do is follow one of the following two paths:

- Keyword: People → Find a Chat
- People toolbar icon → Find a Chat

Don't ever click Chat Now, or you'll wind up in a lobby anyway.

Benefits

- If you find lobbies such as Town Square annoying, you never have to set foot in one again.
- You'll probably get less spam this way.

Creating a Member Room

To create your a new chat room that will be open to everyone on AOL:

> Keyword: People → Find a Chat → Start Your Own Chat → Member Chat

or:

> People toolbar icon → Start Your Own Chat → Member Chat

Double-click the category you'd like your Member Room to be filed under, type a name for it in the box, and click go chat, as in Figure 10-10.

Benefit

- Lets you create a chat room for any specific topic.

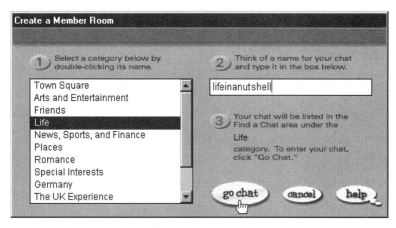

Figure 10-10: Creating a Member chat

Drawback

- This room is open to every AOL member who wants to go there, for better or for worse. Member Rooms are actually a lot like featured rooms, except that AOL would never sponsor a room called "I Got a Hot Wife" or "Bux-omBabes." Those room titles are true examples, so if they made you uncomfortable, you should steer clear of Member Rooms!

If you're itching to make your own room but want to be a bit more selective about who uses it, click **Private Chat** instead of Member Chat, then enter a name for your private chat in the box. If you want to tell people to join you in your Private Room, you'll have to tell them the exact name of it.

See also the "Buddy Chat" and "Private Rooms" sections of this chapter.

Leaving Featured and Member Rooms

To leave a Featured or Member room, either switch rooms or simply close the chat window.

To switch to a different chat room, click **Find a Chat** from within any Featured or Member room. If you're currently in a Member Room, clicking **Find a Chat** results in a list of other Member Rooms (click **Featured Chats** or **Enter a Private Chat** to switch to one of those categories). Double-click a chat room to enter it.

If you're currently in a Featured Room, clicking **Find a Chat** results in a list of other Featured rooms (click **Member Chats** or **Enter a Private Chat** to switch to one of those categories). Double-click a chat room to enter it.

Private Rooms and Buddy Chat

All Buddy Chats are Private Rooms, but not all Private Rooms are Buddy Chats. Confusing? Not really. This section has three subsections that explain it all:

- *Buddy Chat:* We cover responding to Buddy Chat invitations and inviting people to a Private Room by using your Buddy List.

- *Private Rooms:* We talk about other ways to enter Private Rooms and invite people to them.

- *Leaving a Private Room:* Applies to all Private Rooms, no matter how you got there.

Many of the previous sections of this chapter apply to Private Rooms and Buddy Chat. See also: "Chatting," "People in Chat Rooms," "Bothersome Chat Room Participants," "Saving Chats and Chat Rooms," "Chat Preferences," "Stylizing Chats with Rich Text," "Playing and Hearing Chat Sounds," and "Hyperlinks."

Buddy Chat

This section covers starting a Buddy Chat and joining one in progress.

Initiating a Buddy Chat

To start your own Buddy Chat:

> Keyword: BuddyView → Buddy Chat

Buddy Chat is just a Private Room with a different method of invitation. No one else can join you in private chat unless they know the name of the room.

To let people know why you're inviting them to chat, you can invite them with a special message in the Message to Send box, such as "What are we doing this weekend?" There will be a default name of the chat room, such as TiredWritr Chat67, but you can change it to something else. It appears that you can't have any unusual characters (including question marks) in room names, so keep that in mind when naming the room.

To invite one person, highlight the screen name in the visible Buddy List window, then click Buddy Chat.

To invite everyone in a particular Buddy List group (like Buddies, Family, Co-Workers, etc.), highlight the group title (such as Buddies or Family), then click Buddy Chat. Add or delete screen names from the list of Buddies to further tailor your list of invitees.

For instance, Figure 10-11 shows a member highlighting the group title Buddies and clicking Buddy Chat. This will invite TiredWritr, Oreillyfan, British252, and SaraMind to a Buddy Chat.

You can also type the names individually into the Buddy Chat invitation, as in Figure 10-12. When you invite people this way, they need not actually be in your Buddy List.

If your Buddy List isn't already on your screen, Keyword: BuddyView brings it up. To configure your Buddy List to pop up automatically when you sign on, see Chapter 9.

Buddy Chat doubles as a "hey, look at this cool thing I found" feature. Just check the Keyword/Favorite radio button instead of the Private Chat Room

Figure 10-11: Inviting a group to a Buddy Chat with the Buddy List

Figure 10-12: Typing screen names into a Buddy Chat invitation

button, and you can alert the people in your Buddy List to a worthwhile AOL area or URL. Type the AOL keyword or web URL into the box where you'd usually type the chat room name and type a description of the area in the **Message to Send** box.

Benefits of Buddy chats

- Unlike IMs, you can talk to several people at once.

- Unlike featured/member rooms, you choose who gets to be invited.

- Even for one-on-one conversations, many people prefer the chat interface to the IM interface. For example, you can click **Enter** to send your latest comment; even the shortcut to send an IM is two keys (**CTRL-Enter**).

- Buddy chats keep everyone out of the lobby (see also the previous section "The Lobby").

- We've had Buddy Chat business teleconferences with coworkers working from home.

Joining a Buddy Chat

To join a Buddy Chat to which you've been invited, click the Go button on the Buddy Chat invitation. The titlebar at the top of the invitation tells you who the invitation is from. Buddy Chats are invite-only parties, so you should recognize the screen name.

If you click Go and wind up in an AOL area or web page, that's because the sender has used the Buddy Chat feature to alert you to fun things online.

Drawback

- If you're easily offended, beware of following Buddy Chat invitations to random web sites. There's a good chance they'll contain smut.

- Buddy Chat has been discovered by the general population as a method of spamming and sending unwanted social advances. Know that not everyone who invites you to a Buddy Chat is a friend.

The Send IM button is useful if the buddy invitation comes from a screen name you don't recognize. Instead of going into a stranger's Buddy Chat, you can send an IM asking "And you are... ?"

Use the Cancel button if, for whatever reason, you don't want to go there.

Private Rooms

This section covers methods other than Buddy Chat invitations to create and enter Private Rooms. It's a matter of personal preference whether you use these methods or Buddy Chat invitations to create Private Rooms. We also explain both because you might be invited to a Private Room via Buddy Chat or other methods.

Creating a Private Room

> Keyword: People → Find a Chat → Start Your Own Chat → Private Chat

or:

> People toolbar icon → Start Your Own Chat → Private Chat

Enter a name for the room in the box, and click go Chat, as in Figure 10-13.

To avoid intruding or being intruded upon, be creative with the room name. If you try to create a room name that already exists, AOL thinks you've been invited to the existent room and takes you there. For example, we once tried to create a Private Room called "test," and there were already two people chatting when we got there. It appears you can't have any unusual characters (including question marks) in room names, so keep that in mind when naming the room.

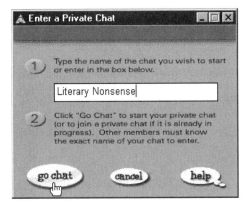

Figure 10-13: Creating or entering a Private Chat room

Benefits

- The benefits of private chats are many, and we've listed them earlier under "Initiating a Buddy Chat."

Drawback

- The room won't appear on any list, so remember its name so you can invite people later. You'll look flaky if you invite someone to a Private Room that doesn't exist.

Inviting with an Instant Message

Another way, besides Buddy Chat, to invite someone to a Private Room is to send them an Instant Message. You can send them a hyperlink to the Private Room:

From any Private Room, click the red Favorite Places heart → `Insert in Instant Message`

You can always send an Instant Message telling the member the name of your Private Room. As long as the member has AOL 3.0 or later, we recommend the hyperlinked option. Then you won't have to bother explaining how to get to a Private Room, if the member doesn't already know.

Entering a Private Room

You've just gotten an IM telling you the name of a private chat room. Now what? Getting there is actually fairly easy. You have a few choices:

- If you're already in a chat room, click `Private Chat` → enter the name of the Private Room → `Go Chat`

- `People` toolbar icon → `Start Your Own Chat` → `Private Chat` → enter the name of the Private Room → `Go Chat`

- `Keyword: People` → `Find a Chat` → `Enter a Private Chat` → enter the name of the room → `Go Chat`

Drawbacks

- "Join me in my private chat room" is often the AOL equivalent of "Why don't you come up to my room and see my etchings?" This could be a benefit, too. Just be aware of it.

- Know the exact name of the room, or you're out of luck: they don't appear on room lists. You could IM the invite-issuer and ask, but you'll look silly. You might want to mark it as a Favorite Place for future reference (see also "Saving Chats and Chat Rooms" in this chapter).

Leaving a Private Room

To leave a Private Room, simply close the chat room window. In Windows 95/98, that means clicking the X in the upper-right corner of the open window. That's it. There's no **Exit** button here to prompt you.

To switch to another Private Room:

From any Private Room click **Private Chat** → enter the name of the Private Room → **Go Chat**

To switch to a Member Room:

From any Private Room click **Find a Chat** → double-click a Member Room to enter it

To switch to a Featured Room:

From any Private Room click **Find a Chat** → **Featured Rooms** → double-click a Featured Room to enter it

Auditorium Chats

Auditorium events consist mainly of celebrity chats (with polls, gameshows, and online auctions scheduled occasionally). Celebrity events are set up so you can chat with other members (the members in your "row" of the auditorium) or ask questions of the celebrity "on stage." They're different from other kinds of chat rooms you'll encounter on AOL, so read or skim this section before venturing into one to make sure you know the ropes.

An auditorium chat might look something like this:

```
ChatHostOnStage:    TiredWritr asks: What are your favorite movies?
TiredWritr:         (24)Hey! They picked my question! Yippee!
BigCelebOnStage:    Why, all of mine, of course.
WristAche:          (24)What an ego!
```

TiredWritr asked her question by clicking **Participate in Event** (see "Asking Questions" in this section). The chat host picked the question and read it to the entire auditorium. The celebrity answered it. The (24) in front of certain comments indicates that the participants are in row 24 in the auditorium; those comments can be read only by other people in that row (not by the people on stage or people in other rows).

The hub of celebrity and other auditorium events on AOL is AOL Live, `Keyword: Live`. It contains schedules and transcripts, which we talk about later in this section of the chapter.

Many of the previous sections of this chapter apply to Private Rooms and Buddy Chat. See also "Chatting," "People in Chat Rooms: Rows and the People in Them," "Bothersome Chat Room Participants," "Saving Chats and Chat Rooms," "Chat Preferences," "Hyperlinks."

Schedules

Auditorium events are like most other events in life: you might stumble into one, but it's better to know when they are and plan ahead.

For a schedule of today's AOL Live celebrity chats, plus schedules (though not necessarily today's) for channel-oriented Conference Rooms, go to `Keyword: Events`.

To receive the weekly AOL Live newsletter, follow this path:

`Keyword: Newsletters` → `AOL Official Channel Newsletters` →
`AOL Live` → `subscribe`

You'll get a weekly celebrity chat schedule in your email box, so you don't have to check the AOL Live area all the time.

To see a monthly schedule, go to `Keyword: Coming Attractions`. You'll know far in advance if any of your favorite celebrities are scheduled to visit AOL. Remember that like all live events, these are subject to change, so don't plan too far ahead.

Transcripts

If you missed a chat or want a copy of a particularly good chat, you can download a transcript of past auditorium events at `Keyword: Transcripts`. For another method of obtaining a copy of a chat, see also "Saving Chats and Chat Rooms" in this chapter.

Entering and Leaving an Auditorium

To enter an auditorium, go to `Keyword: Auditoriums` (plural), then double-click the auditorium of your choice to enter it. `Keyword: Auditorium` (singular) takes you to AOL Live.

AOL claims their auditoriums can hold up to 5,000 participants, but in another section of AOL Live they brag that their most popular events have had over 15,000. Sounds like a fire hazard to us.

To leave an auditorium, click the X in the upper-right corner of the open window.

To switch to another auditorium, you need to return to `Keyword: Auditoriums`.

To switch to another kind of chat room while you're in an auditorium, click the `Home` icon, then click `Find a Chat`. The default is a list of Featured Rooms;

double-click one to switch to it. For Member or Private rooms, click the appropriate button to view a list, then double-click a room.

Rows and the People in Them

Rows are parts of a larger chat room auditorium. All rows can read the comments of the celebrity "on stage," but each row can only read the comments of members in that row. Each row holds up to 16 members.

Changing rows

To move to another row within an auditorium:

From any auditorium click Who's In My Row → Other Row → double-click a row to enter

Like the Online Host says, your comments are only seen by members of your row. You can change rows at any time.

Creating a row

To create a new row within an auditorium:

From any auditorium click Who's In My Row → Other Rows → Create Row → enter a row number → Move to Row

If you and some friends want a row to yourselves, create a row with a very high number.

Viewing people in rows

To view the members in your row, click Who's in My Row while in any auditorium.

To view the members in other rows:

From any auditorium click Who's In My Row → Other Rows → List People

Finding a member in a row

If you want to be able to chat with a specific person during an auditorium event, you can find him with this method:

From any auditorium click Who's In My Row → Find Member → enter the screen name of the member you're looking for → Show Row

Turning off row chat

Turning off chat in an auditorium means you won't be able to read the comments of the other people in your row. You can still read the comments of the people on stage, such as the celebrity guest and the chat host. (And no matter what anyone in your row says, the celebrity can't see it.)

To turn chat off while you're in an auditorium, click Who's in My Row and click Turn Chat Off. The Turn Chat Off button magically transforms into a Turn Chat On button. To turn chat back on, click Who's in My Row, then click Turn Chat On.

Benefit

- You can read the wise words of the auditorium guest without being distracted by the chatter of your row-mates.

Member profiles

To profile a member in your row:

From any auditorium click Who's In My Row → highlight member's screen name → Get Profile

To profile a member in another row:

From any auditorium click Who's In My Row → Other Rows → List People → highlight member's screen name → Get Profile

To profile any member, any time:

Ctrl-g → type member's screen name → OK

Instant Messages

To send an Instant Message to a member in your auditorium row:

From any auditorium click Who's In My Row → Send Message

To send an Instant Message to a person in any row you choose:

From any auditorium click Who's In My Row → Other Rows → List People → Send Message

Asking Questions

To ask a question of an auditorium event guest, click Participate in Event. Type your question in the box and click Ask a Question. Depending on what kind of auditorium event you're at, you could also click Send a Comment, Vote, or Bid.

The chat host sees the questions in the order she receives them. The chat host will probably choose the best questions, but it can't hurt to ask early and get your question at the front of the line. Don't ask anything you'd be embarrassed to ask if the celebrity "on stage" was right in front of you; if you ask a stupid or insulting question, you might get thrown out of the auditorium by the chat host.

Conference Rooms

A *Conference Room* is just a lofty name for a chat room within AOL content areas. Conference Rooms sometimes host chat events with outside speakers; for instance, the Motley Fool financial forum might host a chat with an investment guru.

Popular Conference Rooms are active at other times as well: the Motley Fool chat room is always full of ordinary members chatting it up about stocks and funds. Conference Rooms often have hosts (i.e., moderators) and specific themes (one subject on Monday night, another on Tuesday night, etc.).

Because AOL hasn't documented Conference Rooms to anyone's satisfaction, and because they can be the most useful kind of chat rooms, we've compiled a list of them. You'll find it at the end of this chapter.

Conference Rooms don't have the `Find a Chat` or `AOL Live` buttons that other chat rooms have, but you can still get to those areas using `Keyword: People` → `Find a Chat` and `Keyword: Live`. Missing buttons notwithstanding, Conference Rooms are a lot like other AOL chats, so many of the previous sections of this chapter apply to Conference Rooms. See also "Chatting," "People in Chat Rooms," "Bothersome Chat Room Participants," "Saving Chats and Chat Rooms," "Chat Preferences," "Stylizing Chats with Rich Text," "Playing and Hearing Chat Sounds," and "Hyperlinks."

Some Conference Rooms have a `More Chat` button. It shows the conference room you're in and other chat rooms like it. There might be other chat rooms if a conference room gets too big. For instance, you might see PetChat and PetChat2. To see who's in a chat room, highlight it and click `Who's Chatting`. From there you can get any of the members' profiles or send them Instant Messages (see also "People in Chat Rooms" in this chapter). From the same screen, you can `Search Featured Chats` (see also "Find a Chat" in this chapter).

Some Conference Rooms (like the ones at `Keyword: Thrive` and `Keyword: Astronet`) have an extra icon that looks like a green AOL logo. Click it for a guide to that AOL area's content and chats.

To switch to a Featured, Member, or Private Room, click the `Home` icon on the chat window. You'll be taken out of your Conference Room and sent to `Keyword: People`. Click `Find a Chat` to switch to a Featured or Member Room. Click `Find a Chat`, then `Start Your Own Chat` to enter or start a Private Room.

AOL's Conference Rooms

It's easy to find People Connection chat rooms (`Keyword: People`) and auditorium events (`Keyword: Live`), so easy that we don't list them all here. Conference Rooms are harder to find. They merit some sort of index because you'll typically find conversation there of higher quality: chat events with outside speakers; hosted discussion (i.e., with moderators); and specific themes in areas like business, careers, sports, emotional support, medicine, etc.

Since Conference Rooms are tied in with specific AOL content, they are always subject to change, so don't take this as a canonical list. Generally, once you're familiar with AOL's content areas, you can always find a chat that interests you. But since many members aren't that familiar with AOL content, someone had to document Conference Rooms, and it might as well be us. As far as we know, no one has ever compiled a guide to AOL's many Conference Rooms before. Don't thank us; just send money. (Just kidding. But we're not above suggesting you tell all your friends to buy this book, and buy some more to give out as gifts while you're at it.)

By following the paths below, you'll wind up either in a Conference Room (rarely) or at a front screen containing a link to the Conference Room as well as other information such as schedules and transcripts. We won't pretend that each of these paths will be accurate by the time you pick up this book. The reason for that is that AOL (like all online entities) frequently redesigns the way its areas look. But never fear: as long as you can find an AOL content area, the Conference Room can't be far behind. Use the keywords below, and see Chapter 15, *AOL Content Reference.*

These are the keywords for conference rooms, alphabetically by subject of interest:

Adoption
    Adoption → Conference Center

African-American (see *Black community*)

AIDS quilt
    Names Project → Quilt Chats

Arts
    Culturefinder → Chat
    NYT Chat
    Afterwards → Van Gogh's Ear

Astrology
    Astronet → Chat

Auto Racing
    iRACE → Chat
    Motorsports → Motorsports Chat

Aviation
    AVforum → Chat

Baby boomers
    Baby Boomers → Chat

Bicycling
    Bicycling → Chat Room
    BikeNet → Conference Room and Schedule
    iBIKE → Chat

Black community
    NetNoir → Black Chat
    Black Voices → Chat Rooms

Boating
    Boating Online → Boating Chat

Books
    BarnesandNoble → Community → Chat Room
    BC → Chat
    eChat → Books
    NYT Chat → Books Chat
    TBR → Chat

Cars
    Road → Roadside Chat

Children (see also *Families*)
    KO Chat

Christian community
    COCO → Chat and Live Events

Collecting
    Collecting → Collector's Corner Chat Room

Comics and animation
    DC Comics → click any picture → Chat
    Marvel → Chat
    Japanimation → Anime Café
    Cartoon → Chat

Computers
    Computing Chat → Open Chat Room
    Computing Live
    DOS → DOS Conference Center
    Education and technology: MED → Education Chats
    Mac graphic arts: MOS → Chat Schedule
    Mac music and sound: MMS → Mac Weekly Music Chats
    Macworld → Live Events
    PC animation and video: A & V Forum → Weekly Chat Schedule
    PC Games → Chat Room
    PC graphic arts: PGR → Chat Schedule
    PC hardware: Hardware → Chat Rooms and Schedules
    PC help desk: Help Desk → Help Chat
    PC Music → Conference Center
    PC telecommunications and networking: PTC → Join us for our conferences
    Win → Windows Forum Conference Center
    PDA → Chat Schedule
    Scanning → Artists Chat
    Senior citizen computer users: SeniorNet → Community Center
    Young computer users: YTChat → Chat Room

Cooking
    eGG → Chat
    Cooking Club → Cooking Chat
    FDN → Chats

Crafts
    Crafts Magazine → Chat Today

Cricket
    Cricketer → Chat

Crossword puzzles
    NYT Crossword → Chat

Entertainment, general (see also *Movies, Music,* and *Television*)
   eChat → Etc

Families
   Family Ties → Special Chats
   Moms Online → MO Chat
   Parent Soup → Chat
   Adoption → Adoption Forum Chats
   Roots → Genealogy Chat
   Homeschooling → Conference Center
   Scouting → Conference Center

Fashion
   Elle → Elle Chat

Finance
   PF Live
   Conference Call
   Funds Live
   Sage → Chat
   Fundworks → 401(k) Café
   Beaty → The Chatroom
   IBD → Community → Chat
   MNC → Market News Chat
   Fool → Chat
   BW → Talk and Conferences
   EIU → Global Forum
   Edelman → Chat
   MoneyWhiz → Chat
   Tax → Tax Talk

Fishing
   FBN → Chats → Fly-Fishing Chat Room, Freshwater Chat Room,
   and Saltwater Chat Room

Football
   NFL → Chat

Foreign language
   Bistro (includes chat rooms for speaking Arabic, Chinese, French, German,
   Greek, Hindi, Italian, Japanese, Korean, Russian, Spanish, and Tagalog, plus
   scheduled chats for various other languages)

Games
   PC Games → Chat Room

Gardening (see *Home and garden*)

Gay community
   Gay Chat
   Planet Out → Chat

Genealogy
   Roots → Chats

Golf

    `GOLFonline` → `Chat`
    `iGOLF` → `Chat`
    `Golfis` → `Clubhouse Chat`

Health (see also *Mental health*)

    Health Support
    `Better Health` → `Events, Chats, and Group Meetings`
    `Thrive` → `Chat`
    Addiction and recovery: `A&R` → `Chats and Conferences`
    Alternative medicine: `AHH` → `Chats and Conferences`
    Cancer: `Better Health` → `Events, Chats, and Group Meetings` →
    `Cancer Chat Room`
    Disabilities: `Better Health` → `Events, Chats, and Group Meetings` →
    `Equal Access Café`
    Pain Relief: `Relief` → `Chat`

Hispanic community

    `Hispanic Online` → `Chat Now`

History

    `Civil War` → `Mason-Dixon Line Chat Room`

Home and garden

    `HouseNet` → `Chat at Housenet`
    `Garden` → `Gardening Chat`
    `HomeMag` → `Chat`
    `Met Home` → `Chat`

Horse sports

    `Horse Sports` → `Chat Room`

Humor

    `HO` → `Chat`

Hunting

    `HBN` → `Chats` → `Hunting Chat`

International

    `Bistro`

Jewish community

    `Jewish` → `Chat`

Latino (see *Hispanic community*)

Lesbian (see *Gay community*)

Local

    `Talk of the Town` contains links to chat rooms for Atlanta, Boston, Chicago, Cleveland, Dallas, Denver, Detroit, Greensboro, Hampton Roads, Houston, LA, Orlando, Philly, Roanoke, San Diego, San Francisco, Seattle, South Florida, Tampa Bay, Toronto, Twin Cities, Washington. You can also get to any of these rooms by keywording to the city and clicking chat, i.e., `Atlanta` → `Chat`

Love (see *Romance*)

Martial arts
    MAW Network → Chat

Mental health
    Depression Info → Communicating with Others
    Online Psych → Go to Chat

Military
    MCO → Chat

Money (see *Finance*)

Motorcycling
    Cycle World → Chat Room

Movies
    eChat → Movies links to the following chat rooms: Cinema Chat, Star
    Wars, Critics' Choice, Entertainment Asylum, Hollywood
    Online, Premiere

Music
    eChat → Music links to the following chat rooms: The Nightclub,
    Classical Music, Grateful Dead, Critics' Choice, Mac Music and
    Sound, MTV Yack, Parrot Key, SPINonline, VH1

News
    News Talk → Chat/Message Boards
    NPR → Talk of the Nation → The Control Room Chat
    NYT Chat
    NW → Contents → Let's Talk → Chat

Outdoors
    @outdoors → Chats
    Backpacker → Chat

Paintball
    Paintball → Chat

Parenting (see *Families*)

Pets
    Pet Care → Chat & Message

Photography
    Photography Forum → Chat Room

Politics
    George → Chat

Running
    Runner's World → Chat Room

Queer (see *Gay community*)

Quilting
    Quilting → Quilt Chat

Radio

Ham Radio: Ham Radio → Conference Rooms

National Public Radio: NPR → Talk of the Nation → The Control Room Chat

Religion

Beliefs → Chat

Christian: COCO

Jewish: Jewish → Chat

Romance

Love at AOL → Chat

Romance → Chat

Knot → Chat

School

Alumni: Alumni Hall → Chat Area

College Online → Chat Rooms/Schedules

Homeschooling → Conference Center

Ask a Teacher → [choose school level] → Live Teacher Help

Teachers' Lounge → The Work Room

Science

Astronomy → Planetarium → Enter the Planetarium

Space → Space Talk → Space Chat Room

Seniors

SeniorNet → Community Center

AARP → Chat Rooms

Sewing

Sew News → Chat Today

Sexual health

Thrive → Chat → Sex Chat Room

Shopping

Shop Talk

Skiing

SkiNet → Lift Line Talk

iSKI → Chat

Snowboarding

SOL → Chat

Space

Space → Space Talk → Space Chat Room

Sports (see also listings for individual sports)

Sports Live (includes Sports Chat room and AOL Live auditorium sports events), Sports Rooms (includes Stadium Club, Sports Trivia, The Arena, Press Box, Sports Chat. Specific sports rooms: Active Sports, Baseball, Golf/Bowling, College Football, College Hoops, Cyber Sports, Gymnastics, Hockey, Horse, Lacrosse, Martial Arts, Motor Sports, Other Sports, Pro Football, Pro

Hoops, Skating, Soccer, Sports Card, Tennis, Winter Sports, and Wrestling/Boxing)

ABC Sports → Chat (includes ABC College Football Chat, ABC Sports College Hoops Chat, The Football Huddle Chat, Wide World of Sports Chat, Pit Row Chat, Golf Chatting on the Green, The Paddock Room)

Athlete Direct → choose Chat Rooms from the drop-down menu

CBS Sportsline → Chat

RFsportsbar → Chat Rooms (includes Hockey Chat, AL Chatroom, NL Chatroom, NFL Chat, College Football Chat, NBA Chatroom, College Hoops Chat, PSX Chatroom)

The Sporting News → Chat/Boards (includes Main, NFL, College Football)

STATS → STATS Chat

Thrive → Chat → Get Moving! Chat Room

@outdoors (includes Sports Injury Chat and Outdoors Chat)

WSF → Women's Sports World Chats

Straight Dope (weird facts)

Straight Dope → Chat

Surfing

Surflink → Surf-Chat

Taxes

Tax → Tax Talk

Teenagers

Seventeen → Chat

Book Bag → Chat

Clueless → Cher Speak → Cher Chat

Plug In → Chat

Television

eChat → Television (includes the following chat rooms: Beverly Hills 90210, Days of Our Lives, Frasier, Mad about You, Melrose Place, Remote Control, Seinfeld, Star Trek, X-Files, ABC Daytime, ABC Kidzine, Babylon 5, Court TV, Critics' Choice, Entertainment Asylum, EXTRA, Good Morning, America, Late Show with David Letterman, Nick at Nite: Chatterbox, Nickelodeon, Oprah, Rosie O'Donnell, Soap Opera Digest, and Warner Bros.)

Theater

Playbill → Chat Live Now

NYT Theater → Theater Chat

Travel

Travel Messages & Chat → Chat

AAA → Auditoriums

Cruise Critic → Cruise Café

Family Travel Network → FTN Chat Café

Travel Café

LP → Chat

Travel America → Chat

TV (see *Television*)

Weather
Weather → Chat

Weddings
Knot → Chat

Women's community
Talk Women
WSF → Women's Sports World Chats

Women's magazines
Electra → Chat
Elle → Elle Chat
Mirabella → Let's Talk
Woman's Day → Chat

Woodworking
Woodworking → Shop Talk

Wrestling (WWF)
WWF → Chat and Messages → WWF Chat

Writing
Writers → Chat
Novel → Live Chat

CHAPTER 11

Message Boards

AOL message boards are online discussion groups about specific subjects. They are not conducted in real time (live); rather, participants "post" messages to the board. Posting to a message board is often compared to putting up a notice on a real-life bulletin board, but message boards take this notion one step further. For one thing, a piece of paper announcing free kittens isn't likely to provoke much back-and-forth discussion on any bulletin board. Your "car for sale" sign won't spark a heated debate. And while you might meet some people by having a garage sale, they probably won't become your new pals. All these things can happen when you post to a message board, though. We'd rather compare message boards to back-and-forth email discussions, between large groups of people, about a specific topic in which they all share an interest.

If you're looking to discuss a particular topic, AOL message boards might be the place. A typical message board has a narrow, specific focus. Message boards exist for every television show, rock band, football team, health concern, computer topic, and investment strategy imaginable. "Boston's Best Coffee Shop" isn't the most bustling message board on AOL, but we're impressed it's there. However eclectic your interests, AOL probably has a message board for it (see "Finding Message Boards" in this chapter).

Because the topics of message boards can be so narrow, they are often not as active as other online discussion groups, like newsgroups (see also Chapter 13, *Newsgroups*). Some message boards are busy, generating hundreds of posts every day, and some are so deserted you almost expect to see a tumbleweed roll across your screen. We suspect that message boards have lost some popularity since AOL opened up Usenet newsgroups to its members. AOL message boards do have some advantages over newsgroups, namely that the posts stay a bit more on topic and are more "clean cut" since members have to adhere to Terms of Service. If you're looking for racy content, you're unlikely to find it in message boards (try newsgroups and the Web).

Even if you'd rather jump right into mailing lists, newsgroups, or other Internet discussion, consider using AOL message boards as a training ground. Message boards can acclimate you to some of the conventions of online discussion groups before you venture into the vast, spam-ridden land of Usenet. AOL members have traditionally not been held in high esteem by the old guard Internet community, so it's best to make all your early mistakes among other AOL members. The last thing we want to do is prove the Net snobs right.

If You're New to Message Boards

Those of you who've never used AOL message boards before should see the following sections of this chapter first:

- Locating message boards that cover topics you're interested in can be difficult. Some seem almost hidden. See "Finding Message Boards" in this chapter for help tracking down the right one.

- What good are message boards if you don't know how to read the messages? "Reading Message Boards" shows you how.

- If you want to join a message board discussion, see "Posting to Message Boards" to learn how to participate.

Please take a moment to read the "Newsgroup Terms to Know" section of Chapter 13. The concepts are similar, and you won't be left scratching your head over words you don't understand.

Message Board Essentials

- No one should be forced to remember the elaborate series of clicks that brings you to a message board. See "Keeping Track with Favorite Places" and "Organizing with My Boards" in this chapter for ways to hang onto your message boards. There's no need to traipse all over AOL to follow your message boards when you can do it with just a few clicks.

- See "Marking" in this chapter for ways to keep busy message boards under control and to review posts you've already read.

How Are Message Boards Organized?

There are two kinds of message boards on AOL: old-style and new-style. *New-style message boards* have a background full of colored pushpins, while *old-style message boards* are on a white background. You hardly ever see an old-style message board on AOL any more, so we won't bother with a drawn-out explanation of them. We do, however, provide old-style message board instructions in some parts of this chapter, in case you run across any.

New-Style Message Board Structure

New-style message boards look like Figure 11-1. To start your new-style message board tour, sign on to AOL and go to our sample board: Keyword: Sports

Boards → Tennis → Net Game (Tennis). You'll see a screen full of what appears to be more message boards. These are like old-style message board "topics," since they are subsets of a larger subject (for instance, Martina Navratilova is a subset of the message board "Net Game (Tennis)"). However, in the new-style format, they are separate message boards, not just folders.

To see the list of posts for any message board, double-click the board or click List All. You'll see individual posts, including each one's subject, author, and date posted. To read a post, double-click it, or highlight it and click Read Post. Posts can be sorted alphabetically or by date (see also "Setting Your Preferences" in this chapter).

Some new-style message boards are threaded, which means that posts with the same subject line (like Re: Tennis question) are grouped together on a separate level between boards and posts. To read an individual message in a threaded topic, double-click a message board, then double-click a thread, and *then* double-click a post. However, we've seen truly threaded message boards so rarely that we're going to make this general rule: old-style message boards have boards, topics, and posts; new-style message boards just have boards and posts.

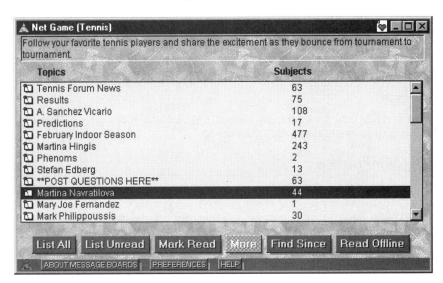

Figure 11-1: A new-style message board

Finding Message Boards

Before you can read or post to a message board, you have to find one that interests you. It's easy to find message boards as long as you know that message boards tend to be associated with AOL content areas. For instance, to find music boards, you'd look in Keyword: Music. To find mutual fund message boards, you'd look in the personal finance channel, Keyword: Personal Finance. You have to poke around in the main area a bit before you find the message board, but you'll find it. Usually you stumble onto interesting message boards because you're already in the related area. It would be an ideal shortcut if AOL had a message board directory so you could find boards quickly (at, say, `Keyword: Message Boards`) instead of wading through AOL's many levels of content. Other online services, such as The Microsoft Network, let you get a list of all their message boards so you can read and subscribe to whichever ones you want in a flash. Until AOL institutes something similar, we direct you to Chapter 15, *AOL Content Reference*, to find AOL areas that might have message boards attached to them.

Once you find a message board, you will want to remember where it is. You can make it a Favorite Place (see "Keeping Track with Favorite Places" in this chapter) or add it to your My Boards area (see "Organizing with My Boards" in this chapter).

Reading Message Boards

Reading message boards is fairly easy. You just sit back and absorb other people's comments. You don't have to contribute if you don't want to. In order to read a post, you must be within an open message board. See "Finding Message Boards" in this chapter if you're having trouble tracking down message boards.

To read a post, double-click it. Alternately, you can highlight the post and click `Read Post`. In old-style message boards, double-click the post or click `Read Message`.

To read the post that's been posted after the current one, click `Next Post->` or `Subject ->>` (depending on the board). In old-style message boards, click `Next Message`.

You can also read backwards by clicking `<-Previous Post` or `<<- Subject` (or `Previous Message` in old-style boards).

The More Button

The AOL message board format can download only 500 posts at a time (to change that default, see "Setting Your Preferences" in this chapter). The `More` button tells AOL to download 500 additional posts. Remember that the default preference is to download the newest 500 posts, so if you want to go further back in time, you have to hit the `More` button. On the other hand, 500 posts is a lot to read, so you might find you never need the `More` button. The `More` button is grayed out when all available posts have been downloaded.

Old-style message boards can display 50 posts at a time and have a `More Messages` button you can use to display 50 more.

There is also a `More` button for every new-style message board post. If a post is particularly long, click `More` to download the rest of it. In old-style message boards, long posts are broken into parts and appear as separate posts.

Reading Posts Offline

You can use Automatic AOL to download or message board posts at a scheduled time, and to write or read message board posts offline. We explain this process in detail in Chapter 21, *Automatic AOL*, in the section "Message Boards."

Sorting Posts

You can choose the order in which you see, and therefore read, message board posts. From any open message board, click the `Preferences` button at the bottom of the window. You can then choose to view the posts in chronological order (`Newest first` or `Oldest first`) or view them alphabetically by selecting, what else, `Alphabetical`.

Number of Days to Keep Posts on the System

An error message stating that a certain post is unavailable usually means that the post is too old to read. The default is to show (or download, if you're using Automatic AOL) posts from the last 30 days. You can make the number of days as large or small as you want, depending on how often you read message boards. Change the number of days by clicking the `Preferences` button at the bottom of any open message board. Fill in the desired number of days and click `OK`.

Posting to Message Boards

Posting to a message board means that you're sending a note to everyone who reads the message board. It's like sending an email message, except that potentially thousands of people can read it, instead of getting it delivered to their email box.

Before you post, we'd like to make some netiquette suggestions:

- Stay on topic. If you post off-topic, you're really sending out "junk posts."
- Be sure your messages contribute to the discussion and aren't just "me too" posts.
- Keep your posts brief.
- Post no advertisements.
- Don't post the same message to more than one group. This is called *cross-posting*. Some people consider cross-posting a form of spam.

Starting a New Subject

When you start a new subject in a message board, you're just posting a message with a new subject line. You are not replying to a particular post that has already been made. Basically, you're changing the subject without interrupting existing conversations. If you want to respond to a post that's already there, in a continuation of the subject that's already been started, see "Replying to Posts," below.

To start a new subject, click `Create Subject` from within any open message board. Type a subject line, type your message, and click `Send`. In old-style message boards, click `Post Another Message` from any open list of posts within a message board. Fill in a subject, type your message, and click `Post`.

Old-style message boards also allow you to create entirely new topics (see "Old-Style Message Board Structure" in this chapter).

Replying to Posts

When you have a response to a particular post, you reply to it. That way, your post has the same subject line (like a title) as other posts addressing the same subject. There are three ways to reply, described in the sections below.

Replying to the entire message board

The standard way to reply is to post a message the entire message board can see. From any open message board post, click Reply. This generates a post with the author and subject fields already filled in. Type your message and click Send. Your message may not appear immediately.

In old-style message boards, click Add Message from any open message board post. The subject field is already filled in. Type your message and click Post.

Replying individually to the author of a post

Sometimes, you may want to respond individually to the author of a post if you have a comment that isn't relevant to the topic of the message board. An example: if someone in a music message board waxes nostalgic about seeing a particular band perform at your alma mater, you shouldn't start up a boardwide, off-topic discussion about your college. If you want to pursue the academic conversation, you should respond to the author privately by clicking Reply from within any open message board post. Check the box next to Email to Author, and uncheck the box next to Post to Board. Write your message and click Send.

This option is not available for old-style message boards, but remember that you can send an email message to the author's screen name simply by clicking the Write toolbar icon and filling in the person's screen name. See also Chapter 8, *Email*.

Replying to an individual and also to the entire board

Sometimes you might want to post a reply to the entire message board and also email a copy of your response to the author of the post to which you're replying. You might do this if you know the author of a post checks his email more often than he reads message boards, and if the reply is also relevant to the board. From any open message board post, click Reply and check the boxes next to both Email to Author and Post to Board.

This option is not available for old-style message boards. If you want to email a copy of your reply to anybody, including the author of the original post, you have to paste a copy of your post into an email message.

Removing Your Own Posts

Unfortunately, when you put your foot in your mouth, there is no easy way to remove one of your own posts. You have to ask someone in charge, such as the *forum leader*, to do it for you. To find the forum leader, go to the area that houses the message board and look for documentation, like staff biographies or "about this area" pages, or a suggestion box. Good luck.

Keeping Track with Favorite Places

Message boards are slippery things. Once you find one (see also "Finding Message Boards" in this chapter), it can be hard to find it again. One solution to this problem is Favorite Places. Another slightly more complicated solution is My Boards; see "Organizing with My Boards" in this chapter.

Don't Lose That Message Board!

You can use Favorite Places to easily remember the location of most message boards. From within any open message board, click the heart icon in the upper-right of the open window. Then click `Add to Favorites`. Now you can return to the board whenever you want by clicking the `Favorites` toolbar icon, selecting `Favorite Places`, and double-clicking the name of the message board.

You won't be able to make a Favorite Place of old-style message boards, but you can make the content area where you found a message board a Favorite Place. As long as you have something to jog your memory, you should be able to find the board again.

Benefit

- Since most message boards don't have keywords, this is a much easier way to navigate to message boards than using the multiclick trails you often have to follow through many levels of an area. Save yourself some time and make it a Favorite Place.

Drawback

- Not all message boards have the heart icon. The new-style ones with the pushpin backgrounds are supposed to, but we've seen some that don't. Old-style message boards never do.

Saving Posts

You can also save message board posts as favorite places, in new-style message boards only. From within an open message board post, click the heart in the upper-right of the open window, then click `Add to Favorites`.

Benefits

- A way to save wise message board posts temporarily. The post eventually expires, breaking your link. (See "Setting Your Preferences" in this chapter to find out how to keep posts around longer than the default 30 days.)

- You can also save message board posts to your hard drive. Copy (`CTRL-c`) the message board text, and paste (`CTRL-v`) it into a new document (in AOL, or Word, or any word-processing program of your choice). Save the file to the desired place on your hard drive.

Tell Your Friends

To share a great message board (or one great post) with your friends, click its Favorite Places heart and select `Insert in Instant Message` or `Insert in Mail`. You could also drag the heart into an open email message or IM window. See also Chapter 17, *Favorite Places*.

Organizing with My Boards

With the special feature of My Boards, you can follow the discussion and post your own messages, either offline or online, to many of AOL's new-style message boards. `Keyword: My Boards` takes you to a history list of each new-style message board you've ever put into the queue to `Read Offline`. It keeps track of message boards you've slated for Automatic AOL downloads (see also Chapter 21). It tells you the date of the last post to the board. Just add a board you like to the list, and then read and post at your leisure without going to the area that houses the board.

Adding Boards to My Boards

To add a board to My Boards, you need to go to the message board of your choice, and click the `Read Offline` feature. This tells AOL to remember that this board is now part of your list of boards in My Boards. From then on, you'll see the board is in your list whenever you go to `Keyword: My Boards`, whether you're signed on as a guest or from your own computer. We hear reports that any message boards you visit are added to your list, but with 4.0, that feature hasn't worked for us.

My Boards has a few bugs to be worked out, such as the fact that you can't use it with old-style message boards, but it has great potential. It is a long-overdue step towards organizing the chaos of AOL message boards, even if you can't use it systemwide.

Reading My Boards offline or online

If you want to read My Boards offline, which is the default, we tell you how in the section "Message Boards" in Chapter 21, *Automatic AOL*. However, most people prefer to read message boards online, while they're signed on to AOL. If you want to switch to online reading, it's easy. Just highlight the board by clicking once, then click `Read Offline` again. You'll see the icon change from a clock to a regular pushpin message-board icon.

A My Boards area with one message board in it, marked to be read online, is shown in Figure 11-2.

Benefits

- Makes navigation faster; one keyword takes you to all the message boards you read.

- Good way to monitor which boards you've slated for Automatic AOL downloading (see the section "Message Boards" in Chapter 21, *Automatic AOL*).

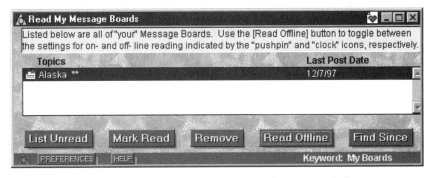

Figure 11-2: Managing your message boards using the My Boards feature

Drawbacks

- Unreliable. Boards sometimes don't come up, only to come up randomly weeks later.
- Can't be used for old-style message boards.

Removing Boards

To remove a message board from My Boards, go to `Keyword: My Boards`, highlight the message board, and click `Remove`.

Benefit

- You can unclutter your My Boards queue by removing boards you've tired of and don't want to visit in the future.

Drawback

- If you want to go back and read the group again someday, you'll have to wade through the AOL maze to find it.

Finding Certain Posts

Sometimes when you're reading a message board, you don't want to see every single post. Here are the different ways to view posts within message boards. All these instructions assume that you've already found a message board and are looking at it:

- *To find posts that have appeared since your last visit to the message board:* Click the `Find Since` button, make sure the `New (since last visit)` radio button is checked, and click `Find`. In old-style message boards, click the `Find New` button.
- *To find all posts you haven't read or marked as read (new-style boards only):* Click the `List Unread` button. (You can also list all unread posts by double-clicking on a message board.)

- *To find posts that have been posted during a certain time period (new-style boards only):* Click the `Find Since` button, click the `From [date] to [date]` radio button, fill in the starting and ending dates, and click `Find`.

- *To find posts that were posted since a specified number of days ago:* Click the `Find Since` button, click the `In last <number> days` radio button, fill in a number of days, and click `Find`. You can find posts from up to 9999 days ago, but keep in mind that AOL didn't actually exist 9999 days (27 years) ago. In old-style message boards, click the `Find Since` button, fill in a number of days, and click `Search`.

- *To find old posts that you've already read:* Click `List All`. You'll see all the posts that have been posted in the past 30 days (or longer or shorter; see "Setting Your Preferences" in this chapter to adjust that setting). In old-style message boards, click the `List Messages` button.

Finding Words and Phrases

Use the `Find in Top Window` function to pinpoint a word or phrase within a huge list of message board threads or within a very long post. To use `Find in Top Window`, click the `Edit` menu, select `Find in Top Window`, type a word or phrase, and click `Find`. This works for both new- and old-style message boards.

Marking

Marking posts, threads, and message boards helps you keep message boards organized and uncluttered. Marking is only available in new-style message boards.

Mark All Read

The `Mark All Read` button tells AOL that you've read a board. The next time you click `List Unread`, you'll only see posts that appeared since you marked the board as read.

Benefit

- Marking an entire message board as read clears all the messages if the board has gotten unmanageably busy since your last visit. Ah...a clean slate!

Mark Read

The `Mark Read` button within a message board tells AOL you've read a certain post or thread. It won't appear the next time you click `List Unread`. If you are looking at a list of message boards, the `Mark Read` button tells AOL you've read the entire message board.

Benefits

- When looking at a list of posts in an open message board window, you can go down the list and use `Mark Read` to get rid of the posts you know won't interest you (for instance, if the subject line is "MAKE $$$ FAST!!!").

- In rare "threaded" new-style message boards, use **Mark Read** if you don't want to read a thread and don't want to see it again.

Mark Unread

This button marks a post as unread. Even if you actually have read it, it will come up when you click **List Unread**. It's like **Keep As New** for email. (See also the entry *keep as new* in Chapter 8, *Email*.)

Benefit

- Posts marked unread stick around even after you leave the board. You can read them again when you come back.

Setting Your Preferences

To adjust the settings that affect your message board experience, click the **Pref-erences** button at the bottom of any open new-style message board window. The **Preferences** screen may say that your preferences apply to all message boards, but these preferences actually apply only to new-style message boards. The **Message Boards Preferences** screen is shown in Figure 11-3.

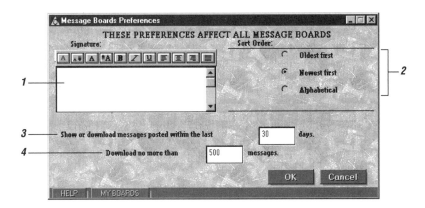

Figure 11-3: Message Boards Preferences screen

Your options are:

1. **Signature**: Text that appears at the bottom of each of your message board posts. See "Using a Signature File" in this chapter.

2. **Sort order**: Choose to view the posts in chronological order (newest first or oldest first) or alphabetical order. The default is **Newest first**.

3. **Show or download messages posted within the last [number] days**: The default is to show (or download, if you're using Automatic AOL) posts from the last 30 days. You can make the number of days as large or small as you want, depending on how often you read message boards.

4. Download no more than [*number*] messages: The default is to download up to 500 posts in any one Automatic AOL session. If you're reading lots of high-traffic groups, then you should probably make the number higher.

Using a Signature File

A signature file (also called a *.sig*) is a text message you can append automatically to each of your message board posts (but only in new-style message boards). Remember that all 11 million or so people who can read AOL message boards can potentially read your signature file, so you should limit the information you supply (for example, giving out your phone number is unwise). An example signature file that is harmless enough to use for message board posts:

```
Jen "TiredWritr" Muehlbauer
http://www.songline.com
Ask me about my new book!
```

Try to keep your signature to four lines or fewer and keep rich-text enhancements to a minimum. Long *.sigs*, such as the multicolored 20-line ones we've seen occasionally, annoy readers, and clog bandwidth.

Creating a Signature

To create a signature file for your message board posts, click the **Preferences** button at the bottom of any new-style message board window. In the box labeled **Signature**, type out your *.sig* as you want it to appear at the bottom of each of your posts. To include rich text, use the style toolbar above the **Signature** box to change your *.sig*'s background color, text color, text size, justification, and style (italic, bold, or underline). To include a hyperlink, drag an area's red favorite-place heart into the **Signature** box.

Once you've created a *.sig*, the default is to use the it every time you post to a message board. To disable it for a particular post, uncheck the **Use signature** checkbox at the bottom of the post.

See also the entry *signatures* in Chapter 8, *Email.*

CHAPTER 12

Mailing Lists

You don't need to go out and search for information on the Internet; you can have it come directly to you, right into your email box. Like message boards and newsgroups, mailing lists serve as a community of individuals who seek information about a particular topic or who want to enjoy like-minded exchange with people from all over. Depending on your interests, you can sign up for mailing lists on cats, books, computer operating systems, the stock market, or just about any other topic you choose; there are literally tens of thousands of mailing lists you can subscribe to.

The basics of mailing lists are pretty easy to get the hang of, too. You use your existing email box, send messages to an email address to sign up, and then sit back and wait while the correspondence pours in. Mailing lists are definitely a cure for an empty email box. They're out of AOL's territory and not covered by the strict rules of TOS, so you are joining largely unpoliced discussions—a freedom many people relish.

Discussion can be one-way, in what's called a *reactive list*. Reactive lists are set up like newsletters or syndicated news services, where information gets broadcast via email to a group of subscribers. Two-way lists, or *interactive lists*, allow subscribers to post messages so that all other subscribers can read them. Interactive lists often generate a lot of discussion, some of which can get heated. Often, there's a live human moderator who filters out spam and completely off-topic messages and sends the good ones to the list.

Compared to open forums like newsgroups, mailing lists can be a pleasure to receive due to the relative intelligence and thoughtfulness of their participants. To help maintain this quality, you should be careful to play by the rules of any list you join. If you're unfamiliar with general online netiquette, be sure to see "Mailing List Netiquette: Know Before You Join" later in this chapter.

One thing we think any AOL member should know is that *netizens*—that is, citizens of the Internet community—have a tendency to think that people with AOL accounts are somehow lacking—lacking Internet savvy, lacking tact, lacking netiquette. We know many AOL members, including ourselves, who prove this stereotype false, and we hope that you'll strive to be a netizen who can also help prove them wrong.

If You're New to Mailing Lists

- Your first goal with mailing lists is to find some that you'd like to receive. Sometimes it's tough knowing what lists are available in categories you're interested in so you'll need help locating them. To assist you in finding lists that match your interests, there are several trustworthy directories you can rely on. See the section "Finding and Subscribing."

- Once you find lists you like, you'll have to sign up to receive mail, a process that's called *subscribing*. The section "Subscribing to a List" tells you how to send the initial email, and how to know what information to include in that email.

- You'll want to avoid being thought ignorant about the rules of mailing lists or rude, so be sure to read over each of the sections in "Mailing List Netiquette: Know Before You Join."

- Finally, you might find that a list isn't for you. Perhaps it doesn't meet your expectations, or you just receive too much mail to keep up with. If you want to leave a list, for whatever reason, you'll need to unsubscribe. See the section "Unsubscribing from a Mailing List" for tips that will help you leave a list without a lot of the common headaches many people encounter.

Mailing List Essentials

Some mailing lists generate a lot of mail (even we're often surprised to find 100 new messages in our email box—per day!). You'll want to be aware that the volume of mail can overwhelm many AOL accounts, due to limits AOL places on the number of messages you can have at any given time. The section that follows, "Mailing Lists on AOL," will save you a lot of headaches if you subscribe to more than one list.

Mailing Lists on AOL

Signing up for a mailing list, or ten, using one of your AOL screen names is easy. First, you have to know how to send and receive Internet email, explained in Chapter 8, *Email*. As with all email, you must use AOL's built-in mail reader. You may one day be allowed to send and receive your AOL email through any MAPI-compliant email program, which includes all of the most popular ones, plus many word processors, spreadsheets, and graphics applications. In case you're curious, MAPI stands for Messaging Application Program Interface, and it's just a certain kind of email standard (like "http" is a web standard). We're not sure when AOL will implement this, but we hear that Microsoft's Outlook Express email client will be the first third-party mail reader allowed.

Too Much Mail? Keep Organized

Mailing lists can generate *tons* of mail. Some lists distribute literally hundreds of messages to each subscriber every day. With all the mail you get, your AOL email box can get extremely full.

The total number of unread messages your mailbox on AOL can hold is 550 items, including mail you have read and mail you have sent. However, you should be primarily concerned with unread mail, since AOL makes room for incoming mail up to the 550-item limit by deleting the archives of sent and read mail on its server.

If your mailbox reaches 550 messages, AOL bounces back (returns) incoming mail to the sender; in this case, the mailing list itself. Returned mail not only deprives you of the mail, but, if mail is bounced back to a list, most list administrators will (1) get annoyed at you, and (2) remove your subscription.

If you read your messages every day, you'll have no problem (other than tired eyes) keeping up. But if you don't, beware! The following is a list of options you can use to keep your mailing lists organized and avoid bouncing mail:

- Regularly check your mail, including reading or deleting all incoming messages. Read mail online or use Automatic AOL to download mail to read at any time (see "Email" in Chapter 21, *Automatic AOL*).

- If you subscribe to more than one list, subscribe using several different screen names. The volume of mail will then be distributed and somewhat less likely to bounce. Of course, this only works if other members of your household haven't pushed you to the limit of five screen names per account.

- Subscribe to the digest version of the list, if the list supports it. Rather than sending out posts one at a time to all subscribers, digested versions of lists include several posts from subscribers in one larger email. Reading the digested version of a list means you're in on the discussion, but mail is slightly delayed until enough posts accumulate to create a digest. We discuss digests below, in "Reading Your Mailing Lists."

- Avoid email altogether by subscribing to the list's newsgroup. Some mailing lists are also offered as newsgroups, in a process that's called *mirroring a mailing list*. You have to go out and get the news, but your email box doesn't fill up. Newsgroups that are also mailing lists are in the *bit.** hierarchy (see Chapter 13, *Newsgroups*).

- Sign up for a free web-based email account so the messages won't ever even come into your AOL account. You go out to the Web to read the messages, and can maintain an extra smidgen of privacy by helping to prevent others from knowing your AOL screen names, too. See Chapter 30, *Privacy*, for information on how to get a web-based email account.

Terms of Service

While AOL claims that its TOS applies to newsgroups, we've been unable to find any evidence that these rules also apply to mailing lists. This makes some sense: with newsgroups, AOL wants to be able to prevent recurring troublemakers from ruining a particular newsgroup. With mailing lists, troublemakers are more easily dealt with by the list's own owners or moderators. Mailing list participants should still follow the list's own rules of conduct, which vary from list to list. See the sections "Get the FAQs" and "Mailing List Netiquette: Know Before You Join" in this chapter for more on how to behave.

Mailing List Netiquette: Know Before You Join

Mailing lists have their own set of implicit and explicit rules to follow when subscribing, participating, and unsubscribing. Before you dive into the complex world of mailing-list discussion groups, here are some tips specifically directed at making your mailing-list experience go as smoothly as possible.

- Research the list before you join. Why waste your time and others by subscribing, then leaving right away? See "Finding and Subscribing" for more on how to find lists that suit your tastes and interests.

- Send subscription and unsubscribe requests to the proper email address, typically called the *administrative address*. Usually, this is an address different from the one that sends you the mailings.

- Follow the list's own guidelines. Read the welcome message you receive when you subscribe. Save it for further reference, for times when you'll need instructions (like how to unsubscribe). We can't say it enough: if there's a FAQ, read it (see also "Unsubscribing from a Mailing List" and "Get the FAQs").

- Read the list for several weeks before posting. Don't assume you know what's appropriate and what's not until you've gained some experience with the list's topics and style.

- Stay on topic. If you post off-topic, you're really sending out junk mail (see also "Posting to a Group").

- Send email to one person only in situations when your answer may not be of general interest to all the subscribers of a list. It is OK to start a side conversation with someone on your mailing list, just not OK to post this sideline to the entire list.

- Beware the AOL 550-piece mail limit. Be sure to read mail regularly (or delete it) so that you'll never bounce mail back to a list. If the list supports *nomail* or *postpone* commands, use them when you're on vacation (see also "Mailing Lists on AOL").

- Don't post a test message to the list. No one wants to see whether your test got through. Post a regular message, and you'll know if it goes through because you typically receive a copy.

- "Me too" replies are usually not appreciated. In general, when responding to a post, be sure you have more of use to say than the material you quote. If you quote two paragraphs, but only add one line of your own, have you really added to the discussion?

- Don't send large files to a list, especially when you can point to a file on the Web or at files others can access, such as an FTP site (see also Chapter 23, *Web Publishing and FTP*).

- Unsubscribe to leave a list. If you delete a screen name or cancel your AOL account (or any account you're using to subscribe to mailing lists), unsubscribe so as not to have mail returned to the list (see "Unsubscribing from a Mailing List").

Finding and Subscribing

While we've said that signing up for a mailing list is as easy as sending out an email, there are still some protocols you have to follow to successfully join it. First you've got to know what lists interest you. Then you've got to follow instructions for sending the initial email. Since most lists are processed by computer, not real people, you'll have to follow the instructions precisely. Getting off a list can be a trial, too, but we discuss that later, in the section "Unsubscribing from a Mailing List."

Locating a List

Why should you learn something about a mailing list before you subscribe? You'll save time and headaches. You'll save time because actually sending out the initial email, responding to the confirmations, reading the email, and then unsubscribing to a list you don't like are pretty much huge wastes of time. You'll save headaches because you can't escape a list if you don't know where to send the unsubscribe email. Some people end up tearing their hair out for months or years as their mailbox fills up with unwanted email. Don't let this happen to you. Read about the list, then sign up.

There are several ways to find mailing lists that might interest you, both on the Web and via email. We've got links to the best of the online resources below.

On the Web

AOL's own *Mailing List Directory* contains extensive descriptions from the list administrators themselves. To see that list go to:

> *http://www.idot.aol.com/mld/production/*

Liszt, a popular searchable database of thousands of list descriptions and information mainly from the lists themselves, can be found at:

> *http://www.liszt.com*

Stephanie da Silva's well-known site *Publicly Accessible Mailing Lists* is at:

> *http://www.neosoft.com/internet/paml*

L-Soft, a producer of list managing software keeps an up-to-date database of lists served with its software at:

> *http://www.lsoft.com/lists/listref.html*

Tile.Net has a searchable database (you'll also get newsgroups in the search) located at:

> *http://tile.net/*

Via mail

How about an email mailing list about email mailing lists? (Say that five times fast!) Subscribe to *New-List*. When you subscribe, you'll get updates every few days about the newest or recently modified mailing lists, along with brief descriptions. Here's what you have to send to subscribe:

```
To: listserv@vm1.nodak.edu
Subject: [type anything here or leave blank]
Body: subscribe new-list your_first_name your_last_name
```

Get the FAQs

FAQs or Frequently Asked Questions are essential reading for any list you plan to subscribe to or for lists you've already joined. FAQs contain the dos and don'ts for a list, what you can post, what's considered to be off-topic (which means, what's beyond the purview of the group), and how to unsubscribe if you want to stop receiving mail. When you sign up for a mailing list, unsubscribing might be the furthest thing from your mind, but believe us, you'll want to know how to leave a list. The FAQ can tell you.

You'll typically find the FAQ attached to the initial email you receive when you subscribe. But many lists have their own web sites where you can learn about what topics the list covers, read the FAQ, and find links to more information on the topic.

To get more information about particular mailing lists, visit Liszt, the Mailing List Directory, at *http://www.liszt.com.*

Subscribing to a List

Ready to sign up? We hope you've read the FAQ, if one exists, or at least consulted some of the web directories we mention in the sections above under "Locating a List." Now you're ready to send off the initial email to CATS-L or DIGVID-L.

Send the initial email

Your first step is to send the initial email that puts you on the distribution list for receiving the list's email. For most lists, signing up involves sending email with the proper administrative address as the subject, and, in the body, something similar to the following: `subscribe` [*list name*] *your_first_name your_last_ name*. You can often leave the subject blank. Why all this precision? As we've said, most lists are run by computers, not humans, so you've got to follow their rules or the program won't understand which list you want to sign up for.

The programs that run most mailing lists are generically called *listservs* or *list servers*. Some of the more common types are Listserv, Listproc, and Majordomo.

These programs control all the mundane tasks related to signing up members, putting accounts on hold, and sending out emails to thousands of subscribers. You send the an email with your requests, and these programs take over.

How do you know what commands to send? Later in this chapter, we include a section called "Quick Reference to Common Distribution List Commands" that covers some of the most common types of commands you send to lists. But our best advice is to follow the sign-up instructions you get from a reliable source. Reliable sources include the directory where you initially located the list (see "Locating a List," earlier), or from the list's very own web site. For instance, if you used *http://www.liszt.com* to locate bowling-L, check for information on where to send the email, what to type in the subject line, and what to type in the body.

The administrative address versus the list address

Most lists have two distinct addresses. The *administrative address* takes care of signing up new members, putting subscriptions on hold, sending out digests, and unsubscribing. It is often *listserv@hostname.com* or *majordomo@hostname.com* (such as *listserv@aol.com*). Others include Listproc, Mailbase, and Mailserv.

The *list address* is the one that accepts email that's forwarded to all subscribers. Don't send administrative requests to the list address. Not only will your request not be processed, you'll annoy all of the subscribers to whom your request has been forwarded (they'll think you're a newbie, at best, or stupid, at worst). Use the list address only when you want to participate in the discussion.

If you follow the instructions you get from the directory, or from the list's own web site, you should have no problem sending your request to the administrative address.

For instance, say you want to subscribe to the net-happenings list (it tells you what's happening on the Net, of course), you'd send the following email:

```
To: listserv@lists.internic.net
Subject: [leave blank or type any character]
Body: subscribe net-happenings your_first_name your_last_name
```

After you send the initial subscribe email, you're not done. You should keep checking your email box for the confirmation message you'll have to read and respond to.

Confirm your subscription

Because the list administrator or owner needs to be sure that you want to sign up for its list, and to confirm the validity of your email address, you often have to reply to a special confirmation mailing. Frequently you have to respond to this confirmation email within a set amount of time, usually 48 hours. This is a precaution that later helps smooth over potential problems (perhaps an evil ex-friend has signed you on to CATS-L knowing that you hate cats; if you don't confirm, you won't start receiving the list's messages).

Save the initial email

The initial email that tells you how to confirm is extremely important for several reasons. Save it. We can't stress this enough. It usually outlines all the commands to send to the administrative address, including how to unsubscribe. You think you'll remember how to leave a list, or that it will be easy to unsubscribe. But you might be wrong. You'll reduce your chances of going wrong and annoying other subscribers if you save and refer back to the initial email. You'll be glad you know how to leave the list or what to do when you want a temporary hold on email while you're on vacation. Our suggestion: put it in your PFC. We put ours into a folder called Mailing List Subscriptions, so we can easily spot them. See Chapter 18, *Personal Filing Cabinet*, for information on how to save a permanent record of email.

Reading Your Mailing Lists

Now that you've subscribed, the messages will start rolling in. Each list is different: some are very busy, with hundreds of separate messages being sent to your email box each day. Others are less prolific; you might get only one post every few days. If you've signed up for a one-way, or reactive list, you might get email only once a week. In any case, be sure you keep in mind AOL's limit on the amount of unread mail you can have in your email box (see "Too Much Mail? Keep Organized" earlier in this chapter for more on AOL's limit).

Too Much Email? Get the Digest

Rather than receiving a separate post from a mailing list each time a participant posts a message, you can often subscribe to a digest version. A digest is a collection of several individual posts that get sent in one email. By requesting the digest version, you cut down on the amount of email you receive. However, the posts are delayed slightly, as the mailing list software waits for message to accrue. Subscribing to a digest is typically outlined in the confirmation message you're sent when you subscribe. Of course, you can check the directory that provided the initial information, or the list's own web site. You then follow the instructions and send the proper command to the administrative address.

If you can't find a reference that tells you whether your list allows digests, you can try to send the digest command to the administrative address anyway. Determine what sort of list-processing software the list uses, then send the proper command: you'll find the commands in the section "Quick Reference to Common Distribution List Commands" later in this chapter.

Too Much Junk?

Unlike newsgroups, you won't have too many problems with junk mail and XXX advertisements coming to you via a mailing list. That's because even publicly accessible mailing lists can limit who joins the list and can remove subscribers who violate a list's guidelines. So people who would send junk mail or advertisements to a list are not likely to be subscribers for long. Still, some junk email will get through.

Currently, with AOL's built-in email client, there's not much you can do about junk mail other than deleting it. But there may be a solution, soon. Lots of email clients allow you to filter your incoming messages so that, for instance, you can remove mail that included "XXX" or "Live Nude" in the subject line, or in the body of the message. Filtering is not one of AOL's email features, but you might be able to filter email based on its content in the future. As we stated earlier in this chapter, AOL is testing the ability to use any MAPI mail reader you choose, which would include the excellent Eudora, Netscape Messenger, MS Outlook Express, and others.

Organizing Your Mail

What happens if you sign up for several mailing lists with the same screen name? Well, you probably get a lot of email, and it's all mixed in together, your CATS-L mail being mixed in with your DIGVID-L mail. Maybe you don't mind all this mixing, but we want a little more organization. Some mail readers allow you to send messages from different senders to separate mailboxes, like separating CATS-L mail from the DIGVID-L mail. But you can't do that automatically on AOL. What you can do it set up a different screen name for each of your lists, so that each list goes to just one name. We call this manual filtering, and we cover it in the "Mailing Lists on AOL" section. You can also follow our suggestions there for getting a web-based email account, thereby avoiding AOL's email box entirely.

Posting to a Group

After you've subscribed to a list and followed the discussion for a while, you, too, might have something to contribute to the discussion. Be sure you understand mailing-list netiquette, which we covered earlier in this chapter in the section "Mailing List Netiquette: Know Before You Join." Look to the list's FAQ for information about what kinds of posts are allowed and what's discouraged.

For just about every mailing list in existence, there are a few things that we can safely say are discouraged: advertisements and chain letters. Never send ads to a list; most don't permit advertisements of any sort. If you still want to post an ad, make sure you've been a member of the list for a while, know the list well, and are certain that the group permits ads.

Chain letters are our personal pet peeve. Chain letters clog the Internet's bandwidth, can clog servers, and annoy us (for the last time: the Good Times Virus is a hoax!). The general rule is not to participate in or forward chain letters. Besides, most people you'll send the chain letter to will have seen it already.

Unsubscribing from a Mailing List

To leave a list, send the correct commands, in email, to the administrative address. Whatever you do, don't send unsubscribe requests to the list address; you won't get off the list, and every other subscriber will see your mistake. See the section "The administrative address versus the list address" if you're unsure about the difference between the general list address and the administrative one.

Below, we present a series of steps to follow to leave a mailing list. Try the first suggestion. If that doesn't work, make your way through the suggestions until you've successfully left the list.

1. Go back to the initial materials you received from the list, such as the welcome message (we told you to save them!). There you'll see how to unsubscribe.

2. Go back to where you initially discovered the list. AOL's Mailing List Directory, Liszt, or the list's own web site usually has instructions on how to leave particular lists (see "Locating a List").

3. Check in the mail headers to see what sort of mailing list-management software your list comes from. Then, use the commands required by that type of software to unsubscribe from the list. Be sure you're sending commands to the administrative address. You might have to experiment a bit here, since it may not be clear what sort of list you're subscribed to. If you're wrong, you'll typically get mail back from the server that says "can't understand the following commands..." For the correct commands for the most popular listserv software, see the tables in the next section.

Quick Reference to Common Distribution List Commands

There are several automated systems for distributing and managing mailing lists. The most popular are listed below along with common commands for how to subscribe, unsubscribe, temporarily halt mailings (great if you go on vacation), view the archives, and others.

The best way to know what sort of list you're subscribed to is to read the welcome message. If you don't have the welcome message, you'll often find evidence in one of the individual mailings, either in the headers or in the body, saying how to subscribe and unsubscribe.

When using list commands, put the administrative address in the To: box. You can leave the Subject: field blank, or type any character if AOL says you can't leave it empty. Put the commands from the tables below into the Body: of the message.

If you know your way around mailing lists but the common commands slip your mind, we present the following tables as a quick reference. This section covers Listproc, L-soft Listserv, Mailbase, Mailserv, and Majordomo/Macjordomo.

Table 12-1: ListProcessor (or Listproc) List Commands

Function	List Command
Subscribe	SUBSCRIBE *listname* Firstname Last-name (e.g., SUBSCRIBE DIGVID-L Jane User)
Unsubscribe	UNSUBSCRIBE [*listname*]
Request a digest verson	SET [*listname*] MAIL DIGEST

Table 12-1: ListProcessor (or Listproc) List Commands (continued)

Function	List Command
Cancel digest	SET [*listname*] MAIL ACK
Temporarily suspend mail	SET [*listname*] MAIL POSTPONE
Resume mail	SET [*listname*] MAIL ACK or SET [*list-name*] MAIL NOACK or SET [*listname*] MAIL DIGEST (use the commands that set up your mail in the manner you want to receive it)
Receive a copy of your own messages	SET [*listname*] MAIL ACK
Don't receive a copy of your own message	SET [*listname*] MAIL NOACK
Get a list of subscribers	RECIPIENTS [*listname*]
Hide your name from the subscriber list	SET [*listname*] CONCEAL YES
Undo the conceal command	SET [*listname*] CONCEAL NO
Get a list of archived files	INDEX [*listname*]
Retrieve a file from the archive	GET [*listname*] [*filename*]

Table 12-2: L-soft Listserv List Commands

Function	List Command
Subscribe	SUBSCRIBE *listname Firstname Last-name* (e.g., SUBSCRIBE DIGVID-L John Doe)
Unsubscribe	SIGNOFF [*listname*] or UNSUBSCRIBE [*listname*]
Request a digest version	SET [*listname*] DIGEST
Cancel digest	SET [*listname*] MAIL or SET [*list-name*] NODIGEST
Temporarily suspend mail	SET [*listname*] NOMAIL
Resume mail	SET [*listname*] MAIL
Receive acknowledgment of your own posts	SET [*listname*] REPRO or SET [*list-name*] ACK (for a shorter automatic acknowl-edgment that your message has been sent to the list)
Don't receive copies of your own posts	SET [*listname*] NOREPRO
Get a list of subscribers	REVIEW [*listname*] F=MAIL
Get a list of subscribers by name	REVIEW [*listname*] BY NAME F=MAIL
Get a list of subscribers by country	REVIEW [*listname*] BY COUNTRY F=MAIL
Hide your name from the list of subscribers	SET [*listname*] CONCEAL

Table 12-2: L-soft Listserv List Commands (continued)

Function	List Command
Undo the conceal command	SET [*listname*] NOCONCEAL
Get a list of archived files	INDEX [*listname*]
Get an archived file	GET [*filename*] [*filetype*] [*list-name*] F=MAIL

Table 12-3: Mailbase List Commands

Function	List Commands
Subscribe	JOIN *listname Firstname Lastname* (e.g., JOIN DIGVID-L Jane User)
Unsubscribe	LEAVE [*listname*]
Receive a digest version	Not supported
Temporarily suspend mail	SUSPEND MAIL [*listname*]
Resume mail	RESUME MAIL [*listname*]
Get a list of subscribers	REVIEW [*listname*]
Get a list of archived files	INDEX [*listname*]
Retrieve a file from the archive	SEND [*listname*] [*filename*]

Table 12-4: Mailserv List Commands

Function	List Commands
Subscribe	SUBSCRIBE [*listname*] *Firstname Lastname* (e.g., SUBSCRIBE DIGVID-L Jane User)
Unsubscribe	UNSUBSCRIBE [*listname*] (UNSUB-SCRIBE [*listname*] [*address*] if you subscribed under a different email address)
Request a digest version	Not supported
Temporarily suspend mail	Not supported
Get a list of subscribers	SEND/LIST [*listname*]
Get a list of archived files	INDEX [*listname*]
Retrieve a file from the archive	SEND [*listname*] [*filename*]

Table 12-5: Majordomo or MacJordomo

Function	List Commands
Subscribe	SUBSCRIBE [*listname*] (e.g., SUBSCRIBE DIGVID-L)
Unsubscribe	UNSUBSCRIBE [*listname*] (UNSUB-SCRIBE [*listname*] [*address*] if you subscribed under a different email address)

Table 12-5: Majordomo or MacJordomo (continued)

Function	List Commands
Request a digest version	SUBSCRIBE [*listname*]-DIGEST (In the same message, unsubscribe from the undigested version by typing on a separate line, UNSUBSCRIBE [*listname*].)
Cancel digest	UNSUBSCRIBE [*listname*]-DIGEST (In the same message, subscribe to the undigested version by typing on a separate line, SUBSCRIBE [*listname*])
Temporarily suspend mail	Not supported
Get a list of subscribers	WHO [*listname*]
Get a list of archived files	INDEX [*listname*]
Retrieve a file from the archive	GET [*listname*] [*filename*]

CHAPTER 13

Newsgroups

Newsgroups or Usenet (the terms are used interchangeably) make up the second largest portion of Internet usage after email. Newsgroups are a global conversation with tens of thousands of participants around the world discussing tens of thousands of topics. No matter what you're interested in, there's bound to be a group for you—computing, travel, hobbies, health, pets, sports, and hundreds of other topics. Depending on the group, you'll find information, advice, gossip, stories, tips, hints, and tricks. If it can be discussed, you'll almost certainly find it somewhere in Usenet.

You can enter the discussion by reading messages others have posted to the newsgroup, or by posting your own messages. Posting involves sending a message to the group, which is set up in much the same way as a giant bulletin board, with new posts being put up at all hours of the day. You'll note that Usenet discussion aims to center around topics. Within topics are shorter, more focused discussions called threads. Within threads you'll find an initial question or comment, then a flurry of replies. The most basic way to read a newsgroup is to move down the list of topics, organized chronologically, picking out the posts that interest you and following the discussion threads. But there's no one way of participating in newsgroups. We know some aficionados who have read them for years, absorbing collective wisdom, without the slightest inclination to say anything. For others, however, sitting quietly in the background isn't their style.

No matter whether you're a talker or a reader, in order to read and post messages, you need a newsreader, which is like an email client in many ways. You receive posts in your newsreader and can, in turn, send your own messages back to the newsgroup itself or to select group members.

Where Are Newsgroups on AOL?

On AOL, newsgroups center around one place (and only one place), Keyword: Newsgroups. From within AOL, you must use AOL's own newsreader to subscribe to and participate in Usenet. There is a less common, but convenient, way to read newsgroups using the Web, which we cover later in this chapter in "Web-Based Newsgroup Locators Are More Powerful."

But back to AOL. Years ago, AOL designed a newsreader that covered the basics and gave its members access to a broad range of newsgroups. AOL made it easy to search through and subscribe to any group of your choice via their easy-to-use graphical interface. Once you had subscribed, you could read any of the posts from the past two weeks, follow threaded discussions, and reply to the group itself, or to individual participants.

To keep things simple, AOL allowed you to view and organize the posts in only three ways. While the simplicity of AOL's newsreader may have been great four or five years ago, other companies have developed newsreaders that are just as easy to use and now far outshine AOL's. AOL's current newsreader is in need of additional, more powerful features, including the ability to filter out certain posts or to see only posts that include particular words or phrases of interest to the user. In addition, AOL's newsreader is further limited by the fact that you can't use it to log onto a company or school server to get local newsgroups that may not be distributed to the Internet.

On the other hand, AOL does carry nearly every newsgroup that exists, which is more than you can say for some other major ISPs or for newsgroup access in most people's workplaces. Too bad this is a case of taking the good with the bad. We wonder what it would take to get AOL's extensive newsgroup coverage combined with a full-featured newsreader?

Allowing us to use third-party newsreaders such as Anawave Gravity, Free Agent, and the ones packaged with Netscape Communicator and MS Internet Explorer would be helpful. Until that happens, the anemic AOL client is the only one you've got.

We show you in this chapter how to make the best of it. For a view of the newsgroups main screen, see Figure 13-1.

Before You Subscribe to a Newsgroup

There's no limit to the number of newsgroups you can read and participate in. Newsgroups are housed on remote computers called *news servers*, in much the same way that web pages are housed on servers. When you want to read a newsgroup, your newsreader downloads the messages from the server and displays them on your computer. As we've said, AOL lets you select from almost every public newsgroup. That means you don't have to worry that a group that's unavailable at your job isn't on AOL; with a search, you'll probably find it and be subscribed in no time.

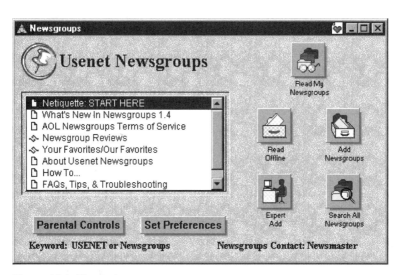

Figure 13-1: The main newsgroup screen

Newsgroups can be moderated or unmoderated. Moderated groups have a person to filter out posts that don't conform to the group's own guidelines. If a topic strays too far from the intended tenor of the group, the moderator may choose to block its appearance in the discussion. In unmoderated newsgroups, nearly anything goes. But—and this is a big but—you are expected to conform to the unofficial netiquette rules (see the "Netiquette" section of this chapter). Be sure to read it if you're unfamiliar with the rules of netiquette; you don't want to get into a very heated discussion, also known as a *flame war*, with your first post.

When you've decided you're ready to subscribe to a group, see the section "Adding Groups"; adding is AOL-speak for subscribing to a group. In this section, you'll find all the options for reading the groups of your choice.

If You're New to Newsgroups

- Be sure to see the section "Newsgroup Terms to Know" in this chapter so you'll be able to successfully speak the language and follow much of what we discuss. In addition, words in this chapter that we define in "Newsgroup Terms to Know" are in a special font, so when you see one, you'll know to come here for its definition.

- Understand netiquette as it applies to newsgroups; see "Netiquette."

- Learn how to locate groups to which you're interested in subscribing: first, you must understand the newsgroup-naming system, which we cover in the entry "Hierarchies (the Newsgroup Naming Scheme)" in this chapter. To locate groups that spark your interest and subscribe to them, see "Finding and Subscribing to a Newsgroup."

- When you're ready to read the posts, go to Keyword: Newsgroups, and click Read My Newsgroups. If you need more detailed instructions on how to read the messages in a newsgroup, see the section "Reading Your News-groups."

Newsgroups Essentials

When you post to a newsgroup, the screen name you use is bound to be inundated with unsolicited email, also known as spam. See "Privacy" in this chapter for our suggestions on how to reduce the risk of getting overwhelmed by spam as a result of your Usenet post. We also include suggestions on how to reduce the chance that current or future employers (or fiancées!) can read and link you to every post you've ever made.

Newsgroup Terms to Know

Charter
> Official description of what a group is about (see "Get the FAQs").

Cross-post
> Sending out a single post to more than one group. Should be done in rare cases only.

Emoticon
> See Chapter 5, *Online Shorthand*.

Flame
> A post to a newsgroup that attacks someone or something. A person who attacks in this manner is called a *flamer*. A series of posts in this manner is a *flame war*.

FAQ
> Information on a group, as in Frequently Asked Questions. Read the FAQ, if available, for guidelines on posting, what to post, and perhaps for answers to your questions (to save regular posters from reading the same questions time and again).

IDG
> Internet Discussion Group. Usenet newsgroups are the typical and primary method of Internet discussion. The others are mailing lists and Internet Relay Chat (IRC).

Lurk
> Read the newsgroup without posting. Helpful if you're new to a newsgroup. Helps you get a feel for the tenor of a group.

Message
> A post or a topic.

Moderated
> A group that has a human filter who screens out inappropriate and unwanted posts before posting them to the entire group.

Netiquette
> Net etiquette. (The terms *FAQs, spam,* and *flame* are highly related.)

Newbie
> A person new to something, or unknowing in its ways and netiquette.

Post
> A newsgroup article or message that anyone with a newsreader can see.

Signature or *.sig*
> Information included in a post that gives information on the person who sent the message including email and web addresses, quotes, and ASCII art. Usually best to keep under 4 or 5 lines.

spam
> Unwanted posts, usually of a commercial nature, or wholly unrelated to the nature of a group.

Thread
> An ongoing discussion about a particular post.

Hierarchies (the Newsgroup Naming Scheme)

Newsgroups are named according to where they fall along a hierarchical organizing scheme. You'll see that Internet names are made up of words or parts of words separated by periods, or dots. Each newsgroup fits into the hierarchical naming scheme, with approximately ten top-level categories covering the bulk of the publicly available groups. For instance, groups whose names begin with "comp." are all computing-related; those with "sci." are in the science hierarchy.

Every time you see a period followed by another word or part of a word, it means you're moving down into a subcategory. What this division means is that names can stretch on and on, as long as they follow the hierarchical naming scheme. The hierarchy works so that as you work your way from left to right in a group's Internet name, things get more specific. The group's aim and discussion topics get more specific the further down they are in the hierarchy. For example, the group *comp.graphics.apps* is more general than *comp.graphics.apps.freehand*. Both groups fall under "comp.", the top level category, "graphics.", the second level category, and "apps" the third level category. The group that includes "freehand" gets even more specific.

For your orientation, here are the main top-level groups (the * in a domain listing indicates any text can follow; for instance, comp.* indicates any group in the "comp." hierarchy):

alt.*
> Alternative groups don't really fit into the grand scheme of Usenet, since you don't have to follow a strict set of guidelines to create a group in the *alt.** hierarchy. Many of the groups are silly, subversive, or simply seek to provide a new and open venue for expression.

bit.listserv.*
> Mailing lists that are also reflected in Usenet appear here.

biz.*
> Groups about business, employment, and work. Advertising is allowed here, although it is strongly discouraged in other parts of Usenet.

---

comp.*

Computer-related topics including operating systems, peripherals, software, databases, and standards.

misc.*

Miscellaneous groups that fit nowhere else or have a different take on a subject.

news.*

Newsgroup-related information as well as current events type news.

rec.*

Recreation, sports, hobbies, travel, and other things to do recreationally.

sci.*

Science and health matters, especially more technical topics for science professionals.

soc.*

Society, social issues, and culture.

talk.*

Discussion and ideas in a chat-like environment.

Finding and Subscribing to a Newsgroup

There are two steps to reading newsgroups. The first is finding suitable groups. The second is signing up for those groups; that is, subscribing to the groups. What to do when you want to join the discussion, but don't know the first thing about which groups you want to read? Our suggestion is to use several web-based tools designed to help you in your quest for your ideal newsgroups. Before we cover the web-based tools, we go over AOL's built-in newsgroup search ability.

Locating Groups

Using AOL's built-in search tool, it's easy to locate newsgroups in areas that interest you. To start an AOL search of the newsgroup names, go to `Keyword: Newsgroups` → `Search All Newsgroups`.

Alternately, follow this path:

`Internet` toolbar icon → `Newsgroups` → `Search All Newsgroups`

Once you're there, type into the search field a word or words that describe the sort of groups you're looking for. All groups with that word in its Internet name are displayed, up to a maximum of 150 groups. Highlight the name of the group and click `Add` to place it on your current lineup.

If you want to see the entire newsgroup list, including those that AOL has deemed potentially offensive and those that include binary downloads like pictures and programs, you must first unlock the Parental Controls (see the sections "Allowing binary downloads using Parental Controls" and "Parental Controls" in this chapter for information on how to unblock your account).

Drawback to AOL's built-in search function

- The AOL newsgroup search function returns all groups that contain your search string, including instances when your string lies in the middle of another word. For instance, typing cat as in domestic cat yields well over 150 hits, including *alabama.decatur.general, alt.education.distance,* and *alt.fan.phoebe-cates.* To limit this, you could type .cat, which shows only the Internet names in which cat is immediately after the . that divides up the newsgroup name.

Web-Based Newsgroup Locators Are More Powerful

When you search for a group via AOL's newsgroup search function, you can't actually get a sense of what the group is about, or search through the text of what people have posted there. If you want a review, or a full text search (to find all the groups that discuss astrology or the Windows Registry) you'll have to look elsewhere. The directories below will help you to make more informed decisions about what groups are worth your time. Of course, if you're rearing to jump right in, there's never a problem with subscribing and then removing your subscription at whim.

AOL Newsgroup Scoop (http://www.aol.com/netfind/newsgroups.html)
A directory containing reviews and ratings of a mere 500 newsgroups. What's good about the AOL Newsgroup directory is that the groups are collected into categories such as computing and health which you can browse for descriptions and ratings of groups that might interest you.

DejaNews (http://www.dejanews.com)
Probably the most comprehensive newsgroup directory. You can search through most of the publicly available newsgroups and read posts going back several years.

Although you won't find reviews of groups at *DejaNews,* you can actually read and post to newsgroups via your web browser. You can choose only to browse, or you can use a new service called My Deja News, which allows you to subscribe to newsgroups, then read and post to them via the Web. To post to a group via *DejaNews* you have to register. But the registration may be worth the trouble: if you hate the AOL newsreader, you've now got this option. In addition, you can use any valid email address when you post, thereby preserving more anonymity and avoiding the increased risk of spam to your AOL account. (For more information on anonymous free email, see the entry **web-based email** in Chapter 8, *Email.*)

Adding Groups

No matter how you've found the name of the newsgroup that interests you (*comp.os.ms-windows.win95.setup* or *rec.pets.cats*) you'll have to add them to your list of subscribed groups in order to be able to reliably read them. Below, we outline each of the options for using the AOL newsreader to add groups (see Figure 13-2).

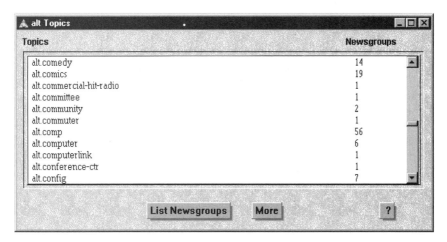

Figure 13-2: Browsing the list of available alt.* groups

Browse the list

Browsing the list is probably the way most AOL users sign up for newsgroups. Essentially, you look at each of the hierarchies until you find a group that strikes your interest.

> Keyword: Newsgroups → Add Newsgroups → double-click the hierarchies to navigate further down until you find the group you want to add → Add button

If you're unsure about whether you want to add a particular group, you can preview it. To preview the group, double-click on its title (don't click the Add button). You'll then be able to see some recent posts and read for yourself if it has something you'd be interested in.

Search the list

We describe how to search all of the newsgroups' titles using AOL's built-in search feature in the section "Locating Groups" earlier in this section. When you use AOL's search function, you'll get a list of groups that include your search word in the title.

Expert add

If you know the exact Internet name of the group, you can type it directly into AOL's newsreader. This is a handy way of adding a group you've decided to subscribe to via a friend's recommendation, or by using one of the web-based directories we highlighted in the earlier section "Web-Based Newsgroup Locators Are More Powerful."

> Keyword: Newsgroups → Expert Add → type the name → Add

Adding the latest newsgroups

If you want to know which groups have been added to AOL's lineup of news-groups since the last time you checked, use this feature.

Keyword: Newsgroups → Add Newsgroups → Latest Groups

What to Do if AOL Says "Invalid Group"

You might get the Invalid Group message when you try to add a group to your list of newsgroups. There are a number of things that can cause this:

- You've misspelled or misnamed the group. Check to make sure you've got the Internet name (i.e., *rec.pets.cats*) correct.

- The group isn't yet on the AOL newsgroup servers. Usually this only happens if a newsgroup is extremely new. Check back in a few days. If you don't find it, send an email request to screen name *Newsmaster* saying that you'd like AOL to add the group to its list.

- Your screen name has been blocked from accessing the group you're trying to add. Check with the person who's in charge of the master account (see "Master Versus Additional Screen Names" in Chapter 3, *Screen Names, Passwords, and Signing On*).

- You've been blocked by the AOL Administrator, probably for some previous violation or as the result of a complaint against posts from your screen name. If you have this problem, contact screen name *Newsmaster* for details.

Get the FAQs

A newsgroup's FAQ is a document that often contains special introductory material about a group. Be sure to read the FAQ for a newsgroup you're interested in to help you get the most out a group. Often it contains essential answers to your commonly asked questions (maybe you won't have to post to the group after all, since the answer you were looking for is contained in the FAQ). The dos and don'ts of a group are also laid out in the FAQ; violate the guidelines here, and you'll not only anger the group's regular readers/posters, you'll risk getting flamed or even banned from the group.

Approximately half the newsgroups publicly available have a FAQ in some form. If there is one it will be posted to the group itself in addition to being publicly available on special web or FTP sites. Go to the Web for some of the most convenient and well organized FAQ archives at *http://www.cis.ohio-state.edu/hypertext/faq/ usenet/top.html*. Keyword: Newsgroups has a "FAQs, Tips, and Trouble-shooting" section, but it's rapidly aging and only marginally useful.

Reading Your Newsgroups

Once you've subscribed to a group (or four), the messages don't come to you, you have to go to the posts. On AOL, this is an easy process. There are two ways to read posts, online or offline. The most common way to read newsgroups on AOL is online. If you choose to read the posts offline, you'll have to download the group's posts using Automatic AOL. Reading offline has the advantage of allowing you to review posts even when you can't sign on, for example if someone is using your phone.

Reading While You're Signed On

This is easy, just make sure you've subscribed (see the section "Finding and Subscribing to a Newsgroup," above), then follow this path:

Keyword: Newsgroups → Read My Newsgroups → highlight group and click List Unread or List All

A window with all your subscribed newsgroups pops up. You might notice that there are some additional newsgroups you're subscribed to. AOL automatically signs you up for some general and how-to newsgroups. You can get rid of them if you'd like (see "Unsubscribing from a Newsgroup" later in this chapter).

To read a particular group, double-click on it to bring up a window with its messages. To read a post, double-click the message or thread that interests you.

Below we review some of your reading options, each of which corresponds to various clickable buttons you'll see as you read your newsgroups.

Listing all the posts in a group

If you've read some of the posts in a group, the next time you list the posts, you see that the posts you've already read aren't visible. That's because AOL shows you only the posts you haven't read. If you want to see all of the posts, including the ones you've read, you need to use the List All function. Here's how:

Keyword: Newsgroups → Read My Newsgroups → highlight the group you want to read → List All

Listing posts in thread

When reading a newsgroup, you might see that some subjects have more than one post. Subjects with more than one post have nested messages inside, called *threads*, in which readers have responded to the post only. To read these threaded posts, click List to see the subject line of all posts in the thread. However, the List function in AOL doesn't work as intended, and only the email addresses of the posters are shown.

Listing only the unread messages

Usually, you'll want to read only those posts you haven't previously read. Double-clicking on the newsgroup title shows you the unread posts. You can also use the List Unread button after highlighting the group:

Keyword: Newsgroups → Read My Newsgroups → highlight the news-group you want to read → List Unread

Marking a newsgroup read

Mark your groups read to see only the newly posted messages the next time you access your newsgroups. This feature is useful if you've perused the current newsgroup, read what interests you, and want to ignore all the remaining posts. You can mark a single group or all groups as read.

While viewing the list of your subscribed newsgroups, mark one group read by selecting the group then clicking **Mark Read**.

Mark all your groups read by clicking **Mark All Newsgroups Read**.

Reading Posts Offline, When You're Not Signed On

While easy to the experienced user, reading a post offline can be a bit difficult to understand at first. Basically, you'll need to set up AOL to download the posts using Automatic AOL. Once you've downloaded them, they'll reside on your hard drive for later reading. Set up your newsgroups by following the steps below, then skip to Chapter 21, *Automatic AOL,* to see how you can download and read your newsgroups. Here's how to get started:

1. Subscribe to your newsgroups in the usual manner (see "Finding and Subscribing to a Newsgroup").

2. Add the newsgroups of your choice to your **Read Offline** list by going to **Keyword: Newsgroups** and clicking **Read Offline** (see Figure 13-3). You should then add groups to the list labeled **Newsgroups to read offline**. Click OK to save your list.

3. Then see Chapter 21, *Automatic AOL,* for detailed instructions on setting up Automatic AOL.

Benefit to using Automatic AOL with newsgroups

- Messages are threaded better, with each thread having its own folder. Thus, discussions are easier to follow when you read newsgroups offline.

Drawback to using Automatic AOL with newsgroups

- If any of your newsgroups are particularly high-traffic, the Automatic AOL session may log you out before it's done retrieving all the posts.

Posting to a Group

Before you contribute anything to a newsgroup, it's essential that you understand the basics of netiquette. Below, we've outlined the most important tenets as they apply to newsgroups.

Netiquette

Every part of the Internet has its netiquette violators, but Usenet violations are more notorious and pernicious than anywhere else. Use these rules. You just might save yourself from an evil flame war or angry posts accusing you of wasting

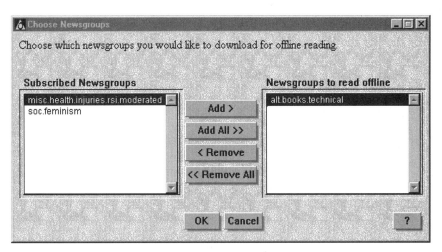

Figure 13-3: Choosing newsgroups for offline reading

everyone's time and being a newbie. Here we've condensed the advice we've sprinkled throughout this chapter:

- Read the group for several weeks to a month before you post. You may find an answer to your question by reading. And you also get a feel for the group—what's allowed and what's not.

- Follow the group's own guidelines. Read the group's FAQ. Approximately half of the newsgroups publicly available have a FAQ in some form. The group often posts its FAQ periodically, so if you're reading the group, you'll see it there. But you can also go to the Web to read specific FAQs. Our favorite place for FAQ archives is *http://www.cis.ohio-state.edu/hypertext/faq/usenet/top.html*.

  Often the FAQ contains essential answers to your commonly asked questions (maybe you won't have to post to the group after all, since the answer you were looking for is contained in the FAQ). The dos and don'ts of a group are also laid out in the FAQ; violate the guidelines here and you'll not only anger the group's regular readers/posters, you'll risk getting flamed or even banned from the group. On Usenet, you can be banned only if the group has a moderator.

- Stay on topic. If you post off-topic, you're really sending out junk posts. Be sure your messages contribute to the discussion and aren't just "me too" posts. Keep your posts brief.

- Post no advertisements (for the most part, only the groups in the *.biz* hierarchy allow ads).

- Don't fuel flames, a.k.a. Internet Wars of Words. Don't post inflammatory material, or respond to it. If you feel a little hot and want to post, hold off. Calm down before you incite a flame war, or add to the fires.

- Keep your signature file short, just as in email (see "Signature" later in this chapter).

- If you have a private response for one person, it may not be of interest to all the readers of a group; consider sending email. However, if your response is of general interest to the whole group, post to the group so the others can benefit from it.

- Don't post the same message to more than one group. This is called cross-posting. Some people consider cross-posting a form of spam. If you have something to say about a particular topic, post only to that group. People don't want to read the same post in multiple groups.

- In posts in which you disclose important content of movies or books, don't just list the information without warning potential readers. In the subject header, say "Spoiler" to warn all readers that you're about to spoil the plot of a new film, or give away a detail of a favorite novel. In addition, the use of spoilers in the subject line of support newsgroups (such as *alt.support.depression*) alerts readers to potentially "triggering" (i.e., traumatic or upsetting) material.

- Never post a test message to a group. If you must test your ability to post, use the group *aol.test* where you can post a mock thread, and see that it got through all right. Don't forget that it sometimes takes a while before the post gets up and is accessible on the server. In addition, many hierarchies have their own *.test.* groups. To locate them, use AOL's Search All Newsgroups function.

Now that you know all about Usenet netiquette, you're ready for the details of how to post, provided in the following sections.

Posting a New Message, in a New Thread

Keyword: Newsgroups → Read My Newsgroups → double-click the newsgroup you want to read → Send New Message

Use the above method when you're posting a wholly new thread to a group. If you're responding to a current post, it's probably best to reply to a post, as described below.

Posting a Reply to a Message, Within an Existing Thread

Keyword: Newsgroups → Read My Newsgroups → double-click the newsgroup you want to read → open the thread you want to reply to → Reply to Group

Be sure to include a very short portion of the message you're replying to so that your message will have a clear context and will be easier for other readers to follow. For instructions on quoting, see the next section.

Quoting From Another Person's Post

When you reply to a post, it's often useful to include a very small amount of relevant material from the message to which you're replying in order to give other readers some context for your comments. This is called *quoting*, and it's easy to do with the AOL newsreader.

To quote, you must be reading a message. Choose `Reply to Group`, highlight the text you want to quote in your reply, and click `Quote`. Figure 13-4 shows a paragraph being quoted.

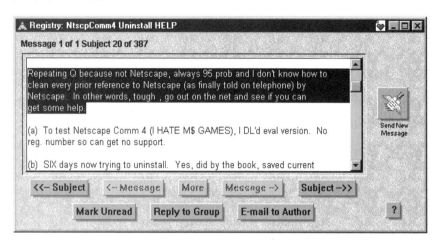

Figure 13-4: Selecting text to quote in a reply

Canceling a Post You've Sent

Oops! If you've made a major mistake—such as posting something inappropriate to a group, posting advertising, or posting to the wrong group—it may be possible for AOL to cancel your post at your request. To cancel, send email to screen name *Newsmaster* and include:

- The date the article was posted
- The subject line of the article
- The message ID of the article, which you can get by going to the newsgroup, opening your message, and looking in the header under `messsage-id`

It's possible to cancel a newsgroup article up to four days after it was originally posted; after that, forget it. To increase the chance that you'll be able to cancel the post, contact the Newsmaster within 24 hours of sending your unwanted post.

Dealing with Attachments

Usually, newsgroups posts are text only. Sometimes, however, posts have attached files, either in the form of text attachments or binary attachments.

Text Attachments

Text attachments are usually regular text posts that are too long for the AOL news-reader. AOL then converts them into text attachments, which are allowable by default in the AOL newsreader. When you download the file, you must then locate that file on your local drive and open it manually, either with AOL's `File` menu → `Open` command or with another text reader (see Figure 13-5).

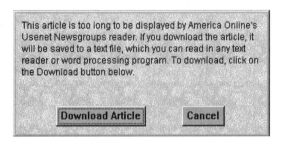

This article is too long to be displayed by America Online's Usenet Newsgroups reader. If you download the article, it will be saved to a text file, which you can read in any text reader or word processing program. To download, click on the Download button below.

Download Article   Cancel

Figure 13-5: Text attachment when a message is too long for the AOL newsreader

Binary Attachments

Binary attachments come in the form of pictures, sounds, and software. They're not just plain old text. By default, AOL blocks binary downloads in newsgroups. That's true for all screen names (even 18+ screen names), presumably to prevent the unsuspecting from happening upon naughty pictures or, less likely, files that could corrupt their computers. In addition, AOL also doesn't reveal some sexually explicit newsgroups when you use the `Add Newsgroups` button to view the list of groups you can subscribe to. For more about the newsgroups list, see the section "Parental Controls" later in this chapter.

To allow access to newsgroups that may include binaries, you must first unlock the Parental Controls.

Allowing binary downloads using Parental Controls

You must be signed on with the master account to change this and any Parental Control. From `Keyword: Newsgroups`, click `Parental Controls`. Clear the `Block binary downloads` checkbox next to the screen name(s) you want to unblock.

Benefit

*   You can get all the binaries you like if you manually unblock binary down-loads. Note that to get the full newsgroups list—including the sexual ones—you'll also have to manually enable the full list of groups. To do that, see the "Parental Controls" section in this chapter.

Drawback

*   Anyone who signs on with your screen name, including your kids, can down-load binaries. Many binaries would make even us blush, and that's hard to do!

To help prevent access, give your kids their own screen names and password protect your own. See "Parental Controls" for more on ways to limit your kids ability to read newsgroups you don't want them to read.

Downloading the binaries

Once the Parental Controls are set to allow subscription to newsgroups with binaries, you can read the messages and download the attached binaries into your local drive. You've got two primary ways of getting the binary attachments, Download File and Download Article, covered below. Figure 13-6 shows what you'll see when you open a post that contains a binary attachment.

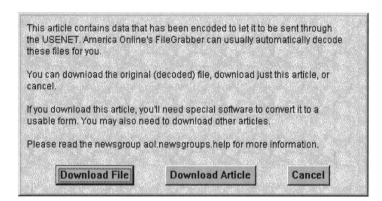

This article contains data that has been encoded to let it to be sent through the USENET. America Online's FileGrabber can usually automatically decode these files for you.

You can download the original (decoded) file, download just this article, or cancel.

If you download this article, you'll need special software to convert it to a usable form. You may also need to download other articles.

Please read the newsgroup aol.newsgroups.help for more information.

[Download File]   [Download Article]   [Cancel]

Figure 13-6: Downloading a binary attachment

Download File button

The easiest way to get the binary onto your computer is Download File. AOL software automatically decodes most binary files and displays them for you as you download.

Download Article button

If you don't want AOL to automatically download the file for you, you can download just the article. Download Article is useful if the file has been broken into many parts and some of those parts are missing. You can download just part of the file and try, with third-party software, to piece the articles together.

Posting a Binary

With AOL, you must first encode binaries before you post them. Encoding turns the binary files into ASCII text (numbers and letters) so that certain newsgroup computers can receive the file. Unfortunately, the people reading your post have to decode your message to turn it back into its original binary file.

Use what's called a *uuencoder program* to change the file into the form that AOL can handle. Uuencode translates or converts a file from a binary format into plain ASCII text. This text can then be handled by older computer systems that may not handle binary files well, and larger files can be more easily divided into multi-part transmissions, which some newservers prefer. You must convert your binaries before using AOL to post to a newsgroup that allows binaries.

We recommend downloading a shareware program, if you don't already have one. Check *http://www.shareware.com* and search on the word "uuencode" for a large list of current programs. We recommend a popular program, WinZip, for your uuencoding needs; get it at *http://www.winzip.com.*

How to post your uuencoded file

Among your subscribed list of newsgroups, go to the newsgroup to which you want to post a binary. If you're not already there, it's at Keyword: Newsgroups → Read My Newsgroups. Select the newsgroup and open it. Click Send New Message to open a window for your uuencoded text. Next, you must cut and paste the text of the binary into a new message window: click the Send New Message button, then paste the uuencoded text into the message field or your outgoing post. Click Send and your binary is on its way.

To be honest, we've been unable to successfully post and then subsequently download a uuencoded file via AOL.

Unsubscribing from a Newsgroup

AOL makes it easy to remove a newsgroup. When you remove the group, you won't see it when you click Read My Newsgroups. The first groups you'll probably want to remove are the ones AOL subscribes you to automatically. To unsubscribe, follow this path:

Keyword: Newsgroups → Read My Newsgroups → highlight the group you want to delete → Remove

Parental Controls

Newsgroups aren't covered under AOL's Terms of Service, and therefore aren't as clean cut as most of what you'll find in AOL-only areas. This can be a good or bad thing, depending on whether you like the rough edges of the Internet or prefer the more whitebread online experience within AOL's walls. In any case, you've got a choice about what you and other subaccount holders can see.

First, to get to the main Parental Controls for newsgroups, you must be signed on with the master screen name. Then follow this path:

Keyword: Newsgroups → Parental Controls → choose screen name → Edit

Alternately, use this path:

Keyword: Parental Controls → Fine Tune with Custom Controls → Newsgroups → Newsgroup Controls → choose screen name → Edit

No matter how you get there, you'll be at the `Blocking Criteria` screen shown in Figure 13-7. From here, you'll be able to modify the newsgroup settings of the screen name you've chosen. We go over all your options below. At any point, click `Save`, and your changes will take effect immediately.

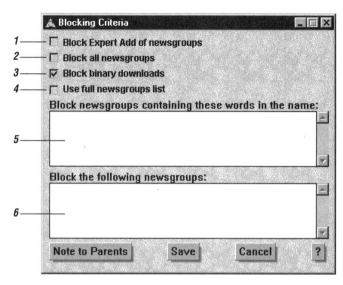

Figure 13-7: Parental Controls for newsgroups

Here are your options on the Blocking Criteria screen:

1. `Block Expert Add of newsgroups`: When this box is checked, the chosen screen name can't add a newsgroup by manually typing in its name. That is, AOL only allows you to subscribe to groups it lists. Because you can limit the types of newsgroups that AOL lists, using `Block Expert Add of newsgroups` prevents the screen name from subscribing to all unlisted groups. Note that Kids Only and Young Teen screen names are blocked by default from all newsgroups. Mature Teen and 18+ screen names are not blocked by default from using `Expert Add`.

2. `Block all newsgroups`: When this box is checked, the chosen screen name has no access to newsgroups. Young Teen and Kids Only screen names are blocked from newsgroups by default; clear the box to allow access to newsgroups. By default, Mature Teen and 18+ screen names can access some newsgroups.

3. `Block binary downloads`: When this box is checked, the chosen screen name can't view binary downloads attached to newsgroup posts. All screen names (even 18+) are blocked by default from viewing binaries. Clear the box to allow the viewing of binaries.

4. `Use full newsgroups list`: By default, when you click `Add Newsgroups` or `Search All Newsgroups`, AOL allows you to see only a subset of the complete listing. We suppose that this is to protect sensitive eyes from

viewing the number of newsgroups—and their names—that contain sexually explicit material. However, the holder of the Master Account can choose to allow any screen name to view the entire list. Even if you can't view the entire list, knowledgeable Mature Teen and 18+ users can use **Expert Add** to subscribe to newsgroups not on the list (that is, unless the accounts have be blocked from using **Expert Add**; see Step 1 of this section).

5. **Block newsgroups containing these words in the name**: Use this feature to keep the chosen screen name from signing up for groups with any given words in the title. For instance, if you want to give your kids access to newsgroups, but don't want to give access to groups containing the words "death" or "taxes," enter those words in the box. Beware when you use this feature, since you block all instances of the string of letters. For instance, blocking "cat" will also block out all *.education.* groups. Clearly, this feature is probably aimed at parents who want to block access to groups that focus on sex. If you're trying to block pornographic images, your best bet is to **Block binary downloads** (which is the default anyway).

6. **Block the following newsgroups**: You must know the exact Internet name of the group you want blocked, then enter the exact name (e.g., *alt.swedish.chef.bork.bork.bork*) in the box.

See also Chapter 28, *Parental Controls*, for more on how to modify other parental options.

Preferences

The defaults are fine, but AOL lets you fine-tune a few things. To modify your newsgroup preferences, go to **Keyword: Newsgroups → Set Preferences**.

The following sections describe the options available to you.

Headers

Headers are lines in a post, usually at the top of the page, in which distinguishing characteristics about a post are highlighted. Headers include the name of the poster, the originating email address, the reply-to address, the groups the message has been posted to, and often, the path the post took to arrive on the news server.

The default on AOL is "no headers," which means you can see only the subject, from, date, and message identification headers at the top of a post. If you want to see more detail about where the post came from, the path it took, what newsgroups it was posted to, and what sort of newsreader sent it, you must change the preferences:

Keyword: Newsgroups → Set Preferences

Below, we provide examples of what you get when you select from among the three options.

Headers at top

You'll see something like this on top of every newsgroup post:

```
Subject: The meaning of life
Path:
lobby01.news.aol.com!newstf02.news.aol.com!portc02.blue.aol.com
!pitt.edu!dsinc!news.voicenet.com!news.idt.net!cam-news-
hub1.bbnplanet.com!cam-news-
feed1.bbnplanet.com!news.bbnplanet.com!tabloid.med.iacnet.com!n
ot-for-mail
From: Joe Foucault <philosopher@liberalartsschool.edu>
Newsgroups: alt.philosophy
Date: Thu, 04 Dec 1997 08:57:50 -0500
Organization: Liberal Arts School Philosophy Department
Lines: 24
Message-ID: <3486B6DE.53A1@liberalartsschool.edu>
Reply-To: philosopher@liberalartsschool.edu
NNTP-Posting-Host: 155.40.13.96
Mime-Version: 1.0
Content-Type: text/plain; charset=us-ascii
Content-Transfer-Encoding: 7bit
X-Mailer: Mozilla 3.0 (Win95; I)
```

Headers at bottom

You'll see the above "headers at top" nonsense at the bottom of every post, and nothing at the top of the post.

No headers

The default. You'll see something like this on top of every newsgroup post:

```
Subject: The meaning of life
From: Joe Foucault <philosopher@liberalartsschool.edu>
Date: 12/4/97 8:57 AM Eastern Standard Time
Message-id: <3486B6DE.53A1@liberalartsschool.edu>
```

Sort Order

The default is oldest first, logical if you want to see what you missed since you last read them. If you don't read very often and just want the latest posts, you can select newest first. Alphabetically lets you follow threads more easily, since they'll be grouped. Alphabetical also helps you segregate some of the spam, since spam often begins with an asterisk or exclamation point.

Name Style

If you don't understand the Internet names, see "Hierarchies (the Newsgroup Naming Scheme)" earlier in this chapter.

With AOL, you can see descriptive names that explain in plain English what the group is about, rather than the traditional, hierarchical Internet-style names. The default is Internet names such as *rec.sport.football.fantasy* or *misc.writing.screenplay*. If you go to English names, you'll see "Rotisserie (fantasy) football play" and

"Aspects of writing and selling screenplays" when you choose `View My Newsgroups`.

We recommend sticking to the hierarchical Internet-style names, since this naming system is employed worldwide and is easy to use. It's also our opinion that the descriptive newsgroup titles are cheesy at best and don't seriously help anyone understand what a group is about.

To change to `Descriptive Newsgroup Titles`, go to `Keyword: Newsgroups → Preferences`.

Filtering

AOL now gives you the opportunity to weed out some of the spam that plagues Usenet. It won't catch every multilevel marketing ploy, but it certainly helps!

AOL, by default, does not filter spam posts. Check the `Filter Junk Posts` box to start bypassing some of the effluent.

Signature

Signatures or *.sigs* in Usenet let other readers know who you are and may give information about your background, your job, or other important information. You can choose to have one, or to just use your email address as the only identifying information.

Every post you make can include the text you place in the signature. If you're going to have a signature, our advice is to include only the information you want millions of people to know about you. Putting your telephone number or address in a signature on Usenet is not recommended. We'd also like to remind you that long *.sigs* can be very annoying, so try to keep them to under four lines of text. Also, be aware that the screen name you use for posting is likely to be harvested by spammers who'll quickly fill your email box with unwanted mail. There may also be signature-collecting spammers, too. See "Privacy" in this chapter for some important tips on how to retain yours and cut spam.

To set up your Usenet signature:

> `Keyword: Newsgroups → Set Preferences`

Place text in the box that you want appended to the footer of all your posts.

Privacy

Discussion groups include Usenet newsgroups, Internet mailing lists, AOL message boards, and any discussion areas or message boards on web sites. The Internet is a great place for open communication, but it is also a place where what you say can be accessed any time, anywhere—a benefit and a drawback.

Assume that anyone, at any time now or in the future, will read what you've posted. Archives can and have been used before by job recruiters to investigate what your interests are, your grammar, and your way of conducting yourself in public.

Another major problem is with unwanted email. Spammers use robots, or automatic programs, that scan newsgroup headers and signatures, pulling any text that resembles an email address. Once you've posted to a newsgroup, your email address is prey to spammers. After collection, your email address is resold to other spammers, and the mail barrage will begin.

Our suggestions:

- Use alternate screen names to post anything you don't want a spammer, a current or prospective employer, your mom, or a journalist to know. Never forget that the searchable Usenet archives at *http://www.dejanews.com* know all and so do the spammers! We suggest you have one screen name for friends, one for business, and one for posting to Usenet.

- Better yet, post to Usenet via DejaNews' special interface, currently at *http://www.postnews.dejanews.com*. You'll have to use an email address, but it can be an address that forwards mail to your real email account, or a free email account, such as one you can get at *http://www.hotmail.com* or *http://www.mailexcite.com*.

Terms of Service

AOL claims that its Terms of Service apply to what its members post to newsgroups. AOL can, will, and has suspended members' access to newsgroups for repeated violations of the following sort:

- Sending chain letters: other members can actually report this violation to AOL, which results in a warning to your account

- Sending commercial articles that "market, advertise, or sell products or services"

- Sending "inappropriate posts," which seem to include posting unrelated topics and points of discussion to a newsgroup

Clearly, each of these violations must be reported to AOL by someone on the Internet or another AOL member, probably a reader or recipient of your bad posts; AOL doesn't go looking for (minor) violators.

Some Additional Notes on Newsgroups and AOL

What follows in the sections below are a few random but important extras that we couldn't fit into any of the main categories.

Making Newsgroups Favorite Places

As with most other AOL and web areas, you can Favorite Place any newsgroup you've subscribed to. Click the heart icon from the window of an open newsgroup to add that group to your Favorite Places menu. Then, to return to that group, just access it from the `Favorite Places` toolbar icon; that way, you won't need to got to `Keyword: Newsgroups`. You can also add the group to the toolbar, if there's room (see the section "Adding and Removing Toolbar Icons" in Chapter 4, *Getting Around AOL: Toolbars and Menus*).

.neighborhood Newsgroups

These are AOL's own newsgroups, just for AOL members. They have never really become widely used. Each state has its own selection of groups, as do many medium and large cities. Inside the state hierarchy, there are five subgroups: events, general, jobs, marketplace, and politics. Each city, town, and regional newsgroup has eight or more subgroups: events, food, general, jobs, marketplace, motss (member of the same sex), politics, and singles.

Examples include:

> *aol.neighborhood.ma.boston.events*
>
> *aol.neighborhood.ma.boston.food*

Searching for a Post

If you're looking for posts on a particular topic, you can search all of Usenet to find it with the brilliant tools provided by the web site *DejaNews*. You can search years' worth of archived newsgroup postings using words or phrases of your choice. The results of your search provide you with a nicely compiled list of posts that include your search words. You can read the posts or you can get information on the person who posted them, including a list of other posts by each author. To search the body of all posts to Usenet go to `Keyword: Find a Newsgroup` or go to *http://www.dejanews.com*.

From within AOL, you can search for words or phrases of your choice in the subject lines of newsgroups you're subscribed to in AOL. You can do this by using the `Find in Top Window` feature. You essentially search all unread messages in your open newsgroup window. Follow this path:

> `Keyword: Newsgroups` → `Read My Newsgroups` → click the newsgroup whose subjects you want to search → `Edit menu` → `Find In Top Window` → type the word you're looking for

PART III

Getting Information

AOL and the Internet can be confusing, anarchistic places. People who are used to looking up information at the library are often shocked the first time they try to find information online. The Internet isn't organized alphabetically or numerically, and at first glance, doesn't appear to be organized in any way at all. Fortunately, one of AOL's strengths is its ability to organize all its content into groups and hierarchies so you can find it easily. The Web is too sprawling for such an approach, but many directories and search engines exist to help you separate the wheat from the chaff, the needles from the haystack, the clichés from the prose.

A true example: just now, we were racking our brains to remember how a certain Beatles song goes. We found the answer on the Web in about three minutes. Isn't technology great? (For the curious, we used the *Ultimate Band List*, *http://ubl.com*, which we mention in Chapter 16, *The Web*.)

Beatles lyrics may not be the most useful resources online, but this example proves that you can find what you want quickly as long as you know where to look. Whether you're searching for stock quotes (Keyword: Personal Finance), a book (*http://www.amazon.com* or Keyword: BarnesandNoble), or an index to make sense of web chaos (*http://www.yahoo.com*), we hope the chapters in this section help you find it.

Chapter 14, *Finding & Searching*: A quick guide to finding people, places, and things on AOL and the Web.

Chapter 15, *AOL Content Reference*: A longer guide to what's on AOL, and the keywords that will get you there quickly.

Chapter 16, *The Web*: Use the Web your way, not just AOL's way.

CHAPTER 14

Finding & Searching

What would a library be if you couldn't find anything in it, if you were without a searchable database or card catalog that listed each of the books on the shelves? Helping you find the information you need is one of the big challenges of libraries and of online services. Things have to be organized and documented in such a way as to make it easy for you to locate what's out there. Libraries are good at that; so is AOL.

One of AOL's more commendable feats is its focus on developing tools to help you find what you want. AOL wants to make things easy for you, especially when you're looking for something. AOL is aggressively building its search capabilities in all areas. For AOL's own proprietary content areas, there's a searchable directory at Keyword: AOL Find. For web sites, they've got a special web site, *NetFind*, at Keyword: NetFind, which uses the Excite search engine to catalog hundreds of thousands of the most relevant web sites in the world.

You've also got easy-to-use tools to help you find businesses, get maps and directions, locate friends, and get telephone numbers. While many of these tools aren't just for AOL members, AOL has formed partnerships with the companies that make these tools to make the tools easier for AOL members to find and use. For instance, you can use the Find menu item on the AOL toolbar and go directly to each of these services. Other ISPs might put links to these on their home pages, but they're not on the toolbar.

Having AOL without knowing how to find stuff is like having a boat and not knowing how to find water: you've got the boat, but you can't really do much with it. While some things on AOL are easy, like finding AOL areas or chat rooms, other things, like finding a newsgroup or mailing list, can be tougher. It's all about knowing where to look. This chapter discusses many of the online directories.

Check the alphabetized entries that follow for our selective collection of resources that will help you find what you're looking for. If you're looking for help using AOL, or getting some AOL technical support, go to Chapter 6, *Help from AOL*. The following quick reference gets you started. We're not long on details, but we take you there so you can begin your search.

access number, AOL

Help menu → AOL Access Phone Numbers

or:

Keyword: Access

For more detailed information, see Chapter 27, *Connecting.*

addresses

Each of the following resembles a searchable, nationwide phone book:

- Keyword: Find a Person (this uses the Switchboard engine that's listed next)
- *http://www.switchboard.com*
- *http://www.whowhere.com*
- *http://www.four11.com*

AOL content areas

Keyword: AOLFind

or:

Find menu → Find on AOL

Search for a phrase, like "baseball statistics" and you'll get a list of related AOL areas. You can read descriptions of these areas then go to the areas themselves. When you're looking for specific information, you can usually find it by checking in the content channels, like News, Sports, and Entertainment, for example. In AOL's channels, you'll find links to both AOL and web resources. If you want to forgo AOL altogether, finding what you want on the Web is easy, too (see the entry *NetFind*).

See also Chapter 15, *AOL Content Reference.*

businesses

Searchable yellow pages, with amazing custom maps and/or directions from your location to the business you're searching for.

http://www.switchboard.com

or:

Keyword: Find a Business

Go to either place for nearly identical information provided by the Switchboard database, the largest business finder on the Web. The AOL version lacks a few of the features of Switchboard's own version, like the ability to use a zip code to narrow the search further.

chats

To find AOL's popular celebrity chats, go to Keyword: Live.

This is the main area for celebrity/auditorium events on AOL. It houses today's schedule (Keyword: Events), this month's schedule (Keyword: Coming Attractions), and other tidbits, such as transcripts (Keyword: Intermission).

To find chats about specific topics (golf, mutual funds, your cat's oral hygiene...whatever), your best bet is Conference Rooms. They're topical chat rooms within AOL channels and content areas. Unfortunately, there is no central Conference Room directory on AOL. You can find the most comprehensive Conference Room directory we know of in the section "Conference Rooms" in Chapter 10, *Chatting*.

mailing lists

AOL's own and rather good directory:

Keyword: Mailing List → Browse the Directory

The much-used, giant mailing-list hub, Liszt, is at:

http://www.liszt.com

For more detailed information, see Chapter 12, *Mailing Lists*.

member, AOL

To find someone via his or her searchable member profile:

People toolbar icon → Search AOL Member Directory

To determine the location of a member who's signed on:

People toolbar icon → Locate AOL Member Online

or:

CTRL-1

NetFind

Keyword: NetFind

or:

Find toolbar icon → Find it on the Web

NetFind is AOL's own search engine, which currently uses the Excite database.

For more information finding on the Web, see Chapter 16, *The Web*.

newsgroups

Keyword: Newsgroups → Search All Newsgroups

For more detailed information see Chapter 13, *Newsgroups*.

Personal Filing Cabinet, searching

My Files toolbar icon → Personal Filing Cabinet → Find

For more in depth in formation, see Chapter 18, *Personal Filing Cabinet*.

random

Not looking for anything in particular? Go to Keyword: Random, click the wheel, and it picks an AOL area... any area.

The first application of this concept was URoulette, which sends you to random web pages. *URoulette* is still around at *http://www.uroulette.com*.

software

Some of it is free, some shareware, some commercial.

Shareware:

Find menu → Software

or:

Keyword: Filesearch

Commercial software:

Keyword: Download Software → Retail Software

For information on how to download, save, and locate files, see also Chapter 20, *Downloading*.

top window, find in

Whenever you're reading some text in a window, you can use the Find in Top Window feature to search for a word or phrase. Note that you can't use Find in Top Window to search web pages or AOL content (see Figure 14-1).

    CTRL-f

or:

    Edit menu → Find in Top Window

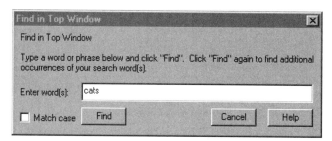

Figure 14-1: Using the Find in Top Window feature

Web

    Keyword: NetFind

or:

    Find menu → Find it on the Web

For more detailed information on finding what you want on the Web, see Chapter 16.

word definitions

    Keyword: Dictionary

The online version of *Merriam-Webster's Collegiate Dictionary* helps you find words and definitions.

CHAPTER 15

AOL Content Reference

AOL keywords are ever-changing, and they number in the thousands. Therefore, we haven't listed *all* of AOL's keywords in this chapter: go to **Keyword: Keyword** if you're interested in the complete list. This is, however, a fairly comprehensive guide to the content you'll find on AOL, and the keywords that will get you there quickly.

We've organized this chapter the way AOL is organized: by channels. The channels are: Computing, Entertainment, Families, Games, Health, Influence, Interests, International, Kids Only, Lifestyles, Local, News, Personal Finance, Research & Learn, Shopping, Sports, Travel, and WorkPlace.

Within each channel, we give you all the keywords you need. Some keywords, like **Keyword: Football**, are pretty self-explanatory. When the keyword is less obvious—which it usually is—we include a one-sentence explanation of the area's purpose. Some keywords appear in the listings more than once if they fall into more than one channel.

As in the rest of this book, our own opinions sometimes reveal themselves in our descriptions of what you'll find at the keyword. They aren't the last word, but they're our words. Where some of AOL's content is concerned, we could have been even more brutally honest, but we've tried not to offend (much).

AOL Today
Keyword: AOL Today

An area that changes according to the time of day, with different news, features, and columnists for morning, afternoon, and night. It spotlights "Essentials" from around the service, such as horoscopes, job hunting resources, parenting advice, and movie reviews. Content such as diet tips (we think we look fine, thanks) and columnists like Joan Lunden don't thrill us; we think AOL Today takes a dangerous step towards making AOL content as banal as network television. What do you think? Plenty of people like most of what's on TV, and we're sure plenty of people like AOL Today.

Computing Channel
Keyword: Computing

You'll usually find more current information on the Web, but your computing interest is probably covered in this fairly comprehensive channel. Each of the words or phrases below is a keyword you can use to go directly to the area.

A&V Forum
> The PC Animation and Video Forum.

Buyer's Guide
> Hardware and software reviews from the likes of ZDNet's *Computer Shopper* and *PC World* magazines.

CE
> No computers here, but Consumer Electronics' reviews of stereos, pagers, and other e-toys.

Companies
> Demos, downloads, and FAQs from the corporate sites of computing companies.

Computing Chat
> Chat rooms, chat transcripts, live-event schedules, and 24 message boards, at last count.

Computing Classifieds
> Buy and sell used PCs, Macs, and peripherals; find Internet and computer service jobs.

Computing Live
> Chat rooms, schedules, and transcripts.

Computing Newsstand
> Computer industry news compiled from AOL and the Web.

Computing Tips
> Some decent PC, Mac, and AOL tips and tricks.

CSS
> No, not Cascading Style Sheets, Computing Super Store. Occasionally some good deals.

Daily Download
> We recommend skipping this gimmick and going right to the source: Download Software.

Download Software
> Hooray! An alphabetical-by-subject organization of AOL's shareware chaos. Retail software, too.

DOS
> If you still dig DOS, this is your place.

FC

Hardware help and G-rated software from Family Computing.

Filesearch → Commerical Software

Online hardware and software store Cyberian Outpost, also found at *http://www.outpost.com.*

Filesearch → Shareware

If you know what shareware/freeware you want, search for it here.

Hardware

Drivers, utilities, and other tricks to make your PC hardware behave.

Help Desk

Help for newbies.

Home PC

The current issue of *Home PC* magazine on the Web and a searchable archive of past issues.

Komando

A web page (*http://www.komando.com*) providing a helpful dose of computer Q&A.

Macworld

Macworld magazine's current and past issues: news, reviews, features, columns, and buyers' guide.

MED

Teaching and learning meet technology and the Internet. Resources were Mac-only at last count.

MGR

The Mac Graphic Arts and CAD Forum.

MMS

The Mac Music and Sound forum for technically minded musicians.

MOS

System 7, or 8, or 3.141596...whatever. Talk Mac hardware and Mac OS here.

On the Net

All about web publishing on AOL.

Online Classroom

Learn about computing topics with instructive chats, tutorials, and books.

OS2

FAQs, news, and Linux information for OS/2 Warp devotees.

PC Games

PC gaming shareware; cheats, add-ons, and fixes for commercial games.

PC Music

The PC Music and Sound forum for technically-minded musicians.

PDA

Personal Digital Assistant/Palmtop tips, reviews, and discussion.

PGR

Resources for PC-using graphic artists.

PTC

The PC Telecommunications and Networking Forum, including LANs, personal connectivity, and viruses.

Win

Recommended utilities, FAQs, Win3.x, Win95, and WinNT. When ripping on Bill Gates, remember Terms of Service.

YT

Computer tips and fun for techie youngsters.

Entertainment Channel
Keyword: Entertainment

The Entertainment Channel brings us bestselling novels, blockbuster movies, and Top 40 music. This probably keeps most of AOL happy, though those of us with more obscure tastes are often left slightly disgruntled. With a bit of searching, however, even we can usually find something we like. Each of the words or phrases below is a keyword you can use to go directly to the area.

ABC

Conglomeration of ABC's soap opera, news, sports, kids', and Oprah content.

ABC Daytime

If you're hooked on *All My Children*, you know where to go.

BC

Book Central offers reviews, tons of message boards, and online reading groups.

Blockbuster

You can buy videos, yes, but also music, books, and games.

Books

The bestseller-oriented front screen for AOL's book areas.

BMG

BMG plugging their artists, but thankfully, not trying to get you to join their CD club. Some good downloads.

Cartoon or CNW

The animated TV you grew up with. Aimed at kids but fun for anyone immature enough.

Celebrity Fix

Celebrity gossip.

Clueless

Like, whatever. We find this area much less fun than the movie that inspired it, but then, we're old.

Comics

Comic books: DC, Marvel, Zombie Detective, Wizard World, manga, etc., etc., etc.

Court TV

For those of you who can't get enough of this week's Trial of the Century.

Critics

Insightful reviews of all forms of media.

Culturefinder

Learn about dance, classical music, and theater.

DC Comics

From classic (*Superman*) to goofy (*Mad* magazine) to weird as hell (Paradox Press).

Dead

We're not Deadheads, but you've just got to admire the friendly community and well-organized area here.

E!

Celebrity news, also located at *http://www.eonline.com*.

Entertainment Weekly

Entertainment Weekly's web site (*http://www.ew.com*) includes the current issue, which is often worth a look.

EXTRA

Celebrity photos, celebrity gossip, celebrity interviews, celebrity downloads...

Frasier

Member interaction is the strength of this area devoted to the TV show *Frasier*.

Friends

More marketing-oriented than fan-driven, but *Friends* junkies will still want to visit.

George

Politics, entertainment, and miscellaneous from *George* magazine.

HO

Hecklers Online, a popular comedy area. We don't think it's funny, but obviously many members disagree.

Hollywood Online

Movie downloads and movie star interviews.

Insomniacs

Wacky but juvenile.

Japanimation

We know the proper term is *anime*, so no angry letters, please. Lots of downloads and a busy chat room.

Late Show

Enough content for obsessive Letterman fans to chew on, and the Top Ten list for the rest of us.

Mad About

Friendly members hooked on *Mad About You.*

Marvel

Interactive stories and other fun content for the kids (or you).

Melrose

Frenzied *Melrose Place* fans examine the show and worship the stars.

Movies

AOL's conglomeration of all its movie areas. A good organizational area but not very useful itself.

MTV

MTV's web site plus some exclusive AOL content.

MuchMusic

In our opinion, Canada's music TV has somewhat better taste than America's. Go see if you agree.

Music

This is where all of AOL's music areas hang their hat.

Music Boulevard

Like Tower and Blockbuster, an online music store.

Nick

Nickelodeon Online (for the younger generation) and Nick at Nite (for the nostalgia-ridden older generation).

Oprah

Oprah's talk show, book club, and...fitness forum?

Parascope

For those of you who personally identify with Fox Mulder.

Playbill

Tour dates, seating charts, and other theatrical information.

Premiere

Big-budget, blockbuster movies.

Pulse

That free magazine you get from Tower Records. You can buy CDs while you're at it.

Reprise

Reprise Records musicians, contests, message boards.

Rolling Stone

The current issue and some interactive extras.

Rosie

Devoted Rosie O'Donnell fans seem to make real friends here.

SOD

Sod? *Soap Opera Digest.* Synopses of all the soaps.

SPIN

This month's *Spin,* tour dates, and downloads.

TBR

The Book Report: trivia, excerpts, reviews, and plenty of literary member interaction.

Trek

Fan forum with convention schedules, episode guides, and trivia.

TV

The couch potato's haven. The main screen for all of AOL's TV areas.

TV Source

Search two-weeks' worth of your local listings.

VH1

Focuses on the musicians you see on VH1: interviews, biographies, chats.

Virgin Records

Tour schedules, chats, biographies, downloads.

Warner

New releases, tour dates, and audio clips from Warner artists.

WB Lot

The Warner Brothers TV network, record label, and other enterprises.

WBnet

WB network shows, stations, photos, and multimedia.

Wizard

Comics area that includes collectible toys, video games, and reviews.

Word of Mouth

A conglomeration of entertainment message boards and chats.

X-Files

Rehash each episode, find Internet resources, and wallow in your crush on Mulder and/or Scully.

Families Channel
Keyword: Families

AOL claims that the Families Channel is vaguely about "helping you with life at home." If you're married with kids, you'll probably find something valuable here; if you're not, your "life at home" will probably go unhelped by this channel. Each of the words or phrases below is a keyword you can use to go directly to the area.

Adoption

Information about all aspects of adoption for adoptees, adoptive parents, and birth relatives.

Babies

A collection of baby-related content, mostly from Parent Soup and Moms Online.

Families Newsstand

Online magazines and the occasional super-cheap subscription bargain.

Family Computing
Family computing forums, *Family PC* magazine, and KidSoft Superstore.

Family Life
Magazine with advice, travel tips, projects for your kids, and reviews.

Family TimeSavers
Looks like repackaged Personal Finance and Shopping Channel content to us, but some may find it convenient.

Family Travel Network
If you're brave enough to travel with children, find out where to go and what to do.

HomeBase
Domestic bliss from all over AOL: home improvement, recipes, pets.

Homeschooling
A small but dedicated community of homeschooling parents.

Kids and Teens
Send the kids to `Keyword: KO`. Send the teenagers to `Keyword: Teens`. Send yourself anywhere else in the Families Channel and skip this area.

Moms Online
One of the two real Families Channel content sources. Trivia games, articles, parenting advice, and the Kid of the Day. Where are Dads online?

Parent Soup
The other of the two real Families Channel content sources. Baby names, games, expert advice, and activity ideas.

Parental Controls
Filtering and blocking your child's account. See Chapter 28, *Parental Controls*, for details.

Parenting
Isn't "Parenting" what the whole Families Channel is all about? Looks like more repackaged content to us.

Roots
`Keyword: Roots`, presumably because AOL thinks its members can't spell "genealogy." Some good resources here.

Scouting
Boy Scouts and Girl Scouts resources, mostly message boards.

Games Channel
Keyword: Games

The most important thing to know about the Games Channel is that "Premium" translates to "costs $1.99 per hour." These charges are levied on top of your regular monthly fees, and even during your New Member free time. Fractions of hours are billed at 3.3 cents per minute. Secondary screen names are, by default, blocked from Premium areas (even if they have General access). To unblock secondary accounts or block your primary account:

> Keyword: Parental Controls → Premium Services → Block
> Surcharged Services checkbox

You can only unblock Young Teen and Mature Teen accounts. Kids Only accounts can't be unblocked: you'll see that each Kids Only account checkbox is grayed out. We've divided these games areas into Free and Premium (surcharged). Each of the words or phrases below is a keyword you can use to go directly to the area.

Free

ANT
> Antagonist Inc., an abrasive games area geared towards teenage boys.

AT
> Antagonist Inc.'s trivia counterpart.

Boxerjam
> The word games Out of Order and Strike-A-Match.

Brainbuster
> Trivia game with some challenging, obscure questions.

Games Celeb
> We never thought we'd see game-show hosts put on a pedestal. Stay far, far away.

GIX
> Sparsely populated area for paper-and-pencil role-playing and strategy games.

Mac Games
> Mac game hints, help, and downloads.

NTN
> Trivia games on a multitude of subjects.

OGF
> The Online Gaming forum covers noncomputer gaming such as role-playing, collectible card games, and chess.

Parlor
> Random games conducted in People Connection chat rooms.

PC Games
> PC gaming shareware; cheats, add-ons, and fixes for commercial games.

RJ Casino
> The name implies poker, but it's actually bingo.

Slingo
> A strange slots/bingo hybrid that's fun if you like board games and word games.

Trivia Forum
> Trivia games run in People Connection chat rooms.

Unlimited Adventures
Modules and updates for a commercial Dungeons and Dragons-esque computer game.

VGS
Arcade games from home systems like Sony, Sega, and Nintendo.

Wipeout
Yet another interactive trivia game.

Premium (Surcharged)

Air Warrior (for Macs) and **Air Warrior II** (for PCs)
World War II flight simulation game.

BattleTech
A multiplayer strategy/action game.

Bridge
Choose a bridge game from one of two companies.

Catchword
Create words from random letters in this competitive word game.

Classic Cards
Hearts, spades, whist, and contact bridge.

Harpoon
Naval strategy game.

Incredible Machine
Build a better mousetrap (or any other apparatus) than your opponent.

Legends of Kesmai
Medieval action game.

Magestorm
Action, roleplaying, combat game.

Online Casino
Poker and blackjack.

Splatterball
Virtual paintball.

Virtual Pool
It's like a pool hall, but without the smoke...or the pool.

Warcraft 2
This game has been commercially popular for a while, but now you can kill Orcs online, too!

WorldPlay Backgammon
For the cost of a few hours of this surcharged game, you could just buy the board game.

Worldplay Cards
Cribbage, gin, spades, hearts, whist, and bridge.

Health Channel
Keyword: Health

The Health Channel organizes all its content into topical areas with intuitive keywords. Each area has content from AOL health areas and the Web, most of which appears to be reliable and well-organized. Of course, the support groups, where you can contact other people with similar dilemmas, are popular. For this channel, the keywords usually say it all, so we won't belabor the point by giving synopses of most areas. Each of the words or phrases below is a keyword you can use to go directly to the area.

Addictions
> Recovery from a variety of addictions.

AHH
> The alternative medical forum.

Allergies

Alternative Medicine

Better Health
> A wealth of information on many topics.

Bones
> Arthritis, back ailments, chronic pain, and muscle/joint illnesses.

Cancer

Caregiving
> Caring for children, the elderly, and the ill.

Children's Health

Dental

Diabetes

Diet

Digestive Disorders

Disability

Eating Well

EN&T
> Ear, nose, and throat problems.

Glenna
> A supportive community for cancer sufferers and loved ones.

Health News

Health Support
> Speakers and support groups.

Healthy Living

Heart

Illness

Infection

Kidney

Medical Experts

Medical Reference

Men's Health

Mental Health

Online Psych

Pain Relief

Relationships

Seniors Health

Sexuality

Stress Management

Thrive
   Food, sex, and healthy living tips.

To Your Health
   A free, weekly health newsletter.

Vision

Wellness

Women's Health

Influence Channel
Keyword: Influence

This channel aspires to have lots of taste, although it contains content usurped primarily from other AOL channels or gathered from the Web. We find some of the content fascinating and thought-provoking, but we still mock this channel mercilessly for its grand title. Each of the words or phrases below is a keyword you can use to go directly to the area.

Barnes and Noble
   A place to buy your books.

BC
   Book resources for every genre and topic.

Book Report
   Reviews, author events, and extensive message boards.

BW
   Business reports, profiles, and a six-year archive of *Business Week* back issues.

Classical
   A collection of classical music resources for beginners and experts.

Culturefinder
Kind of like Arts for Dummies, but a good starting point for learning about dance, classical music, and theater.

Digital City
Local information for many major cities, mostly on the East and West coasts.

Drudge
90s muckraker Matt Drudge gossips about politics and entertainment.

eGG
The Electronic Gourmet Guide is the place for tasty recipes.

Elle
Fashion, fitness, beauty, and models.

Entertainment Weekly
The magazine itself is interesting; however, the Influence Channel spotlights the annoying celebrity-gossip angle.

FDN
The Food and Drink Network: restaurants, cooking, smoking, and booze.

Fool
The investment area with a sense of humor. One of the few AOL areas that lives up to its hype.

George
Politics, entertainment, and miscellaneous from *George* magazine.

Met Home
Magazine with features like mansion tours and fancy home decorating ideas.

Mirabella
Women's magazine about relationships, beauty, health, fashion, and culture.

NW
The contents of *Newsweek* magazine.

NY Observer
What's going on in New York City.

Playbill
Broadway tour dates, seating charts, and ticket information.

Salon
Movies, books, news, media, and entertaining columnists we like to read (*http://www.salonmagazine.com*).

Smithsonian
The *Smithsonian* Magazine.

T&L
Features from the writers at *Travel & Leisure* Magazine.

Times
If you like the *New York Times*, you'll like it online—even if you just download the daily crossword.

Wine Country

Plan your trip to California wine country.

Worth

Daily market snapshots, financial columns, and the current issue of *Worth* Magazine.

Interests Channel
Keyword: Interests

"Interests" is a pretty broad category, encompassing many hobbies and pastimes. If you don't know where to look for a particular area, Interests is a good bet (and if you still can't find it, look in the Interests Channel's `Keyword: Hobby`). Each of the words or phrases below is a keyword you can use to go directly to the area.

AutoCenter

Car reviews, insurance advice, and loan information.

Aviation

Air shows, careers, and photos.

Boating

Maintenance tips, boat shows, and sportfishing events.

Books

Links to all of AOL's many book areas. Reviews, best-seller lists, reading groups, and an online bookstore.

Car and Driver

The magazine online, with auto reviews and advice from driving experts.

Car Stereo Review

Help with car stereos.

CigarAficionado

The glorification of a cancer-causing agent (in our humble opinion) at *http://www.cigaraficionado.com*.

Civil War

Civil War history.

Collecting

Stamps, dolls, coins, antiques, and other collectors to meet.

Cooking Club

Recipes from professional chefs and other AOL members, as well as cooking ware to buy.

Crafts Magazine

Quilting, knitting, and ceramics.

Cycle World

Product tests, racing information, and classifieds for bike enthusiasts.

eGG

The Electronic Gourmet Guide is the place for tasty recipes.

FDN
The Food and Drink Network: restaurants, cooking, smoking, and booze.

Flying Mag
Weather reports, aviation news, and columns by flying gurus.

Food
The hub of food and drink on AOL with links to all of the food-related content.

Garden
Gardening content collected from all over AOL.

Ham
CBs, ham radio, shortwave, and scanners.

Hobby
Message boards and downloads for many pastimes.

Home
Martha Stewart, eat your heart out. An aggregation of AOL's domestic content.

HomeMag
Magazine for buying, building, remodeling, and/or decorating a house.

HouseNet
Another home-improvement area.

MAW Network
Both the athletic and movie-oriented aspects of martial arts.

Met Home
Magazine with features like mansion tours and fancy home decorating ideas.

Motorsport
Auto racing news, results, and chats.

Novel
A place for writers to gather, but mostly an advertisement for the man who runs the area.

Pet Care
Good resources for owners of dogs, cats, horses, birds, farm animals, fish, reptiles, amphibians, and other animals.

PhotographyForum
Thinly veiled Kodak ad with information for photographers.

Pictures
Learn how to save and edit your photos on the computer.

Pop Photo
Photography magazine providing product reviews, technical information, and tutorials.

Quilting
Quilting lessons, swap listings, exhibits, and chats.

Road and Track
Read the results of road tests, buyers guides, and automotive news.

Sew News
> Fabrics, fashion, sewing machines, and tips.

Stereo
> Product reviews on home and car stereo systems.

Thrive@eats
> A bit of valuable healthy-eating advice, but mostly just an ascetic, thinness-above-all attitude.

Video Online
> Tests and reviews of VCRs, DVD players, camcorders, and other home electronics.

Wine Spectator
> A web site (*http://www.winespectator.com*) for knowledgeable wine drinkers.

Woman's Day
> Cooking, homemaking, health, and time-saving tips, geared mostly toward mothers.

Woodworking
> Tool reviews, tips, and a woodworking community.

Writers
> Resources and chats for aspiring writers.

International Channel
Keyword: International

For this channel, we'll be listing all the content areas with a short synopsis. Just about every country you could think of has its own area, and we don't have room to list them all. But rest assured that Keyword: [country or continent name] usually gets you where you want to go. Each of the words or phrases below is a keyword you can use to go directly to the area.

Anthems
> Download national anthems from all over the world.

Bistro
> Foreign-language chat rooms.

Foreign Dictionary
> Searchable dictionaries for a huge number of languages.

GG
> Information on international food, plus recipes.

Global Meeting Place
> All of the International Channel's meeting-people content (pen pals, international flirting, etc.).

International Access
> How to sign on to AOL from abroad.

International Store
> Consumerism from all over the globe.

Intl Business
Currency exchange rates, international business etiquette, and financial news.

Intl Classifieds
Study abroad, international jobs, and other classifieds. Fairly sparse as of this writing.

Intl Cultures
Looks like repackaged content from all over the International Channel to us.

Intl Games
Trivia, language games, and Name That Flag.

Intl Love
Find a long-distance relationship, then find out how to deal with it.

Intl News
News, international newspapers, time zones, and weather.

Intl Sports
This looks pretty much like the Sports Channel to us, but there is a bit of additional international content.

Intl Travel
Planning help, etiquette tips, transportation, and tourist traps.

Intl Weather
International weather forecasts and maps.

Royalty
Share your adulation of monarchs, especially the British ones.

Special Delivery
Find international penpals.

Tell Us
A place to trade family immigration stories and traditions.

Kids Only Channel
Keyword: Kids Only

These are the main sections of the Kids Only Channel. See also Chapter 28 for more about children and AOL. Each of the words or phrases below is a keyword you can use to go directly to the area.

KO Central
An index of all the kids' areas on AOL.

KO Chat
Kids' chat rooms, complete with safety rules.

KO Create
Inspiring the kids to write, draw, and make web pages.

KO Find It
An alphabetical list of all the Kids Only areas and a truly awful slideshow.

KO Games

Contests, trivia, stories, and games.

KO HH

Homework help: dictionary, encyclopedia, thesaurus, and help from teachers.

KO Sports

Scaled-down sports content for the youngsters.

KO SS

Kids Only Shows and Stars: because you're never too young to start worshipping your TV.

KO Web

A slightly simpler web interface.

Lifestyles Channel
Keyword: Lifestyles

AOL gets into the identity politics game, with areas for your religion, generation, sexual orientation, gender, race, nationality, and other demographics. If it can be considered a "community," it's here, though we think Keyword: Oprah's community of talk-show fans is reaching a bit. Each of the words or phrases below is a keyword you can use to go directly to the area.

AARP

Information for folks over 50.

Ages&Stages

Meet people from your generation.

Astronet

Horoscopes (we hope this is just for fun, but things look so serious).

Black Voices

Close knit African-American community.

CNS

Catholic News Service.

CO

Christianity Online: chats and religious information.

College Online

Mainly links to college directories, and chats. It's unclear whether this area is supported or was put up and forgotten.

Communities

An aggregate area for religious, ethnic, gay and lesbian, self improvement, and women-centered areas on AOL.

Elle

Fashion, fitness, beauty, and models.

Ethnicity

Separate communities for Hispanics, African Americans, Native Americans, Asian Americans, and Americans of European descent.

Jewish
> Culture, food, religion, and holidays.

Knot
> Wedding advice, tips, and plenty of opportunities to buy.

Love at AOL
> Find a match via personals and dating services.

MCO
> Military City Online: a highly regarded forum where enlisted men and women find resources, news, and community.

Moms Online
> Who doesn't need some help with mothering (including fathers)?

NAMES Project
> The AIDS Memorial Quilt as a fundraising and awareness tool.

NetNoir
> Business, education, music, and sports, not necessarily in order of importance.

Online Psych
> Support groups, diagnosis, and treatment information, and a good deal of information from experts.

OnQ
> The more serious of the two queer areas on AOL with news, travel, entertainment, and chat forums.

Oprah
> Her booklist, inspirational aphorisms, and community of followers and fans.

Parent Soup
> Meet other parents and get expert advice.

Planet Out
> More irreverent than OnQ, Planet Out has a daily radio show and movie recommendations, as well as news and community groups.

Religion
> Your religion is probably covered here. Some good communities have been built up over the years.

Romance
> Find a mate in the community that suits you best.

Rosie
> A gathering place for fans of Rosie O'Donnell and her show.

Self Improvement
> An aggregate area for help with stress management, relationships, and other problems of living.

Teens
> If your son or daughter is too old for the Kids Only Channel, maybe he/she will like the areas here.

Thrive
> Food, sex, and healthy living tips.

Top Model

>Fashion inanities.

Women

>Work, family, and health resources for women with a pro-woman and feminist slant.

Local Channel
Keyword: Local

This channel consists solely of **Keyword: Digital City**. The cities and regions with their own areas are in the table below. Each of the following places is a keyword:

Atlanta

Boston

Chicago

Cleveland

Dallas

Denver

Detroit

Greensboro

Hampton Roads

Houston

LA

Orlando

Philly

Roanoke

San Diego

San Francisco

Seattle

South Florida

Tampa Bay

Toronto

Twin Cities

Washington

News Channel
Keyword: News

We truly like getting news as it happens. Often, the web site or the AOL area has information, streaming video, and related links to a news story the day before you'll see it in your local paper, or hours before you'd see it on TV.

Many of these areas, such as ABC News and the *New York Times,* have a large number of subareas which also have their own keyword. We give you the main keyword (such as `Keyword: ABC News` or `Keyword: Times`); you can explore the subareas for yourselves. Each of the words or phrases below is a keyword you can use to go directly to the area.

`ABC News`
: Video clips and news of all kinds from ABC.

`Business News`
: Collected business news from around AOL.

`Buzzsaw`
: Sometimes amusing, sometimes lame, current-events humor.

`InToon`
: A daily political cartoon from Mike Keefe.

`Life News`
: Family, health, and weird news.

`Newstalk`
: News chats, message boards, and surveys.

`NW`
: The contents of *Newsweek* magazine.

`Politics`
: A collection of political news stories.

`SportsNews`
: Sports news stories. True sports fans will want the Sports Channel instead.

`Times`
: The entire *New York Times,* including the crossword and *The New York Times Magazine.*

`USWorld`
: News headlines and features from America and abroad.

`Weather`
: Local and worldwide weather; browse weather maps, forecasts, and ski reports. (There is also a `Weather` icon on the Welcome screen that gives you your local weather, based on the local-access numbers you used to connect.)

Personal Finance Channel
Keyword: Personal Finance

The Personal Finance Channel used to scare us because it is filled with hard-core stock and money-management information that overwhelmed our senses. But we've come to appreciate it and benefit from its collective wisdom. Maybe we'll even become more financially stable as a result. This channel is popular with small- and big-time investors alike, and has something of interest even if you're just getting started. Each of the words or phrases below is a keyword you can use to go directly to the area.

AAII
> The American Association of Individual Investors, for broker-free traders.

Banking
> Bank online; choose from 21 different banks.

BankRate
> Research interest rates on credit cards, mortgages, loans, CDs, and MMAs.

Broker
> Invest and trade online; choose from seven online brokers.

BW
> The current issue and years of archives from *Business Week* magazine.

Chartomatic
> Get often-updated graphs of Dow, NASDAQ, and S&P 500 activity.

Company News
> Enter a company's ticker symbol to search a 14-day news archive.

Consumer Reports
> The same objective reviews as in the print magazine.

DP
> Learn technical analysis, if you dare.

Disclosure
> Understand the public company filing process and fundamental data.

Edelman
> Some good money-management advice and a fair amount of blatant self-promotion.

EIU
> International economic, political, and business analysis.

Fool
> Informative, entertaining investment advice from one of AOL's most popular areas.

Funds Live
> Mutual Fund message boards and chat.

FundWorks
> All about investment clubs, fund managers, and pumping up your 401(k).

Historical Quotes

Research the past performance of potential investments.

Hoovers

Capsule descriptions of over 1,000 companies. Additional services for subscribers.

IBD

Daily business newspaper with concise news briefs and in-depth columns.

Insurance

Down-to-earth articles and links to insurance companies.

MNC

News about stocks, bonds, funds, currencies, mutuals, futures, and the economy.

MoneyWhiz

Too broke to play the market? This is the personal finance area for you.

Morningstar

Stock reports, a U.S. equities guide, and a mutual fund database.

Mutual Funds

Collected mutual fund information from around AOL.

NYSE

New York Stock Exchange news and listings, and a beginners' investment guide.

Online Investor

Help for stockholders who trade online.

PF Live

Live events, daily chats, and forums.

PF Newsletter

Free newsletters that help you manage your money.

PS Money

Parent Soup's money expert answers questions about family finances.

Quotes

Set up an online portfolio; check your stocks and funds.

Real Estate

Mortgages, apartments, and online househunting.

Sage

Our favorite of the many mutual-fund areas on AOL.

Traders

The Shark Attack Trading Forum, a tongue-in-cheek look at daily trading.

Tax

Everything you need to survive April 15.

Worth

Economic, business, and finance news from *Worth* magazine.

Research & Learn Channel
Keyword: Research & Learn

One of the most useful AOL channels, if you know what's there. Many of the areas below are collections of other areas; `Keyword: More References`, for example, includes both `Keyword: Thesaurus` and `Keyword: Dictionary`. We've listed mainly the larger areas for the sake of organization and brevity. Each of the words or phrases below is a keyword you can use to go directly to the area.

`Ask-A-Teacher`
> Post your question or get live help from a teacher.

`Astronomy`
> For anyone fascinated by the sun, stars, and planets.

`Courses`
> For-credit and noncredit courses at reasonable prices. Since we haven't tried them, we can't personally attest to their quality.

`DCL`
> Look up literary terms, mythological references, and other academia in the *Dictionary of Cultural Literacy.*

`Dictionary` or `Collegiate`
> The searchable *Merriam-Webster Collegiate Dictionary.*

`Education`
> College preparation, financial aid, study skills, and information for parents and teachers.

`Encyclopedias`
> Search *Compton's Living Encyclopedia, Grolier Multimedia Encyclopedia*, and *Columbia Concise Encyclopedia.*

`Fact A Day`
> The word and quote of the day, the weird fact of the day, and what's happened on that day in history.

`Geography`
> Maps, weather, and time zones.

`History`
> Biographies, the History Channel, the Civil War Forum, folk tales, other historical resources.

`Law`
> All about the law, politics, and government.

`More References`
> This is possibly the most practical area on AOL. Dictionaries, encyclopedias, newspapers, homework help, quotations, and plenty more.

`PhoneBook`
> An online white pages, yellow pages, congressional directory, and other phone and address resources.

Reading

Book reviews, style guides, quotations, and literary resources.

RL Arts

Architecture, art, dance, fashion/costumes, film, museums, music, opera, and theater.

RL Business

Mostly search engines for various Personal Finance Channel and WorkPlace Channel resources.

RL Consumer

Advice about cars, home finance, real estate, taxes, and other consumer matters.

RL Health

A medical dictionary and lots of content from the Health Channel.

RL Sports

Content from the Sports Channel and the Web, plus cooking and bartending information.

Science

Scientific American magazine, science fair guides, and many individual subjects.

Space

Everything to do with space exploration.

Straight Dope

Truly strange facts from Cecil Adams. Worth a look.

Thesaurus

The searchable *Merriam-Webster Thesaurus*.

Your Career

Resume tips, help-wanted ads, and career advice.

Shopping Channel
Keyword: Shopping

We think this channel gets enough hype from constant in-your-face ads all over AOL, so we're not going to shove it down your throat in this book. But it can be convenient to shop online, so be aware that you can buy many items from AOL at Keyword: Shopping.

Sports Channel
Keyword: Sports

Like the Health Channel, most of the Sports Channel is well-organized, with self-explanatory keywords. You're a smart person, and you don't need us to tell you what can be found at Keyword: Baseball. In the cases where the keyword doesn't say it all, we add our own synopsis. Each of the words or phrases below is a keyword you can use to go directly to the area.

@outdoors

ABC Sports
    In-depth coverage of college football, Monday Night Football, and other major sporting events.

AOL Bike

Athlete Direct
    Read athletes' journal entries and chat with sports stars.

Auto Racing

Backpacker

Baseball

Bicycling Magazine

Boating Online

Bowling

Boxing

CBS SportsLine
    Up-to-the-minute news and scores (*http://cbs.sportsline.com*).

Cheerleading

College Basketball

CFB (college football)

Cricketer
    For Britain's favorite sport, cricket.

Edelstein
    Pro football analysis and picks.

Extreme Sports
    Snowboarding, aggressive skating, face-first rock-diving, etc. (just kidding about the last one).

Fans
    News and community for fans of the big six.

FBN (fishing)

Field & Stream

Fitness

GFB
    Fantasy basketball league.

GFBase
    Fantasy baseball league.

GFF
    Fantasy football league.

GFH
Fantasy hockey league.

Golf

GOLFonline

Grandstand
Message boards and live chats for almost every sport.

GS Sports Cards

Gymnastics

HBN (hunting)

Hockey

Horse Sports

iBIKE

iGOLF

Inline Skating

iRACE (auto racing)

iSKI

Martial Arts

More Sports
If the sport of your choice doesn't have its own keyword, you'll probably find it here.

MTN Bike (mountain biking)

NFL

NTN Sports
Real-time sports trivia games.

Outdoor Adventure
Find places for camping, kayaking, and other outdoor activities.

Outdoors
Any sport you can do outdoors: backpacking, biking, snowboarding, and so on.

Paintball

Pro Basketball

Pro Football

Rodeo

RSD (scuba diving)

Runner's World

Running

Sail

SCUBA

Skiing

SkiNet

Soccer

SOL (snowboarding)

Speed Skating

Sports LIVE
Chats, message boards, and live events with athletes.

SportsFan
News, editorials, the latest odds and point spreads, and more.

SportsSuper
The Sports Superstore for athletes, outdoors enthusiasts, and fans.

STATS
Get the latest sports information just minutes after it happens.

Surflink

Tennis

TransWorld (snowboarding)

TSN
An in-depth look at baseball, football, basketball, and hockey.

WSF
A forum for woman athletes.

WWF (World Wrestling Federation)

Travel Channel
Keyword: Travel

Travel is one of the great online success stories given its balance of useful advice and commerce. Get advice from travel experts, airline schedules and fares, then reserve your airline tickets, vacation packages, and hotel deals instantaneously. Consult the Travel Channel before you start planning your next trip. It sure beats a trip across town to the travel agent. Each of the words or phrases below is a keyword you can use to go directly to the area.

AAA
Car care tips, scenic drives, and plenty of help for AAA members.

B&B
A guide to bed and breakfasts everywhere.

Bargain Box
Inexpensive airfares, hotels, and car rentals.

Cruise Critic
Cruise reviews and the Cruise Selector, which helps you choose one.

Destination Focus
Vacation planning for a different destination every week.

Family Travel Network
Are we there yet? Where to go and what to do with your kids.

Golfis
Golf vacation packages.

Great Escape
The Travel Channel's free newsletter points you to deals and new destinations.

InsideFlyer
More than you need to know about frequent flyer miles and points.

LP
The well-written, fun, and down-to-earth Lonely Planet guides.

MCL
Photo developing from Mystic Color Labs.

Outdoors
Any sport you can do outdoors. Not much travel-related content here.

Over the Rainbow
Planet Out's guide to safe, fun trips for gay and lesbian travelers.

Preview Travel
Buy plane tickets, or reserve hotels and rental cars. Useful!

Rick Steves
Your guide to avoiding European tourist traps.

RPMC
How to plan your vacation around music, sports, and other events.

Ski Zone
Ski conditions and vacation spots.

T&L
Features from the writers at *Travel & Leisure* magazine.

TA
Discount airfares, hotels, car rentals, and vacation packages.

Travel America
Visiting U.S. national parks, zoos, and tourist spots.

Travel Corner
Correspondents in more than 200 countries help you decide where to go.

Travel File
Vacation packages, with a focus on active vacations involving, for example, golfing or skiing.

Traveler
Bargains and tips for the independent traveler.

Wine Country
Plan your trip to California wine country.

WorkPlace Channel
Keyword: Workplace

We'd prefer more resources for workers and less for business owners, but we're glad to see this channel exist as a resource for getting, switching, or inventing a job. Each of the words or phrases below is a keyword you can use to go directly to the area.

About Work
Advice and discussion on all aspects of working for a living.

Business Classifieds
The categories are Merchandise, Investments, Services, and Opportunities.

Business Dinner
Topical chats every weeknight at 8 p.m. EST.

Business Know-How
A popular business strategies area.

Business News
News about the economy, the markets, various industries, and international business.

Business Research
Search copyrights, trademarks, news archives, patents, and press releases.

Business Talk
Job-related message boards and chats.

Business Travel Center
Information such as airport details, maps, and international business etiquette.

BW
The current issue and years of archives from *Business Week* magazine.

Career Research
Looks a lot like **Keyword: Business Research**.

CCH
A useful area for owners of both small and large businesses.

Changing Direction
How to make switching careers relatively painless.

Company Research
Company reports, earnings estimates, and financial statements.

EIU
International economic, political, and business analysis.

Finance Center
A collection of tax and personal finance areas.

Find a Job
Résumé and cover letter help and many job listings.

Gonyea

Career profiles, want ads, a résumé bank, and other job-hunting resources—many for a fee.

Guerrilla

Marketing tips for anyone looking to advertise.

HOC

Computing and financial help for home-office workers.

Hoovers

Capsule descriptions of over 1,000 companies. Additional services for subscribers.

Inc

Inc. Magazine, a guide for starting or running your own company.

Incorporate

How to incorporate your business.

MLM

The Multi-Level Marketing area.

Online Business

Using the Web for fun and profit—mostly profit.

PrimeHost

Get your business a web page. See also Chapter 23, *Web Publishing and FTP*.

Professional Forums

Message boards and articles for many professions; each job has its own keyword.

Startup

A collection of AOL areas of interest to new entrepreneurs.

Your Business

A hub of information for business owners.

Your Career

A hub of information for employees

CHAPTER 16

The Web

We could have written an entire book about the World Wide Web, but instead we've tried to write a concise chapter you can use to get a handle on the basics and understand how the Web works with AOL. We cover AOL's built-in browser, and what you should do if you want to use other ones. To conclude the chapter, we provide a quick guide to some of the standout web sites you might want to visit.

The latest version of AOL comes with a built-in Microsoft Internet Explorer (MSIE). The current version shipped with AOL is MSIE3.0, but we understand that MSIE4.0 is forthcoming. If you have a higher version of MSIE installed on your machine, AOL will use that version; you needn't worry that AOL will downgrade your browser. It used to be that AOL devised its own browser, but it left a lot to be desired. Now, however, the nuts and bolts of the AOL browser are identical to what you get direct from Microsoft, complete with support for Java, ActiveX, and streaming audio and video.

However, MSIE has a slightly different face if used from within AOL. Typically MSIE has a toolbar and icons that include features you use to navigate backwards and forwards through sites; a favorites listing that stores, well, your favorite sites; and a history icon that shows you each of the pages you've visited over the past several weeks. AOL's MSIE retains some of these features, but its toolbar has been replaced with the hybrid AOL/Web toolbar. Herein lies the crux of the potential problem: do you like AOL's version of MSIE, or do you prefer another browser?

Avid AOL users might love this hybrid toolbar, since it closely marries the functionality of AOL and the Web in one interface, and it's very easy to use. On the other hand, people accustomed to standalone browsers may miss some of the interface and features that AOL has chosen to leave off its MSIE. These "power" users might desire more control over the way their browser looks and functions. The good thing about AOL is that you can choose either path, the built-in MSIE or an alternate browser you run in tandem with the AOL software.

In this chapter, we cover the merits of both the integrated MSIE and the MSIE standalone version. We also touch on alternate browsers you can use with AOL, most notably Netscape's.

These are the sections you'll find in this chapter:

- "The Web via AOL."

- "To Use or Not To Use AOL's Integrated Browser."

- "Using AOL's Browser": Includes launching the browser and adjusting the browser's settings.

- "Using Alternate Browsers": Downloading, installing, configuring, and using Netscape Communicator or a nonintegrated version of Microsoft Internet Explorer.

- "About Plug-Ins": An explanation of the browser plug-ins that come with AOL, where to download new versions of them, and where to find all the plug-ins you want.

- "Web Site Overview": A brief guide to web sites you should know about, if you don't already.

The Web via AOL

Before we tell you about using the Web via AOL, let us remind you that AOL is, and probably always will be, an online service. AOL existed for years before the Web appeared, with members dialing in to AOL's private network to communicate with other members. AOL then began to expand its services to include some Internet services, including Internet email, FTP, and newsgroups. Later, as the Web was born and began to grow in popularity, AOL added web access to its list of services.

What all this means is that AOL is both an online service, with private, subscriber-only areas, and an Internet service provider. AOL offers features and content the Web doesn't. We hardly believed our ears when told this, but some AOL members never venture onto the Web. They're happy with AOL's proprietary content areas. However, for anyone who wants the Web, AOL offers unfettered access.

Here's how the Web works with AOL: anything that's publicly available on the Web is available to AOL members using a web browser. Any screen name you have that's 18+ can access any public site on the Web. If you use the integrated browser, Mature Teen, Young Teen, and Kids Only screen names are blocked by default from certain web content. However, holders of the master screen name can override these blocks by allowing access via Parental Controls if they desire. On the other hand, if non-18+ screen names use a standalone browser, they can access any site. Later in this chapter, we show you how to modify your standalone browsers so that they'll use AOL's Parental Controls, too.

For the More Technically Inclined

Even though AOL web access is nearly the same as most other ISPs, there are two slight differences, not in content, but in how this content is brought to the member. Note that these differences only come into play when using the integrated version of the browser. We list them in order to fully document the ins and outs of AOL; they're not of much importance to the majority of AOL users.

The main difference is AOL's use of *caching*, which means that AOL may store some text, graphics, or other data from a web site on its own servers. Caching speeds up the time it takes to get a site to your browser and reduces the lengthy data retrievals by AOL members to some web sites. To the AOL member, there won't be any noticeable effects of caching, other than faster web access. You also won't have to worry that you're getting a stale version of a frequently updated site: AOL gives you the latest version of a site since it always checks the site for more recent information before deciding whether to use the cached version. In addition, hits from AOL members are reported to the web site; webmasters aren't losing valuable hit information from AOL users.

The other difference—a counterpart to AOL's caching methods—is that AOL may compress graphics it sends to members browsing with the integrated MSIE. While AOL claims that this further speeds up browsing, you can turn the feature off in the browser preferences if you want your graphics to be exactly what everyone else sees. If you want a faster web experience, keep compression on.

An aside for nervous webmasters: if you've got a web site, and you don't want AOL to cache, don't freak out. You pretty much have to allow caching by using the *Date, Last-Modified,* and *Expires* header lines in your web pages. Or just set *Expires* to now. But these are programming issues we don't cover in this book; see AOL's Webmaster Website at *http://webmaster.info.aol.com/* for more information.

To Use or Not To Use AOL's Integrated Browser

We'll come right out and say that we prefer to use a standalone browser rather than AOL's integrated one. But we realize some people prefer the ease of use of the integrated one, for the reasons that we list below.

When you use a standalone browser, you essentially use AOL only to connect to the Internet, then start up your external browser and run it on top of AOL. In the section "Using Alternate Browsers" later in this chapter, we cover just two, those offered by Netscape and Microsoft, but you can use any browser that's compatible with your system, including a new guy on the block named Opera.

Benefits to Using AOL's Integrated Browser

- *AOL's browser is always launched:* Any Web hyperlink you follow from within AOL brings up the default, integrated MSIE browser. You can't use your alternate browser as AOL's default browser. Essentially, following a link from within AOL is easier if you stick with the integrated browser. We elaborate this in the next point.

- *No cutting and pasting to get where you want to go:* AOL has done its best to weave web content seamlessly into its proprietary content, so it doesn't usually differentiate proprietary hyperlinks from web hyperlinks. From within AOL, if you click something that opens AOL's integrated web browser, you have two choices: live with it and use AOL's browser to view that particular page, or copy the URL from AOL, launch your standalone browser, paste the URL, and reload the page from there.

- *Integrated Favorite Places:* If you like having your AOL and web favorite places all in one place, stick with the integrated browser. You can have a mixture of AOL Favorite Places and web favorite places, which you can organize as you choose. If you use a standalone, you won't have integrated favorites.

- *Easier Parental Controls:* If you prefer to use the extremely easy AOL Parental Controls for the Web, you might be better off sticking with the integrated browser—and using no other browser on your system. On the other hand, configuring a standalone browser to use parental controls is easy, although, admittedly, a bit more work. See Chapter 28, *Parental Controls*, for more on how to use Parental Controls for both the integrated and standalone browsers.

Benefits of Using an Alternate Browser

- *More features:* AOL's browser may be convenient, and it's a lot faster and more functional than it used to be, but standalones have better bookmarking, better history-keeping, better toolbars, and more extensive customization. We go into detail about some of these points in the rest of the items listed below.

- *Better bookmarking:* Some people prefer the flexibility of Netscape Navigator's method of saving web sites (Bookmarks) or the standalone Internet Explorer's method (Favorites) to AOL's own Favorite Places. Your collection of marked web sites can grow into the hundreds or even thousands. That's when AOL Favorite Places really show their weaknesses.

- *Better history trails:* With AOL's integrated browser, you can use a drop-down menu to see only the last 25 sites visited. But with the latest standalone MSIE, you can go back for weeks to see exactly which pages you've browsed. Netscape's Communicator also lets you view a more extensive history than the integrated browser.

- *Freedom of choice:* Some people prefer Netscape Navigator to any form of Internet Explorer because they like the features better, or for philosophical, anti-Microsoft reasons. Like we've said, if you browse a site with AOL's integrated browser, you're using MSIE.

- *More easily upgraded:* New browser versions appear every few months, it seems. If you like to have the latest, a standalone browser is essential.

Using AOL's Browser

As we said in the introduction to this chapter, AOL's integrated browser has the meat and bones of Microsoft's Internet Explorer inside, with AOL's own skin outside. Essentially, AOL has placed its own toolbar onto MSIE without compromising the core ability of the browser to present web pages, use style sheets, display frames, run Java applets, encrypt information, etc. In these ways and more, the integrated browser is just like the standalone.

You've got a choice between several methods of going to a web site with the integrated browser. The numbers below correspond to those in Figure 16-1.

---

1. Use the `Internet` toolbar icon. Click the icon, then select `Go to the Web`. The integrated browser is launched, and you're taken to your default web page. To go anywhere, you'll have to follow a link from the home page, or type a new URL into the dual Web/AOL Keyword box (as in Number 2 below).

2. Type the URL (web address) into the dual Web/AOL Keyword box on the new 4.0 toolbar. If you're having trouble finding this box, just look for the long white box in the toolbar that says, `Type Keyword or Web Address Here and Click Go`. For example, if you want to go to the O'Reilly web site, at *http://www.oreilly.com*, simply type *www.oreilly.com*, and AOL launches the integrated browser and takes you to the site. No need to type in the *http://*, since the browser adds that for you.

3. You can also keyword to a web site. Keywording is handy if you don't want to touch the mouse. First, get a keyword window by typing `CTRL-k`, then enter the URL (starting with *http://*) in the `Keyword` box and hit `Enter` to send it.

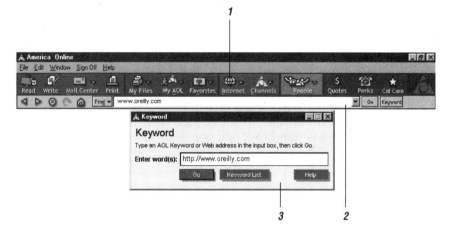

Figure 16-1: Three ways to get to the Web using the integrated browser

Setting Web Preferences

Just as with any web browser, AOL's integrated MSIE gives you a huge number of preferences for customizing your web browsing. In many ways, the preferences for the integrated MSIE are identical to the standalone's preferences, although AOL doesn't allow modification of the defaults for several of the options.

Web preferences are more complicated than other AOL preferences, because they're based on the settings for Microsoft's Internet Explorer. With the integrated version of MSIE, the preferences aren't as extensive (and therefore complicated) as they could be. The downside to the preferences, if you want a lot of control over the settings, is that AOL has set some preferences in stone, which, if you used the standalone MSIE, you'd be able to modify.

To get to the preferences screen for the integrated MSIE, you must go to the My AOL toolbar icon, select Preferences, then click WWW.

To change the preferences for the standalone MSIE, you must go to the View menu, then choose Internet Options.

Browser Main Options

For the integrated version, there are several tabbed sections to the web preferences, including General, Security, and Web Graphics. Each of these has subsections. To get to the preferences in these instructions, you'll follow the path, tabbed main section, followed by subsection. For example, to find the General → Multimedia section we talk about, click the General tab and look at the Multimedia section of the screen.

Be aware that when you change the preferences of your AOL integrated browser, those changes may also take effect in the standalone version of MSIE that came bundled with Windows, and vice versa.

What we list below are a few of the most necessary highlights of web preferences. The first word in the path is the tab; the second corresponds to the section we're referring to. Note: these paths are for the integrated version of MSIE3.0 only. If you've installed MSIE4.0 on your system, you see a slightly different interface, but the concepts should be identical. We strongly recommend you read the complete reference to web preferences in Chapter 29, *Preferences*.

General → Multimedia
>   The defaults are to show pictures, play sounds, and play videos. You can disable any multimedia option by clearing the checkbox next to it. If you've got a modem slower than 28.8 K-bps, you might want to disable sounds and videos, and even pictures, which helps load your pages faster. When disabled, you can still see multimedia, but you have to double-click on the image outline to load it.

Navigation → Customize
>   Your default start page (the one that pops up as soon as you launch your browser from the Internet toolbar icon) is *http://www.aol.com*. You can change that to any web page of your choice, or leave it blank if you don't want any page to automatically load (leaving it blank saves time).

Security → Content Advisor
>   In the bundled MSIE, there are special settings from the Recreational Software Advisory Council (RSAC) that helps you set your browser to filter out objectionable material. See the section "Security tab" in Chapter 29, *Preferences*, for information on your options.

Web Graphics
>   The default is to Use compressed graphics. That means that when you use AOL's integrated browser, graphics from the Web are compressed by AOL so they can load faster. Compressed images may be of slightly lower quality than a web site's native images, but they do load faster, and function exactly as the site's own uncompressed images.

Using Alternate Browsers

If you've already installed AOL or you've got Windows 95/98, you've probably already got at least one standalone browser somewhere on your computer. It came with your operating system, or it was installed at the same time AOL was installed (even if you didn't know it at the time!); it's called Microsoft Internet Explorer. If you want to use this version of Internet Explorer as your browser, it's easy. Just sign on to AOL, then locate MSIE on your computer. You'll find an icon labeled The Internet on your computer's desktop, or you'll see it from the Start → Programs menu. Once you've established a live connection with AOL, run the standalone browser.

If you don't want to use the version of Internet Explorer that's most likely already on your machine, you'll have to install an alternate browser. Preferably, you've got Netscape on disk, but if you don't have any CD-ROMs from which you can install an alternate browser, you'll have to download one from the Internet. Below, we discuss a few web browsers and where you can get them.

Netscape Navigator

You can download the latest version of Netscape Navigator from the Netscape web page at *http://home.netscape.com/download/*.

If you think you'll want to use Netscape applications to publish web pages or send email (once AOL allows MAPI-compliant email clients), download the entire Netscape Communicator suite. If all you want is a browser, look for Netscape Navigator Standalone. Double-click the file you just downloaded and follow the on-screen instructions.

Netscape Communicator and almost all of the suite's components, including Composer, are now free.

To use Netscape Navigator as your browser, sign on to AOL and launch Netscape Navigator/Communicator from the desktop icon or the Windows Start → Programs menu. You'll run the browser over the top of your AOL connection.

Internet Explorer

You've most likely got some version of MSIE on your computer. But there may have been a few updates you've missed. You can download the latest version of Internet Explorer at this Microsoft web page: *http://www.microsoft.com/ie/download/*.

This page has good instructions for downloading and setting up whichever version of Internet Explorer you choose. Consult the same web page to order an Internet Explorer CD, if you'd rather not wait through the painfully long download. If you request the CD, you might wait a few weeks, or months, however. Currently, Microsoft IE is free. You have to decide what the true cost is.

To use standalone Internet Explorer as your browser, sign on to AOL and launch MSIE from your desktop or the Windows Start → Programs menu. The browser runs on top of your AOL connection.

Other Browsers

Netscape Navigator and Internet Explorer are by far the most popular browsers, but there are others to choose from. Browsers other than Netscape and Internet Explorer are often smaller and faster, but much less full-featured, and sometimes display web pages incorrectly. These browsers may not be right for most people, but if you're short on hard drive space or RAM, or you root for the little guy, you might want to investigate them:

* Hot Java: *http://java.sun.com/products/hotjava/*

* Mosaic: *http://www.ncsa.uiuc.edu/SDG/Software/Mosaic/*

* Opera: *http://www.operasoftware.com*

About Plug-Ins

When you install AOL, several of the most popular and useful plug-ins are automatically installed. Plug-ins expand the capabilities of your browser, giving it special audio, video, or animation capabilities. When you reach a site that requires the use of a plug-in you already have, you don't usually need to do anything; the plug-in launches automatically. If you don't have the plug-in, you'll usually be given the opportunity to download and install it immediately.

Here are the plug-ins that come with the integrated browser:

* *QuickTime:* Plays any downloaded QuickTime (*.mov* or *.mpg*) movie while you browse the Web. QuickTime VR lets you play with QuickTime virtual-reality panoramas and objects.

* *RealAudio Player:* Plays streaming audio; adapts to the speed of your Internet connection.

* *Shockwave Essentials:* Provides two applications that your browser loads automatically if it senses relevant content: Shockwave Director, an advanced application for multimedia, games, and streaming audio; and Shockwave Flash, for small, fast web animation.

* *VDOLive:* Plays streaming video and sound; adapts to the speed of your Internet connection; often used for live events and news broadcasts.

In the event you don't get these plug-ins, or you learn that a newer version exists (due to the lag time between creation of the AOL installation download or CD), you can go directly to the makers' web sites:

* For QuickTime: *http://quicktime.apple.com/*

* For RealAudio Player: *http://www.realaudio.com*

* For Shockwave Essentials: *http://www.macromedia.com*

* For VDOLive: *http://www.vdonet.com*

If you need additional plug-ins, Netscape's web page has a good list at *http://home.netscape.com/comprod/products/navigator/version_2.0/plugins/index.html*.

Web Site Overview

Here are a few useful—and fun—sites covering many topics. Use the search engines to explore the rest of the Web's vast offerings.

Search Engines

Yahoo! (http://www.yahoo.com)
> This is where every web newbie should start. It's a well-organized index for web pages.

AltaVista (http://altavista.digital.com)
> A great search engine that scours the Web and Usenet for any word or phrase—the only problem is sorting through all the results.

Excite (http://www.excite.com)
> A web directory and search engine. We're fans of My Excite, one of many personalized web services out there, which puts together a web page with your choice of news topics, sports scores, horoscopes, and more.

Lycos (http://www.lycos.com)
> A web directory with original content and interactive site ratings.

Metacrawler (http://www.metacrawler.com)
> Metacrawler takes your search phrase and runs it through AltaVista, Excite, Infoseek, Lycos, Webcrawler, and Yahoo. Wow.

People and Places

Four 11 (http://www.four11.com)
> Helps you track down people's email addresses. There's no guarantee the email address you get is a current one, but it's worth a shot.

Switchboard (http://www.switchboard.com)
> Switchboard helps you find people (phone numbers, addresses, and email addresses) or businesses. It has searchable white and yellow pages, with amazing custom maps or directions from your location to the business you find. Personal information appears to be provided by the phone book, so you won't find unlisted numbers (or people whose phone service is in someone else's name) here.

WhoWhere (http://www.whowhere.com)
> Another people-finder. This one looks for email addresses, street addresses, and phone numbers. Other features allow you to price cars, track down your ancestors, and find personal home pages.

Mapblast (http://www.mapblast.com)
> Enter an address; get a street map of it.

Mapquest (http://www.mapquest.com)
> More maps, plus door-to-door driving directions.

All Apartments (http://www.allapartments.com)
> National apartment-hunting, plus other moving resources.

Discussion Groups

America Online Mailing List Directory (http://www.idot.aol.com/mld/production/)
Despite coming from AOL, this is actually a pretty good directory of an under-documented topic.

Liszt (http://www.liszt.com)
The much-used and giant mailing-list hub. Search their database for lists and follow the directions to subscribe.

DejaNews (http://www.dejanews.com)
DejaNews has excellent background materials and is probably the most comprehensive newsgroup directory. They've also got archives of years' worth of postings to Usenet, so if you're looking for posts on a particular topic, be sure to stop there. You can also read and post to newsgroups from here.

AOL Newsgroup Scoop (http://www.aol.com/netfind/newsgroups.html)
This is a directory containing reviews and ratings of 500 newsgroups.

Usenet FAQs (http://www.cis.ohio-state.edu/hypertext/faq/usenet/top.html)
Planning to read or participate in a Usenet newsgroup? Look here for the FAQ before you do anything else.

Software

Download.Com (http://www.download.com)
Of course, there are many sites from which to download files, but this one is fairly extensive (and the easiest to remember!).

GetRight (http://www.headlightsw.com/getright.html)
If you plan to do a lot of downloading from the Web, you should investigate GetRight. It's a shareware utility that resumes interrupted web downloads (see also the entry **interruptions** in Chapter 20, *Downloading*).

Happy Puppy (http://www.happypuppy.com/)
Games galore. The best thing is that you can download trial versions of all the most popular games. Just be prepared for long download times over a modem, since some of these puppies are huge.

Computing and Internet

C/net (http://www.cnet.com)
Goliath site for computing and Internet news, programming how-tos, downloads, and buying advice.

WebReview (http://www.webreview.com)
Articles, tools, and tutorials for professional web workers, or anyone who wants their site to look professional. Animation, web authoring, style sheets, dynamic HTML, audio, video, JavaScript, CGI, Perl: it's all here. WebReview is produced by Songline Studios, Inc., an affiliate of O'Reilly & Associates.

HotWired (http://www.hotwired.com)
Like its print counterpart, *Wired* magazine, HotWired is flashy and brainy. You'll find news, reviews of new tools, tutorials for beginners and experts, and the inside scoop on the Internet.

ZDnet (http://www.zdnet.com)
This mega-publisher puts out news, reviews, computer-buying advice, and downloads. There's also ZD University, where, for a few bucks a month, you can take all the computer-related classes you have time for.

Whatis.Com (http://www.whatis.com)
Haven't a clue about the difference between a Zip drive and ActiveX control? Whatis.Com includes scores of definitions for computer-related terms.

Newspapers and Webzines

New York Times (http://www.nytimes.com)
From the giant, intelligent newspaper comes a web site that includes just about everything you can get in the print version—only for free. If you want the crossword, you'll have to get that from the NYT AOL area (`Keyword: NYTimes`).

Salon (http://www.salonmagazine.com)
Reportage, cultural analysis, books, film, TV, sex, and motherhood are just some of the realms covered by these opinionated authors, artists, and intellectuals.

Finance

Motley Fools (http://www.fool.com)
The hugely popular AOL area for the individual investor also has a web site.

Financial Times (http://www.ft.com)
International and business news articles, and a searchable archive of the past 30 days' stories.

Sports

NBA.com (http://www.nba.com)
A multimedia-rich site for pro basketball fans. Read the news, get the scores, and email the players.

NFL.com (http://www.nfl.com)
Stats, standings, news, detailed information on each NFL team, multimedia, and a page for kids.

Major League Baseball@BAT (http://www.majorleaguebaseball.com)
The American and National Leagues, scores, and a digest with features like players' journals and a virtual ballpark tour.

NHL.com (http://www.nhl.com)
Hear live broadcasts of games, watch game highlights, and find out what hockey legends are doing today.

ESPNet SportsZone (http://espnet.sportszone.com)
News, features, columns, and stats for every sport you can think of.

Kids

Yahooligans! (http://www.yahooligans.com/)
An index and search engine of kid-friendly web sites.

The Web

Disney.com (http://www.disney.com)

A slick site full of games for kids and tips for parents. We should warn you that many features are members only, and membership costs $5.95 per month.

KidsCom (http://www.kidscom.com)

Kids can play games, chat, find an email pen pal, and learn about other countries. We like this site because it clearly designates its ads and links so younger kids don't get confused.

Travel

Expedia (http://www.expedia.com)

Make plane, hotel, and rental car reservations with Microsoft's online travel agent.

PreviewTravel (http://www.previewtravel.com)

You might also know it as Keyword: Preview Travel, but we like it enough to mention it twice. Plane, hotel, and rental car reservations.

Travelocity (http://www.travelocity.com)

And, because it never hurts to get a second (or third) opinion, another online reservations system. This one lets you choose your own airplane seats.

Arts and Entertainment

Amazon.com (http://www.amazon.com)

You might already know about Keyword: Barnes and Noble, but this is the other online bookstore.

BookWire (http://www.bookwire.com)

Book reviews, publishing industry information, original fiction, literary links, and author events in your town.

The Internet Movie Database (http://www.imdb.com)

No movie lover should miss it. All about every movie, actor, cinematographer, producer, costume designer...you get the idea.

MovieCritic (http://www.moviecritic.com)

Get personalized movie recommendations based on how you rate movies you've seen.

CultureFinder (http://www.culturefinder.com)

An accessible guide to theater, dance, classical music, jazz, and art.

The DJ (http://www.thedj.com)

We love their 60 diverse radio stations. Way better than your local radio stations, and no commercials.

AudioNet (http://www.audionet.com)

Listen to CDs, live radio, seminars, and interviews.

The Ultimate Band List (http://ubl.com)

A huge directory of sites dedicated to musicians, from the legends to the ones you've never heard of.

PART IV

Getting Organized

What would life be like if you could always find what you're looking for, had all your documents in order and waiting for your perusal, and had records of all of your correspondence going back for years? Well, you'd probably be president of the United States, but barring that, you'd be amazing. Of course, that sort of organization isn't within the grasp of us mere mortals. But AOL gives you a couple of tools that, used properly, can help you stay organized and sane. We wouldn't be anywhere without Personal Filing Cabinet, with searchable records of the years' worth of emails in there. While AOL's standard tools aren't the most full-featured, they get the job done. In this part, we show you all the ways to use them, as well as the tips and tricks.

Chapter 17, *Favorite Places*: "Get Back. Get Back. Get back to where you once belonged..." (Lennon/McCartney)

Chapter 18, *Personal Filing Cabinet*: Put it all in here: records of email, newsgroups, downloads, and favorite files.

CHAPTER 17

Favorite Places

Have you ever come across a web site or a handy tool on AOL, but then forgotten how to return later? Favorite Places is one of the best ways you can get organized on AOL. Use it to help you return to the places you visit frequently, or places that you want to go back to at any point in the future. Primarily, Favorite Places take you back to where you've been, functioning like the Bookmarks feature in Netscape Navigator or the Favorites in Internet Explorer.

Besides helping you know where you've been and keeping your journeys organized, there are two other uses for Favorite Places that involve sharing a Favorite by sending it in email, or by dropping it into an Instant Message or chat window. We show you how in this chapter.

In AOL 4.0, Favorite Places has been greatly improved: you can now see them in a drop-down menu from the `Favorites` toolbar icon. That means you no longer have to open a separate window to see them, giving you faster access and less clutter. Favorite Places are completely customizable, allowing you to add and delete places at will. If you ever update your AOL software, you can take your favorites with you. In addition, you've got some privacy, since each screen name has its own Favorite Places; you won't get yours all mixed up with your kids'.

Before you get started, there's one final note: you can't use Favorite Places when you're signed on as a guest. Why? Because all your Favorite Places are stored on your own computer.

Two Ways to See Favorite Places

There used to be only one way to view your Favorite Places, and that was through a separate Favorite Places window, similar to that shown in Figure 17-1. But with 4.0, you no longer have to open the separate window to get to your favorite places. You can use the `Favorites` drop-down menu on the toolbar, shown in Figure 17-2. Each way of viewing your Favorite Places has its advantages. If you want to organize your favorites by moving them around, or dragging and drop-ping them into folders you've created, you must use the separate window. On the other hand, if you just want to jump quickly to a Favorite Place, it's easiest to use the drop-down `Favorite Places` menu to go there directly.

Figure 17-1: A Favorite Places window to organize and edit your favorites

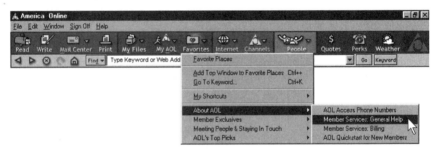

Figure 17-2: The toolbar/menu view of Favorite Places

Here are the paths to follow to get to the two views of Favorite Places:

• To get the Favorite Places window go to the `Favorites` toolbar icon, then highlight `Favorite Places`. The standalone window then opens, as shown in Figure 17-1. In this figure, you can see we've highlighted `AOL Access Phone Numbers`. With a double-click, we go directly there. In Figure 17-1, you'll also notice the buttons, `New`, `Edit`, and `Delete`, which allow you to add your own folders, move favorites, rename, and delete them. All that's covered later in this chapter.

• To use the `Favorites` drop-down menu, just click the `Favorites` toolbar icon, then move down to the list of your favorites and your favorites folders. Folders with favorites in them have arrows pointing to the right; moving your mouse over these menu items opens them so you can see the nested favorite places inside. When you've highlighted the favorite you want to go to, click it.

In the example in Figure 17-2, we've selected Member Services General Help in the folder About AOL.

Adding a Favorite: Just a Click Away

Any time you want to mark a place for later viewing, just click the heart icon in the upper right of the open window, then click Add to Favorites. That creates a permanent record you can come back to at any time. You can make a favorite out of almost all of AOL's windows, including web pages open in the integrated browser.

Favorite Placing Web Sites

If you use the integrated browser, you'll see the heart icon in the titlebar of the browser window, the same as for any other window inside AOL. However, you can't use AOL's Favorite Places with standalone browsers. Instead, you can use the very well-designed Favorites in MSIE or the Bookmarks in Netscape to keep your list of favorites. We think the standalone browsers are better since they have more extensive options and filing systems for all your web sites.

Getting Organized

You might notice when you install AOL that some favorites are already in there. AOL starts you out with several folders full of Favorite Places that include access numbers and member help areas, and areas that AOL wants to highlight. Some of these include links to AOL's partners, who'll try to get you to buy something. You might not agree that these default favorites are even close to your favorites. We'll show you how to delete them.

To organize your Favorite Places, you must have the standalone Favorite Places window open. You can't rearrange any folders or favorite places from the Favorites drop-down menu. To get to the Favorite Places standalone window:

> Favorites toolbar icon → Favorite Places

Using folders

You can put your Favorite Places into categories that make sense to you. Whenever you add a Favorite Place, it lands at the top of the list. The more Favorite Places you add, the longer the list becomes. Using folders is a way of breaking up the long list into more manageable categories. Here's how to create a new folder:

> Favorites toolbar icon → Favorite Places → highlight any folder → New → New Folder

Moving things around

Once you're in the Favorite Places folder, drag and drop the favorites into the locations and folders that are most convenient for you. Create additional folders of your own and/or eliminate AOL's default Favorite Places. Figure 17-3 shows the use of drag and drop to rearrange items in the Favorite Places folder. We're putting a favorite place into the Books! Books! Books! folder we created earlier.

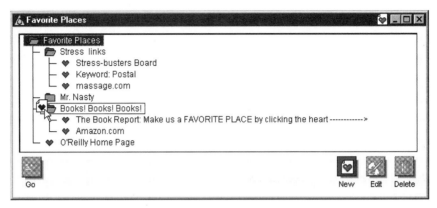

Figure 17-3: Moving items within the Favorite Places folder

Renaming stuff

You can rename folders or individual Favorite Places to make them easier to use. Sometimes, you'll find that the title of a favorite goes on and on. For instance, here's what we got recently when we made Barnes and Noble a Favorite Place: "BarnesandNoble@aol The World's Largest Bookseller Online Home Page." You can shorten it to something that's easier for you, such as "Barnes and Noble." Editing the name of a favorite won't affect where it goes.

> **Favorites** toolbar icon → **Favorite Places** → highlight item to be renamed → **Edit**

You can also edit the Internet address of the Favorite Place; just be sure to use a valid URL and include the *http://* or *aol://* protocol at the beginning. If you don't use the full URL, AOL can't follow the path correctly.

Deleting folders and favorites

If you delete a folder, you delete all the Favorite Places inside. If you want to save some of the Favorite Places inside a folder you want to delete, be sure to move them into other folders first. Just highlight the favorite or the folder you don't want, then click **Delete**. You can't restore deleted favorites (unless you find the items again and add them).

Sharing Your Favorites

You might think that favorites are just for you, but they make sending links to a web site or AOL area extremely easy. After all, if you have something you like, wouldn't it be even more fun to share? Send Favorite Places in just about everything you do on AOL, including email, chat, and Instant Messages. When you send the link, the recipient sees blue underlined text, which she can then click on and go directly to.

There are many ways to send Favorite Places on AOL, the two most common ways being dragging and dropping the heart icon into the open window where you want the link to appear, clicking the heart icon, then choosing what sort of method to use to send it. We'll explain how these work in the sections that follow.

Emailing

You've got three options for sending a hyperlinked favorite place to anybody with an email address.

- Click any heart icon in the open window → `Insert in Mail` (see Figure 17-4).

    AOL then launches a new `Write Mail` window, and inserts the hyperlinked Favorite Place. Just address and send your mail in the normal way.

Figure 17-4: Choosing what to do with a Favorite Place

- Drag any heart icon into an open email message.

    If you've already got an email message open, the easiest way is to drag and drop, which is also best for times when you want to add several links to one email; just keep dragging and dropping the hearts into the body of the message. With this method, you can also choose what the hyperlink name will be. Choose and highlight some text in the body of the message you want hyperlinked. Then drag a heart into the message. Your highlighted text turns a hyperlinked blue.

- Click the blue heart icon in the `Write Mail` window → highlight, then click the Favorite Place you want to send (see Figure 17-5).

    From an email you're currently composing, you can use the email favorites feature to insert one of the Favorite Places into the mail, without actually going to the area. In Figure 17-5, we've highlighted "The Book Report" to send as a hyperlink.

Chatting

You can send a Favorite Place into the main chat window for all participants to see. Just drag and drop the Favorite Place heart icon into the small chat window, and click `Send` (see Figure 17-6).

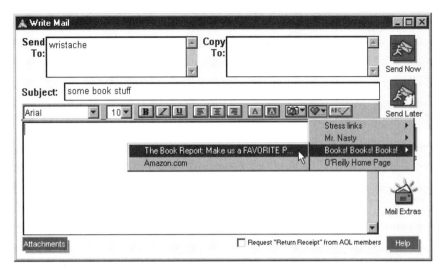

Figure 17-5: The blue heart icon in the Write Mail window

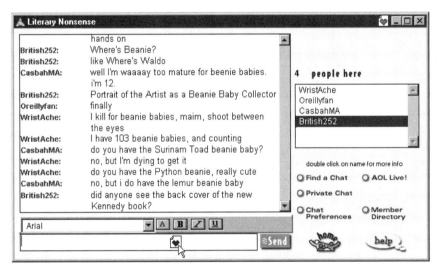

Figure 17-6: Dragging and dropping a Favorite Place into chat

Don't forget about TOS; you can't send vulgar hyperlinks into a chat room (see Appendix D, *Terms of Service*).

Benefits

- Chatting about a site is easy when you can follow the link with just one click.

- Chats among friends or colleagues in Private Rooms are easy to manage when you can take everyone on a tour of favorite sites or projects.

- Parents can decide whether they will allow their children to see links in chat (see "Chat" in Chapter 28, *Parental Controls*).

Drawback

- You never know where the link will take you; you're taking the risk of seeing something you'd rather not see.

Instant Messaging

You've got two ways to send a hyperlinked Favorite Place in IMs:

- Click the heart icon → `Insert in Instant Message` → type the screen name of the person → `Send` (see Figure 17-4).
- If you've already got an IM window open and you want to send a link, drag and drop it into the window (see Figure 17-7). It automatically becomes blue and hyperlinked.

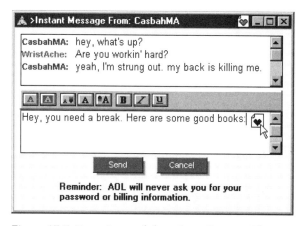

Figure 17-7: Dragging and dropping a Favorite Place into an open IM window

Benefit to sending an IM

- You can send any Favorite Place link to any other member who accepts IMs and hasn't blocked you. Links include AOL areas, message boards, chat rooms, private chat rooms, and web sites.

Drawback

- A child (or anyone) who has IMs enabled could follow a link to something he doesn't want to view. Your best bet to avoid what some may consider offensive material is not to follow a link from someone you don't know.

Additional Tricks with Favorite Places

Since the goal of Favorite Places is to help save you time and keep you organized, AOL lets you put Favorite Places on your desktop, and create your own customized toolbar icons and keyboard shortcuts to favorite areas.

Favorite Places on Your Desktop

A Favorite Place on your desktop not only takes you right to the area with one click, it also launches AOL, and signs you on. If you don't have your password saved, you have to type it in. But once your computer connects to AOL, you're taken right to the area represented by the Favorite Place. Figure 17-8 shows the Today's News Favorite Place on the desktop.

Figure 17-8: A Favorite Place icon on the desktop

Drag any heart icon from any open window to the desktop. You can even drag and drop items from your standalone Favorite Places window to the desktop.

Benefit

• One-click access to your favorite AOL and web areas, even if you aren't signed on.

Drawbacks

• Anyone who uses your computer will see your AOL Favorite Places on your desktop.

• If you store your password, other users can go directly from the desktop to your favorite areas with your account.

Favorite Places on your Toolbar

See "Adding and Removing Toolbar Icons" in Chapter 4, *Getting Around AOL: Toolbars and Menus.*

Keyboard Shortcuts to Your Favorite Areas

See "Creating Your Own Keyboard Shortcuts" in Chapter 19, *Keyboard Shortcuts.*

CHAPTER 18

Personal Filing Cabinet

More than just a repository for your old junk, your Personal Filing Cabinet—or PFC, as it is frequently called—is what you can use to keep organized and sane. It is your memory of mail sent and mail read. You can search its contents and locate that special note from your old college friend or find an email that includes the long-forgotten password confirmation to a web site you subscribed to.

Your PFC is literally like a filing cabinet, a place to store documents for later retrieval. It resides as a file on your hard drive, which is convenient because you'll always have access to your PFC, whether you're signed on to AOL or not. If you upgrade to a new version of AOL, you can take your older PFC with you. In addition, the PFC expands to accommodate as many files and records as you have room for on your hard drive.

Each screen name comes with its own PFC, so that you won't get a record of your mail or your newsgroup postings all mixed in with your spouse's or your kids'. The 4.0 version includes a new feature that lets you password-protect your PFC, to keep out prying eyes.

The PFC can be useful, but you have to make it useful. Organization is made, not born. You have to turn on some of your PFC's best features, such as saving copies of mail you send and receive. In its default state, the PFC doesn't do much more than sit there, unused. In this chapter, we start with the basics of where it is and how to move stuff around in it, then move on to customization and using more than one PFC.

If You're New to Personal Filing Cabinets

To start out, you'll have to get to your PFC and open it up for viewing. Go to the toolbar icon **My Files**, then select **Personal Filing Cabinet**. You see a window similar to the one in Figure 18-1, only your own saved documents are inside. This is how you access your PFC, unless you're signed on as a guest, in which case you won't have access.

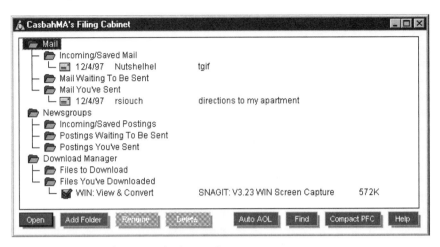

Figure 18-1: A sample Personal Filing Cabinet

The whole concept of the PFC is that of file folders and individual documents. Each document is in a folder. Folders can be inside other folders. The section "Keeping Organized" helps you understand how to set up and then organize your PFC in the way that works best for you.

When your PFC is born—that is, in the default state—it just sits there, not doing much of anything. The first thing we recommend is that you set up your PFC to save all your incoming and outgoing mail. It's easy to change the preferences; see the section "Saving Email."

Since you store things in your PFC, like you store socks in your chest of drawers or files in your filing cabinet at work, you might want to keep some things under lock and key, so to speak. AOL now allows you to require a password to gain access to your PFC's contents; see the section "Password Protection."

PFC Essentials

As your PFC grows to include more saved mail, records of downloads, Automatic AOL mail, newsgroup posts, and the like, it definitely takes up more hard disk space. Your PFC is automatically set up to regulate the amount of drive space it occupies, but if you're running low on space, you might want to manually override these limits or do a little spring cleaning. To manage your PFC's size, check out both "Keeping Organized" and "PFC Preferences." You should be able to keep the size of your PFC as small and manageable as you'd like it.

If you want to use an older version of your PFC, or you want to open a PFC from a dormant account—or even from a screen name that no longer exists—you can. But you'll have to do it manually. We show you how in "Transferring an Old PFC to a New Location or Account."

Open Your PFC

When was the last time you went down in the basement to take a peek at all the files and papers you've stored in there? The PFC is supposed to help you make order out of chaos, but to get things going, you've got some work to do. Start by opening your PFC at **My Files** toolbar icon → **Personal Filing Cabinet**. You'll see a window like the one in Figure 18-1.

What you can store in your PFC:

- Incoming/saved mail
- Mail waiting to be sent
- Mail you've sent
- Incoming/saved newsgroup postings
- Newsgroup posts waiting to be sent
- Newsgroup posts you've sent
- A list of files you've marked "Download Later"
- A record of files you've downloaded

Once something gets into your PFC, it's there until you delete it (unless a catastrophe happens upon your PC, like a flood or an especially pernicious virus that deletes the contents of your hard drive; both are uncommon, but you get the point).

AOL doesn't automatically save anything in the PFC except for records of files waiting to be downloaded and files you've downloaded. This is why we say that you have to set up your PFC to make it useful, since it clearly doesn't come that way. In the sections that follow, we cover saving email and keeping records of newsgroup activity.

Saving Email

You can configure your PFC to automatically save email you've read, save email you've sent, or both. We don't know what we'd do without this feature. It has gotten us out of jams when we needed to go back to old email we've sent out to resend it to people who've lost it. Had they turned on this feature of the PFC, they wouldn't have to come crawling back to us with their request for a copy.

To Save Email You've Read

We've told you elsewhere in this book that email is the most popular activity on the Internet, and surely it is the most popular use of AOL. For some reason, however, AOL doesn't have email saving on by default. That essentially means that unless you turn on saving in the PFC, you won't be able to access read email three days after you've read it. That's when AOL yanks it from its server.

The cure: keep a record in your PFC.

> **My AOL** toolbar icon → **Preferences** → **Mail** → check the box **Retain All Mail I Receive in My Personal Filing Cabinet**

Benefits

- You'll be glad to have a record of all the mail you read, especially if you subscribe to mailing lists (see Chapter 12, *Mailing Lists*). Never forget how to unsubscribe to a mailing list again!

- The record of email can be organized any way you like, and messages you've read can also be deleted.

- Never ask someone to resend important email again!

Drawbacks

- Even the spam you've read goes into your PFC. You must then open the PFC and delete it (see "Deleting Folders or Documents").

- If you send and receive a lot of mail, your PFC can become huge, taking up disk space. If this is a problem, you'll have to delete files from your PFC when it gets too full.

To Save Email You've Sent

If you also want to keep a record of the mail you send out, you'll have to enable that at the same place as for mail you've read.

> My AOL toolbar icon → **Preferences** → Mail → check **Retain All Mail I Send in My Personal Filing Cabinet**

Benefits

- You can resend a message that didn't arrive at its destination, or that the recipient lost after reading it.

- You save the time of manually saving copies of important mail you send out.

- You can organize your saved message in your PFC in any way you choose (see "Keeping Organized").

Drawbacks

- If you send a lot of mail, your PFC can take up many megabytes of disk space.

- If you don't like the chronological organization of the AOL PFC, you'll need to manually organize the messages (see "Keeping Organized").

Newsgroups and the PFC

You can download newsgroups into your PFC while you sleep, then read them and respond at your leisure. While easy to the experienced user, reading a post offline can be a bit difficult to understand at first. Basically, you need to set up AOL to download the newsgroups posts using the Automatic AOL feature. You tell AOL to download your subscribed newsgroups, then you'll find them in your PFC where they stay until you delete them. Here's how to get started:

1. Subscribe to your newsgroups in the usual manner (for instructions see "Locating Groups" in Chapter 13, *Newsgroups*).

2. Once you've subscribed, you have to configure Automatic AOL. See Chapter 21, *Automatic AOL* "Newsgroups" for detailed instructions.

Keeping Organized

Think of the PFC as a real filing cabinet, full of folders, and within those folders, individual files. In the ideal filing cabinet, everything that was similar or used for the same purpose would be found in the same folder. You can set up your PFC in this way, using folders that you create and name.

Depending on whether the individual documents are email, newsgroup posts, or other saved text documents, AOL puts things into different places. Notice that, by default, there's a `Mail` folder, a `Newsgroups` folder, and a `Download Manager` folder. There are folders within these folders, too. It is pretty obvious where AOL puts the documents by default: incoming and saved email goes into the `Incoming/Saved Mail` folder; mail you've sent out goes into the `Mail You've Sent` folder. Downloaded newsgroups each have their own folder inside the main `Incoming/Saved Postings` folder in the `Newsgroups` folder. Open or close a folder by double-clicking on it. When you open a folder, it springs open to reveal the other folders inside.

Adding Folders

It's your computer, they're your files. Why not organize them the way you want them, not just in AOL's default folders? If you get email from Mom and Granddad you want to save, you can put them into special folders; that way you have one place to look when you need to refer back. Create as many folders as you need to keep organized. Note: you can have folders inside of folders *ad nauseum*, but why would you want to do that to yourself?

> `My Files` toolbar icon → `Personal Filing Cabinet` → click where you want to add the new folder → `Add Folder`

You'll be prompted to name the new folder. If the folder doesn't end up where you want it, drag and drop it into place. The next entry on dragging and dropping shows you how.

Dragging and Dropping to Put Items in Their Place

Dragging and dropping is a standard way to move files around on most graphical computers, especially Windows and Macs. So it's no surprise that you can organize your files in your PFC by dragging and dropping them, swapping folders and placing files where you choose.

To drag and drop an item, click on it once, and hold down the mouse button. While holding down the mouse button, move the item to its new location. You should see a document icon as you move it. Release the mouse when it is where you want it. Note: you can't move the default nested folders, such as `Incoming/Saved Mail`, to other folders, but you can move them within the `Mail` folder.

If you want to drag and drop more than one item you'll have to use the CTRL or Shift keys on your keyboard:

CTRL

> Hold down CTRL and click once on as many individual items as you want to highlight. When you've highlighted the last item, let go of the CTRL key and drag and drop the documents into their new location. If you hold down the CTRL key while you drag and drop, only copies of your items are moved, leaving the originals in their original locations.

Shift

> Use Shift to highlight multiple items in a series with just two mouse clicks. Hold down Shift, then click on the first and last items in a series. When you click the second item, all the items in between are highlighted. Drag and drop them in the usual manner. Unlike CTRL, holding down Shift while dragging won't copy the files.

Deleting Folders or Documents

If you save all your incoming and outgoing mail or use Automatic AOL for your newsgroups, you'll find that your PFC gets really big really fast. Deleting items is the only way to get rid of them. Thankfully, you can delete entire folders, if you wish, or just the documents inside them.

> My Files toolbar icon → Personal Filing Cabinet → Delete

You've got a lot of ways to delete items:

Delete a single item

> Select the item you want to delete.

Delete multiple items

> Hold down the CTRL key and click on any items to select. If you make a mistake, you can just click the item again to deselect.

Delete multiple items in a series

> Hold down the Shift key and click the first item and then the last in the series; all items between the two are selected.

Benefit

• Keep your PFC organized and take up less local disk space.

Drawback

• You have to delete items manually from the PFC window if you've checked save mail read or save mail sent in your email preferences (see "Saving Email").

See also "Warning Before Deleting," later in this chapter.

Filtering Email

Don't hold your breath for automatic filtering, a feature found on just about every other email reader. As we've said many times in this book, AOL is slated to allow the use of Microsoft's Outlook Express email client in the future, but it's hard to tell when that will be.

Until then, you'll have to organize your email (and your other files) by hand, through dragging and dropping, which can be, excuse us, a real drag. The sections above tell you how to create new folders and organize their contents.

Finding Stuff in Your PFC

Good thing AOL lets you search for words or phrases in your PFC, otherwise, you might never find that old email. The Find icon is right in the PFC window.

My Files toolbar icon → Personal Filing Cabinet → Find

When you choose Find in your PFC, you have a series of choices. Select the option that corresponds with the way you want AOL to search, then enter your search word and click Find Next. You have the following options:

- Titles Only: Looks only in the headers of email and newsgroup posts.

- Full Text: Looks for matches in the body of the email and posts, too.

- All Folders: Exhaustive search of all items in both open and closed folders.

- Open Folders Only: Limit your search and the time it takes to wait while searching. When you use this feature, be sure that the folder you want to search is actually open.

In addition, using find in top window is an alternate way to search the message headers of your open PFC. From the Edit menu, select Find in Top Window.

See also *top window* in Chapter 14, *Finding & Searching.*

PFC Preferences

You've got a number of ways to make your PFC work the way you want it to. The following sections cover the options. The main Personal Filing Cabinet Preferences window is shown in Figure 18-2. Get there by following this path:

My AOL toolbar icon → Preferences → Personal Filing Cabinet

PFC Size

Reduce the amount of space the PFC takes up on your local drive. Consider compacting when you've just deleted a bunch of files from your PFC (see Figure 18-2). This is similar to defragmenting your hard drive. By default, AOL lets you know when your PFC has reached 10 MB, and asks if you want to compact it. Can't hurt to say yes.

If you're running out of room on your hard drive, you can compact your PFC or delete individual files and folders if you don't mind losing those records.

My Files toolbar icon → Personal Filing Cabinet → Compact PFC

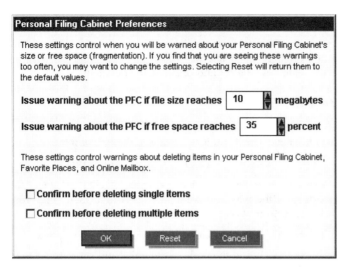

Figure 18-2: Personal Filing Cabinet Preferences

Benefits

- The less space the PFC takes up on your hard drive, the more you'll have free for other bloated applications and files.

- If you want to reduce the amount of hard-drive space your PFC occupies (with stale email you'll never read again anyway) you can delete some files (see "Deleting Folders or Documents").

- When you set the size, you're setting it only for the current screen name, not for all names in your account.

Drawback

- If your maximum size is small, you'll get the warning all the time. Raise it and/or delete items from your PFC to cure this annoyance.

Limiting Free Space

By default, you get a warning if your PFC free space reaches 35% (see Figure 18-2). If you want to increase or decrease this amount, type in a new number. If you delete a lot of files from your PFC, you'll find that AOL is always telling you when there's free space. To get less frequent warnings, increase the default to over 50%. Compacting your PFC regularly can save on hard drive space.

My AOL toolbar icon → Preferences → Personal Filing Cabinet

Warning Before Deleting

By default, you get a warning before you delete items from your PFC, your online email box, and your list of Favorite Places (see Figure 18-2). The warnings can help you if you don't know what you're doing, or if you have fast and loose fingers. But when you delete items often, you'll probably find the warnings annoying, and you'll want to turn them off. Here's how:

- Single items: My AOL toolbar icon → Preferences → Personal Filing Cabinet → clear the box Confirm before deleting single items

- Multiple items: Follow the same path as above, but clear the box Confirm before deleting multiple items.

Benefit of turning off default delete confirmation

- Save time by not having to click OK every time you want to delete an item from your PFC, email queue, or your Favorite Places.

Drawback to changing the defaults

- You could accidentally delete something that you wanted to keep.

Password Protection

Keep your saved email, newsgroup posts, and download history from prying eyes by passwording your PFC. The password is the same one you use to sign on to your account. So if someone knows the password to your account, that person can also use that password to get into your PFC. Note that you must be signed on with the account whose PFC you're trying to password protect. Follow the path below to get to the Store Passwords screen (see Figure 18-3):

> My AOL toolbar icon → Preferences → Passwords → check the box that corresponds to the screen name whose PFC you want to password protect

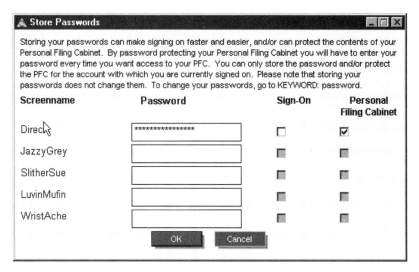

Figure 18-3: Password protecting a Personal Filing Cabinet.

Drawback

- If you've stored your password to sign on, be careful. Anyone who signs on with your account can gain access to your PFC by turning off passwording. Someone could simply clear the `Personal Filing Cabinet` box on the password preferences screen. Don't store your password to sign on if you want a secure PFC.

Restore Your Old PFC

What happens when you delete a screen name? Does your PFC go "poof"? No, you've still got it on your hard drive, although you can't get to it in the normal way, by signing on, since the sign on screen name no longer exists. You've got two options:

- Restore the deleted screen names (see "Creating and Managing Screen Names" in Chapter 3, *Screen Names, Passwords, and Signing On*). When you restore, your PFC will often be salvaged as well. If the PFC is still on your local drive, the recreated screen name can again access it.

- Manually move the old PFC with some file-manipulation tricks (see the section below, "Make a Copy by Hand: Keeping PFC Up to Date on Multiple Computers"). With this method, you'll still have access to your files, and you won't have to restore the deleted screen name.

Transferring an Old PFC to a New Location or Account

There are two ways to transfer your old PFC to a new account or to a new version of the AOL software. When you upgrade to a new version of AOL, you can transfer your PFC. You can also copy your PFC and move it from machine to machine. Transferring when you upgrade is the only easy way to move a PFC. Copying it takes some knowledge of the Windows Explorer, and copying and renaming files on your PC.

Make It Automatic When Installing, Reinstalling, or Upgrading

During the set-up process, you are presented with options that allow you to transfer the contents of an existing PFC into a new PFC. The following steps are presented during installation:

- When you're beginning to install and given four options (joining as a new member, upgrading, adding a new copy of AOL, adding an additional copy of AOL), make sure you choose `Upgrading to a new version of AOL`.

- When asked to `Choose Account To Upgrade`, make sure you choose the version of AOL that contains the PFCs you want to transfer. A PFC is automatically transferred for each screen name you have set up.

- When asked to Select Downloaded Files Action, choose either MOVE or COPY. This transfers your old downloads, Preferences, and PFC contents to your new, upgraded version of the AOL software. The PFC still appears in the old account, too. As long as you stick to using one PFC, it's always the one that's most up to date. However, if you use two different installations of AOL, like at home and at work, the saved contents of your PFCs reflect the documents you open using a particular computer. For instance, your PFC at work and at home won't automatically contain the same saved mail. Copying by hand helps take care of this problem, but it isn't the easiest or most elegant solution.

Make a Copy by Hand: Keeping PFC Up to Date on Multiple Computers

If you don't transfer the old PFC when you upgrade, don't worry: you can still use it later. You just have to learn a bit about how AOL uses its PFC files and a trick or two. We call this trick the *manual copy method*. Learn it and you'll be able to move PFCs around, from computer to computer, never missing an important archived file. Any time you want access to the contents of more than one PFC—an old one, or one from another screen name, or one from a deleted screen name—you can use the manual copy method.

PFCs get out of sync. Say you have one copy of your AOL account on your laptop, one at home, and one at work, just to check your email when you're bored. If you store mail and other items in your PFC, you'll begin to notice that different items are on different computers. That's because the PFC is on your local hard drive, not AOL's network. When you open and save an email with your work computer, it won't be opened and saved on your laptop or your home PC (that is, unless you use the email reader's Keep As New button, and reopen the mail in the other computers—but that defeats the time-saving purpose of the PFC). Using manual copy won't let you merge all these out-of-sync PFCs, but it's the next best thing.

When you manually copy your PFC, it becomes an archive. You won't have access to the copy via the usual method of My Files toolbar icon → Personal Filing Cabinet. Instead, with the manual copy method, you'll rename this PFC and access it within AOL using File menu → Open. Essentially, you're going to transfer files in Windows folders themselves, not via the AOL software.

For example, I want to open the PFC for my work screen name, WristAche, on my machine at home. Using my work PC, I copy it to disk, rename it *Wrist-Ache.pfc*, then open it at home in AOL via File menu → Open. In this section, we go over how to do just that, step by step. Before we get to those details, here are some important caveats to remember:

- By using the manual copy method, you'll end up with two—or more—PFCs: the one that you use in the typical way, via the My Files toolbar icon → Personal Filing Cabinet; and the older, copied PFC you have to access via File menu → Open in AOL.

- A copied PFC, like *WristAche.pfc*, is an archive only. You can view and use the files, even delete them, but nothing new can be added. New mail, newsgroups, saved files, and records of your downloads go into your regular PFC.

Here are the exact steps to follow to manually copy a PFC:

1. Go to Windows Explorer (Windows `Start` menu → `Programs` → `Windows Explorer`).

2. Determine which version of AOL on your computer contains the PFC you want to transfer, and double-click it to open it. If, for instance, the AOL program is located in a folder titled */AOL 30/*, double-click on the */AOL 30/* folder.

3. Double-click the */Organize/* folder which should lie in the */AOL30/* folder.

4. Locate a file called *your_screen_name* (that is, if your screen name is Wrist-Ache, the file will be called *WristAche*). It should be right in the */Organize/* folder, but sometimes it's in a folder called */your_screen_name/*.

   If you have several screen names, make sure you choose the file that corresponds to the PFC you want to copy. The full path from Steps 2–4 should be similar to *C:/AOL30/organize/your_screen_name* where *C:/* is the location of your hard drive and */AOL30/* is the folder that houses the installation of AOL you want to copy the PFC from. Your actual directory names may differ.

5. Right-mouse-click the *your_screen_name* file and select `Copy`.

6. Navigate to your desktop, right-mouse-click the desktop, and select `Paste`.

7. Right-mouse-click the *your_screen_name* file and choose `Rename`. Rename it *your_screen_name.pfc* replacing *your_screen_name* with a screen name currently in use.

8. Launch AOL. You don't need to sign on.

9. To open the archive PFC, follow this path in AOL: `File` menu → `Open` → find the Desktop in the drop down menu → *your_screen_name.pfc*.

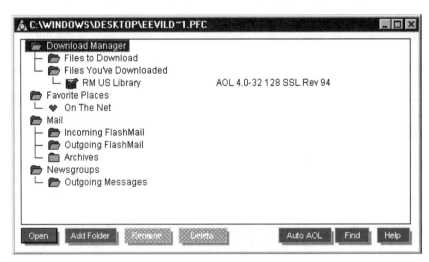

Figure 18-4: The transferred PFC, opened via File → Open

10. You will be looking at a copy of your old PFC, shown in Figure 18-4. You can keep it on the desktop for future reference. Or, even better, you can drag

and drop (or copy and paste) the archive's contents into your new PFC (My Files toolbar icon → Personal Filing Cabinet). Notice that this PFC file is located in the desktop folder in Windows, as evident by the path at the top of the window that begins C:/

PART V

Becoming an AOL Power User

In computer circles, the phrase *power user* refers to a someone who really knows the ins and outs of the program or system she's using. Part of being a power user is taking advantage of *power tools,* often-hidden features that make your software run better. Whatever a specific computer power tool does, a comparison to home-improvement power tools is apt: a saw gets the job done, but a chainsaw is a power tool that gets the job done faster and more easily. Likewise, the ability to type CTRL-1 and see if a member is signed on is a tool; being able to put that member in your Buddy List is a power tool.

We've explained AOL power tools and scattered power-user tips throughout every chapter in this book, but the seven chapters in this part are where we really get into chainsaw country. Most AOL members don't know about the tricks we explain in these chapters, but there's no reason why they shouldn't. These power tools are part of what makes AOL a good ISP for beginners *and* experienced users, contrary to the belief that AOL is only good for training newbies.

You don't have to be a computer geek to be a power user. Even if you're just starting out, skim through these chapters and we guarantee you'll find information you can use. If nothing else, read Chapter 22, *Billing*, and make sure you're not spending too much money on AOL.

After you've been on AOL for a while and know the ropes, you're definitely ready to become an AOL power user. We thought we knew it all, but writing these chapters still taught us a lot. We hope you'll learn even more by reading them.

Chapter 19, *Keyboard Shortcuts*: Pick up some keyboard shortcuts so you can put down your mouse.

Chapter 20, *Downloading*: Downloading a file isn't that hard. What's hard is uncovering AOL's great download utilities.

Chapter 21, *Automatic AOL*: Perhaps the greatest invention for busy people since programmable VCRs.

Chapter 22, *Billing*: Learn how to avoid customer service and maybe save some money.

Chapter 23, *Web Publishing and FTP*: We'll tell you how to make a web page, as long as you promise not to make it blink.

Chapter 24, *Telnet*: It's old, it's ugly, and you've probably never heard of it, but it can be quite useful.

Chapter 25, *Third Party Add-Ons*: Software that can boost AOL's performance.

CHAPTER 19

Keyboard Shortcuts

Sore hands? Sore wrists? This is the age of Repetitive Stress Injury (RSI), including maladies such as carpal tunnel syndrome and tendonitis. After a few hours using your computer, you may notice that your wrists are sore, or your hands are numb. The only surefire way to ward off RSI is to spend less time computing. Fortunately, there are other preventative measures as well. For instance, use your mouse less often. We've found that our mousing hands usually hurt much more than our nonmousing hands. Therefore, this chapter is about navigating AOL (or Windows) with minimal mouse use.

Our favorite method of mouse avoidance is keyboard shortcuts. In this chapter are two tables: both list keyboard shortcuts and the tasks they perform. Table 19-1 lists keyboard shortcuts in alphabetical order; Table 19-2 lists tasks in alphabetical order. Some of these shortcuts are general Windows shortcuts, but some are unique to AOL. We'll also show you how to create up to ten of your own customizable AOL keyboard shortcuts.

One of us has grown fond of the Windows feature MouseKeys. It allows you to use your numeric keypad in place of the mouse. It takes some getting used to, and slows you down at first, but a combination of MouseKeys and keyboard shortcuts decreases your wrist pain greatly. Unfortunately, there is no such feature for Macs.

It's best to accustom yourself to keyboard shortcuts first, maybe making a few of your own, and then, if you're feeling adventurous, trying out MouseKeys. You might notice that in addition to saving your wrists, keyboard shortcuts save time.

At first, you'll still find yourself reaching for the mouse to perform any task, but you're going to have to reteach your brain how to use a computer. It's like breaking any habit: challenging, but possible. We suggest leaving your mouse slightly out of reach to remind you to use keyboard shortcuts whenever possible. Your hands and wrists will thank you.

Shortcut Keys (or, How I Learned to Stop Mousing and Love the Keyboard)

Before we jump into our charts showing all of AOL's keyboard shortcuts, we're going to show you an easy way to figure them out on your own (Windows only). When it comes to menus and toolbar shortcuts, AOL gives you some visual cues by underlining the letter in the menu item that you'll need for the shortcut. For instance, in Figure 19-1, note that the M in Mail Center is underlined. That means Alt-m opens the Mail Center toolbar icon's menu. Underlined letters in menus and toolbar icons are there to remind you which keyboard shortcut to use. As a rule, underlined letters in menus or toolbars always mean that the Alt key and the underlined letter are to be struck. The key you hit will always be lower-case, even if the underlined letter is uppercase.

Figure 19-1: The underlined letter M

When you use a shortcut key to select an AOL toolbar icon or open an AOL menu, you have options for even more keyboard shortcuts. In Figure 19-2, you see that you can use Alt-s to open the Sign Off menu. Note that the n in Switch Screen Name and the S in Sign Off are underlined. Each option within a menu has one letter underlined, and this is the letter you hit on the keyboard to perform that task. Within an open menu or toolbar menu, you need hit only one key to perform a task (it's n, not Alt-n or CTRL-n). So, in Figure 19-2, if you hit the s key, you're signed off; if you hit the n key, you switch screen names.

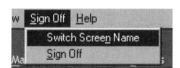

Figure 19-2: Underlined letters in the Sign Off menu

We've given you two ways to look up keyboard shortcuts: alphabetically by shortcut key and alphabetically by task. Mac users: The CTRL key usually corre-lates to your Command key.

Table 19-1: Keyboard Shortcuts Alphabetically by Key

Shortcut Key	Task
Alt	Highlights menubar; navigate with arrow keys and use Enter to choose an option (see also F10)
Alt-a	Selects MY AOL toolbar icon
Alt-c	Selects Channels toolbar icon
Alt-d	Selects Find toolbar icon
Alt-e	Opens Edit menu

Table 19-1: Keyboard Shortcuts Alphabetically by Key (continued)

Shortcut Key	Task
Alt-f	Opens `File` menu
Alt-F4	Signs you off and exits the application in one fell swoop
Alt-h	Opens `Help` menu
Alt-i	Selects `Internet` toolbar icon
Alt-m	Selects `Mail Center` toolbar icon
Alt-p	Selects `People` toolbar icon
Alt-s	Opens `Sign Off` menu
Alt-v	Selects `Favorites` toolbar icon
Alt-w	Opens `Window` menu
Alt-y	Selects `My Files` toolbar icon
CTRL-a	Selects all text
CTRL-b	Bolds (or unbolds) selected text in a document
CTRL-c	Copies text
CTRL-Enter	Sends email and Instant Messages; doesn't initiate them but sends them within an existing IM conversation
CTRL-Esc	Opens Windows 95 `Start` menu
CTRL-f	Finds a given word or phrase in the topmost open window
CTRL-F4	Closes topmost window (don't confuse with `Alt-F4` and log yourself out)
CTRL-F6	Toggles between windows in the open application, including minimized ones
CTRL-g	Pulls up a window, in which you can enter a screen name to get that member's profile
CTRL-i	Initiates Instant Message; doesn't italicize selected text (see also `CTRL-t`)
CTRL-k	Pulls up a window, in which you enter an area's keyword to go directly to that area
CTRL-l	Pulls up a window, in which you enter a screen name and see which chat room the member is in
CTRL-m	Opens a new Write Mail window for composing email
CTRL-n	Creates new text document; good for composing a document when you don't want to open an email window
CTRL-o	Opens a file
CTRL-p	Prints an open text file or graphic file (but not an AOL area)
CTRL-r	Reads new email
CTRL-s	Saves the topmost open text or graphic file (but not an AOL area)
CTRL-t	Italicizes selected text in a document
CTRL-Tab	Toggles between open windows (including minimized ones)
CTRL-u	Underlines selected text in a document
CTRL-v	Pastes text
CTRL-x	Cuts text

Table 19-1: Keyboard Shortcuts Alphabetically by Key (continued)

Shortcut Key	Task
CTRL-z	Undo
CTRL =	Checks spelling
CTRL +	Selects the topmost open window as a Favorite Place; you can then choose to add it to your Favorite Places, add it to an email message, or add it to an Instant Message (this only works if the topmost open window has a red heart icon in the upper right; use numeric keypad or CTRL Shift =)
Esc	Stops incoming text and graphics when they're loading too slowly for your taste
F10	Highlights menubar; navigate with arrow keys and use Enter to choose an option (see also Alt)

Table 19-2: Keyboard Shortcuts Alphabetically By Task

Task	Shortcut Key
Channels toolbar icon, select	Alt-c
Edit menu, open	Alt-e
Email, compose	CTRL-m
Email, read	CTRL-r
Email, select Mail Center toolbar icon	Alt-m
Email, send	CTRL-Enter
Exit	Alt-F4 (also signs you off)
Favorite Place, add to current list	CTRL + (use numeric keypad or CTRL Shift =)
Favorites toolbar icon, select	Alt-v
File, create new text document	CTRL-n
File, open	CTRL-o
File, print	CTRL-p
File, save	CTRL-s
File menu, open	Alt-f
Find in top window	CTRL-f
Find toolbar icon, select	Alt-d
Help menu, open	Alt-h
Instant Message, initiate	CTRL-i
Instant Message, send	CTRL-Enter
Internet toolbar icon, select	Alt-i
Keyword, go to	CTRL-k
Mail Center toolbar icon, select	Alt-m
Member, get profile	CTRL-g
Member, Instant Message	CTRL-i
Member, locate (only works if member is in a chat room)	CTRL-l

Table 19-2: Keyboard Shortcuts Alphabetically By Task (continued)

Task	Shortcut Key
`My AOL` toolbar icon, select	`Alt-a`
`My Files` toolbar icon, select	`Alt-y`
Navigating menu bar	`Alt` or `F10` brings you to menubar; use arrow keys to navigate
`People` toolbar icon, select	`Alt-p`
Sign off	`Alt-F4` (also exits application) `Alt-s`, then hit the `s` key
`Start` menu, open	`CTRL-Esc`
Text, bold	`CTRL-b`
Text, copy	`CTRL-c`
Text, cut	`CTRL-x`
Text, italicize	`CTRL-t`
Text, paste	`CTRL-v`
Text, select all	`CTRL-a`
Text, spellcheck	`CTRL =`
Text, stop incoming	`Esc`
Text, underline	`CTRL-u`
Text, undo	`CTRL-z`
`Window` toolbar icon, select	`Alt-w`
Window, close topmost	`CTRL-F4` (don't confuse with `Alt-F4` and log yourself out)
Windows, toggle between open windows in an application	`CTRL-Tab`
Windows, toggle between open windows in an application	`CTRL-F6`

Creating Your Own Keyboard Shortcuts

To create your own keyboard shortcuts, start here:

> `Favorites` toolbar icon → `My Shortcuts` → `Edit Shortcuts`

In the `Shortcut Title` field, name the shortcut. In the `Keyword/Internet Address` field, type the keyword or URL you want the shortcut to take you to. The `Key` column tells you which two keys to use for the shortcut. Click `Save Changes`.

Benefits

- You can have up to 10 homemade keyboard shortcuts.

- Like any other keyboard shortcut, saves wear and tear on your hands and wrists.

- Allows you to replace AOL's 10 lame shortcuts (like `Sign On a Friend`) with shortcuts you can actually use.

Drawback

- It's hard to create a shortcut for an area that doesn't have a keyword or a URL. For our clumsy solution, see the next section.

Creating Keyboard Shortcuts for Areas with No Keyword

You can also make this work for chat rooms, message boards, newsgroups, and non-keyworded areas-within-areas, but only if the URL is short enough. Because this is confusing, we're giving you step-by-step instructions.

1. Go to the area you want to create the shortcut for.

2. Click the red heart icon in the upper-right corner.

3. Click `Add to Favorites`.

4. Go to your Favorite Places folder (`Favorites` toolbar icon → `Favorite Places`).

5. Single-click the item you want to create a keyboard shortcut for.

6. Click the `Edit` button.

7. Highlight the text in the `Enter the Internet Address` box. It should start with *aol://*.

8. Copy the text, using `CTRL-c` or `Edit` menu → `Copy`.

9. Click OK.

10. Use the same path as the one for creating your own keyboard shortcuts (`Favorites` toolbar icon → `My Shortcuts` → `Edit Shortcuts`).

11. In the `Shortcut Title` field, name the shortcut. In the `Keyword/Internet Address` field, paste the AOL URL (the one that starts with *aol://*). The `Key` column tells you what keys to use for the shortcut.

12. Click `Save Changes`. If the AOL URL is short enough, you've created a keyboard shortcut for that area.

Using MouseKeys

AOL's graphical interface has a lot of keyboard shortcuts built in, but you often can't avoid clicking, double-clicking, and dragging. MouseKeys is a Windows option that allows you to navigate with your numeric keypad instead of the mouse. We know that MouseKeys doesn't have much to do with AOL per se, but with so many millions of AOL members signing on with Windows 95/98, we think it's worthwhile to show those members another way to move around AOL.

Enabling

To enable MouseKeys:

Windows `Start` menu → `Settings` → `Control Panel` → `Accessibility Options` → `Mouse` tab → check `Use MouseKeys`

If you decide you hate MouseKeys, go to the same place and clear Use MouseKeys to turn it off.

When MouseKeys is turned on, a mouse icon appears on the lower-right corner of your Windows toolbar, in your system tray. We'll call that the *mouse tray icon*.

Configuration

To configure MouseKeys, double-click the mouse tray icon or follow this path:

> Windows Start menu → Settings → Control Panel → Accessibility Options → Mouse tab → Settings

Your settings options are:

- Use shortcut: The shortcut to turn MouseKeys on and off is Left Alt-Left Shift-Num Lock. Using this shortcut is convenient, but makes a very strange noise.

- Top speed: We recommend a high speed.

- Acceleration: For maximum control, we recommend a slow acceleration

- Hold down CTRL to speed up and Shift to slow down: We've never used it, but it can't hurt to have it enabled.

- Use MouseKeys when Num Lock is [on/off]: This doesn't really matter.

- Show MouseKey status on screen: This refers to whether or not you want to see the mouse tray icon. We like having this enabled, especially since MouseKeys occasionally inexplicably turns itself off.

Getting to Know MouseKeys

To navigate, use the arrow keys on the numeric keypad to move the mouse in the direction you want it to go. The 7 (Home), 9 (Pg Up), 1 (End), and 3 (Pg Dn) keys move the cursor diagonally. If it moves too fast or too slow, adjust the settings (see "Configuration"). Here are the common MouseKey equivalents:

- To single-click, press the 5 key.

- To double-click, press the + key.

- To use the right mouse button, press the minus (-) key, then press the 5 or + key (to single-click or double-click).

- To go back to the left mouse button, press the * key.

- To hold down your mouse button (for dragging), press the 0 (Ins) key. The mouse tray icon will now have a black left button (if you don't have a mouse tray icon, see "Enabling").

- To drag (once the mouse button is held down), press the navigation (arrow) keys.

- To release the mouse button (after dragging), press the Del key.

CHAPTER 20

Downloading

Downloading simply transfers files from a remote location (AOL, newsgroups, email, the Web) to your computer. It's an easy and cheap way to get screensavers, games, sound clips, pictures, and computer programs of all sorts. With a little exploration, you can find a huge variety of files for every interest and need. Most files are free to download, so downloading is financially risk-free. As a bonus, the AOL download client has some unique features you won't find anywhere else (we cover these in the "Downloading Essentials" section of this chapter). True, there's a chance that downloading could give your computer a virus, but that's easy to prevent (see *viruses*). All in all, downloading is a pretty great idea.

Though we're enthusiastic about the wide variety of files available for download, the variety can make downloading somewhat complex. Because there are so many places from which to download and so many different files to download, we've organized this chapter alphabetically so it's easy for you to look up the information you need. Don't even know what information you need? The "If You're New to Downloading" section below tells you which entries to read to learn the basics.

We use some terms in this chapter you may not recognize. *Binaries* are any non-text downloadable files, such as pictures or computer programs. *Encoded* files (often binaries) have been scrambled so that AOL can't read them. When you unscramble an encoded file, you are *decoding* it. AOL then can read the decoded file and show it to you. Think of decoding as translating a sentence from a language you don't know to English: the sentence says the same thing either way, but in its translated form, you can read it.

There are also a few terms we don't use much in this chapter, but which you need to know once you actually start downloading: freeware, shareware, and payware. Those are three different kinds of computer software, and your downloading journey will be easier if you understand the difference between them. *Freeware* is the term for files that are free to download and free to keep. *Shareware* is software that's free to download. You're supposed to pay for shareware if you're going to keep it, though it would be naïve to assume that everyone does. If you keep shareware without paying for it, it's usually illegal. The cops won't come after you, so let your conscience be your guide. *Payware* is software you have to pay for. Usually you can't download payware; you purchase it and receive it on floppy disk or CD. It's becoming an increasingly popular practice to buy payware online with your credit card number.

A note to AOL 3.0 users: many downloading features explained in this chapter exist in 3.0, but are located in different places. Your download manager is located under the `File` menu, and your preferences are located in the `Members` menu. Buttons might have slightly different names, but you should be able to figure them out.

If You're New to Downloading

- The first thing you'll need to know is where to find downloadable files. See *locating files to download*.

- For the easy, no-frills way to download, see *download now*.

- If you still need step-by-step downloading instructions after you read this chapter, you can find a downloading tutorial at `Keyword: Download 101`.

- Did you skip the introduction to this chapter? Go back and read it, because we explain several terms you need to know when using this chapter.

Downloading Essentials

- Our favorite feature of AOL's Download Manager: if your AOL download is interrupted (call waiting, computer crashes, etc.), you can resume your download where you left off (see *interruptions*).

- You can click `Download Later` to download big files at any scheduled time (see *Automatic AOL*).

- You can decompress (unzip) files with a click of the mouse or configure AOL to decompress files automatically as soon as you sign off (see *decompressing*).

- You don't have to sit in front of your computer for hours watching huge files download. Just check the `Sign Off After Transfer` box.

- Many people worry that downloading files gives their computers viruses. This isn't usually the case, since most software on commercial web sites and in AOL's own software libraries has been thoroughly checked for viruses (see *viruses*).

- Downloading via modem can be slow. See *Automatic AOL* to schedule downloads for times when you don't need your computer or your phone line.

- Files from AOL's software library (`Keyword: File Search` and `Keyword: Download Software`) can be outdated; if getting the newest version of a program is important to you, look for it on the Web instead.

attachments

See *email attachments* in this chapter.

Automatic AOL

Automatic AOL is a feature used primarily for scheduling AOL tasks, and can be useful for downloading. Set up AOL to download large files while you're at work or asleep, which frees your phone line for when you need it. It's also nice to be able to download five files at once, instead of downloading and waiting five separate times.

When you're within any AOL file library, you are presented with two ways to download a file: Download Now or Download Later. To select a file for Automatic AOL downloading, click Download Later.

We won't repeat our lengthy Automatic AOL setup instructions here. For more information, see Chapter 21, *Automatic AOL*, especially the "Downloading" section.

See also *Download Manager*.

binaries

Binaries are, basically, any file that isn't plain text. That could be pictures, sounds, movies, or computer programs. In the realm of downloading, the word "binaries" is usually associated with lewd pictures on Usenet newsgroups.

Downloading binaries from your email, AOL file libraries, or the Web is simple. It's just like downloading a text file. AOL makes it even easier for you by automatically displaying images and playing sound files as soon as they finish downloading. Other binaries need to be located on your hard drive and double-clicked.

Binaries are only complicated when you're reading a newsgroup, or if the binary has been encoded. For help with those situations, see *newsgroups*.

See also *images* and *sounds*.

compressing

When you compress, you make several documents into one, or make a large document into a small one.

To send multiple email attachments, you used to have to compress (or zip) them into one file. With AOL 4.0, Windows users can send multiple attachments with ease; AOL automatically compresses them for you (see also *email attachments* in this chapter). This has been possible on Macs for a while.

If you want to compress files for other purposes, you'll need a utility such as PKZip or WinZip. Mac users should use StuffIt. You can find compression utilities at Keyword: File Search or *http://www.download.com*.

decompressing

When you use the download manager to download files ending with the suffix *.zip*, AOL is set up by default to automatically decompress them when you sign off. You can disable this feature, which forces you to manually decompress using Download Manager or an external client such as WinZip or PKUNZIP. Mac users: your compressed files end with the suffix *.sit*, and, if you disable automatic decompression, you have to use a client such as StuffIt to decompress files.

Decompressing Automatically on Exit

Automatic decompression on sign-off is the default. The decompressed files are placed in the *C:\America Online 4.0\download* directory, or whichever directory you've designated (see also **directory**). To enable or disable this feature, follow this path:

> MY AOL toolbar icon → Preferences → Download → Automatically Decompress Files at Sign-off checkbox → OK

Benefits of automatic decompression

- You don't have to bother decompressing later, either with AOL or another decompression utility, such as PKunzip.

- You don't even have to think about decompressing the file. It just happens. This is especially useful if you don't know the first thing about decompressing files.

Drawbacks

- If you just want to exit AOL quickly, you'll still have to wait a brief moment while the files decompress.

- If you download a rogue file, such as a Trojan horse or *.zip* file with a virus in it, AOL runs it, thereby giving the program a chance to do damage. (See **Trojan horses** in Chapter 8, *Email*, for information on avoiding rogue files.)

To Manually Decompress a File That Ends in .zip

> My Files toolbar icon → Download Manager → Show Files Downloaded → highlight the file you want to decompress → Decompress

Figure 20-1 shows how to decompress a previously downloaded file.

Benefits

- The Decompress button in Download Manager is second easiest way to decompress (having AOL do it automatically when you sign off is the easiest).

- You don't have to bother with decompression utilities. The same is true when you decompress automatically on exit from the AOL software.

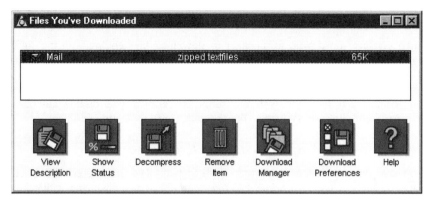

Figure 20-1: Decompressing a previously downloaded file

To Delete zip Files Automatically After Decompressing

The default is for AOL to leave your *.zip* files alone after you decompress them. To have AOL delete your *.zip* files after decompression (or change back to the default):

> MY AOL toolbar icon → Preferences → Download → Delete ZIP files after decompression checkbox → OK

Benefit of deleting zip files

- Saves disk space by deleting zip files after you've decompressed them.

Drawback

- If something goes wrong with the program associated with the *.zip* file and you have to reinstall, you'll have to redownload, since you won't have the *.zip* file anymore

delete previously downloaded file

To trim the list of files in your Download Manager:

> My Files toolbar icon → Download Manager → Show Files Downloaded → highlight the file you whose listing you want to remove → Remove Item

Benefit

- Keeps your download directory uncluttered.

Drawback

- You delete the file information, not the actual files. The files you've downloaded will still be in the folder(s) you downloaded them into. To delete those files, go to the directory on your hard drive where you saved the files.

directory, default

The default directory for AOL 4.0 for Windows 95/98 downloads is *C:\America Online 4.0\download*. To view or change the default directory, do one of the following:

*   My Files toolbar icon → Download Manager → Select Destination → locate a directory on your hard drive and highlight it → Save

*   MY AOL toolbar icon → Preferences → Download → Use this directory as default for downloads → enter directory name (or click Browse to locate a directory on your hard drive) → OK

Benefit

*   You can keep all your downloads in one spot (like *C:\download*). This is useful if some of your downloads come from outside AOL (external web browsers, other ISPs).

Drawback

*   Changing your default download directory could confuse you later, especially if you're looking for downloads you sent to the previous default directory. See *locating files after downloading* in this chapter.

download later

See **Automatic AOL** and **Download Manager**.

Download Manager

The Download Manager is an important and underutilized tool. To access it, click the My Files toolbar icon and select Download Manager.

The Download Manager lets you put files you want to download in a "to-do" list. Then you can download them all at once, either during the same session or another time entirely (see also **Automatic AOL** in this chapter). You can also use the Download Manager to view a list of files you've already downloaded, their description, and the directory you downloaded them to. With the Download Manager, it's easy to decompress your files, resume an interrupted download, and adjust your downloading preferences. The main Download Manager screen is shown in Figure 20-2.

Downloading Files in Your Download Manager Queue

My Files toolbar icon → Download Manager → Download

This means you're downloading the files right now, not scheduling the download for another time. See **Automatic AOL** in this chapter for information about downloading later.

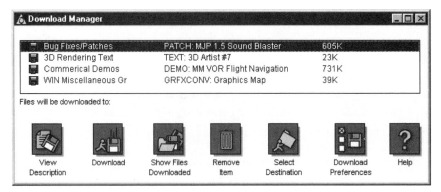

Figure 20-2: The Download Manager interface

Turning Download Manager confirmation on and off

Whenever you add anything to your Download Manager queue, you'll get a long, annoying confirmation screen that says:

> The file has been added to your download list. To view your list or start the download, select 'Download Manager' below (or select from the file menu).

The default is to give you this confirmation screen all the time. To disable or enable confirmation:

MY AOL toolbar icon → Preferences → Download → Confirm Additions to My Download List checkbox → OK

Benefit of disabling

• After seeing the confirmation once, that's probably enough. You'll relish the chance to turn it off.

Removing a File from Download Manager's Queue

My Files toolbar icon → Download Manager → highlight the file you want to remove → Remove Item

"Unmarks" the item; that is, removes it from the list of files to be downloaded by the Download Manager. This function used to be called "Delete item," which was a misnomer since it didn't actually delete anything.

Benefit

• You can change your mind about downloading that huge file before you start.

Marking Files for Later Download with Download Manager

To mark a file for later download with Download Manager, just click the Download Later button instead of the Download Now button when you're about to start downloading.

"Marking" files just means that you put them in the Download Manager's queue of files to download. You can have as many files as you'd like in your Download Manager. Whenever you want to download an item, click **Download Later**, which adds it to your queue. When you activate Download Manager, they should all download at once.

See also *compressing*, *interruptions*, and *preferences*.

download now

From any file library, double-click the file you want to download. Click **Download Now**. A window pops up; here, you can change the default name of the file and which directory on your hard drive it is saved to. Click **Save**.

A **File Transfer** window opens. A bar starts filling up with blue; the blue indicates how much of the file has been downloaded. Text under the blue bar tells you approximately how much time is left in the download, which is useful for long downloads. The time may be inaccurate if your connection is very fast (like a cable modem or a connection through your office LAN) or slow (a 9600-baud modem).

You will see a pop-up window that tells you the download is finished. The file has now been downloaded to your computer.

email attachments

An attachment is a file that arrives along with an email message, but which is not part of the email message itself. People use attachments to send pictures, word-processing files, programs, sounds, and many other files that can't be included in the body of the email message. You can also use attachments to send text files larger than AOL's outgoing mail limit of 31K.

You should know that if you're sending only to other AOL members, you can send and receive pictures without using attachments (see *images* in Chapter 8, *Email*). We also can't tell you enough times: be cautious when downloading attachments from people you don't know (see also *Trojan horses* in Chapter 8, *Email*).

To download an email file attachment you've received, open the email message and click **Download Now**.

In the headers of the email, you'll see the name of the file, its size, and approximately how long it will take to download. When downloading very large attachments, you might want to click **Download Later**, so you can download them with Automatic AOL at the end of the session or some other time (see also "Email" in Chapter 21, *Automatic AOL*).

Please note that when you attach multiple files to one email message, the multiple attachments are automatically compressed (sometimes called zipped) into one *.zip* file for the recipient. This isn't a bad situation for you since zipping speeds the delivery of the email and the time you spend downloading, and you can set up AOL to do decompress attachments for you automatically.

Email Attachments in Automatic AOL

To download email attachments during your Automatic AOL sessions:

> `Mail Center` toolbar icon → `Set up Automatic AOL (Flashsession)` → `Download files that are attached to unread mail` checkbox

This is the only way you can get a virus via email, so we don't recommend it (see also ***Trojan horses*** Chapter 8, *Email*).

MIME (.mme) Attachments

If you receive an email attachment with the suffix *.mme*, it's in what's called *MIME format*. This happens when the AOL email reader can't figure out how to decode an attached file. You'll have to download the file and decode it yourself. Many decoding programs are MIME-capable, such as Wincode for Windows and Decoder for Macs. You can find the latest versions of these and other decoders at *http://www.download.com* and *http://www.shareware.com*.

---

file information, retaining

The default is to retain information about your last 100 downloads. To make this number anything from 1 to 1,000:

> `My AOL` toolbar icon → `Preferences` → `Download` → `Retain Information About My Last [number] Downloads` → `OK`

This refers to the number of files stored in the Download Manager's `Show Files Downloaded` folder. To view the files:

> `My Files` toolbar icon → `Download Manager` → `Show Files Downloaded`

---

finish later

Once you've started downloading a file, you can click the `Finish Later` button under the blue status bar to pause the download. The partially downloaded file is kept in your Download Manager. To later pick up the files where it left off:

> `My Files` toolbar icon → `Download Manager` → highlight partially downloaded file → `Download`

Benefit

- You can stop downloading and resume the download later or during another session. It picks up where it left off; try that with Internet Explorer or Netscape Navigator!

FTP

FTP stands for File Transfer Protocol—a set of commands that are used to transfer a file from one computer to another. Most people have traditionally used FTP to access and download files from a public server. FTP is so integrated with the Web these days that you don't need to know much about FTP. In fact, you may have already used your browser to download from an FTP site without even knowing it.

We cover FTP in more detail in Chapter 23, *Web Publishing and FTP.*

images

The default is to automatically display graphic files as they're downloading. To disable this option (or enable it again):

> MY AOL toolbar icon → Preferences → Download → Display image files on download checkbox → OK

Displaying on download works with *.avi, .art, .jpg, .bmp,* and *.gif* files. The alternative is to use a separate graphics viewer, such as Internet Explorer or QuickTime Picture Viewer, after you sign off.

Benefit of displaying on download

- You don't have to bother with *.gif* or *.jpg* viewers; AOL just pops that image up as soon as it's downloaded.

Drawbacks

- This doesn't work with Automatic AOL or Download Manager. It only works if you're taking the "Download Now" route.

- Can slow down your online session.

interruptions

When your download gets interrupted, you can pick up where it left off later. We're not sure that any other online service has this feature, which can be found at either of the following:

- My Files toolbar icon → Download Manager → highlight the interrupted file → Download

- My Files toolbar icon → Personal Filing Cabinet → Files to Download folder → right-mouse-click the interrupted file → Download

Don't delete the already downloaded portion of the file, or you won't be able to resume downloading where you left off.

Benefit .

- It saves you time, because you don't have to start all over again, say, if you decide to use your phone line, or you lose your modem connection.

Drawbacks

- It doesn't work 100% of the time. Then you do have to start all over again. So it goes.

- It doesn't work for web downloads. The good news is, software exists that lets you resume interrupted web downloads. See *Web*.

locating files to download

AOL has a number of download libraries that include both shareware and commercial software. A few channels have their own comprehensive software libraries, and there are some reliable places on the Web to locate downloadable software. We briefly tell you what you'll find in each of these realms.

Most of the information in this chapter applies to downloading from AOL file libraries. For additional information about other download sources, see *news-groups* and *Web*.

AOL's Main Download Library

You can find files in AOL's main download library by searching or by browsing.

To search, go to `Keyword: File Search` and click `Shareware`. The best way to find what you want is to make your search narrow. First, check the box next to a category: Applications, Development, DOS, Education, Games, Graphics & Animation, Hardware, Music & Sound, OS/2, Telecommunications, or Windows. Choose a timeframe (files uploaded in the past week, past month, or any time). Enter a specific search phrase, but don't get too specific or you might not get the most current version of the software. For instance, searching for `QT16.exe` gets you QuickTime for Windows, but not the newest version, which is called QT32. Searching for `quicktime for windows` will be more helpful.

To browse, go to `Keyword: Download Software`. The categories you can look through are Animation & Video, Business & Finance, Desktop Publishing, Development & Programming, Education & Reference, Fun & Games, Graphics, Home & Hobby, Internet, Music & Sound, Networking & Telecommunications, Personal Digital Assistants, and Utilities & Tools. If you don't know specifically what you're looking for, this is a better bet than `Keyword: File Search`, even though the two have the same files.

AOL Channel Download Libraries

The Personal Finance Channel has a number of useful resources gathered at `Keyword: PF Software`. The categories of software are: Best Picks, Download Tools, Accounting, Career and Job Hunting, Demo Programs, Financial Planning, Home Management, Investment Programs, Loan Calculators, Organizers and PIMs, Portfolio Management, and Real Estate. Also a weekly newsletter and software reviews.

The Sports Channel's well-organized file library is at `Keyword: Sports Libraries`. The categories are: Toolbox, New Files, First Round Picks, Baseball, Basketball, Bowling, Boxing, Extreme Multimedia Library, Football, Golf, Gymnastics, Hockey, Horse Racing, Horse Sports, Lacrosse, Martial Arts, Motor Sports, Roller Skating, Soccer, Sports Cards Collecting, SportsMart, Tennis, Winter Sports, Wrestling, and Other Sports.

Many individual AOL content areas have their own download libraries, from Japanimation Station's anime video clips to the Pet Care forum's collection of horse noises to About Work's fax templates. Explore AOL's content areas (see Chapter 15, *AOL Content Reference*) and you're sure to find plenty to download.

Download libraries on the Web

Of course, there are innumerable web pages from which to download. You should note that you can't use AOL's download tools or the download manager when you download from the Web, so you won't have access to its features. A couple of our favorite sites for useful computing tools are *http://www.download.com* and *http://www.shareware.com*.

locating files after downloading

If you just know you downloaded that file but you can't find it, check here:

My Files toolbar icon → Download Manager → Show Files Downloaded → click the file you want to locate → Show Status

You'll see the directory into which the file was downloaded.

Benefit

*   Makes it easy to find previously downloaded files if you change your default directory occasionally—or if you're just forgetful.

MIME

See *email attachments* in this chapter and *MIME* in Chapter 8, *Email*.

newsgroups, downloading from

Downloading from newsgroups can be a tricky business. First you'll have to unblock your account, then you'll have to figure out the best way to get files from the newsgroup to your computer. We help you with both these problems.

Allowing Binary Downloads from Newsgroups

By default, all accounts are set up to block binary downloads from newsgroups. You can, however, turn this blocking off:

Keyword: Newsgroups → Parental Controls button → click the radio button next to the appropriate screen name → Edit → clear the box next to Block binary downloads → Save

You must be signed on with the master account (see also "Master Versus Additional Screen Names" in Chapter 3, *Screen Names, Passwords, and Signing On*). By the way, if you're wondering where all the raunchy *alt.binaries.** groups are, check the box next to Use full newsgroups list.

Downloading from Newsgroups

AOL walks you through this process. When you read a post with a binary attached, you'll be prompted to Download File. Do so. The file is saved on your hard drive. Graphic binary files (.art, .bmp, .gif, and .jpg) are automatically displayed (if they aren't, see *images*). Sound files are downloaded, and then a sound player application pops up. Click the arrow button to play the sound clip.

Sometimes, you get a message that a file is too large to be viewed by AOL. Click Download File to download it, then open it in a word-processing program (like Microsoft Word) or text reader (such as Notepad).

Encoded Binaries

When you read a newsgroup post with an encoded binary attached, a dialog box prompts you to either Download File or Download Article.

When you click the Download File button, the file downloads and is decoded automatically. A player pops up for sound/multimedia files, and images are automatically displayed (unless you've altered the default preferences; see also *images*). We strongly recommend this option.

If you click the Download Article button, you're doing it the hard way. You need to decode the file yourself with a decoding utility. If you don't already have a decoding utility, you'll have to find one at Keyword: File Search or a web page. We like Wincode, a program we found at *http://www.download.com*. Decoders tend to be fairly easy to use, but they're all different, so you're on your own. You might as well click Download File and let AOL do the work for you.

Benefits to decoding manually

- You can see the download...eventually.

- One encoded file could contain several smaller, encoded files. When you decode manually with Download Article, you see all the files. When you let AOL decode the file automatically with the Download File button, you only see the first file. Usually, when more than one file has been encoded, the subject or body of the newsgroup post says so.

Drawback

- By the time you download the decoding program and get it working, you've probably forgotten what you wanted to download in the first place.

Parental Controls

To adjust downloading Parental Controls:

    Keyword: Parental Controls → Fine Tune with Custom Controls
    → Downloading → Download Controls

Your options, and what they really do are:

- **Block AOL Software Library Downloads**: Disables downloading from AOL software libraries, and even blocks kids from reading the file descriptions; at least they won't know what they're missing. Incidentally, this probably isn't necessary, since AOL file libraries have (supposedly) been screened for objectionable content. Unless you set Kids Only Access, too, your kid can still download from anywhere on the Web.

- **Block FTP Downloads**: Does just what it says (if you don't know what FTP is, see *FTP*). The catch is that it only works for FTP'ing through AOL's FTP client. If an external client is used, your child can FTP.

Another Parental Controls option is to restrict your child's web access:

> Keyword: Parental Controls → Fine Tune with Custom Controls → Web → Web Controls

If you choose Access Kids Only Sites, your child is only able to see (and thus download from) web sites approved for 6- to 12-year-olds. Young Teen access allows access only to web sites that have been deemed appropriate for that age group. Mature Teen blocks selected sites. However, filtering schemes aren't foolproof; not every site can be screened or blocked (see also Chapter 28, *Parental Controls*).

When you are done adjusting Parental Controls, click OK.

There is a Parental Control for newsgroups that affects downloading. By default, all accounts are set up to block binary downloads from newsgroups. To turn this blocking off:

> Keyword: Newsgroups → Parental Controls button → click the radio button next to the appropriate screen name → Edit → clear the box next to Block binary downloads → Save

---

pausing

See *finish later*.

---

pictures

See *images*.

---

preferences

To adjust your Download Preferences:

> My AOL toolbar icon → Preferences → Download

or:

> My Files toolbar icon → Download Manager → Download Preferences

The Download Preferences screen is shown in Figure 20-3.

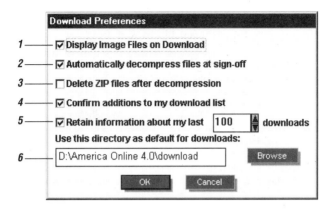

Figure 20-3: The Download Preferences screen

This information can be found elsewhere in the chapter, but for your convenience, we've gathered all the downloading Preferences together.

1. **Display Image Files on Download**: The default is to automatically display graphic files (*.art, .avi, .bmp, .gif,* and *.jpg*) as they're downloading. The alternative is to disable this option and use a separate graphics viewer after you sign off.

2. **Automatically decompress files at sign-off**: When you download compressed (zipped) files, the default is for AOL to automatically decompress them when you sign off. The decompressed files are placed in the */aolxx/download* folder. If you disable this option, you have to decompress the files manually, either with the Download Manager's **Decompress** button or with a separate decompression utility, such as PKunzip.

3. **Delete ZIP files after decompression**: The default is to have this option disabled: AOL leaves your *.zip* files alone after you decompress them. If you enable it, AOL deletes your *.zip* files after decompression, which saves hard drive space but makes it impossible to ever reinstall the software contained in the *.zip* file.

4. **Confirm additions to my download list**: The default is to give you a long, annoying confirmation screen whenever you add anything to your Download Manager queue. Disabling this option means you won't see that confirmation screen anymore.

5. **Retain information about my last [number] downloads**: The default is to retain information about your last 100 downloads. This refers to the number of files stored in the Download Manager's **Files You've Downloaded** folder. To view the information, use the Download Manager's **Show Files Downloaded** button.

6. **Use this directory as default for downloads**: The default directory for downloads is *C:\America Online 4.0\download*. To change the

default directory, use the **Browse** button to navigate to the directory of your choice, then click **Save**.

When you are done adjusting Download Preferences, click OK.

read description

When you are in any AOL software library, you can highlight a file and click the **Read Description** button—or double-click the file—to learn more about the file. You learn information such as the time it takes to download the file, the equipment you need to use it after you download it, and the number of times it has been downloaded (called the *download count*). Information for some files is more complete than for others, depending on who uploads the file.

remove item

The **Remove Item** button within the Download Manager removes a file from the Download Manager's queue of files to download. See also *Download Manager*.

sign off after downloading

If you've just started downloading a large file, you have two options:

- Watch the file download, then sign off or stay signed on after it has downloaded completely.

- Click the **Sign Off After Transfer** checkbox, walk away from your computer, and get on with your busy life. When the file is done downloading, AOL signs off your account.

sound

If you're looking for downloadable *.wav* files, try **Keyword: File Search →**
Shareware. Check the **Music & Sound** box and enter any search phrase (such as the name of a favorite movie or band) in the box.

There are also many web pages devoted entirely to sound files. There is an index of those pages at *http://www.yahoo.com/Computers_and_Internet/Multimedia/ Sound/*.

When you download a sound from any AOL software library, it is played instantly (assuming you have a sound card and speakers). Sound files downloaded from the Web or chosen to **Download Later** won't be played automatically (see *Automatic AOL* and *Download Manager*). In those cases, you have to locate the downloaded *.wav* file on your hard drive and double-click to hear it.

We think changing the `File's Done` download sound is an excellent use for *.wav* files (these instructions are for Windows 95/98 users):

> Windows `Start` menu → `Settings` → `Control Panel` → `Sounds` → scroll down to the `America Online` section to locate `File's Done`, then highlight it → `Browse` → locate file on your hard drive → `OK`

Figure 20-4 shows us replacing `File's Done` with a new sound.

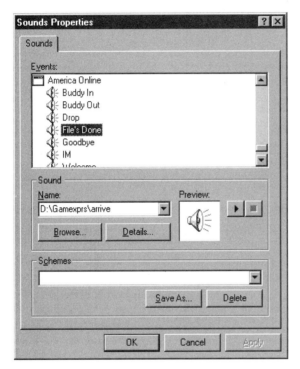

Figure 20-4: Changing the File's Done event sound in Windows

stopping

To stop any download in progress, click the `Cancel` button.

If you need to stop downloading but want to resume eventually, click the `Finish Later` button. See also *finish later*.

Many people hate those automatic "updates" AOL forces you to download sometimes when you sign off. You know the ones: they end in *.utf* and are accompanied by a window explaining that this download is for your own good. There is no real way to stop these downloads other than `CTRL-Alt-Delete`. You might as well let the download run its course.

view downloaded files

To see a list of files you've downloaded on AOL:

> `My Files` toolbar icon → `Download Manager` → `Show Files Downloaded`

Each item in `Files Downloaded` is part of a list of the files you've downloaded. These items are not actual files; those are located in your *download* directory.

See also *directory* and *locating files after downloading*.

viruses

Some people are afraid to download because they don't want to risk getting a computer virus. Relax! Most software on commercial web sites and in AOL's own software libraries has been thoroughly checked for viruses. Besides that, there are two basic rules you can follow to keep your computer safe from viruses:

- Never download email file attachments from strangers. And think twice about downloading a file attachment with an *.exe* extension, unless you trust the source.

- Use a virus-scanning program (such as McAfee VirusScan) to check all downloaded files for viruses.

See also *viruses* and *Trojan horses* in Chapter 8, *Email.*

Web, downloading from

Downloading from the Web is fairly self-explanatory. You usually are told "click here to download" or some other kind of instruction. When you're asked to choose a download directory and filename, you can save downloaded files from the Web into the same directory as your AOL downloads; then they're all in one place. See also *default directory*.

You can't use Download Manager when you download from the Web, even if you're using AOL's integrated web browser.

If you plan to do a lot of downloading from the Web, you should think about downloading GetRight, a shareware utility available at *http://www.head-lightsw.com/getright.html.*

GetRight resumes interrupted web downloads the same way the Download Manager resumes interrupted AOL downloads (see also *interruptions*).

zip files

See *compressing* and *decompressing*.

CHAPTER 21

Automatic AOL

Automatic AOL (formerly known as FlashSessions) automates tasks such as sending email, retrieving email, downloading files, sending posts (for both Usenet newsgroups and AOL message boards), and retrieving posts. Automatic AOL does this by signing on to your account (if you're not already signed on) and executing the tasks you've told it to.

Automatic AOL is, in some ways, a vestige. Automatic AOL's heyday was the time before unlimited access and flat fees. Because signing on to AOL was like calling long distance, people used Automatic AOL to save money by spending less time online. They'd spend minutes downloading a day's worth of newsgroup postings, then spend hours reading them offline, for free. They could spend a free 15 minutes writing a long email offline, then sign on for 10 seconds to send it. Today, only members on the Limited and Light Usage price plans save money with Automatic AOL (see also Chapter 22, *Billing*).

Another time Automatic AOL was popular was during the busy-signal crisis that followed the switch to flat-fee pricing. Everyone enjoyed the luxury of signing on for unlimited periods of time at only $19.95 per month, and as a result, modem lines got tied up, and it became difficult to connect to AOL. Crafty members avoided busy signals by writing email offline, then setting up Automatic AOL to sign on and send it at a low-traffic time. While Automatic AOL was signed on at, say, 4 a.m., it could also be busily downloading newsgroup posts, new email, and message board posts, all of which could be read offline the next day (perhaps while you incessantly redialed your modem?). AOL has improved their modem capacity, but if your city still has busy signal problems, you should use Automatic AOL this way.

Today, most members have unlimited online time and no busy-signal woes, so Automatic AOL has fallen out of fashion. However, it's still useful for freeing up your phone line. If your phone is in use for most of your waking hours, or if you want to keep your phone line open for incoming calls, you can use Automatic AOL to perform tasks late at night or while you're at work. With Automatic AOL, you can write email offline while you wait for a phone call, download large files in your sleep, or read all your favorite newsgroups while someone else in your house uses the phone.

We don't use Automatic AOL much anymore, but we think it's a great feature. You never know when you might need it!

The main screen for Automatic AOL settings is shown in Figure 21-1.

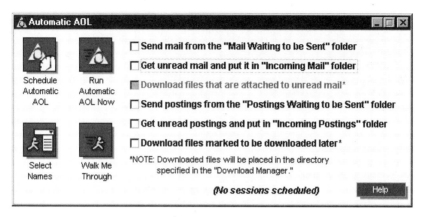

Figure 21-1: Automatic AOL preferences

If You're New to Automatic AOL

- The easiest way to set up Automatic AOL for the first time is to let AOL walk you through it. See "The Easy Way."

- You can't use Automatic AOL while you're signed on as a guest (i.e., from someone else's computer where your screen name does not appear on the Sign On screen).

- Your computer must be on and the AOL application must be open for Automatic AOL to work. You can be signed on, but you don't have to be (see "Scheduling").

Automatic AOL Essentials

- Unless you store your password, you won't be able to schedule Automatic AOL sessions for another time. See the "Screen Names and Passwords" section of this chapter. You also need to check the Enable Scheduler box for a scheduled Automatic AOL session to work.

- If you schedule an Automatic AOL session for the middle of the night, make sure the sound of your modem won't disturb you (or anyone else in your home). You can turn your modem connect sound down or turn it off.

  From the Sign On screen click Setup → Connection Devices → highlight the modem you want to modify → Edit → select the option from the Speaker volume drop-down menu → OK.

- We're willing to bet that the most popular Automatic AOL activity is retrieving new email during scheduled sessions. See "Email" for instructions.

- Automatic AOL settings and preferences apply to all screen names on your account. (Each screen name, however, has its own Personal Filing Cabinet, and thus has its own incoming/outgoing mail folders, incoming/outgoing newsgroup post folders, and Download Manager.) However, Automatic AOL only runs for the screen name or screen names you select. See also "Screen Names and Passwords" in this chapter.

- We often suggest that you schedule Automatic AOL sessions for the middle of the night. However, keep in mind that approximately once a month AOL shuts down for maintenance at 4 a.m. EST. There is no set schedule for this, so you're just going to have to take your chances. The worst thing that can happen is that your Automatic AOL session fails, and you try again another time.

The Easy Way

We've written this chapter with a bias towards setting your preferences manually. If you want a more step-by-step, tutorial-oriented approach, your best bet is to have AOL give you a "walk-through." The first time you set up Automatic AOL, the path to follow to get a walk-through is this:

Mail Center toolbar icon → Set up Automatic AOL (Flashsessions) → Continue

AOL asks you a series of questions about how you want Automatic AOL to be set up.

After that, when you want to adjust your Automatic AOL settings, you can still be walked through, but the path is slightly different:

Mail Center toolbar icon → Set up Automatic AOL (Flashsessions) → Walk Me Through → Continue

The on-screen instructions are so clear that we're not going to waste your time going over them here. However, we'd like to remind you to see the sections of this chapter that pertain to performing specific Automatic AOL tasks; just telling Automatic AOL to do something isn't enough. To cover all the bases, see the following subsections of the "Individual Automatic AOL Tasks" section: "Downloading," "Email," "Message Boards," and "Newsgroups."

The rest of this chapter covers configuring Automatic AOL manually.

Setting Up Automatic AOL

The first time you set up Automatic AOL manually, you perform these steps in order. After that, you can adjust your settings in any order. Just remember this path:

My AOL toolbar icon → Preferences → Auto AOL

It brings you to your main Automatic AOL preferences screen, shown in Figure 21-1.

Choosing Automatic AOL Tasks

Just check the boxes next to the tasks you want to perform. However, checking the boxes doesn't ensure that those tasks will get done. To cover all the bases, see the following subsections of the "Individual Automatic AOL Tasks" section: "Downloading," "Email," "Message Boards," and "Newsgroups."

Screen Names and Passwords

Your Automatic AOL session can include one screen name or all five. Just be aware that if you select more than one screen name for Automatic AOL, your Automatic AOL settings and preferences apply to all selected screen names. For example, let's say TiredWritr and CasbahMA are two screen names on your account. You select them both for Automatic AOL. You can't have TiredWritr's Automatic AOL session retrieve new email and *not* have CasbahMA's Automatic AOL session retrieve new email. If you set preferences for one Automatic AOL screen name, you set preferences for all Automatic AOL screen names.

Another important thing to know is that you need to store your password to schedule an Automatic AOL session for another time. This is different (and safer) than storing your password for one-click sign on, which we explain in the section "Passwords" in Chapter 3, *Screen Names, Passwords, and Signing On.*

The first time you set up Automatic AOL, this is the path to select screen names and save their passwords:

> Mail Center toolbar icon → Set up Automatic AOL (Flashsessions)
> → Expert Setup → Select Names

Subsequent times you set up Automatic AOL, this is the path to select screen names and save their passwords:

> Mail Center toolbar icon → Set up Automatic AOL (Flashsessions)
> → Select Names

Whichever path you have to take, you see a screen that lists all the screen names on your account, like the one shown in Figure 21-2. Check the boxes next to the desired screen name(s). For each screen name you've checked, enter the screen name's password in the Password box. Click OK.

If you're online when you activate Automatic AOL, it runs only for the screen name you're using, no matter how many you've selected. To activate Automatic AOL for all the screen names you've selected, you must be signed off (see "Scheduling").

Benefit of selecting screen names

- If you're only using one screen name, you'll only have to do this once, ever.

Drawbacks

- If you have multiple screen names, you'll have to make sure the right one is checked.

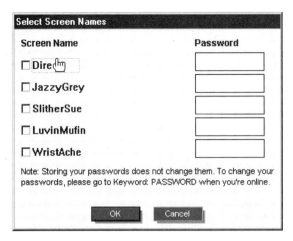

Figure 21-2: Storing passwords for Automatic AOL

- All screen names are able to change Automatic AOL settings, which affect every screen name using Automatic AOL. You should check to make sure other people using your account haven't changed the settings.

- If you share a multiple-screen-name account with other people, make sure they know how to select their own screen names for Automatic AOL (using the path we've given above). Otherwise, they might be confused as to why Automatic AOL never works for their screen name. Worse yet, if you don't have your PFC passworded, other screen names might get confused and mistake your Automatic AOL email and downloads for theirs.

- Automatic AOL redials your modem for every screen name. This could get annoying if you haven't turned your modem sound off (see "Automatic AOL Essentials" for instructions).

Benefit of storing passwords

- Storing your password allows you to schedule sessions for whatever time you wish. If you don't store your password, you'll have to physically sign on to AOL to activate Automatic AOL, which defeats the purpose if you're doing it to avoid connectivity problems or to free up your phone line. See also "Scheduling."

Drawback of storing passwords

- If you store your password for Automatic AOL, anyone who can turn on your computer can run Automatic AOL and read your email.

Scheduling

Scheduling an Automatic AOL session for another time is like setting your VCR to record a TV show you won't be there to watch. You fiddle with the controls a bit, then let the machinery do all the work. There are two ways to schedule a session:

set the controls manually or let AOL walk you through the steps. Either way, you can be signed on or signed off when you schedule your sessions.

If you've never set up Automatic AOL before, this is the path to follow:

Mail Center toolbar icon → Set up Automatic AOL (Flashsessions) → Expert Setup → Schedule Automatic AOL → check Enable Scheduler → OK

After you adjust your Automatic AOL settings once, the path you follow to adjust settings subsequent times is different:

Mail Center toolbar icon → Run Automatic AOL (Flashsessions) Now → Schedule Automatic AOL → check Enable Scheduler → OK

No matter which path you follow, you have to choose days, starting time, and frequency of Automatic AOL sessions. The on-screen instructions are adequate. Just remember to leave the AOL application open, though not signed on, at the scheduled time, and make sure you've selected screen names and stored your password (see "Screen Names and Passwords" in this chapter).

Benefits

- Gets things done when you're out, asleep, or won't need your phone for anything else.

- Helps circumvent connectivity problems.

Canceling Scheduled Sessions

To cancel your future Automatic AOL scheduled sessions:

Mail Center toolbar icon → Set up Automatic AOL (Flashsessions) → Schedule Automatic AOL → clear the box next to Enable Scheduler → OK

You don't have to clear the boxes next to the days of the week, you just have to clear the box next to Enable Scheduler. All future scheduled Automatic AOL sessions are canceled, not just the one that is coming soonest. Check Enable Scheduler to resume your Automatic AOL schedule.

To skip an individual session or two while leaving your overall Automatic AOL schedule intact, just exit the AOL application or turn your computer off. Whenever you exit the AOL application you're reminded that you have Automatic AOL sessions scheduled. Some people find this confirmation annoying; some find it helpful. Either way, the only way to get rid of it is to cancel all your scheduled sessions.

Activating Automatic AOL

To begin an Automatic AOL session (whether you're signed on or off, and whether or not you've scheduled a session):

Mail Center toolbar icon → Run Automatic AOL (Flashsessions) Now → Run Automatic AOL Now → Begin

If you were online when you started the session, you'll be signed off as soon as the session is over if you check the Sign Off When Finished box.

Benefit

- You can write a ton of mail or newsgroup postings offline and then jump on for one quick Automatic AOL session to send them all, immediately, in minutes.

Drawback

- If you're using Automatic AOL to avoid heavy-traffic times or get things done while you're out, this option doesn't help you, since you have to be present to do it.

Individual Automatic AOL Tasks

All these instructions assume you've used the previous sections of this chapter to set up Automatic AOL. None of these instructions will work if you haven't told AOL to perform the task you want it to do (download files, retrieve email, etc). If you haven't chosen Automatic AOL's tasks yet, do so now:

> MY AOL toolbar icon → Preferences → Auto AOL → check the boxes next to the tasks you want to perform

Downloading

When you're within any AOL file library, you are always presented with two ways to download a file: Download Now or Download Later. To select a file for Automatic AOL downloading, click Download Later. You get a pop-up screen, where you can click Download Manager to see your queue of files marked for Automatic AOL download. You can also click OK; the file is still put in the Download Manager queue.

Benefit

- Instead of downloading files while you're online, you can mark them for later download. This saves time, especially when downloading large files.

The file is downloaded during your next Automatic AOL session into whichever directory you've set for downloads; the default for AOL 4.0 is *C:\America Online 4.0\download*. To view or change your default download directory, follow this path:

> MY AOL toolbar icon → Preferences → Download → Use this directory as default for downloads: → OK

If you want to, you can configure Automatic AOL to download files that are attached to incoming email, but we don't recommend it:

> MY AOL toolbar icon → Preferences → Auto AOL → check Download files that are attached to unread mail

This checkbox is grayed out until you check the `Get unread mail and put it in 'Incoming Mail' folder` checkbox.

Benefit to downloading email attachments with Automatic AOL

- Email and attached files are downloaded at the same time. You won't have to sign back on to retrieve email attachments.

Drawback

- Downloading email attachments is the only way you can get a virus via email, so our official advice is: don't do it! (see also *viruses* and *Trojan Horses* in Chapter 8.)

Email

Most people use Automatic AOL to send and retrieve email if they use Automatic AOL at all. Fortunately, it's easy.

Reading email offline

If you have set up AOL to retrieve your unread email (see "Setting Up Automatic AOL"), you won't have to do anything else except read it. To read mail you've downloaded during an Automatic AOL session:

> `Mail Center` toolbar icon → `Read Offline Mail` → `Incoming/Saved Mail`

or:

> `My Files` toolbar icon → `Offline Mail` → `Incoming/Saved Mail` folder

Benefit of having Automatic AOL retrieve unread email

- If, like many AOL users, email is your main priority, this is a way to make sure that connectivity problems never interfere with your online experience. Just set up Automatic AOL to retrieve your email at a wildly off-peak hour (like 5 a.m.) and you're set.

Writing mail offline

To write email offline in preparation for an Automatic AOL session:

> `Write` toolbar icon → write your message → `Send Later` button

Clicking `Send Later` instead of `Send Now` is shown in Figure 21-3.

By default, when you click `Send Later` you see this message:

> `Your mail has been placed in the "Mail Waiting to be Sent" folder of your Personal Filing Cabinet. To see your outgoing mail, click Mail Folders. To send your outgoing mail later, click Auto AOL.`

The email is sent during your next Automatic AOL session.

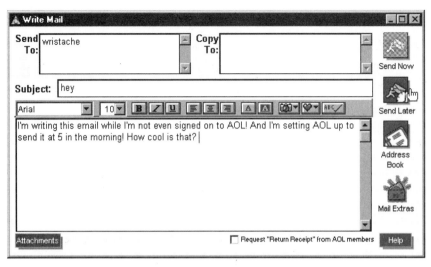

Figure 21-3: When writing email offline, click Send Later instead of Send Now

It's probably not a bad idea to see the above confirmation message the first few times you use Automatic AOL, but after that, you might find it easier to ditch it. To enable or disable email confirmation:

> `Mail Controls` toolbar icon → `Mail Preferences` → `Confirm when mail is marked to send later` checkbox

You have several other options when you write email offline, which we explain below.

If you decide you don't really want to send that email after all, you can delete it from Automatic AOL's queue by following one of these paths:

- `My Files` toolbar icon → `Personal Filing Cabinet` → `Mail Waiting To Be Sent` folder → highlight mail → `Delete`

- `My Files` toolbar icon → `Offline Mail` → `Mail Waiting To Be Sent` Folder → highlight mail → `Delete`

- `Mail Center` toolbar icon → `Read Offline Mail` → `Mail Waiting To Be Sent` → highlight mail → `Delete`

This not only takes the email out of Automatic AOL's queue, it deletes it entirely. If you want to save a copy of the mail, open it first and save it to a different directory.

As long as your outgoing email hasn't been sent yet, you can edit it in one of these ways:

- `My Files` toolbar icon → `Personal Filing Cabinet` → `Mail Waiting To Be Sent` folder → highlight mail → `Open`

- `My Files` toolbar icon → `Offline Mail` → `Mail Waiting To Be Sent` folder → highlight mail → `Open`

- Mail Center toolbar icon → Read Offline Mail → Mail Waiting To Be Sent → highlight mail → Open

To reply (offline) to mail you've read (offline):

- Mail Center toolbar icon → Read Offline Mail → double-click Incoming/Saved Mail folder → double-click any message to read it → Reply → Send Later

To see the list of email that will be sent during your next Automatic AOL session:

- My Files toolbar icon → Personal Filing Cabinet → Mail Waiting To Be Sent folder

- My Files toolbar icon → Offline Mail → Mail Waiting To Be Sent folder

- Mail Center toolbar icon → Read Offline Mail → Mail Waiting To Be Sent

To save sent mail in your Personal Filing Cabinet, you must set your email preferences to do so:

MY AOL toolbar icon → Preferences → Mail → Retain all mail I send in my Personal Filing Cabinet checkbox

You can also reread sent mail (for up to three days after writing it) this way:

Mail Center toolbar icon → Sent Mail

Message Boards

Most people don't think to use Automatic AOL with message boards, but it's possible to read, write, and reply to messages offline.

Reading message boards offline

To have Automatic AOL download message board posts, you must mark the message boards of your choice for offline reading. To do this, click the Read Offline button from within any new-style message board. Selecting message boards for Automatic AOL retrieval and offline reading is shown in Figure 21-4.

Use Keyword: My Boards to keep track of which boards you're reading offline. A clock icon indicates you've chosen to read it offline. Click Read Offline again to switch it back to regular online reading.

See also the section "Organizing with My Boards" in Chapter 11, *Message Boards*.

To read the posts you've already downloaded:

My Files toolbar icon → Personal Filing Cabinet → Newsgroups folder → Incoming/Saved Postings folder → *message_board_name* folder

or:

My Files toolbar icon → Offline Newsgroups → Incoming/Saved Postings folder → *message_board_name* folder

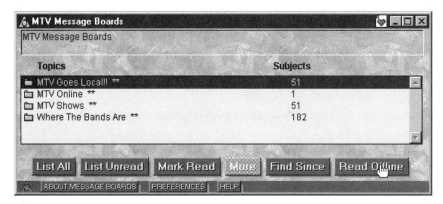

Figure 21-4: Selecting a message board to read offline

To adjust the number of posts to download during your AOL sessions, click **Preferences** from any open message board. You'll see a space where you can fill in a number of posts to download. The default is not to download more than 500 posts in any one Automatic AOL session. You can go up to 999 posts per session.

Benefit

- If you're reading lots of high-traffic groups, you can increase the maximum number.

Drawback

- Increasing the maximum number of posts may cause you to download an unmanageably large number of posts. In most cases, 500 should actually be plenty. Try increasing the number gradually until you find a number of posts per session that agrees with you. Or try scheduling more frequent AOL sessions.

Posting to message boards offline

To start a new thread offline:

> **My Files** toolbar icon → **Personal Filing Cabinet** → **Newsgroups** folder → **Incoming/Saved Postings** folder → *message_board_name* folder → **Create New Posting** → **Send Later**

or click **New Message** from any open post you've just read.

To reply (offline) to a post you've just read (offline):

> From any post you've just read → **Reply to Group** → compose your post → **Send Later**

To reply to the author of a particular post instead of replying to the whole group (this won't get posted to the message board):

> From any post you've just read → **Reply to Author** → **Send Later**

If you decide you don't really want to post a certain message after all, you can delete it from Automatic AOL's queue:

> My Files toolbar icon → Personal Filing Cabinet → Postings Waiting To Be Sent folder → highlight post → Delete

or:

> My Files toolbar icon → Offline Newsgroups → Postings Waiting to Be Sent folder → highlight post → Delete

This not only takes the post out of Automatic AOL's queue, it deletes it entirely. If you want to save a copy of the post, open it first and save it to a different directory.

As long as an outgoing post hasn't been sent yet, you can edit it:

> My Files toolbar icon → Personal Filing Cabinet → Postings Waiting to Be Sent folder → highlight post → Open

or:

> My Files toolbar icon → Offline Newsgroups → Postings Waiting to Be Sent folder → highlight post → Open

Message board posts you send via Automatic AOL are automatically saved in your PFC. To view them:

> My Files toolbar icon → Personal Filing Cabinet → Newsgroups folder → Postings You've Sent folder

or:

> My Files toolbar icon → Offline Newsgroups → Postings You've Sent folder

Newsgroups

Reading and posting to newsgroups with Automatic AOL is a lot like using Automatic AOL with message boards. You can read, write, and reply to posts offline. If you love newsgroups, it's actually easier to read them with Automatic AOL. Why? Automatic AOL downloads all the messages and responses, and organizes threads for you. AOL's simple newsreader doesn't sort messages as well as Automatic AOL.

Reading newsgroup posts offline

To have Automatic AOL download newsgroup posts, you must select newsgroups for offline reading. You must choose from newsgroups you're already subscribed to (see Chapter 13, *Newsgroups*, if you don't know how to subscribe).

Select the newsgroups from which Automatic AOL should retrieve new posts:

> Keyword: Newsgroups → Read Offline → highlight a newsgroup → Add → OK

You could also click Add All to select all your newsgroups for Automatic AOL downloading.

To read the posts you've downloaded:

> **My Files** toolbar icon → **Personal Filing Cabinet** → **Newsgroups** folder

Benefit

- Reading newsgroups can be time-consuming. Downloading them to read offline keeps your phone line free; that is, unless you subscribe to scores of traffic-intensive newsgroups.

Drawback

- If any of your newsgroups are particularly high-traffic, the Automatic AOL session may log you out before it's done retrieving all the posts. Message boards allow you to adjust the number of posts to download in an Automatic AOL session, but newsgroups don't. You'll just have to set more frequent Automatic AOL sessions to get all the posts.

Writing newsgroup posts offline

To start a new thread:

> **My Files** toolbar icon → **Personal Filing Cabinet** → **Newsgroups** folder → **Incoming/Saved Postings** folder → *newsgroup_name* folder → **Create New Posting** → **Send Later**

or from any open post you've just read, click **New Message**.

To reply to a post you've just read:

> From any post you've just read → **Reply to Group** → **Send Later**

To reply to the author of a particular post (this won't get posted to the message board):

> From any post you've just read → **Reply to Author** → **Send Later**

To reply (offline) to a post you've read (offline):

> **My Files** toolbar icon → **Personal Filing Cabinet** → **Newsgroups** folder → read any post → **Reply to Group** → **Send Later**

If you decide you don't really want to post that message after all, you can delete it from Automatic AOL's queue:

> **My Files** toolbar icon → **Personal Filing Cabinet** → **Postings Waiting To Be Sent** folder → highlight post → **Delete**

or:

> **My Files** toolbar icon → **Offline Newsgroups** → **Postings Waiting to Be Sent** folder → highlight post → **Delete**

This not only takes the post out of Automatic AOL's queue, it deletes it entirely. If you want to save a copy of the post, open it first and save it to a different directory.

As long as an outgoing post hasn't been sent yet, you can edit it:

My Files toolbar icon → Personal Filing Cabinet → Postings
Waiting to Be Sent folder → highlight post → Open

or:

My Files toolbar icon → Offline Newsgroups → Postings Waiting
to Be Sent folder → highlight post → Open

Newsgroup posts you send via Automatic AOL are automatically saved in your PFC. To view them:

My Files toolbar icon → Personal Filing Cabinet → Newsgroups
folder → Postings You've Sent folder

or:

My Files toolbar icon → Offline Newsgroups → Postings You've
Sent folder

Automatic
AOL

CHAPTER 22

Billing

As soon as your free trial period ends, you start dealing with AOL's billing process. You are placed on the Standard Unlimited price plan, which bills you $21.95 per month for unlimited access. This is pretty easy, and you probably won't think about it much.

You might be wondering why we devoted an entire chapter to a simple topic such as billing. The answer is: because it's not as simple as it looks. After you read this chapter, you'll truly be an informed AOL consumer.

This chapter has three parts:

- "Don't Pay More Than You Have To": We tell you which groups qualify for AOL discounts and show you how to avoid additional AOL charges.

- "Know Your Price Plans": Depending on your circumstances, you may not have to pay $21.95 a month.

- "Account Information Online": When something goes wrong with your AOL bill, or when you have a question, your first instinct might be to call customer service. However, you'd be amazed at how much time you can save taking care of billing bureaucracy online.

Don't Pay More Than You Have To

The only clever way we know to dodge the monthly fee entirely is to work for AOL, but you probably don't want to do that. We do, however, have a few tips that might help you save some money.

See if You Qualify for a Discount

American Association of Retired Persons (AARP) members, which includes anyone over 50 years old, are eligible for unlimited access at $19.95 per month (that's 10%

off the regular rate). For details, go to Keyword: AARP → Member Benefits →
AARP Discount on AOL.

As of this writing, no other oft-discounted group (like students) gets a discount
from AOL.

Beware of Premium Areas

Premium areas (mostly games as of this writing) incur a $1.99 per hour surcharge
(on top of your regular monthly fees, and even during your New Member free
time). Fractions of hours are billed at 3.3 cents per minute. We don't recommend
spending much time (and therefore money) in Premium areas, since we think AOL
and the Web provide enough entertainment on their own, at no additional fee (see
also Chapter 15, *AOL Content Reference*, and Chapter 16, *The Web*).

Premium areas make themselves abundantly clear, so don't worry about accidentally stumbling into one. Afraid your kids will be tempted? Don't worry: secondary
screen names are, by default, blocked from Premium areas. To change the default
and allow secondary screen names access to Premium areas, see Chapter 28,
Parental Controls.

Beware of Surcharges

You incur additional surcharges when you use surcharged 800/888 numbers or
connect from another country (and sometimes from Alaska). See Chapter 27,
Connecting, for information on finding local access numbers that are free.

Put Your Account on Hold or Cancel

You can save money by putting your account on hold if you're not going to use it
for more than a month (for instance, if you're going on a long vacation). Call
AOL's billing customer service at 1-888-265-8003 and ask them about the "hold"
plan. Under this plan, you pay $2.95 per month to keep your account active.
You're not supposed to sign on during the time the account is on hold, but your
email box still receives email. If you do sign on to AOL during this time, you'll be
charged $2.50 per hour for access. So if you sign on and check your email for five
minutes, it costs you about a quarter.

If you're going to be gone for less than six months, you can cancel your account.
Your screen names are not released for six months after you cancel. When you get
back, you'll have to call AOL customer service at 1-800-827-3338 and tell them that
you want to rejoin.

For more information about canceling your account, see Chapter 31, *Canceling
and Suspending Service.*

Hassle AOL if You Must

If you feel that your bill has been fouled up, you could try complaining at
Keyword: Credit (intended mostly for people getting billed by the hour, like
Light Usage or Limited Plan members). Usually, we advocate avoiding telephone
support at all costs, but in this case, we think it might be the better way to argue

about your bill. The billing customer service number is 1-888-265-8003 at the time of this writing.

Know Your Price Plans

An important part of spending no more than you have to is knowing the difference between all of AOL's price plans. It's so important that we've given price plans their own section of this chapter. We've heard that 75% of AOL members are on the Standard Unlimited Plan; so are we, and we wouldn't want it any other way. But if you spend only one hour a week online, why pay for unlimited access?

Standard Unlimited Plan

This is the $21.95 per month, all-you-can-eat plan. It is the most common price plan, and the one that AOL now automatically signs you up for when you join.

Benefits

- Unlimited access and no hourly rates. You (or your entire household) can use AOL all day and all night without paying extravagant fees.

- It's reliable. Unlike your long-distance bill, you never have to wonder how much your AOL bill is.

Drawbacks

- If you're not online very much, you may be better off with the Limited or Light Usage Plans (explained later in this section).

- If you have the capital (and the commitment), go for the One Year Plan; you'll save $24 per year.

Bring Your Own Access Plan

This plan costs $9.95 per month. The catch is that you have to connect to AOL through a non-AOL Internet connection, such as a LAN (TCP/IP connection) at work, or a dial-up account with a local ISP.

Benefits

- Like the Standard Usage Plan, it offers unlimited usage and no hourly rates.

- It's always easy to connect to AOL via TCP/IP, and you'll get a faster connection.

- Depending on your ISP and where you live, it can be easier to connect to other ISPs than to connect to AOL.

- If you're hooked on AOL features that you don't get with your other Internet connection, the Bring Your Own Access plan makes staying on AOL more affordable.

- On an altruistic note, the more people that connect with Bring Your Own Access, the easier it is for others in that neighborhood to connect via modem.

Drawback

- If you use AOL's access numbers—if, for instance, you want to connect to AOL and your other ISP isn't working—you'll get an hourly surcharge of $2.50 per hour ($6 an hour for surcharged 800 numbers).

For more about TCP/IP access, see also Chapter 27.

Light Usage Plan

The Light Usage Plan is for those with excellent self-control. It's $4.95 per month for the first three hours; $2.50 for each additional hour.

Benefit

- If you're online for three hours or fewer every month, this is a good deal.

- Automatic AOL makes it easier to perform tasks offline and spend less time signed on (see also Chapter 21, *Automatic AOL*).

Drawback

- If you go over your allotted three hours, the fees could get exorbitant. We recommend timing your online hours for a month or two before switching to this plan. To see how many hours your account spends online per month, see "Account Information Online."

Limited Plan

If the Light Usage Plan is a bit too restrictive but you're not online enough to need unlimited access, the Limited Plan might be a good compromise. It's $9.95 per month for the first five hours; $2.95 for each additional hour.

Benefit

- If you're online for five hours or fewer every month, this is a good deal.

- Automatic AOL makes it easier to perform tasks offline and spend less time signed on (see also Chapter 21).

Drawback

- Like the Light Usage Plan, if you go over your allotted hours, you'll pay. To see how many hours your account spends online per month, see "Account Information Online."

One Year Plan

This plan is a $239.40, prepaid one-year subscription. It used to be $215.40 per year, but the price went up in April 1998. Members already on the one-year plan in April 1998 kept the original price, but pay the higher price when their yearly membership runs out and must be renewed.

30 days before your one-year membership expires, AOL emails you and tell you. You are automatically re-enrolled in the one-year plan unless you change your price plan within 72 hours of the end of the one-year period.

AOL also used to have a two-year plan, but it was suspended in 1997.

Benefits

- Like the Standard Unlimited Plan, you get unlimited access and no hourly rates.

- At $19.95 per month, it's $24 cheaper per year than the Standard Unlimited Plan.

- You pay once a year and don't have to think about monthly bills.

Drawbacks

- You have to commit to a full year on AOL. Maybe that kind of commitment isn't worth the $24 savings.

- It might be easier for you to pay $21.95 a month than $239.40 up front.

Invoice Billing

Invoice billing is not, strictly speaking, a price plan, but it can be considered one. It is only available to businesses with at least five separate AOL accounts (not just five screen names). If your business needs an invoice, not just a charge on a credit card, this is your only option. The Account Manager receives a monthly bill listing all the charges from each individual account, including the time each account spent online. Invoice Billing carries a $500 "pre-payment" surcharge, and after that each individual account costs $24.95 per month; $14.95 per month on the Bring Your Own Access Plan, or $299.40 per year.

Account Information Online

Don't touch that (phone) dial! Of course, sometimes you'll have to call customer service and face the Muzak, but we'd like to help you avoid it whenever possible. There are several ways to reduce billing red tape by checking or changing your account information yourself.

Changing Your Billing Information

Your billing information includes the name, address, and phone number that appear on your bill. To change that information:

Keyword: Billing → Change Your Name or Address

Note that changing your phone number here only changes information in AOL's database; it's not the same as changing your local access number (see also Chapter 27).

Changing Your Billing Method or Price Plan

There are two ways to pay for AOL: bill your credit card (the default), or have your charges deducted from your checking account. When you have your charges deducted from your checking account, you pay for the convenience with a $5-per-month surcharge.

To change your billing method or change the credit card you pay with:

> Keyword: Billing → Change Billing Method or Price Plan → enter your password in the Current Password box → Continue → click Checking Account or Credit Card, then follow the instructions

You're supposed to be able to use the same path to change your price plan, but that wasn't working for us as of this writing. We suggest you try the online method of changing price plans (Keyword: Billing → Change Billing Method or Price Plan) anyway, in case AOL gets its act together by the time you read this. If that doesn't work, you're going to have to surrender and use telephone support at 1-888-265-8003.

Understanding Your Bills

Find out when your billing period ends, how much you owe, how much time you spend online, and more. You probably won't ever need some of this information, but it's good to know where to find it.

Billing summary

Your billing summary tells you the start of your next billing period, your current balance, the amount of last month's bill, and other miscellaneous information about free online time. It's not information most people need to know on a regular basis.

To check your billing summary:

> Keyword: Billing → Display Current Bill Summary

Billing terms

To check your billing terms:

> Keyword: Billing → Display Your Billing Terms

What the "terms" are, and what they really mean:

- Your next billing date is the day that you'll be billed, and also the end of this "month's" billing period.

- Free minutes each month shows you how much (if any) free online time you have each month. Unused free online time doesn't roll over to the next month.

- Monthly fee is what you're paying per month. You should already know what this is based on the price plan you selected.

- Daytime hourly rate and evening hourly rate: This doesn't apply to most people, so you'll probably see zeroes in these fields. Daytime and evening hourly rates apply to companies that provide AOL to their employees. A company's employees can be charged less for signing on to AOL during work hours and more for signing on at night, or vice versa.

Hours spent online

To see how many hours your account spent online last month:

> Keyword: Billing → Display Your Detailed Bill → Last Month's Bill

To see how many hours your account has spent online so far this month:

> Keyword: Billing → Display Your Detailed Bill → Current Month's Bill

For either month, click the Request Email Copy button at the bottom of the screen to have a copy of the information emailed to your screen name.

Benefits

- You can monitor your usage if you're on the Limited or Light Usage plan.
- Keep tabs on how many hours your kids spend on AOL avoiding their homework.

CHAPTER 23

Web Publishing and FTP

Is it true that everybody's got to have a web page? It would seem so, given that there are millions of individuals who have pictures of themselves and their families up on the Web, along with poetry, personal mottos, and odes to their favorite celebrities. No matter that the term "vanity page" is pejorative; you might have something of interest to share with people that would be perfectly published on the Web. Life, liberty, the pursuit of happiness, and your own personal web presence: aren't those the pillars of our nation?

Sarcasm aside, this chapter is all about how to get your web pages up on your AOL server space. In our effort to be as complete as possible, we include a great deal about FTP, or file transfer protocol, the method that you'll use to publish your documents to the Web. Without FTP, you couldn't publish anything to your server space on AOL.

We move from discussing the simplest methods of putting documents up on your server space to examining tools with more advanced features. If you wonder whether you'll be able to successfully publish something, just remember one thing: web publishing is like chess or golf: you can "play" at any level.

Here's what we cover in this chapter:

- "What Is FTP?": This section gives you some insight into this standard means of moving files, creating directories, and organizing them on another, networked computer. We also cover the reasons why you'd want to use this space.

- "About AOL Server Space": This short section tells you how much you've got and where it's located.

- "Some Basics of Web Publishing": Go here if you don't know the first thing about putting a page on the Web. We include a reference section that includes online resources that can help you with coding and design.

- "Putting Stuff in Your Server Space": This section covers several web publishing tools:

  Personal Publisher
  The easiest way to get on the Web. For the beginner, AOL provides a form-driven way to put up basic pages via `Keyword: Personal Publisher`.

  AOL's built-in FTP client
  AOL's offered this for years, but hasn't got around to updating it much. We don't recommend it, but you can use it for quick uploads.

  AOLPress for basic and intermediate web sites
  Freely distributed to anyone on the Web, it's a versatile editor that creates nice-looking web pages using a drag-and-drop interface. This gets a high recommendation.

  Third-party tools for basic, intermediate, and/or advanced pages
  We cover using the hundreds of alternative available web publishing and FTP tools. We show you how to find freeware, shareware, and commercial web page-creation applications, many of which give you fine control over your web documents with professional features. Using Netscape's Composer as an example, we take you through the rudiments of uploading a page.

While this chapter has a lot of information in it, we left out a great deal in order to keep the focus on AOL and our advice for using it better. You won't find information on how to design pages, code HTML, or create graphical images. That stuff is better left to more detailed documentation that accompanies the tools themselves or is covered in the hundreds of tomes on web publishing that have been printed in the last few years. For books on the fundamentals of web publishing, see the bibliography at the end of this chapter. Online how-tos are also covered in the section "Learn Web Publishing Online."

What Is FTP?

The File Transfer Protocol is a set of commands that transfer a file from one computer to another. Before the Web came along, before hypertext transfer protocol (http), there was FTP, and it was the way to move files around between the world's computers. FTP is still very popular, and in fact, you might encounter it without knowing it when you are browsing the Internet. Many times, if you click a link from a web site to download a program, you begin to download the file using FTP.

A computer that stores the files that can be transferred via FTP is called an *FTP server* or *FTP site*. It used to be that you'd fire up your FTP program and point it to an FTP site, such as *ftp.oreilly.com*, to get a file or a program. While FTP-only sites still exist, they're being overshadowed by the higher profile, all-in-one communications network that is the Web. Why go to O'Reilly's FTP site, when you can get more information from their web site, often with links to the same FTP downloads on the FTP site, too?

So now what is the primary use of FTP? As it has always been, the main use of FTP is to control and manipulate files on remote computers—that is, computers that might be in the next city, state, or across the world. FTP is indispensable if you want to put any document on a server, including your free server space on AOL. Once uploaded, anyone with an Internet connection can gain access to whatever you've placed there, in your very own site.

What can you put there? Web pages, in the form of HTML files and their associated graphic and sound files. You're not limited to web pages, though. Put any file you choose there, like a word-processing document, spreadsheet, or a program you've created. Share pictures with friends, without emailing them out individually: just upload the pictures to your server space at *ftp://members.aol.com/Your_Screen_Name,* then tell friends where to find them with any browser or FTP client, including the one built into the AOL software. If you've got a scanned photo of your most recent vacation, you could upload it, then tell your friends to go to *http://members.aol.com/TiredWritr/vacation.jpg* or *ftp://members.aol.com/TiredWritr/vacation.jpg* to see it.

Among AOL members, we suspect that server space is underutilized: most don't know what it is or that it even exists! When members do use the space, it is primarily for serving web pages. File sharing is just as useful and handy, but not many people think to put a file (like a spreadsheet or vacation photo) into their FTP space instead of emailing it out scores of times or putting it on the front of their home page for the whole world to see.

While the built-in AOL FTP tools are serviceable, we recommend using a third-party tool if you intend to do any amount of FTPing. We recommend several friendly clients later in this chapter, in "Putting Stuff in Your Server Space."

About AOL Server Space

In the sections that follow, we describe what you get in your AOL server space, including your URL, the 2MB limit, and AOL's domain name hosting service.

Benefits to basic AOL server space

- Quickly share files and/or set up your web site.

- Included in your monthly fee for AOL, each account has up to 10 MB of space, 2 MB per screen name.

- There are no limits on how many megabytes of traffic your server space incurs (although if you start getting a lot of traffic, and AOL checks this and finds that you've put up something that violates the Terms of Service, it may be removed).

- Accessible by both the Web (http) and FTP (ftp) protocols, so you can get to your files by typing *http://members.aol.com/your_screen_name* or *ftp://members.aol.com/your_screen_name.*

- Access to some seriously easy-to-use—although not high-powered—tools from within AOL. Get your basic web pages up in a flash.

Drawbacks

- 2 MB per screen name may not be sufficient for users who have large web sites or scores of graphical images. See "How Much Is Two Megabytes?"

- AOL supports only a few basic CGI scripts. See "CGI."

- AOL's built-in FTP client is extremely limited. To maintain any but the most rudimentary web site or collection of files, we recommend using an alternate client. See "Putting Stuff in Your Server Space."

- Proprietary extensions to some web publishing programs, such as Microsoft Front Page, won't work on AOL. An extension contains programming that broadens the capabilities of a more basic program. In order to function properly, these extensions have to be installed on the server, which AOL doesn't allow.

It's All About Directories

Just like the computer you're working on, your server space on AOL is based on a hierarchical directory system. Basically, that means that there are files in folders (i.e., directories), and folders within folders. It all keeps things from getting too cluttered. Could you imagine what your hard drive would look like if all of the thousands of individual files were just floating around, not organized in some way? It would be nearly impossible to find anything you wanted.

Here's an example of a hierarchy of folders in the server space of our screen name CashahMA. The path */cashbahma/hobbies/publications/* would represent the directory */publications/* inside */hobbies/* inside our main directory of *cashbahma*. We—or anyone who's accessed our server space—can go in and view all the documents in */publications/* without having to view any of what's in */hobbies/*.

If you have trouble understanding the hierarchical directories in your server space, just remember that it is exactly like the folders within folders system that your computer uses to display the contents of your hard drive.

Within your AOL server space, you set up these directories yourself, depending on how you want to organize things. We discuss files and folders in more depth in the section "Basic File and Directory Management."

Your URL

Once you upload something to your AOL space, whether it is a web page or just a file, your address on the WWW will be one of two things:

- *http://members.aol.com/Your_Screen_Name/*

- *ftp://members.aol.com/Your_Screen_Name/*

If you're using a web browser that also supports FTP, you can use either of these protocols. For instance, if my screen name is CasbahMA, then my URL is *http://members.aol.com/casbahma/*, or I could get there via *ftp://members.aol.com/casbama/*. If I'm going to FTP with an FTP-only client, I'd FTP to the host, *members.aol.com*, then enter the directory (usually called changing directory) to */casbahma/*.

If I've uploaded a page called *nutshell.html,* the URL to that is *http:// members.aol.com/Casbahma/nutshell.html.*

If I've uploaded a file called *vacation.jpg,* the URL is either *ftp://members.aol.com/ casbahma/vacation.jpg* or *http://members.aol.com/casbahma/vacation.jpg.*

You can also have multiple directories inside your main directory. For example, if I've got another directory called */hobbies/* and inside I have a web page called *writing.html,* the URL is *http://members.aol.com/CasbahMA/hobbies/writing.html.*

Note: watch those cases! The screen-name portion of the path is not case sensitive. However, all trailing portions are. That means *index.html* and *INDEX.HTML* are not equivalent, while *CasbahMA* and *casbahma* are equivalent. You should keep this in mind when designing your web page. We recommend keeping it all lowercase.

How Much Is Two Megabytes?

The answer depends on your goals. We estimate that 2 MB of plain HTML is equivalent to 200 text-only HTML pages. However, almost no one these days publishes text-only web sites. Graphical images can take up a lot more space than bare HTML, so when you add a variety of images, you'll be reducing 200 pages to significantly fewer. If, for example, you limit your unique graphics on each page to 50 KB each, you've got room for 20 pages. To some people, 20 pages is more than they could fill in a lifetime.

If you're more prolific, you can create up to four other screen names and create sites with pages linked among the screen names. The URL for the site changes slightly as you move between pages under different screen names, but otherwise, all else is identical. Essentially, with each account, you've got a total of 10MB server space on AOL. And you've got unlimited traffic. We think that's a bargain compared to many services that limit the traffic or charge extra for it when your site's popular and you exceed the limits.

CGI

If you want more than a bunch of pages that just sit there, CGI might be for you, because it allows dynamic communication between the browser and the server. The Common Gateway Interface (CGI) is a convention that allows information to get passed back and forth from the web server to an application on the server that processes the information. It enables visitors to the site to send unique information to the web server that determines what unique results are returned to the visitor. For example, CGI scripts let web sites poll users, or have them send information via a form.

Your server administrator usually puts the CGI scripts on the web server or gives you a directory where you can place your own. AOL allows the use of only three preset CGI scripts, prohibiting all others. As of this printing, the following CGI programs are available on *members.aol.com*:

A web traffic counter
Tracks the number of people who visit your web site on AOL.

Email forms

Allows visitors to send you information via an input form.

Guestbook

Allows you to set up an ever-growing file to which visitors can add information

If you're looking for other functionality that would require modifying anything in the CGI-bin, such as the extensions for Microsoft FrontPage, you're out of luck with AOL.

For more information on the CGI programs that AOL supports, go to AOL's at WWWAdmin Home Page at *http://members.aol.com/wwwadmin/index.htm*.

AOL's PrimeHost Domain Hosting Service

If you want your URL to be something like *www.MySite.com*, you can spend $99 a month for AOL's PrimeHost service. In addition to the monthly fee to AOL, you also have to cough up a one-time fee of $100 to InterNIC to register your domain name for two years. There is no minimum contract, unlike some cheaper hosting services. If you want to shop and compare before you jump in with PrimeHost, you could follow some of the links in Yahoo, under web hosting: *http://www.yahoo.com/ Business_and_Economy/Companies/Internet_Services/Web_Services/Hosting/*.

Whether you use AOL's PrimeHost or not, InterNIC registers your domain name. Find them at *http://www.internic.net*.

What you get with PrimeHost:

- You can create your site quickly with templates if you choose; though they're not amazing, they get the job done for small businesses.

- You get 50 MB of server space for your site with 1,500 MB of activity/downloads a month. AOL claims that's enough for about 50,000 hits per month. A single page of your web site could incur several hits, as each graphic and HTML document is counted as a separate hit. Please note that all of these numbers are merely estimates, based on averages. If your site has a huge number of large graphical images, and/or gets a lot of traffic, you'll reach the 1,500-MB transfer limit more quickly than if your site has few graphics and/or little traffic.

- You can set up email accounts at your domain, and have mail forwarded from these aliases to another ISP mail account, such as your AOL email account.

Some Basics of Web Publishing

The most basic outline we can give to sum up how to publish using AOL is this: (1) design and create your page(s) and (2) upload it to your AOL server space. Traditionally, your server space on AOL was called the *FTP space*, but since AOL also runs HTTP on the same servers, it's better called simply *server space*. Sometimes, AOL refers to it as *My Space*, but we think it's childish, even cheesy, and won't be part of that. In this book you might see your server space referred to as FTP space, especially when we're talking about FTPing something there.

Skip this section if you're already familiar with HTML, WYSIWYG and text-editing tools, and FTP. If you're not, we'll outline these for you, and point you to further information.

HTML

The basic language of the Web is Hypertext Markup Language or HTML, which tells a web browser how to present the details of the page so that it looks like something meaningful, rather than a jumble of programming code. Whether you know it or not, any page you put up on the Web for browsing is going to have some HTML coding in it. HTML is fairly easy to learn, but can get boring: inserting special tags around elements in your documents so that the browser knows how to present something, deciding what's text, what's a table, what's bold, audio, video, and so on.

We don't cover HTML here. Rather, we point you to other resources in the sections "Learn Web Publishing Online" and "Recommended Books for More Advanced Web Publishing."

Editing Tools

As we mentioned earlier, when you're designing a web page, you can "play" at any level. Some HTML pros use only a text editor, such as the Windows Notepad, typing in their HTML and JavaScript by hand. Others prefer to use what's called a WYSIWYG editor, which stands for What You See Is What You Get. With a WYSIWYG tool, as you set up a page, it looks much like it would to the person browsing it—that is, what you see when you lay out your page is what you get when you upload and browse the page from a web browser. WYSIWYG tools are easy to use; however, you often sacrifice control over the code. For most beginning web publishers, losing a little control over the code isn't a problem; they're just happy they didn't have to put all the tags in by hand.

As you begin to know more about layout and about coding your own documents, you might want to graduate to a text editor, or to a more advanced WYSIWYG editor. We cover some editing tools in the section "Third-Party Web Publishing Tools."

FTP

Once you create your pages you have to get them on a server. You send the documents to AOL servers using FTP—whether you use the built-in AOL tools, a third-party FTP client, or a web browser that has publishing capabilities (most of them do, now). Before you upload your first page to your AOL server space, you have to prepare it for the first use. This isn't hard: essentially you access it for the first time, and AOL automatically sets aside server space for that screen name. We present the many options for the first access of your server space.

AOL claims that you can use only AOL itself—at Keyword: FTP, Keyword: My Place, or Keyword: Personal Publisher—to set up your server space. But we've discovered otherwise. You can use any third-party client, as long as you're also connected to AOL at the time.

To set up your server space you've got four options:

- Keyword: My Place → Go to My Place
- Keyword: FTP → Go to FTP → select *members.aol.com* in the listbox → Connect → OK
- Keyword: FTP → Go To FTP → Other Site → type members:/*your-ScreenName* → Connect → OK
- Use a third-party FTP client or automated Web page publisher pointed at *ftp:// members.aol.com/your_screen_name/*

Figures 23-1 and 23-2 illustrate the process of using the built-in AOL FTP client to set up the server space for TiredWritr. To start, AOL creates the */screen_name/* directory. Within the */screen_name/* directory, a private directory is also created by default, in which you can store items that only you can access (see "Basic File and Directory Management"). A short *README* file with the latest copy of the AOL FTP FAQ is also installed. We recommend you read the FAQ, which usually has the most up-to-date practices for using AOL's server space.

For more detailed information on working with AOL's built-in FTP tools, see "Basic File and Directory Management." If you decide to use AOL's built-in FTP client, you definitely want to take a look at how to manipulate documents the AOL way.

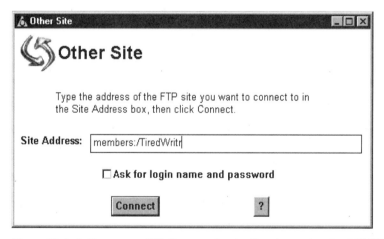

Figure 23-1: Setting up an FTP directory for the first time using the AOL FTP client

Learn Web Publishing Online

It's not surprising that the Web is the quickest, cheapest, most up-to-date way to get information on web publishing. Why spend cash on a five-inch-thick book when you're just starting out? Using the Web itself, you can read some background information, take tutorials, and instantly view the code that's behind it all.

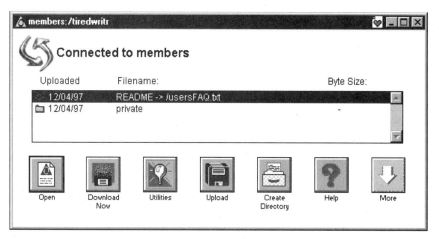

Figure 23-2: Setting up your AOL server space as viewed with the AOL FTP client

Clearly we're advocating the "Just do it" method of learning HTML. Below is a very small selection of some decent sites that cover web publishing.

Keyword: On the Net
Jump from this one place to all of AOL's web publishing information.

Keyword: Online Classroom → Web and Internet
Free classes include "HTML Basics," "Using AOLPress," and "Counters, Guest-books, and Forms."

Web Review (http://www.webreview.com)
Developer's web resources, tutorials, and advances in web publishing. Published by an O'Reilly affiliate, Songline Studios (Curt and Jen work for Songline).

Yahoo's directory to the WWW (http://www.yahoo.com/Computers_and_Internet/ Internet/World_Wide_Web/)
Lists hundreds of links to web how-to sites.

CNET Builder.Com (http://www.builder.com)
A guide to HTML editors, Java, and CGI; also includes useful downloads.

Putting Stuff in Your Server Space

Whether you know HTML or not, you can still get your pages online. But you need the right tools. Below we cover AOL's own tools first, with Personal Publisher being the easiest way to get a page on the Web, not counting having a friend or paid pro do it for you. Then we list other, more advanced tools both to upload your pages and to lay them out. Most of them are WYSIWYG editors that also FTP your documents up into your AOL server space.

Here's our advice: unless you've got only a few files to upload, or a minuscule, static web site, you'll save tons of time with a third-party FTP client and a nice HTML editor to lay out your pages. The FTP client speeds up the process of uploading the myriad files of your web site, while the extra features in HTML editors help you create nicer-looking pages. AOLPress is great at helping you lay out pages, and allows you to upload entire web sites with one click. WS_FTP also lets you upload entire directories with just a click or two. We cover both of these in the sections that follow.

Personal Publisher for AOL 4.0

Keyword: Personal Publisher or My AOL toolbar icon → Personal Publisher

Personal Publisher is essentially a form-driven way to get basic pages up onto your AOL server space at *members.aol.com*. You needn't know a single HTML tag: you simply fill in the blanks with your own information, and Personal Publisher codes the HTML. This is great for kids, or for people who just want to experiment with the rudiments of web publishing or get something up quickly. Business people are better off with AOLPress or the full-featured HTML editor of their choice (covered in the following entries).

To get started with Personal Publisher, you've got a choice of extremely basic templates, such as Personal, Business, Greeting, or a blank page. In any case, you're asked for information to fill in the page. AOL walks you through, asking for a title, background color, image(s) of your choice, personal information, and hyperlinks. Once your page is complete, you can view and edit the page, adding more text, images, or links as you wish. If you know a little basic HTML, you can add it manually, too, and tell Personal Publisher where this free-form HTML should go.

Basic File and Directory Management

If you go beyond the scope of Personal Publisher, you need to know a little about manipulating files, putting them into directories, and uploading. But it's all easy, and a lot of the things you have to do are similar to managing files on your hard drive, as we said in an earlier section, "It's All About Directories."

The most basic unit you'll be working with is a file, something that could be graphic, a sound file, or the text that makes up a main page of a web site. Those individual files are placed into folders, called *directories*.

Use AOL's built-in FTP client to create, delete, and rename files and directories, as well as create special */incoming/* and */private/* directories that have special uses. If you use third-party clients, which we encourage, these directions won't apply: you have to follow the program's own instructions. Note, however, that AOL doesn't allow some tools, like Netscape Communicator, to create new directories. So if you want to publish something into a new directory using Netscape Communicator, you'll have to create a new directory with AOL's built-in FTP tool first.

Benefits to AOL's built-in FTP client

• Handy way to go directly to your server space; no other applications needed.

• Good if you want to modify just one or two files in a rush.

Drawback

- You can only upload or download one file at a time with the built-in client. AOLPress and other third-party web publishing tools (described in later sections) allow you to modify multiple files simultaneously and have more features.

To create a directory

Keyword: FTP → Go to FTP → select the entry *members.aol.com* →
Connect → OK → Create Directory → type the directory name you
want to create → Continue

You can create as many directories as you'd like, nested inside other directories. Some people prefer a number of different directories to help them stay organized, such as folders for graphics, sounds, or parts of their web site. Figure 23-3 shows how to use the AOL client to create a new directory, *NewWork,* in the AOL server space.

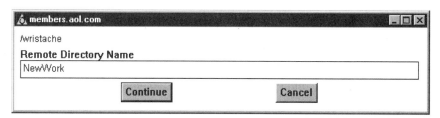

Figure 23-3: Creating a new directory using the AOL client

Any other person world-wide who knows your URL can access all of the files in your server space, except for those in your */private/* directory, explained below.

To create an incoming directory

Keyword: FTP → Go To FTP → select the entry *members.aol.com* →
Connect → OK → Create Directory

Follow the same steps you would follow to create any directory (see the previous section, "To create a directory"), but name this one *incoming*. People who have Web or FTP access and who know your URL may upload files into your *incoming* directory. They won't be able to upload files into any other directory on your site. Note that what they upload counts as part of your 2-MB limit.

To create a private directory

A private directory is created when you initially use AOL's own FTP client to create your topmost *Your_Screen_Name* directory. What you've got, essentially, the first time you go to your FTP space is a *Your_Screen_Name* directory and a *private* directory within that.

Only you can access your *private* directory. In addition, you must be signed on to AOL at the time you attempt to access your private directory or any of the files inside it.

To delete a directory

> Keyword: FTP → Go to FTP → select the entry *members.aol.com* → Connect → OK → Click on the directory you want to delete → Utilities → Delete → OK

Deleting a directory removes the folder and all its contents. You can't undo a delete.

To delete a file

> Keyword: FTP → Go To FTP → Other Site → type members:/*your_screen_name* → Connect → OK → select the file you want to delete → Utilities → Delete → OK → OK

Once you've deleted a file, it can't be restored.

To rename a directory

> Keyword: FTP → Go to FTP → select the entry *members.aol.com* and click Connect → OK → click on the directory you want to rename → Utilities → Rename → type the new name → OK

This is pretty self-explanatory. But be careful about renaming a directory that may house pages of your web site. Changing a directory name may break links in your web pages, since the directory that they're linked to has a different name.

To rename a file

> Keyword: FTP → Go To FTP → Other Site → type members:/*your_screen_name* → Connect → OK → select the file you want to rename → Utilities → Rename → type the new name → Continue → OK

Renaming a file that's linked to in one of your web pages breaks the link: you must also update the link with the new filename.

To open a file

> Keyword: FTP → Go To FTP → Other Site → type members:/*your_screen_name* → Open → select the file you want to open

Double-clicking a file also opens it. We prefer using local copies of the files, rather than downloading the ones in the server space. We just modify the local file, then overwrite the one on the server. Overwriting saves time, since you don't have to open and then download the file from AOL.

To overwrite a file

> Keyword: FTP → Go To FTP → Other Site → type members:/ *your_screen_name* → Upload

You can overwrite the files in your server space simply by uploading a file to a destination in your server space that has an identical filename. Overwriting saves you from having to delete an old file before replacing it. Be careful that you don't accidentally overwrite a file that you wanted to keep.

AOLPress

Keyword: AOLPress or *http://www.aolpress.com*

AOLPress is a free WYSIWYG web-publishing tool from AOL. It allows easy uploading of web pages or entire web sites via a graphical user interface that's easy to use, even for a novice web publisher. Figure 23-4 shows AOLPress' graphical interface. The web site has full details on downloading, installing, and using AOLPress.

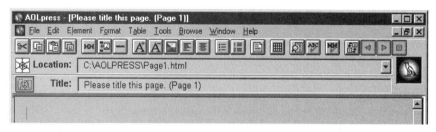

Figure 23-4: The AOL Press toolbar

AOLPress has a lot of features and is an excellent tool for anyone who wants to create professional looking web sites using just a little know-how. We're not going to cover all of the features and functions of the program. Instead, we recommend that you take the online tutorial that walks you through the rudiments. The tutorial is easy to use and allows you to modify practice web pages as you learn. Get to the tutorial via a link from the main AOLPress web site at *www.aolpress.com*.

Some things you should note when using AOL press

You must be signed on to AOL when you want to publish your pages with any publishing tool, including AOLPress.

AOLPress recognizes when you've reached your 2-MB limit for a given screen name and returns a *Failed* response if you exceed that limit. To circumvent this limit, upload other web pages via other screen names, linking within the pages to the appropriate screen names (i.e., one web site may reside at both *members.aol.com/screen_name1/* and at *members.aol.com/screen_name2/*).

To upload a page

File → Save as

Creating the pages is nearly as easy as creating a new document with your word processor. Uploading, however, gets a bit tougher, especially for the novice, and it's not as easy as AOLPress documentation would have you think. First, you must start with a web page or a set of pages that you want to upload to AOL. When

WWW & FTP

you choose File → Save As, you're given the option of saving to your local disk (which we recommend before uploading, just in case anything goes wrong) or to a remote computer. A screen appears that gives you a choice as to where you want the file(s) to be uploaded (see Figure 23-5). Choose the remote system (by default *members.aol.com* is one of your choices). At this point, you'll have to manually type in the screen name directory *your_screen_name*. That's easy enough.

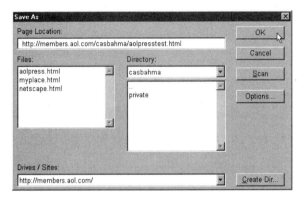

Figure 23-5: Publishing your page with the "save as" command

In the Page Location box, part of the path will already appear, usually as *http:// members.aol.com/name_of_your_page.HTML*. Here's where things get a bit tricky. Ideally, the *your_screen_name* directory would appear just after *members.aol.com*, but it doesn't. You have to insert the cursor just before the name of your page and type in your screen-name directory. That would look like:

http://members.aol.com/your_screen_name/name_of_your_page.HTML

If you want to add subdirectories, you can type the new directory name into the Page Location box. Position the cursor at the insertion point, such as:

http://members.aol.com/your_screen_name/new_directory/name_of_your_page.htm

Third-Party Web Publishing Tools

Besides the choices you've got from AOL, you can use any of the hundreds of applications from other software vendors to publish web pages to your AOL server space. Just as with AOL's own tools, you need to tell the software where to upload the pages. That means you must include the full path of the server space, including the *your_screen_name* directory and any other directories you want.

Each of these programs has its own interface and many of the details are unique, so we're not going to tell you exactly how to use them. However, this section is intended to do two things: (1) help you point these publishing tools toward your AOL server space, and (2) help you find the applications that are right for you.

Here's the basic way to get to your server space:

- Point your web publishing tool or FTP client to *http://members.aol.com/your_ screen_name* or *ftp://members.aol.com/your_screen_name*.

- When you upload, you must be signed on to AOL at the same time, via the same PC. Essentially, you'll run the publishing tool over your AOL connection.

It's extremely easy to use Netscape Communicator, Internet Explorer's FrontPage Express, or a host of other free or commercial publishing suites to publish web pages to your AOL server space. With many of these clients, the steps are similar to those required by AOLPress: you design the pages in the WYSIWYG editor, then upload them with a click or two.

Where to download the software

Below we list just a few of the application available to you. We link mainly to the main page of these companies, so you'll often have to look around for a link from that page to their products.

- Netscape Composer: *http://www.netscape.com*

- Microsoft Front Page (Express): *http://www.microsoft.com/ie/*

- Hot Dog: *http://www.sausage.com*

- HomeSite: *http://www.allaire.com/*

- HotMetal Pro: *http://www.sq.com/*

Uploading with Netscape

Netscape Composer (see Figure 23-6), part of the Communicator suite, is very easy to use. We've chosen it as our example because it's popular and freely down-loaded from Netscape's web site at *http://www.netscape.com*. If you use another application that could be just as easy to use, such as Microsoft Front Page Express, the details differ, but the general principles are the same:

1. You must be logged into AOL with the screen name you want to publish to.

2. From the Composer, open (or create) the web page you want to upload, and click the Publish icon.

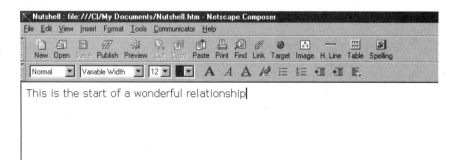

Figure 23-6: Preparing a page to be uploaded using Netscape Composer

3. You're then prompted with a `Publish:` window (shown in Figure 23-7). In the box `HTTP or FTP Location to publish to`, type the server space that you want to publish to, such as `http://members.aol.com/`*`your_ screen_name`*. Leave the `User name` and `Password` fields blank.

4. Click `OK` and Composer uploads your page. Note that you must upload to a valid directory path. AOL won't allow the Composer to create a new directory (folder) in your server space. So you'll have to create the directories beforehand; see "Basic File and Directory Management" for information on how to create directories.

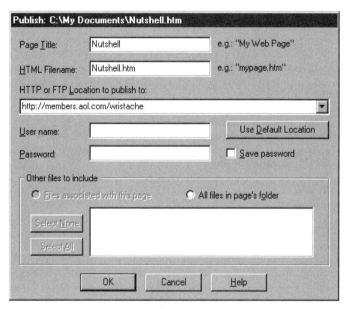

Figure 23-7: Using the Publish screen in Composer to direct files to the server space of user WristAche

Save Time with FTP Only

If you've already created the pages—either in an HTML editor, or by hand-coding them in a word processor—you might just want to publish (and manage) your documents using an FTP client. A standalone FTP client moves scores of files and even entire directories full of files from your computer to the AOL server space. You can rename, delete, and overwrite in seconds. That way, you won't have to keep uploading individual pages, one after the other, as you do with some of the applications like Netscape Communicator. Our favorite FTP-only application is WS_FTP, at *http://www.ipswitch.com/Products/WS_FTP/index.html*.

Recommended Books for More Advanced Web Publishing

So, you've dipped your toes into the web-publishing pool. But what happens when you're ready to create some pages that are well-coded stars? At the risk of blatant self-promotion, we offer up the following books by O'Reilly & Associates and Songline Studios as well-written and highly-regarded guides to creating for the Web:

- *HTML: The Definitive Guide* by Chuck Musciano and Bill Kennedy

- *Designing with JavaScript: Creating Dynamic Web Pages* by Nick Heinle

- *GIF Animation Studio: Animating Your Web Site* by Richard Koman

- *Designing for the Web: Getting Started in a New Medium* by Jennifer Niederst with Edie Freedman

- *Web Navigation: Designing the User Experience* by Jennifer Fleming

CHAPTER 24

Telnet

Telnet is a method of connecting with people and resources outside of AOL. You telnet within a client, which is an application that performs commands that allow it to talk to other computers, much the same way a web browser is an application that talks to other computers. You use AOL and Telnet as your connection to another computer, just as you use AOL and a web browser as your connection to the Web.

It was a big deal when AOL added Telnet to its Internet services, but that was before the Web exploded in popularity and size. People who used to get their online information via Telnet now get the same information from the Web. The Web is easier, and the text-only Telnet just can't compete with the graphic design of most web sites. However, if you're using a slow modem, you might grow to love Telnet just because it's so much faster than the graphics-rich Web.

No matter how fast your modem is and how much you love the Web, there still may be times when Telnet comes in handy. You might telnet to a non-AOL email account, an Internet chat, your local library, or a role-playing game. See the "Places to Telnet" section of this chapter for a partial tour of the land of Telnet.

If You're New to Telnet

Make sure you see the sections "What Do You Need to Telnet?" and "Using Telnet" before you attempt to connect to any Telnet sites.

Telnet Essentials

- For the sake of convenience, we sometimes refer you to `Keyword: Telnet` to download clients and get information. However, `Keyword: Telnet` doesn't appear to be updated very often. We suggest searching it to find the names of software you want, then searching for the most recent version of that software on the Web (at a site such as *http://www.download.com* or *http://www.shareware.com*).

- The easiest way to telnet through AOL is to use the built-in Windows 95/98 Telnet client (see "Windows 95/98 Telnet").

- Some organizations, as a security measure, don't allow you to telnet to their computers from remote sites. In other words, you might be able to check your email through Telnet at work, but you might not be able to telnet to your office from home.

What Do You Need to Telnet?

If you have AOL 4.0, you need two things: a Telnet client and your AOL software. A Telnet client is an application that performs commands that let your computer talk to other computers, much in the same way a web browser is an application that talks to other computers.

To get a Telnet client, use either the one that comes with Windows 95/98, or if you don't have Windows 95/98, download one. We cover both options below.

For Telnet to work, you need a file called *winsock.dll.* Both AOL 3.0 and AOL 4.0 come with their own *winsock.dll,* so you needn't download a special file.

Windows 95/98 Telnet

Conveniently, Windows 95/98 comes with a built in Telnet client. A Windows 95/98 Telnet window is shown in Figure 24-1.

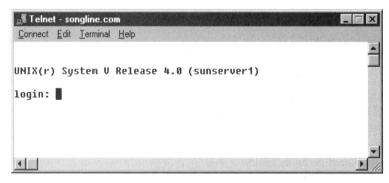

Figure 24-1: Telnetting through the built-in Windows 95/98 Telnet client

Telnetting through AOL with Windows 95/98 is incredibly easy. Just sign on to AOL and follow this path:

Windows 95/98 Start menu → Run . . . → type Telnet

You are then presented with the Windows 95/98 Telnet client. To telnet anywhere (see "Places to Telnet" for ideas):

Telnet Connect menu → Remote System . . . → type the address in the Host Name box → Connect

Methods of exiting the remote system vary (typing logout, exit, and quit are only a few possibilities). But exiting Windows 95/98 Telnet is easy enough:

Telnet Connect menu → Exit

Benefit

- You don't have to download or install a client. It's built right in.

Downloading and Installing a Telnet Client

If you choose not to use the Windows 95/98 client, or if you don't use Windows 95/98, you have to download a Telnet client. The only problem with that plan is that each client has its own commands and features, and we can't give you a comprehensive guide to all of them. Just make sure you read the documentation and use your common sense.

The easiest way to download and install a Telnet client (or a MUD, IRC, or any other kind of Net client) is to download one from Keyword: Telnet. Once you've downloaded a client, you have to install it. It's generally the same as installing any downloaded program (for downloading help, see Chapter 20, *Downloading*). To download the file:

Keyword: Telnet → Go To Net Clients

If the file ends in *.zip*, decompress it:

My Files toolbar icon → Download Manager → Download → Show Files Downloaded → highlight the file → Decompress

Then run the *.exe* program:

Windows Start menu → Run . . . → Browse . . . → locate the file on your hard drive and double-click it

As we said in the introduction of this chapter, however, Keyword: Telnet is outdated. If you don't mind a challenge, you're better off searching web sites such as *http://www.download.com* for a Telnet client. One good, free Telnet client is NCSA Telnet, available for PCs and Macs at *http://www.ncsa.uiuc.edu/SDG/Homepage/telnet.html*.

Benefits of downloading from the Web

- Wider selection of Telnet clients.

- More recent versions of Telnet clients.

Drawback

- If the download is compressed (that is, if it ends in *.zip* or *.sit*), you have to decompress it yourself. You'll need a utility such as WinZip, PKunzip, or StuffIt. Unless you're already familiar with these utilities, you might prefer to stick with AOL's download libraries. See also **decompressing** in Chapter 20, *Downloading*.

Using Telnet

To use Telnet to connect to a remote site, you must be signed on to AOL or be signed on to an ISP. When you connect to a remote site via Telnet, you won't see a `Sign On` screen like you do on AOL. You'll probably see a screen with instructions and a login prompt. For example:

```
Welcome to the BBS.
Login as 'Guest' to check things out, or 'New' to create an
account.
Name:
```

or:

```
UNIX(r) System V Release 4.0 (your_domain@your_college.edu)
login:
```

Every remote site is different, so be sure to follow the on-screen instructions.

Some Telnet sites want you to establish an account, including a username (like your AOL screen name) and a password. You'll sign on to those Telnet sites by entering a name and password, like you do on AOL. Choosing your password at a remote site is, in many ways, like choosing your AOL password: choose something obscure, don't use a word that appears in the dictionary, try to use at least one number in it, and never tell anyone what it is. It's also a bad idea to use a password you've already used for something else (like your AOL password).

Places to Telnet

Telnet may be archaic, but it's versatile: use it to check email, do research, play games, and chat with others.

Your Non-AOL Email

Who says you can't check your email from halfway across the country? Here are two Telnet scenarios:

- You're on a business trip or working from home, and you need to check your (non-AOL) work email account. If you have a computer with AOL on it, you can access your work email, too. Just sign on to AOL through a local access number (see also Chapter 27, *Connecting*). Once you're on AOL, use Telnet to connect to your work email. Caveat: your office, as a security measure, may not allow you to Telnet to your email from outside the office, or they might limit where remote logins can come from. You might want to talk to your system administrator at work before you try to telnet to work email from another place.

- You're a college student at your parents' house for Thanksgiving, and you want to check your school email. Sign on to your parents' AOL account and telnet to your university email account. Like the above work scenario, you might be prevented from connecting for security reasons, but we think this is rare on the college level.

You can't telnet to your AOL email, but you can check it from the Web. See also the entry *web-based email* in Chapter 8, *Email.*

Libraries and Other Useful Things

One task Telnet can do that the Web can't do better is search library catalogs. This is useful if you're looking for a book on a specific topic (you can also search an online bookstore like *http://www.amazon.com,* but depending on the subject you're looking up, libraries can be more extensive than any bookstore). Find out if your local library has the book you want. Some libraries even allow you to reserve books online. You can find a partial list of Telnet-accessible libraries at U.S. public libraries: *http://www.einet.net/hytelnet/US000PUB.html.*

If yours isn't listed there, try local resources like your city's official web page. For instance, we work in Cambridge, Massachusetts, so we used the City of Cambridge web site (*http://www.ci.cambridge.ma.us/libraries.html*) to track down Telnet information on our local library system. We discovered that to connect to the Boston area's Minuteman Library Network, all we had to do was telnet to *mln.lib.ma.us* and log in as `library`.

As for other useful things Telnet can do, the list is long. Whether you're intrigued by NASA databases or Chaucer bibliographies, you'll find an abundance of random information available via Telnet. To explore the vast, miscellaneous offerings of Telnet-accessible resources, try this web page, *http://www.einet.net/hytelnet/SITES2.html.*

Each resource's page gives you rudimentary instructions, such as what to type at the `login` prompt. Like we've said, you can probably find most of this information on the Web, but not all of it, and finding it via Telnet is faster on slow modems than waiting for web pages to load.

Bulletin Board Systems

Now we're getting into not-so-useful but potentially fun territory. Bulletin Board Systems (BBSs) resemble message boards (see also Chapter 11, *Message Boards*) and newsgroups (see also Chapter 13, *Newsgroups*) in that people carry on conversations by "posting" messages about specific topics. Like message boards and newsgroups, these conversations don't happen in real-time (live). BBSs' identifying features are:

- BBSs aren't threaded by subtopic. You read the posts in chronological order.

- BBSs are divided into topical forums, much like message boards are divided into topical folders, and Usenet is divided into topical newsgroups.

- BBSs tend to be moderated, usually with some people (called *sysops*) running the system as a whole and individual people moderating each forum.

- BBSs "scroll" faster than message boards and newsgroups. For instance, many BBS forums can hold 150 posts, so post #151 deletes post #1. Depending on the traffic of the BBS, you might have to log in often to keep up.

- Some BBSs come with a feature that allows you to have real-time conversations with individual users, much like AOL Instant Messages (see also Chapter 9, *Instant Messages and Buddy Lists*).

To connect to a BBS, use your Telnet client to connect to the BBS's address. If this concept confuses you, compare your Telnet client to your web browser and compare a BBS's address to a web page's URL. For lists of Telnet BBSs, try this web site: *http://www.thedirectory.org/Telnet.htm*.

Internet Chat

Internet Relay Chat (IRC) is a text-based system of real-time conversation about any topic imaginable. IRC is divided into *channels*, which we've heard compared to AOL chat rooms. There are even private channels, just like there are private chat rooms (see also "Private Rooms and Buddy Chat" in Chapter 10, *Chatting*).

You don't actually Telnet to IRC, but you do something very similar. You use IRC via an IRC client, which is usually a lot like the *client* (i.e., certain kind of computer program) you use to telnet or to read newsgroups. To find downloadable IRC clients, try *http://www.yahoo.com/Computers_and_Internet/Internet/Chat/IRC/Software/*.

After downloading, you use your IRC client (software) to connect to an IRC server (another computer on the Internet). Here are a few servers:

- *irc01.irc.aol.com*
- *irc02.irc.aol.com*
- *irc03.irc.aol.com*
- *irc04.irc.aol.com*
- *irc05.irc.aol.com*
- *irc06.irc.aol.com*
- *irc07.irc.aol.com*

Before you connect, you should read the IRC information at *http://www.irchelp.org*.

An interesting tidbit: AOL claims that their Terms of Service apply to IRC, though we're not sure how they intend to enforce that. See also Appendix D, *Terms of Service*.

*MUDS, MUSHes, and other MU*s*

MU* refers to MUDS, MUSHes, MUCKs, and MOOs. All of these are text-based, real-time, interactive, online environments. They are generally related to role-playing games, though there some are MU*s for other topics and some just for socializing. In role-playing MU*s, you play a character, though you can go out of character to chat with other players about nonrole-playing topics. In the social MU*s, you play yourself, but you make up a name (like your AOL screen name).

A few new acronyms often used in MU*s (see also Chapter 5, *Online Shorthand*):

- OOC: Out Of Character
- RPG: Role-Playing Game

*A brief guide to the various MU*s*

MUD stands for Multi-User Dungeon, or Multi-User Domain. MUDs tend to be hack-and-slash, combat-oriented role-playing games. Some MUD varieties (like TinyMUDs) are less combat-oriented and more closely resemble MUSHes.

MUSHes are a variation on MUDs (as far as we know the letters MUSH don't stand for anything, it's just a play on the word MUD). Role-playing MUSHes tend to be less combat-oriented and more social than MUDs. They also have the advantage that players can build their own text-based role-playing environments (we don't have any experience in this arena, but we're assured that it's pretty easy). Some MUSHes are just for socializing, not role-playing.

MUCK supposedly stands for Multi-User Construction Kit. MUCKs tend to be more free-form, sometimes themed, with less of a focus on building your own environment. MUCKS are often catch-alls for people's wild-and-crazy MU* ideas; for instance, you'd participate in a MUCK to develop an idea you don't think would adapt well to the MUD or MUSH format. A significant number of MUCKs are just for socializing, not for role-playing.

MOO stands for MUD Object-Oriented. They are mainly for social interaction (not role-playing) and for building your own environment.

Though you can (usually) connect to MU*s via Telnet, experienced users often prefer the additional features that specific clients can have. You can find out more about MU* clients at this web site, *http://www.netaxs.com/~jgreshes/clients.txt*.

To download a client from the Web or to learn everything you ever wanted to know about MUDS, MUSHes, MUCKS, and all the rest, try: *http://www.yahoo.com/Recreation/Games/Internet_Games/MUDs_MUSHes_MOOs_etc_/Indices/*.

CHAPTER 25

Third Party Add-Ons

Have you ever wished AOL had more or better features? Don't sit around waiting for AOL to improve things! There is plenty of software out there that lets you take the law (or at least your AOL experience) into your own hands. These renegade software programs are called *add-ons*.

Add-ons are third-party programs, which means they are created by companies other than AOL, or by individual people. Their expansion of AOL's existing abilities can make your AOL experience better, quicker, and easier. Many members can't imagine using AOL without them. The downside: AOL doesn't support them, and we often find them more trouble than they're worth.

Some older add-ons, like redialers and spell checkers, have become obsolete over time as AOL has improved its own features. We've skipped add-ons whose only features are now integrated into the AOL 4.0 software.

We can't guarantee that all these add-ons will be compatible with AOL 4.0, nor can we guarantee that they'll do what they promise. At the time of this writing, many of them were already 4.0-compatible—we've noted those—and we assume that most of the rest will be 4.0-compatible by the time you read this. We recommend you visit each add-on's web page for more information about its 4.0 compatibility.

We're sure more add-ons will be created as AOL 4.0 ages and gains even greater popularity. To find the latest AOL add-ons, go to a download web page such as *http://www.download.com* and search for AOL. Or, go to Keyword: File Search, click Shareware, click Past Month radio button, and search for aol add-on.

You have to download all these add-ons. If you don't understand how to download, see Chapter 20, *Downloading*, especially the entry *Web*.

Add-Ons

Some Add-On Capabilities

Since the best add-ons have features that don't exist in AOL's natural state, you might not even know what some of these features are. Here, we explain three common add-on capabilities.

Anti-Logoffs

Sometimes when you're downloading a large file, playing a game, or browsing the Web, AOL thinks your account is idle and disconnects you. You get an idle warning first and are asked to click OK, but if you're using a non-AOL web browser, for instance, you might miss the warning. In addition, whether you're idling or not, AOL asks you if you want to stay signed on every 46 minutes.

An *anti-logoff* utility is software that keeps you from being disconnected from AOL. Anti-logoff add-ons click OK when AOL asks if you want to stay online, and they work for both the idle warning and the 46-minute timer.

There has been some confusion and debate about whether anti-logoff programs are against Terms of Service (TOS). Whether they're officially permitted or not, AOL frowns upon anti-logoff utilities because they may encourage people to hog modem lines and stay signed on to AOL while they shower, cook dinner, etc. If you use an anti-logoff utility, use it for good (web browsing, downloading), not evil (staying signed on waiting for email while you read *War and Peace*).

Macros

A *macro* is, essentially, a set of commands, clicks, or keyboard strokes that can be done with a single command or keyboard stroke that you customize. Macros can speed up your online experience if there are certain sets of commands you use regularly. AOL doesn't have macro capability built in, but some add-ons provide it.

Auto-Reply

An *auto-reply* program sends an automated response to people who Instant Message you. You might want to tell people who IM you things like, "Can't talk now; I'm working" or "I can't come to my IM right now because I'm downloading an enormous file."

Hopefully you wouldn't ever need to say "Can't talk now; I'm walking the dog" or "Sorry, I'm grocery shopping." See our point about modem-hogging in the previous section, "Anti-Logoffs."

You might be interested to know that AOL's Instant Messenger client for the Internet supports auto-reply. They call it "away."

See also Chapter 9, *Instant Messages and Buddy Lists*.

The Add-Ons

This section provides a list of popular AOL add-ons, their web sites, their features, and their cost, if any.

AOLPress (http://www.aolpress.com)
> Some members consider this web publishing tool an add-on. (Freeware) See also Chapter 23, *Web Publishing and FTP*.

AOL SuperFreeTools (http://www.cdhnet.com/scree/aolsft.htm)
> Clears the stuck AOL hourglass, provides anti-logoff, auto-replies to IMs and Buddy Chat invitations, breaks into full chat rooms, and much more. Some features are compatible with AOL 4.0. (Freeware)

CRoom (http://members.aol.com/tartanhelp/croom.html)
> Allows you to customize your chat room interface. Probably a must for chat addicts! (Shareware, $19.95)

GetRight (http://www.headlightsw.com/getright.html)
> Resumes interrupted web downloads the same way the Download Manager can resume interrupted AOL downloads. (Shareware, $17.50)

PowerMail (http://www.bpssoft.com/PowerMail/index.htm)
> Souped up email in the form of style templates, form letters, letterheads, signatures, address book replacement, macros, and other email features. (Shareware, $35; $28 if you register before your free evaluation period ends; $23 for registered PowerTools users)

PowerTools (http://www.bpssoft.com/PowerTools/index.htm)
> An extremely popular add-on that gives you enhancements, such as gathering all Instant Messages into one window, customization of AOL's toolbar, a sound-file manager, automatic logging of chat rooms and Instant Messages, macro capability, a more advanced Favorite Places list, tools to break into full chat rooms, custom windows (such as IM, Keyword, and Locate), a master keyword directory, a session timer and alarm clock, and a few more. Power-Tools has been updated for AOL 4.0. (Shareware, $29.95; $23.95 if you register before your free evaluation period ends)

PowerWatch (http://www.bpssoft.com/PowerWatch/index.htm)
> Keeps track of how much time you, or your children, spend online. There's also an automatic timer setting which parents can use to limit their children's online time. (Shareware, 19.95; $14.95 if you register before your free evaluation period ends)

Stay Connected (http://www.inKlineGlobal.com)
> An anti-logoff utility, compatible with AOL 4.0. (Shareware, $19.95)

SweetalkPro (http://www.sweetalk.com/html/body_sweetalkpro.htm)
> Anti-logoff, Instant Message auto-reply, macro capabilities, and more. (Shareware, $19.95)

Terminator (http://www.tpasoft.com/term/term_main.html)
> An anti-logoff utility, compatible with AOL 4.0. (Shareware, $5)

Add-Ons

TransAOL (http://members.aol.com/VinceDeb/)

Lets you send and receive AOL email via your U.S. Robotics Pilot (personal digital assistant). (Freeware)

Way To Go (`Keyword: WTG`)

Includes macro capability and tools to customize the AOL interface. Some of the features are obsolete, like the ones that sound a lot like Buddy Lists, Automatic AOL, and the online clock. It has supposedly been updated for 4.0 compatibility, but we couldn't find any documentation of its new features. (Shareware, $25)

PART VI

Configuration

If you've come this far in this book, you've done an amazing amount of work improving how you use AOL. You've installed and set up your account, maximized your abilities to communicate with your friends and colleagues worldwide, learned more efficient ways to navigate and find things on AOL and the Web, gotten yourself organized, and become an AOL power user. Now we're going to go into even more detail. In the next six chapters we've condensed the nitty gritty behind-the-scenes of AOL, getting further under its hood, so that if you choose, you can further optimize it to work better for you.

It seems that every operating system, online service, web browser, and word- processing application has an infinite number of options and preferences you can change to suit your needs. AOL is no exception. Throughout this book we've been giving you some context for each of the ways you can use and modify AOL, and with this section we take that a step farther. Think of it as your reference for changing a feature, or as a tutorial you read through to better understand how AOL works, and the many ways that you can make it your own.

This part of the book, more than any other, is intended to be read in piecemeal fashion. Jump around among the next six chapters depending on your needs. Read a small section, or read an entire chapter. Parents have a chapter just for them. The privacy chapter is one of our favorites, since most people's primary online concern is the safekeeping of their personal information. We show you how to keep both your integrity and sanity.

Chapter 26, *System Requirements*: What does your computer need to satisfy the demands of AOL's bloated software?

Chapter 27, *Connecting*: Making your modem (or your TCP/IP connection) behave, and traveling with AOL.

Chapter 28, *Parental Controls*: Decide what your kids can see, and make sure AOL can't control what *you* see.

Chapter 29, *Preferences*: Hold the pickle, hold the lettuce, hold the annoying advertisements. Here's our synopsis of everything you can tweak on AOL.

Chapter 30, *Privacy*: Don't get paranoid; get smart about your options.

Chapter 31, *Canceling and Suspending Service*: We help you say goodbye to AOL, temporarily or forever.

CHAPTER 26

System Requirements

There's no denying that AOL 4.0 is a large, memory-intensive program. Unless your hardware is fairly new, your computer will sputter and die at the mere thought of running AOL 4.0. Even if your hardware is state-of-the-art, you still may have trouble multitasking with AOL 4.0 (that is, running other applications at the same time). To be fair, we point out that AOL is not solely responsible for the multitasking problem: most Windows 95/98 applications hog hard-drive space and memory, so when you put two or three together, it's bound to be a drain on system resources.

If your computer and all its components are five years old and you want to run AOL, you have three options: upgrade some of your hardware, run an older version of AOL (such as 3.0), or reconsider whether AOL is really for you. (see also Appendix A, *AOL as an ISP*).

In this chapter, we evaluate AOL 4.0's system requirements, i.e., what kind of hardware AOL officially recommends you have before trying to run 4.0.

Hard Drive

AOL recommends, for both the 16- and 32-bit versions of AOL 4.0, that you have 30 MB of hard disk space available. We'd suggest more, like 60. You want to have some extra drive space available after you install AOL, otherwise your system will slowly grind to a halt. Essentially, as the browser and AOL's own caches fill up, you'll have less space on your drive to use for virtual memory.

Modem

AOL recommends, for both the 16- and 32-bit versions of AOL 4.0, a 14.4 or faster modem. With a graphics-intensive program like AOL, the faster the better. No matter which ISP you use, the fastest modem possible will decrease your frustration with slow-loading web pages.

Monitor

AOL recommends, for both the 16- and 32-bit versions of AOL 4.0, a 640×480 monitor with 256 colors or more. Not only is a 16-color palate ugly, it can make some text illegible and prevent some text and graphics from appearing where they should. The size of your monitor also affects AOL's functionality if you want to customize your toolbar: your monitor resolution must be at least 800×600 if you want room to add your own toolbar icons. At 800×600 resolution, you'll have to remove one of the icons before there is room for yours; we removed the Weather toolbar icon. At resolutions of 1024×768 or more, you have plenty of extra room for your own toolbar icons.

Processor

AOL recommends a 486 or better for AOL 4.0 16-bit versions on Windows 3.x; a Pentium or better for AOL 4.0 32-bit versions on Windows 95/98. It's physically possible to run AOL 4.0 for Windows 95/98 on 486 machines—we do it every day—but it requires patience. We've heard complaints about AOL 4.0's system-resource-draining ways from people running processors as fast as the Pentium 166-MHz.

RAM

AOL recommends 16 MB for AOL 4.0 16-bit versions on Windows 3.x and AOL 4.0 32-bit versions on Windows 95/98. Of course, the more RAM you have, the faster AOL runs. And we don't recommend multitasking if you're running AOL 4.0 on a 486 with 16 MB of RAM—talk about slow! With a faster processor, such as a Pentium, you can get away with less RAM and still have adequate speed and multitasking.

CHAPTER 27

Connecting

When you're not connected to AOL's network of computers, all you've got is a bunch of software that just sits on your hard drive taking up space. Connecting to AOL takes many forms, but by far the most popular is via a modem. This chapter walks you through modems, describing what they are and how to set yours up to work optimally with AOL. Along the way, we cover all there is to know about dial-up access numbers, which are what your modem dials to get you connected. Finally, we cover the many alternate ways you can connect to AOL, ways many AOL users aren't familiar with, but that can save a lot of trouble and effort.

Use this chapter to troubleshoot problems with your connection, if you move around a lot and need additional access numbers, or if you want to find ways into AOL that help you avoid the dial-up network—and busy signals—altogether.

This chapter is divided into the following sections:

- "Understanding Modems" and "Dialing In: You Need an Access Number (or Two)." In these two sections, we discuss the rudiments of what modems do, and how you use access numbers with AOL. If you don't know anything about modems or how they work, use these brief sections as the bedrock from which you can build further understanding.

- "Connection Setup" and "Adding and Modifying U.S. and International Numbers and Locations" deal with identifying your modem, adding a new modem, and setting up new access numbers. You should also come here when you need to know how to add new access numbers, such as times when you're on the road, or you move to another city.

- "No Local Access Numbers?" helps you use 800/888 numbers or choose an alternate way of connecting to AOL.

- "Adding a New Modem" shows you what to do when you upgrade your modem.

- "General Modem Settings" is for modifying the modem sound, the dialing prefixes, using touch-tone service, and all the other little ways to customize and maximize your modem connection.

- "For Experts Only: Your Options in Detail" is a brief outline for those of you who want to bypass AOL's walkthrough and zero right in on changing all aspects of your setup by hand.

- "Modem Problems" tells you where to get answers if you're having trouble with your modem.

- "Alternatives to Dialing In to AOL" shows you all the ways to use TCP/IP to get into AOL, including your Internet access at work, other dial-up access providers, ISDN, or via cable modems. This is also the place to come to if you want to keep AOL, but don't want to dial up over AOL's network for some reason (e.g., busy signals). Additionally, you should be familiar with these types of connections if you access AOL from work or school.

Understanding Modems

The capacity of analog modems has increased significantly in the last five years, going from 2400 bits per second (bps) to the current 56 kilobits per second (56,000 bps), an increase of more than 2,000 percent. Despite the fact that there are faster, albeit more expensive, ways to transmit data (cable modems, ISDN, and digital satellite, to name a few), analog modems have remained accessible and relatively cheap, and as a result are what most people use to access AOL.

You've got a number of current modem options, which we've divided into two categories:

33.6-, 28.8-, 14.4-, and 9600-baud modems
These modem capacities are all admissible by AOL, with 14.4 baud being the slowest modem AOL recommends for use with 4.0. If you use anything slower than a 14.4, you're going to be waiting around for a while every time you try to do anything, including simply reading AOL email, due to the graphics explosion that's happened on AOL and the Web. If, like most people, you're going to go the modem route, we recommend at least a 28.8. But the 56K is faster.

56K modems
For most of 1997 and part of 1998, there were two major, but incompatible, 56K modem protocols, x2 and K56flex. AOL and other major ISPs allowed access via both of these protocols, each having their own access numbers due to the incompatibility (that is, you couldn't use an x2 modem at home to dial into a K56flex on AOL's side).

You can expect AOL to continue to have access via both x2 and K56flex in most cities during the near future. In early 1998, the International Telecommunications Union (ITU) ratified a 56K standard that should ensure that 56K modems manufactured in the future are compatible. If you purchase a new 56K modem now, it most likely adheres to this standard. However, many people purchased these modems before the standard and will have to upgrade to the standard (contact your modem manufacturer if you don't know how to upgrade yours). Until most people upgrade their x2 and K56flex modems to the ITU standard, AOL and other ISPs will have to continue offering two ways to connect at 56K.

During the initial set up, AOL automatically detects the type of modem you have, and adjusts its software settings to enable the modems on its end to talk to the modem attached to your computer. If the automatic process goes well, AOL's modems successfully send and receive data to and from yours.

But things can go wrong: Auto Detect might make a mistake in identifying your modem. Sometimes that's not a problem, because you'll be sending and receiving data using a generic modem profile. But often, if your modem is misidentified, you'll have a poor connection or none at all. And who wants to use a generic modem profile when a profile tailored to your modem will most likely minimize data transfer problems and maximize speed?

We know from experience that modem connections really give some users a headache, especially when connections are frequently lost, despite everything seeming to be OK during the initial set up. Later in this chapter, we describe how to set up your modem and optimize its settings. If you don't like what Auto Detect has come up with, you can manually tell AOL your modem make and model.

Dialing In: You Need an Access Number (or Two)

Access numbers are the phone numbers your modem dials to connect you to AOL. Think of it as dialing a friend's home phone number: you dial him, and he answers on the other end of the line. You should have several AOL access numbers set up, in case one of them is busy or malfunctioning (we explain how to set up access numbers later in the chapter). Having multiple access numbers is like having multiple numbers for your friend: his home phone, work phone, pager, and fax number. Whether you're trying to reach AOL or a friend, the rule is the same: the more dialing options you have, the more likely you are to get through. You might rely on one most of the time, but it is always nice to have the others handy.

The phrase "access numbers" may be irrevocably linked in AOL members' minds with the phrase "busy signals." AOL has been wearing the Busy Signal Albatross around its neck for some time now, but we can honestly say that we haven't had problems dialing in since AOL started running those Steve Case "We're working hard to serve your needs" commercials. Of course, we can't speak for everyone, and we've heard some less-than-impressive reports from other parts of the country.

AOL will always be playing catch up when it comes to access numbers and modems; the more popular AOL becomes, the more modems they'll need. Of course, AOL realizes their dilemma, and plans for growing usage, but unexpected surges in subscribers or usage could cause busy signals. If you're currently getting a lot of busy signals, you might be able to sign on at night, when everyone else is asleep; see Chapter 21, *Automatic AOL*, for some ways to sneak onto the service.

Access Number Essentials

In the sections below, we cover the basics first—getting to know how AOL thinks of access numbers as being part of locations like home, work, etc. Then we have sections on some rather specific issues involving access numbers themselves. If you already know something about organizing your access numbers, you could skip to one of the sections below:

- If you'll be using AOL from more than one place, you'll want to add more "locations." To add an additional location (Grandma's House, Paris, or any-where you want) and a set of access numbers for that location, see "Adding and Modifying U.S. and International Numbers and Locations." This is espe-cially useful when traveling with a laptop.

- To add more access numbers to a location, see "To Add a New Location."

- If you'll be traveling somewhere that doesn't have its own local access num-bers, your only way to connect may be through a surcharged access number. See "No Local Access Numbers?" for details and caveats.

Dial-In Alternatives

What happens when you don't want to dial in to AOL? Maybe you've got a super-fast cable modem or ISDN, but you don't want to give up your old AOL account? Maybe you just don't like AOL's busy signals, but you still want AOL. Or you want some quick access from work, where your employer already has a high-speed Internet pipe set up for you. You've got options. You can subscribe to AOL under the "Bring Your Own Access Plan" (see also Chapter 22, *Billing*). Any way you choose to get in, you connect to the Internet using another Internet service, then run AOL over that connection.

TCP/IP is the way to access AOL that avoids AOL's own dial-up network. TCP/IP is a protocol that handles traffic on the Internet. There are a lot of TCP/IP options open to you if you want to access AOL that way; we cover them in greater detail later, in the section "Alternatives to Dialing In to AOL."

Connection Setup

Now let's get started with setting up your access numbers. Note that your modem may already be set up. If you've upgraded from another version of AOL, you probably won't have to touch the setup, since your old preferences and access numbers will have been transferred over. If you haven't used your new software yet, see Chapter 2, *Installing and Upgrading*.

However, use the instructions below if you need to update or reset your modem connections. We suggest you read through the following section from start to finish to get a feel for what your options are.

In general, using AOL's Auto Detect feature for setting up both your modem and the access numbers it uses is the easiest way to get your connection started or to add a new location, such as access numbers for a new city. More advanced options include directly modifying the access numbers and adding new numbers to AOL by hand if you already have a list of numbers you like.

It All Happens Via the Sign-On Screen

To begin any connection setup or modification, you must be signed off of AOL and be at the Sign On screen. The sign on screen is present both when you start up the AOL software, and—looking slightly different—when you sign off. If you don't see it, go to the Sign On menu and choose Sign On Screen. Now you're ready to set up your modem and access numbers:

From the Sign On screen → Setup

Connection Setup Main Options

Once you click Setup from the Sign On Screen, you're taken to the America Online Setup window, as shown in Figure 27-1. In setting up and adjusting your modem and connection options, there are four choices.

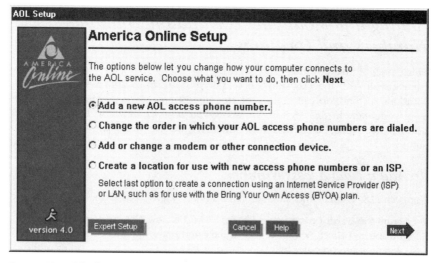

AOL Setup

America Online Setup

The options below let you change how your computer connects to the AOL service. Choose what you want to do, then click **Next**.

⦿ Add a new AOL access phone number.

○ Change the order in which your AOL access phone numbers are dialed.

○ Add or change a modem or other connection device.

○ Create a location for use with new access phone numbers or an ISP.

Select last option to create a connection using an Internet Service Provider (ISP) or LAN, such as for use with the Bring Your Own Access (BYOA) plan.

version 4.0 | Expert Setup | Cancel | Help | Next

Figure 27-1: The four primary options at the main access number setup screen

By choosing one of the four options we explain below, you can easily set up AOL to work with your modem, find new access numbers, make new locations if you take your computer on the road, or configure AOL to bypass its own dial up network and use an Internet connection you already have. Your options are:

- Add a new AOL access phone number: Allows you to get new dial-up numbers either to replace or to supplement old ones. In addition, you can add numbers to an existing location, such as the default Home location, or you can create a new location, such as Paris or Work, to which the new numbers are added. Note that you need more than one location only if you take your computer on the road.

- Change the order in which your AOL access phone numbers are dialed: AOL dials the numbers in the order they've been placed in the list, so that if the first number encounters a busy signal, AOL will move on to the next number, and so on, until a connection is made. If you find that one of your numbers is consistently busy, you should lower its position so that it is dialed after two or more other numbers have been tried first. In addition, you can delete numbers altogether here.

- **Add or change a modem or other connection device**: Use this when you've installed or upgraded your modem. AOL will automatically detect the type of modem you have, or you have the option of telling AOL the make and model.

- **Create a location for use with new access phone numbers or an ISP**: Use this option if you want to connect over your LAN at work, or want to use the Bring Your Own Access plan (BYOA) for connecting to AOL using another ISP. In addition, you can add new locations and dial-up numbers using this step, although it is the same as using the **Add a new AOL access phone number** option described above.

Adding and Modifying U.S. and International Numbers and Locations

Since one of the advantages of AOL as an ISP is that there are local access numbers all over the U.S. and the world, you'll want to add new numbers and locations so that you can dial in toll-free almost any place you find yourself and your computer. In this section, we show you how to add new access numbers, add new locations, delete locations, and sign on using one of the locations you've set up.

To Add a New Access Number

For both U.S./Canada and international numbers, there's one place to go:

From the **Sign On** screen → **Setup** → **Add a new AOL access phone number** → **Next** → choose the country and enter the area code of the place where your computer will be located → **Next** → select a location from the drop down box → highlight a number and click **Add**, then **OK** (repeat until you have at least two access numbers) → **Sign On**

While you're adding the new numbers, you can rename the location, or add a new location by choosing **Add Location** from the **Add numbers to this Location:** drop-down box. We explain how to add a new location in more detail in the section below, "To add a new location."

Once you've entered your location and area code, you'll be taken to a screen that asks you to **Select AOL Access Phone Numbers**. This is where you must examine the list of dial-up numbers and determine which are the best for you, which we explain in the tips below. Figure 27-2 shows the **Select AOL Access Phone Numbers** screen.

The next sections give a couple of tips on getting the best numbers.

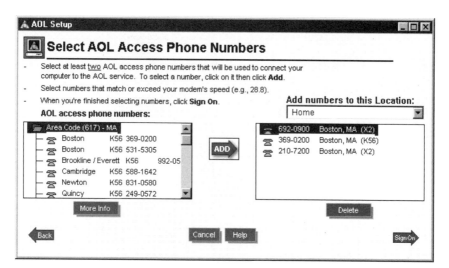

Figure 27-2: Adding new access nmbers to the "Home" location

Choose numbers that are toll free

Dialing in to local, toll-free numbers is always preferable to dialing numbers that happen to be in an adjacent suburb or city. You'll save on toll charges that some local phone companies impose for local calls not included in your basic monthly fee, but which aren't quite "long distance" either. Below we explain how the process of selecting the best number works. Here's one place where many AOL members initially fail, since they assume all the numbers listed are toll free. They may be, but it all depends on where you're calling from.

Once you give AOL the area code (or the international city code), you're presented with local numbers and the modem speeds those numbers serve. Here's what to do to select the best new numbers for your location:

Look for your town. In almost all cases, your town or one near it will be listed. It's a pretty safe bet that those numbers are in that local calling area. However, you may find that some of the numbers are outside what your local phone company considers your local calling area, even if it's in the same area code. It's your responsibility to make sure that any numbers AOL dials are local.

For example, if you live in a large urban area, you might find that your telephone plan has a "free" calling area as well as additional areas—nearby villages, towns, or even adjacent neighborhoods—that aren't really long-distance calls, but for which the phone company charges a small fee. What happens when the AOL number you choose is outside this calling area? Your local phone company may charge you an added toll to call these numbers. This is not an AOL fee since AOL won't charge you for using an access number that's not local to you.

Check the numbers with your phone company to confirm if you're unsure. Or look in your local phone book to see which local exchanges are included in your monthy telephone plan. If you can't find a number that's a local, nontoll call for you, it's often possible to get a larger local area from your local phone company.

Use an access number with at least the capacity of your modem

If you've got a 14.4, choose a 14.4, 28.8, 33.6, or x2 or K56flex access number. The modem capacity is listed next to the city, before the phone number. When you dial in, AOL recognizes your modem speed, and adjusts data transfer rates accordingly.

Benefits of additional numbers

- Adding more numbers gives you a better chance of connecting; if one number is busy, AOL has alternatives.

- If you upgrade your modem to one with higher capacity, you want to find new access numbers that can match this increase. You don't want to be using an access number that's limited to 28.8 if you have a modem that has more capacity than that.

- If you're going to be traveling, adding new local access numbers before you go may be cheaper than using the surcharged 800 number. (Remember that you first have to create a new dialing location for each city; for this, see the previous section.)

- Access numbers are dialed in the order you've added them. Uppermost are dialed first. Drag and drop each number to put the best (read: least busy) at the top of the listing.

- With older versions of AOL, you have to use your modem to connect to an 800 number every time you want to look up a new access number. In AOL 4.0, almost all of the access numbers are stored on your hard drive. Occasionally, you'll choose a country for which AOL needs to dial the 800 number to get the access numbers.

Drawback

- There is a small chance you won't be able to find any access numbers in your area. See "No Local Access Numbers?"

To Add a New Location

New locations, such as Home2, Work, or even Paris or Kalamazoo are easily added at any time. Just repeat the setup process that you'd use to add a new access number, but choose Add Location from the Add number to this Location: box. Here's the full path to add a new location:

> From the Sign On screen → Setup → Add a new AOL access number → highlight the location you want to modify → Add Number → select a country and enter an area code in the Area Code box → Next → select Add Location from the Add numbers to this Location: drop-down box

You can then name your new location anything you'd like. Remember that it will appear among the choices in the drop-down box on the Sign On screen. Next, add your dial-up numbers in the usual fashion by highlighting them and clicking Add. When you've added at least two numbers, click Sign On to save your new location and your new access numbers.

Benefits of additional locations

- Set up locations for all the places you log in from: home, work, friends' and relatives' houses, vacations you take anywhere in the world. You can gain access to your account no matter where you are, usually—not always—with a toll-free local access number.

- No matter what exotic locale you're headed for, you'll always have your email.

Drawbacks

- You need to remember to change the location in the Select Location drop-down box on the Sign On screen each time you log on in a new place. AOL can't read your mind about what location you're at!

- Beware of intense surcharges on some international numbers: Globalnet numbers have surcharges of up to $24 an hour in some areas. AOLNet international numbers are usually $3.95 per hour. To find out what each number will cost you (which AOL really should tell you when you set up the number!), check Keyword: International Access → Search for a number.

- If you can't find any local access numbers for the country you'll be going to, see "No Local Access Numbers?" in this chapter.

To Sign on With One of Your Locations:

Sign On screen → Select Location drop-down menu → highlight the location of your choice → Sign On

Figure 27-3 shows using the drop-down menu on the Sign On screen to select Paris from among our Locations.

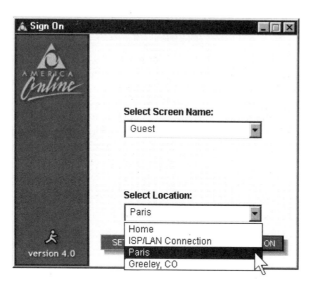

Figure 27-3: Selecting "Paris" from the drop-down menu on the Sign On screen

To Delete Any Location

You might want to delete a location because you no longer use it (say, after a one-time business trip, or a move across the country). If you leave them in place, they won't do any harm, but cleaning up never hurt. Figure 27-4 shows how to delete "Paris" as a location. If you choose to delete a location, follow this path:

> Sign On screen → Setup → Expert Setup → Locations tab → highlight the location to delete → Delete

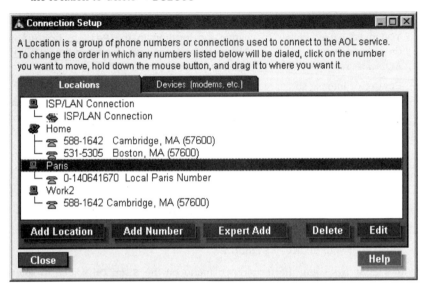

Figure 27-4: Preparing to delete the Paris Location

Using Expert Add (If You Already Know the Number)

Using `Expert Add` is a quick way to add a new number to a location if you already have the number ready. `Expert Add` won't look up numbers for you, so you need to get the number from a friend or perhaps from AOL (they publicized some additional numbers during 1997's access crunch, and people who frequented `Keyword: Access` could use them; other people knew nothing about them). Use `Expert Add` if you want to avoid the walk-through method: for instance, you can immediately tailor all the settings from one screen, including setting the number of times to dial the number, the COM port, or dialing prefixes for call waiting or an outside line.

Follow this path to enter your new access number or new location manually:

> From the Sign On screen → Expert Setup → Locations tab → highlight the location you want to add the access number to → Expert Add

No Local Access Numbers?

In the rare instance that there are no local numbers in your area, your options are:

- Use a surcharged 800 number (see "Surcharged 800 Numbers").

- Use another ISP with a local access number and sign on to AOL via TCP/IP. Accessing AOL via TCP/IP is often called the "bring your own access plan," and it's about half the price of a standard AOL account (although you have to pay your local ISP, too, which may make the total cost more than the standard AOL rate). See "Alternatives to Dialing In to AOL."

- Contact your local phone company about the possibility of widening your local calling area. Often, for just a few extra dollars a month to your local telephone company, you'll have a calling plan that's broad enough to include local AOL numbers, say in an adjoining town or suburb.

Surcharged 800 Numbers

You used to think that 800 numbers were, by definition, toll free. AOL shifts your paradigm by having 800 numbers that currently cost 10 cents a minute. The call won't show up on your phone bill (that's the 800-number part), but your AOL account will be billed (that's the surcharged part). Here are the numbers: 1-800-716-0023 or 1-888-245-0113. In Canada, use 1-800-318-2265. You set them up just like any other number; we outline the process below. Figure 27-5 shows how to set up surcharged 800 numbers in a new location that we've called "800 Number."

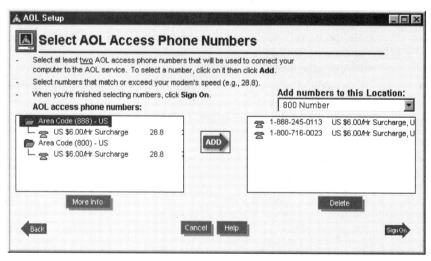

Figure 27-5: Setting up your AOL account to dial surcharged 800 numbers

Remember, it's cheaper if you can find a local access number; see "Adding and Modifying U.S. and International Numbers and Locations."

To set up a new Location that dials the 800 or 888 number:

From the Sign On screen → Setup → Add a new AOL access number →
Next → enter 800 or 888 in the area code box → Next → name the location
(for instance, "800 number") by choosing Add Location in the Add number
to this Location: box → highlight the number you want to use → Add →
Sign On

To use the surcharged number:

From the Sign On screen → select the Location drop-down menu →
choose the location that contains the 800 or 888 number

Benefits to surcharged 800/888 numbers

- If there are no local access number in your area, or if you are traveling, you
  can still connect to AOL from any place you find a phone jack.

- These numbers, except the Canadian number, work from anywhere in the
  United States, Puerto Rico, or the U.S. Virgin Islands. Or you can dial in from
  other countries in a pinch, but you're better off finding numbers in those
  countries (see "Adding and Modifying U.S. and International Numbers and
  Locations").

- 800 numbers connect at speeds up to 28.8.

Drawbacks

- You are charged an added fee (currently 10 cents per minute) for connecting
  with these numbers, even if you use them during your free trial period. The
  fee is added to your AOL bill; it's not a phone company charge.

- If you use the Bring Your Own Access billing plan, you get charged just as
  much: 10 cents per minute (see also Chapter 22, *Billing*). In the cases of multiple surcharges, the highest one applies.

- If you're traveling, a better option is to look up the local access numbers for
  that area. See "Adding and Modifying U.S. and International Numbers and
  Locations" and follow the instructions for adding a new location and access
  numbers.

Adding a New Modem

Adding a new modem is rare. AOL makes it easy to update the modem drivers
with Auto Detect, in which AOL scans your computer looking for new modems,
then automatically sets itself up to work with the modem. The feature Expert
Add is useful if AOL fails to properly identify your modem make and model.

The Expert Add feature is useful to configure AOL to work with your new
modem. Follow this path:

From the Sign On screen → Setup → Add or change a modem or other
connection device → Next

AOL scours your computer in order to identify your modem. From there you've got two options:

- **Accept the modem AOL has detected**: AOL tells you the type of modem it thinks you have. Make sure you confirm that AOL did, in fact, detect the correct make and model. If so, click `Next`. If AOL got it wrong, choose the option we outline next, `Change modem`.

- **Change modem**: Tell AOL what type of modem you've got by locating it from a huge list. Refer to your modem's documentation if you're unsure of the exact make and model. Figure 27-6 shows the `Change Modem` screen where you manually select your new modem from the lengthy, scrollable list. Once you select it from the list, you can choose to modify the speaker volume, port, or speed by clicking `Settings...`

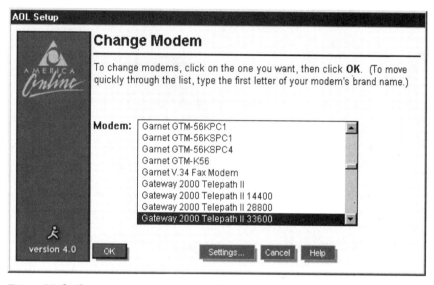

Figure 27-6: Choosing your modem from Change Modem, rather than using Auto Detect

General Modem Settings

There are times when you want more control over the modem and access number settings. Perhaps you've grown tired of hearing the modem dialing followed by the high-pitched squeal that signals a connection has been made. You can turn off the sound! In addition, you can set the dialing prefixes, disable call waiting, and maybe speed up your modem connection. Most of the settings we describe in this section can be modified via a single screen, shown in Figure 27-7.

If you want to modify a default setting, you have to get to the `Connection Setup` screen. Follow this path:

> `Sign On` screen → `Setup` → `Expert Setup` → highlight the dial-up number you want to edit → `Edit`

Note that this only changes the preferences for one number. If you have more than one access number, you have to repeat the steps for each of them.

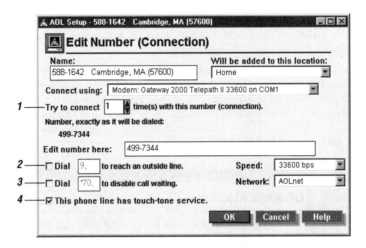

Figure 27-7: Adjusting general modem settings by editing an existing access number

We describe some of the settings below. The numbers correspond to the numbers in Figure 27-7.

1. *Redialing*: By default, each access number gets redialed once before moving to the next number in the current Connection Location. AOL tries the number up to nine times before moving to the next number. Use the arrows to increase or decrease the number of times AOL tries to dial this number.

2. *Outside line*: Oftentimes, especially in offices, you'll have to dial a prefix (e.g., 9) to get an outside line. Check the box `Dial 9, to reach an outside line`. Type a new number into the default box if 9 is not the way to reach an outside line from the phone system you intend to use. Be sure that there's a comma after the number (e.g., `9,`) so that AOL waits to get the outside line.

   Remember to edit each number in this location; otherwise, you won't be able to dial out if AOL tries subsequent access numbers.

3. *Call waiting*: If you don't disable call waiting when you're online, the signals from incoming calls cause interference in the line, and you'll probably lose your connection to AOL. Call waiting is restored when you sign off of AOL. Check the box `Dial *70, to disable call waiting`. Type a new number into the default box if *70 is not the way to disable call waiting in your area. Be sure that there's a comma after the dialing prefix (e.g., `*70,`) since this comma tells AOL to pause for a moment to ensure call waiting is off.

   You'll also have to edit each access number in this location; otherwise, you'll still get bumped by incoming calls when you use other numbers.

Special note about call waiting: if you have a voicemail system on the line that uses a broken or stuttering tone to signal that you've got new voice messages, AOL might read this as "no dialtone," and consequently won't dial out successfully. There are a couple of remedies, though. You can call your phone company and ask them about disabling the broken/stuttering tone, or you can enter three commas `,,,` before `*70,` in the `Dial *70, to disable call waiting` box. The commas signal AOL to pause before attempting the next move, thus allowing the broken tones to cease.

4. *Tone versus pulse dialing:* Touch tone dialing is the default. For connecting via a pulse line, clear the box `This phone has touch-tone service`. Be sure to edit each number, otherwise you won't be able to dial out if AOL tries subsequent access numbers. If you also have call waiting on a pulse line, you'll have to manually adjust the prefix for disabling it; usually it's 1110. Check with your local phone company if you're unsure.

A Few More Modem Options

Listed below are preferences that can be applied to the modem, and don't have to be changed for each of your dial-up numbers. You can select the modem you're using and direct AOL to another port, change the port speed, and adjust the speaker volume. Most likely, the only one you'll really want to adjust is the modem volume, which you can shut off if you're annoyed by all the dialing and screeching every time you dial up AOL. You'll be taken to the `Expert Edit Modem` screen, similar to that shown in Figure 27-7:

From the `Sign On` screen → `Setup` → `Expert Setup` → `Devices (modems, etc.)` tab → highlight the modem you want to edit (there's probably only one) → `Edit`

The following are your options on the `Expert Edit Modem` screen:

- `Connected to port`: A port is a place on your computer where one device, in this case your modem, can physically connect to another device. During Auto Detect, AOL automatically locates the port, but you can change it if you needed to. To change the port where AOL looks for your modem, select the COM port from the `Connected to Port` drop-down menu. Note that this does not change what COM port your modem is actually using. It only tells AOL where to look.

- `Port speed`: During Auto Detect, AOL senses and records the true port speed of your modem into this setting. The default number AOL comes up with is adequate. However, modem wisdom says that a trick to maximize your connection speed involves choosing a port speed of up to twice the printed speed on the modem. We're not sure if you really get a faster connection, but we use this trick, and have noticed no adverse effects. Typically, your modem attempts the fastest connection it can, reducing its capacity if the connection is experiencing interference. If you do experience connection problems, reset your port speed to match exactly the modem speed.

- `Speaker volume`: To make that shrill modem connect sound lower or louder, or, better yet, to turn it off, select the option from the `Speaker volume` drop-down menu. Your options are `Off`, `Low`, `Normal`, and `Loud`. This method of volume control is an improvement with AOL 4.0. It was possible to adjust the modem sound in older versions of the AOL software, but it involved editing your modem string by hand. No matter what your system-wide modem sound setting are, AOL uses the settings you specify here.

Advanced: Manually Edit Your Modem String

If you know what you're doing, you can manually edit the *modem string*, the set of commands AOL uses to communicate in your modem's language. If you don't know what you're doing, you could accidentally disable AOL's ability to properly talk to your modem. When something goes wrong after you've manually adjusted the modem string, be prepared to use the Restore Defaults button so AOL can go back to the settings it knows and trusts. Figure 27-8 shows the screen where you can make the adjustment. To get there, follow this path:

From the Sign On screen, click Setup → Expert Setup → Devices (modems, etc.) tab → highlight the modem whose commands you want to modify → Edit → Edit Commands

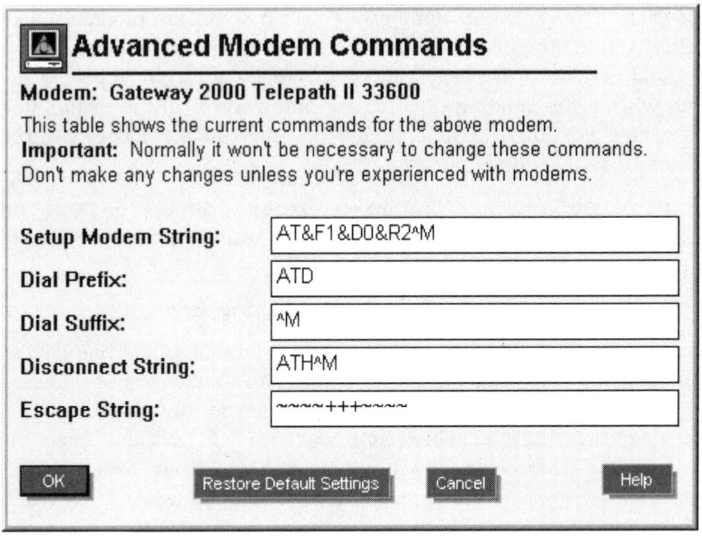

Figure 27-8: Preparing to manually edit the modem strings

For Experts Only: Your Options in Detail

In the interest of completeness, we've included this section as a way of explaining what you can do when you choose Expert Setup. You can modify all of your AOL connection settings by hand, if you use a bit of common sense and want to poke around on your own. AOL has made it easier and quicker to use their walk-through to set up your access, so we don't see the need to use Expert Setup as often these days as we used to in AOL 3.0. Still, it's nice to be able to go in and adjust all of the settings if we want to.

Here's what you'll see when you use **Expert Setup**:

Locations

From the `Locations` tab, you've got several options that help you set up numbers that you can use from different locations. The following numbers correspond to the numbers in Figure 27-9:

1. `Add Location` allows you to store new cities or groups of access numbers, for use at any time. Say you're going to Paris and want local dial-in access. Just add a new location and then add new local access numbers as prompted. AOL brings up a list of numbers available in the area you've chosen. Select from them and add at least two to the list (each access number increases your chance of a successful connection).

2. `Add Number` connects you to AOL and brings up a listing of current access numbers. Select several for each location to maximize your chance of signing on (see Figure 27-9).

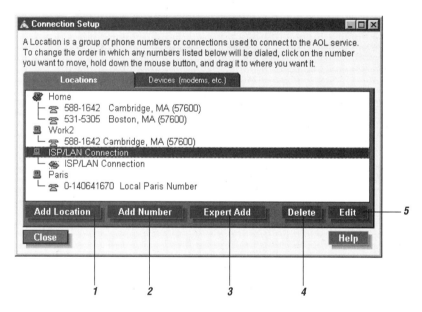

Figure 27-9: The Locations tab in Expert Setup

3. `Expert Add` allows you to type in an access number and choose the location to which you want the number added. You can also modify the entries found via the `Edit` button (see `Edit` below).

4. `Delete` removes the item you've highlighted, whether it is a single access number or an entire location.

5. `Edit` allows you to directly change or modify the access number, add a dialing prefix to get an outside line or disable call waiting, change the connection speed, or change the Connection Location.

Once you've added `Locations`, you can then choose from among them when you sign on. For instance, choosing Paris from the drop-down list at the `Sign On` screen is depicted in Figure 27-3 in the section "Adding and Modifying U.S. and International Numbers and Locations."

Devices (modems, etc.)

Devices are primarily related to the type of hardware your computer uses to access AOL. Again, you've got only two options here, either a dial-up modem—preferably the exact make and model attached to your computer—or TCP/IP, which requires a connection to the Internet via a LAN or via an alternate ISP. Figure 27-10 shows the `Devices (modems, etc.)` section under `Expert Setup`.

When you set up your new Locations, you should select the correct `Device`. If your Location is work, and you will access AOL via your company's LAN, you don't want to select `Modem`; most likely you'll select `TCP/IP` (see the section at the end of the chapter, "Alternatives to Dialing In to AOL"). If you're traveling, and you'll be using AOL over a phone line, select Modem.

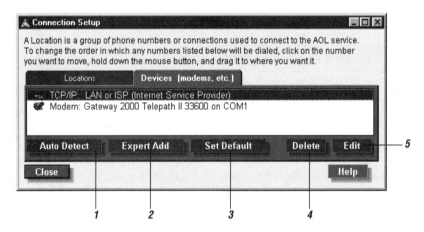

Figure 27-10: The Devices (modems, etc.) tab shows your computer's connection methods

The following numbers correspond to the numbers in Figure 27-10:

1. `Auto Detect` searches your PC and its hardware for all the ways to connect. You can use it if you installed a new modem.

2. `Expert Add` allows you to choose the type of connection (TCP/IP or modem) and the access numbers.

3. `Set Default`. Highlight the type of connection you most often use, and click `Set Default`. The result is that when you create new Locations, AOL prefers this connection device.

4. **Delete** removes the connection device driver you've highlighted. It is no longer available as a connection. Use **Auto Detect** or **Expert Add** to restore removed **Devices**.

5. **Edit** allows you to change directly the COM port, port speed, and modem speaker volume. From within **Edit**, click **Edit Commands** to directly modify the modem strings (for an explanation of these preferences, see "A Few More Modem Options" earlier in this chapter).

Modem Problems

If you're experiencing a modem problem, always check the connections first. Check each of the items in the list below:

- Be sure that the phone line coming from the wall jack is connected to the modem input slot that's labeled either "Line," "Jack," or "To Wall."

- Test the line from the wall jack with a phone; listen for a dial tone (this is a pretty basic step, but one that some people miss: if the phone line is dead, it's obvious you'll never get a modem connection).

What to look for with external modems:

- Is the modem's electrical power cord securely plugged in? Is the modem turned on?

- Check all modem cables and be sure that they're securely connected to your PC.

Reporting Modem Problems

If you can get online, AOL recommends you use their online help, rather than typing up their support lines with nonemergencies: **Keyword: Access →
Report a Problem**.

Of course, if your problem is access, you probably can't get online. Then you should call tech support: 1-800-827-3338.

If your problem is not being able to find an access number near you (or near the place you'll be traveling to), you can complain at **Keyword: Access → Request Access Numbers**.

After you let AOL know that you'd like a local access number, don't hold your breath. These things can take years. For some other access alternatives, see "No Local Access Numbers?"

Alternatives to Dialing In to AOL

You can spare yourself the trouble of using AOL's own dial-up access numbers or get speedier access when you connect using TCP/IP. In the **Select Location** drop-down box on the **Sign On** screen, AOL labels this the **ISP/LAN** Connection. In addition, AOL often calls connecting via TCP/IP the Bring Your Own Access Plan (BYOA).

Why would you want to have AOL and another Internet connection? Well, you might want to keep your AOL screen name around forever, since everyone already knows you by it. Or you might like to have AOL for your kids, even if you have some other ISP for yourself. Maybe you have an AOL account at home, but you want to use it at work over your LAN, too. Or you can't give up your Buddy Chat with your family across the country who has AOL, or your kid in college. Whatever the reason, you can keep your account with AOL alive, using it over another Internet connection of your choice.

With Bring Your Own Access, you pay another company to access the Internet, from which you can access AOL for a lower rate per month, currently $9.95, which is less than half the rate you'd be charged if you dialed directly into AOL's own network. What it comes down to, technically, is that you need a SLIP or PPP connection through which you have access to TCP/IP. Any time you can connect to the Internet, you can use TCP/IP to connect to AOL.

TCP/IP is how we access AOL at work, and we can tell you, the speed going both up and downstream is many times faster than the top analog modem speed (56KBps), and there are no busy signals when we use our own connection. You can also access AOL via ISDN if you've got the right phone line from your phone company and a local ISP that's ISDN-capable (AOL currently doesn't accept direct ISDN connections). If you're using TCP/IP and another dial-up ISP to connect to AOL, your speeds won't be any faster than if you dialed AOL directly, but you won't hit AOL's busy signals (you might, however, encounter your ISP's busy signals).

Benefits to TCP/IP

- Speed: If you're on a LAN at school or work (not a dial-up connection), ISDN, or cable modem, you'll almost always have access to AOL that's many times faster than you could get through a modem connection.

- You avoid times when AOL's own network is plagued by busy signals, even if you dial in to your local ISP.

Drawbacks

- If you dial into another ISP, you may have to contend with their own busy signals, shoddy network-connection issues, and/or poor customer service. When you lose your Internet connection, you lose AOL (and it won't be AOL's fault).

- If you dial into another ISP, you have to pay them, and pay AOL a lesser charge (currently $9.95/month). Could get expensive.

About the Bring Your Own Access Plan

You can use the BYOA plan only if you have another Internet connection, through an ISP, cable company, or LAN at school or work. You must not access AOL via any AOLNet or SprintNet dial-up access numbers or through the surcharged 800 or 888 numbers, or you are charged an additional fee. Once you switch, you use your standard AOL software, with no modifications. Just be sure you've set AOL to sign on using ISP/LAN.

To switch to this plan:

Keyword: Billing → Change Billing Method or Price Plan

Use Another Internet Service Provider

First you've got to choose your ISP. Get recommendations for local ISPs from people you know or check a web site called 'the list' at *http://www.thelist.com* for scores of local ISPs that might suit you better than AOL's own network, AOLNet. You might get a great company with lots of local numbers, install a cable modem, go for ISDN, or use some other form of connecting to the Internet. After you sign up with the local ISP, change your connection type to ISP/LAN from the Sign On screen, as we describe below. And don't forget to save yourself some money by switching to the Bring Your Own Access Plan.

Benefits

• You might encounter fewer busy signals than on AOLNet.

• ISPs often provide additional services such as server space for web site hosting and email boxes.

Drawbacks

• You might choose an ISP with more busy signals than AOL.

• Your ISP may not have toll-free access numbers all over the country, or even the world, as AOL does.

• AOL can't help you with technical difficulties you might experience with your connection to your local ISP; you have to call the ISP for customer service (which could be better or worse than AOL's).

• If you lose your connection to your ISP, you lose the connection to AOL.

How to configure AOL to work through your ISP

There are several steps to signing on to AOL via ISP/LAN and an ISP or cable company:

1. Configure AOL to use ISP/LAN. AOL usually does this for you the first time you set it up. Often, AOL detects your modem, making that one of the Locations while adding an ISP/LAN connection to your options, too. This is convenient, just in case you ever need to use it.

   If you don't see ISP/LAN Connection in the drop-down box on the Sign On screen, don't worry. Adding a location is easy. Just follow this path:

   From the Sign On screen → Setup → create a location for use with new access phone numbers or ISP → Next → add a custom connection (for example, TCP/IP) → Next → OK

2. Now that you have ISP/LAN as an option, you must always remember to select it from the drop-down menu on the Sign On screen.

3. Sign on to your local ISP in the manner specified by the ISP. You have to use the ISP's own instructions for setting up your connection, dialing the access

numbers, and signing on to their service, whether you're using a dial-up modem, cable modem, ISDN, or your Internet connection at work.

4. Once your connection has been made, start AOL, select `ISP/LAN` from the `Select Location` drop-down menu if you haven't already done that, and sign on to AOL in your usual manner.

Notes on Alternative Connection Methods

Below, we give a quick overview about how you'd use AOL with cable modems, ISDN, and over a LAN at work. With any of the following methods of connecting to the Internet, you must always remember to choose `ISP/LAN` from the drop-down box on the `Sign On` screen, or else AOL is going to try to dial up. To prepare AOL for these methods, follow the steps in the previous subsection.

Cable modem

AOL is fully compatible for use with cable modem systems. You need only configure AOL to sign on via TCP/IP as described in the previous section.

As with any ISP, you should connect in the manner they require, leave their software running, then launch AOL. Chances are that your cable modem connection to the Internet is permanent—that is, when your computer's on, you're connected. Your connection to AOL will be significantly faster than any other method of access.

ISDN

Currently, you can't dial into AOL directly via ISDN. The only way to connect to AOL using ISDN at this time is if you have ISDN access with your local ISP. You must first connect to the Internet via your ISDN-capable ISP, then access AOL via TCP/IP.

Local Area Network

When you first install AOL on a PC where the only way to connect is via a LAN, AOL automatically detects your network card and sets up AOL for TCP/IP. All you need to do is confirm that you want TCP/IP. If at some point you want to add a modem to that PC and want to switch to dial-up, you have to either rerun the setup (with the modem installed on your computer) or manually, but easily, add a new location.

Note that if you've got a notebook computer with a modem/network card combo, AOL usually identifies and sets up both ways to connect during installation.

CHAPTER 28

Parental Controls

If you're using this book, you're probably not the kind of person who has a knee-jerk reaction to every rumor you hear about the online world. Not everyone out there is a sicko. Most of the millions of people online, both on AOL and on the Internet, are just like you: they have their quirks, but they're not out to harm anyone. Some people have a hard time understanding that objectionable material found online can also be found just about anywhere else, and probably in the same quantity.

We think the Internet and AOL are great places for kids to learn, play, and interact with others. But just as you pay attention to what your kid is up to while he plays in the park or watches TV in the next room, you have to be aware of what your child is doing online. You can maximize the richness of your child's experience by being an attentive, interested participant in his or her online endeavors.

Probably the best piece of advice we can give to parents is: participate in your child's life, both online and offline, and everything should turn out fine. Use common sense paired with the advice we give in this chapter, and you shouldn't worry too much.

If you're an adult who's come to this chapter because you suspect that AOL censors your account, you're right. Skip to the "Chat" and "Newsgroups" sections of this chapter.

Safety Tips for Kids Online

Here are our top tips for keeping kids of any age safe online. Make sure you understand them and even discuss them with your child:

- Keep your kids informed. They can't see the person on the other end, so they shouldn't assume that they're always talking to a kid. It may be an adult posing as a kid.

- Remind them not to give out their telephone number, home address, or school name no matter who asks. There might be rare times when it is appropriate to give out this information, but you should consider making it a policy that your child discuss it with you before giving out such information.

- You should never give out your password to anyone and neither should your children. Make sure they understand that there are some things that should be kept secret, even from their best friends. Though you may usually instruct your child to listen to grownups, let him know that someone asking for his password is an exception, even if the grownup claims to work for AOL.

- Become familiar with the online world yourself. You can watch out for your child if you yourself know what the dangers are (see also Chapter 30, *Privacy*).

- Use AOL's Parental Controls for kids between ages 6 and 16. AOL has two levels of controls you can use to help you tailor what your child can do with his or her account. You can even strengthen or relax these setting as you wish with Custom Controls. We explain these controls in the "Using AOL's Built-In Parental Controls" section that follows.

- Keep track of what your kids say in their profiles. Obviously, you don't want them giving out your home address or other personal information. You might also suggest that your adolescents not reveal their gender and age. In particular, predators have emailed children and adolescents asking if they want to be "models." Clearly, these people are up to no good. To profile your child, type CTRL-g and enter your child's screen name. Most of all, help your child create her profile, and make sure she understands what not to say online.

- You've probably already told your kid not to get in a car with a stranger. Tell him not to meet online friends in person without first discussing it with you. No matter how old you are, it's best to meet online acquaintances in public places with other people around.

- Encourage your kids to tell you about bad language or times when they're uncomfortable online.

When your child enters a Kids Only chat room, guidelines appear to remind him what to do and what not to do. But the only way you can be sure your child is having a safe experience is to go online with him and explore together.

Creating a Separate Screen Name

In order to use Parental Controls (explained in the "Using AOL's Built-In Parental Controls" section of this chapter), you have to create separate screen names for your children. That way, you can block them from certain activities without blocking your account, too. To create a secondary screen name for your child:

Keyword: Names → Create a Screen Name

Once you've created the name, AOL prompts you to choose the level of access for your child. For more information on the categories "Kids Only," "Young Teen," and "Mature Teen," see "Kids' and Teens' Screen Names."

Along with each screen name comes a password. Your child can change his or her password at any time by going to `Keyword: Password` or selecting `Passwords` from the `My AOL` toolbar icon. So, if you want access to that screen name, you have to be sure you ask your child periodically what the password is. The only way to avoid this is to store your child's password so she can sign on without typing it and not tell her what it is (see "Passwords" in Chapter 3, *Screen Names, Passwords, and Signing On*).

If you want to change your own or your child's password, you must first sign on with the screen name whose password you want to change. Then follow this path:

`Keyword: Password` → `Change Password` → enter old and new passwords, following the on-screen instructions → `Change Password`

Limiting Your Child's Online Time

To keep tabs on how much time your kids have spent online this month, follow this path:

`Keyword: Billing` → `Display Your Detailed Bill` → `Current Month's Bill`

Even if you're on an unlimited billing plan, you'll see how many hours each of your screen names has spent on AOL this month.

If your kids are spending too much time online, the obvious first step is to sit down with them, discuss it, and set some limits. Failing all else, there is software that controls how much time your kids spend on AOL. PowerWatch is an AOL add-on that allows you to monitor or limit your child's online time. It also has its own method of restricting children's web access. PowerWatch is shareware and costs $19.95 to register ($14.95 if you register before your free evaluation period ends). You can find out more about PowerWatch at *http://www.bpssoft.com/Power-Watch/index.htm*.

See also Chapter 25, *Third Party Add-Ons*.

Content for Children, Teenagers, and You

The Kids Only Channel (`Keyword: Kids Only`) is just what it sounds like: kid-friendly content and chats. AOL takes a number of steps to ensure that children accessing the service with "Kids Only" accounts are exposed only to specially designed content and specially moderated kid-only chats. See also Chapter 15, *AOL Content Reference*, for a list of the main areas in the Kids Only Channel.

If your kids are too old for the Kids Only Channel—for instance, anyone in junior high school is sure to rebel against it—you might want to suggest `Keyword: Teens`. It's a little fluffy, but age-appropriate as far as we can tell (of course, we can't personally guarantee the seemliness of any AOL content). We especially like `Keyword: Book Bag`, a book-review area that treats teenagers like young adults, not big kids.

In the Families Channel (Keyword: Families), parents find resources for their youngsters and teens, guides to areas AOL has deemed kid-safe, and tutorials on how to use Parental Controls. Even if your kids aren't online, it's a great parenting resource. Incidentally, screen names that are set to "Kids Only" can't access the Families Channel, just the Kids Only Channel. Teens have access to all AOL channels, including the Families Channel.

Using AOL's Built-In Parental Controls

On AOL, you can set up each screen name to have 18+, Mature Teen (17-18), Young Teen (13–16), or Kids Only (6–12) access. To change the access of your child's screen name, you must be signed on with your AOL account's primary screen name. The primary (or "master") screen name is the one you choose when you first create your AOL account. It's always the uppermost screen name in the sign-on screen drop-down menu.

The "Kids' and Teens' Screen Names" section contains a quick-reference guide to what each of the four parental control settings are, as defaults. The following sections ("Premium Services," "Chat," "Instant Messages," "Downloading," "Newsgroups," "Email," and "Web") allow you to adjust the level of access each screen name has to individual parts of AOL.

You can reach any of the Parental Controls in this chapter through the Parental Controls front screen at Keyword: Parental Controls (shown in Figure 28-1). AOL 4.0 users can also select Parental Controls from the My AOL toolbar icon, or click the Parental Controls icon on the Welcome screen.

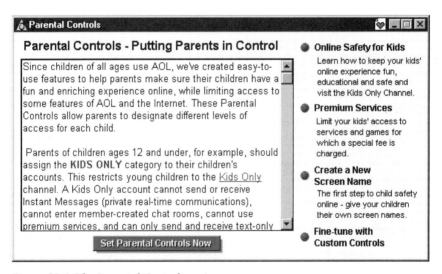

Figure 28-1: The Parental Controls main screen

If you're using Parental Controls, you shouldn't store your account password (see also the section "Passwords" in Chapter 3, *Screen Names, Passwords, and Signing*

On), since storing it allows your kids access to the master settings. Don't underestimate kids' ability to sign onto your account and change the controls around.

Kids' and Teens' Screen Names

Giving your child a kids' or teen screen name is the easiest way to enact Parental Controls. To change a secondary account to Mature Teen, Young Teen, or Kids Only:

> Keyword: Parental Controls → Set Parental Controls Now →
> for each screen name, select 18+, Mature Teen, Young Teen, or Kids
> Only → OK

Below is a quick-reference guide to what each of the four parental control settings (18+, Mature Teen, Young Teen, and Kids Only) are. You can use Custom Controls to change any of these settings (see "Chat," "Instant Messages," "Downloading," "Newsgroups," "Email," and "Web").

Controls selected by default for 18+ screen names are:

- Chat: Block hyperlinks in chat
- IM: No restrictions
- Downloading: No restrictions
- Newsgroups: Block binary downloads
- Mail: Allow all mail
- Web: Access all web content

Controls selected by default for Mature Teen screen names are:

- Chat: Block hyperlinks in chat
- IM: No restrictions
- Downloading: No restrictions
- Newsgroups: Block binary downloads
- Mail: Allow all mail
- Web: Access to all web sites, except for those deemed inappropriate for the 17- to 18-year-old age group

Controls selected by default for Young Teen screen names:

- Chat: Block member rooms; block hyperlinks in chat
- IM: No restrictions
- Downloading: No restrictions
- Newsgroups: Block Expert Add of newsgroups; block all newsgroups; block binary downloads
- Mail: Allow all mail; block file attachments and pictures in email
- Web: Access to only young teen sites

Controls selected by default for Kids Only screen names:

- Chat: Block all chat rooms; block member rooms; block hyperlinks in chat
- IM: Block Instant Messages
- Downloading: Block FTP downloads
- Newsgroups: Block Expert Add of newsgroups; block all newsgroups; block binary downloads
- Mail: Allow all mail, block file attachments and pictures in email
- Web: Access to Kids Only sites; all others blocked

Premium Services

Premium areas, such as games, incur a $1.99 per hour surcharge as of this printing. These charges are levied on top of your regular monthly fees, and even during your New Member free time. Fractions of hours are billed at 3.3 cents per minute.

Secondary screen names are, by default, blocked from Premium areas (even if they have 18+ access). To unblock secondary accounts or block your primary account:

> Keyword: Parental Controls → Premium Services → Block Surcharged Services checkbox → OK

You can only unblock Young Teen and Mature Teen accounts. Kids Only accounts can't be unblocked; you'll see that in Figure 28-2, each Kids Only account checkbox is grayed out.

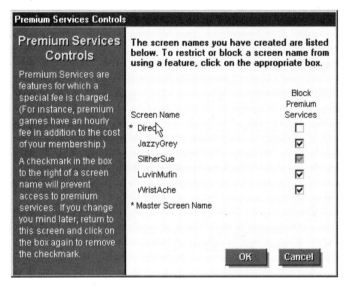

Figure 28-2: Premium Services controls

Chat

To adjust chat controls:

> Keyword: Parental Controls → Fine Tune with Custom Controls → Chat → Chat Controls

Figure 28-3 shows the screen where you can adjust your child's chat options.

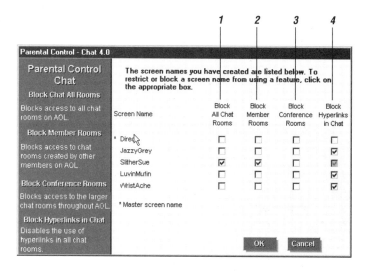

Figure 28-3: The Parental Control Chat customization screen

Your options, and what they really do, are described below (you can combine one or more of these). The numbers correspond to the numbers in Figure 28-3.

1. **Block All Chat Rooms**: "All rooms" means People Connection rooms: Public Rooms, Member Rooms, and Private Rooms. However, you can still enter Private Rooms via a Buddy Chat invitation.

2. **Block Member Rooms**: Blocks Member Rooms and Private Rooms. The Buddy Chat loophole doesn't work here.

3. **Block Conference Rooms**: Conference Rooms means chat rooms within channels/content areas—even the Kids Only Channel!—but not including auditoriums. (See also "Conference Rooms" in Chapter 10, *Chatting*.)

4. **Block Hyperlinks in Chat**: This means you can't see hyperlinked text, but you can see the referring URL in plain text. (See also "Hyperlinks" in Chapter 10, *Chatting*.) Kids Only accounts can never accept hyperlinks in chat.

When you are done customizing your screen names' chat controls, click OK.

An easy way to block your child from chats is to create a Kids Only screen name for him:

> Keyword: Parental Controls → Set Parental Controls Now → click Kids Only → OK

This blocks IMs (though you can still have a Buddy List) and blocks all chats outside the Kids Only Channel, including Buddy/Private chats. Your kid may hate you, but this is the most comprehensive option.

Downloading

To adjust downloading controls:

> Keyword: Parental Controls → Fine Tune with Custom Controls
> → Downloading → Download Controls

Figure 28-4 shows the Parental Control Downloading screen.

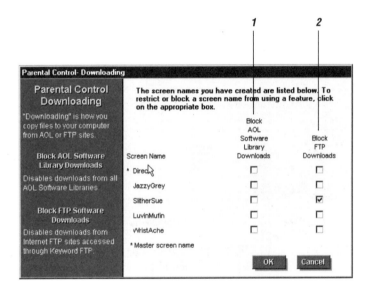

Figure 28-4: The Parental Controls Downloading customization screen

Your options, and what they really do, follow. The numbers correspond to the numbers in Figure 28-4.

1. **Block AOL Software Library Downloads**: Disables downloading from AOL software libraries and even blocks kids from reading the file descriptions; at least they won't know what they're missing. Incidentally, this probably isn't necessary, since AOL file libraries have (supposedly) been screened for objectionable content. Unless you set Kids Only Access too, your kid can still download from anywhere on the Web (keep reading to block your child's web access).

2. **Block FTP Downloads**: Does just what it says (if you don't know what FTP is, see also Chapter 23, *Web Publishing and FTP*). The catch is that it only works for FTPing through AOL's FTP client. If an external client is used, your child can FTP.

When done customizing your screen names' download controls, click OK.

Another way to restrict your child's download access is to restrict the web sites he can access:

Keyword: Parental Controls → Fine Tune with Custom Controls → Web → Web Controls

If you choose Access Kids Only Sites, your child can only see (and thus download from) web sites approved for 6- to 12-year-olds. Young Teen or Mature Teen access only allows access to web sites that have been deemed appropriate for that age group. However, we have our doubts about the screening process (see "Web" in this chapter).

Instant Messages

To adjust Instant Message controls:

Keyword: Parental Controls → Fine Tune with Custom Controls → Instant Messages → IM Controls

See Figure 28-5 for a view of the Parental Control Instant Messages screen.

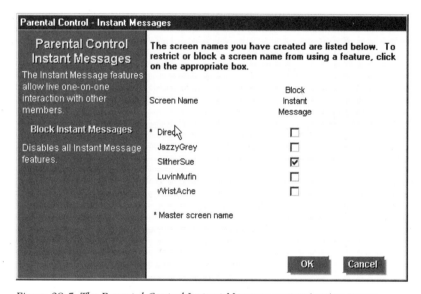

Figure 28-5: The Parental Control Instant Messages customization screen

Kids Only accounts can't send or receive Instant Messages. All other accounts (18+, Mature Teen, and Young Teen) have IMs automatically enabled.

When you are done customizing your screen names' IM controls, click OK.

Email

To adjust email controls:

> Keyword: Mail Controls → Set Up Mail Controls → click the radio button next to the appropriate screen name → Edit

or:

> Keyword: Parental Controls → Fine Tune with Custom Controls → Mail → Mail Controls → click the radio button next to the appropriate screen name → Edit

See Figure 28-6 for a view of the Mail Controls screen.

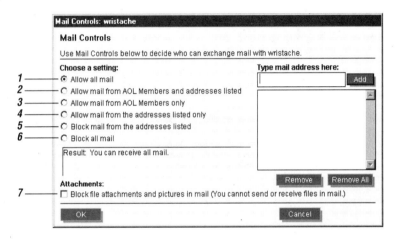

Figure 28-6: Mail Controls options

If you're signed on with your master screen name, you can use Mail Controls to restrict the email received by any screen name in your account.

No matter what Mail Controls preferences you set, you won't receive email from any address on AOL's list of known spammers. See also the entry *Preferred Mail* in Chapter 8, *Email.*

The following numbers correspond to the numbers in Figure 28-6:

1. Allow all mail: You receive email from anyone who sends it to you. The default setting for all screen names (18+, Mature Teen, Young Teen, and Kids Only).

2. Allow mail from AOL Members and addresses listed: You can receive email from any AOL member, plus any Internet addresses you specifically enable.

3. Allow mail from AOL Members only: You won't be able to receive email from the Internet, but you can receive email from any AOL member. If you think this option prevents spam, you're wrong: many spammers have AOL accounts.

4. **Allow mail from the addresses listed only**: You choose the addresses (AOL and/or Internet) that you want to receive email from. All other email is blocked. You can use this to limit your child's incoming email to a set list of friends and relatives.

5. **Block mail from the addresses listed**: You choose the addresses (AOL and/or Internet) that you never want to get email from, ever. This is a good option if someone has been harassing you (remember, though, that they can change screen names and send you email that way), or if you get spammed by a non-AOL email address.

6. **Block all mail**: Like it says, nobody can send you email. This is a good option for screen names you're using in chat rooms and other spam-attracting places (see also "Annihilating Spam" in Chapter 7, *Essential AOL Survival Tips*).

7. **Block file attachments and pictures in mail**: This is the default for Young Teen and Kids Only screen names. Use it if you're afraid that your children will be emailed pornography or computer viruses. For adults, we recommend ignoring this option and simply never downloading files from strangers.

When you are done customizing your screen names' email controls, click OK.

Newsgroups

To adjust newsgroup controls:

> Keyword: Newsgroups → Parental Controls → click the radio button next to the appropriate screen name → Edit

or:

> Keyword: Parental Controls → Fine Tune with Custom Controls → Newsgroups → Newsgroup Controls → click the radio button next to the appropriate screen name → Edit

These paths lead you to the Blocking Criteria screen, where you can modify the newsgroup settings of the screen name you've chosen. Click Save, and all changes take effect immediately.

The following are your options on the Blocking Criteria screen. The numbers below correspond to the numbers in Figure 28-7.

1. **Block Expert Add of newsgroups**: When this box is checked, the chosen screen name can't add a newsgroup that isn't included in the list under the Add newsgroups button. The list of newsgroups can be longer and typically more sexually provocative if you check Use full newsgroups list (see below). Kids Only and Young Teen screen names are blocked by default from Expert Adding newsgroups (but they're also blocked by default from using newsgroups at all). Mature Teen and 18+ screen names are not blocked by default from Expert Adding newsgroups.

2. **Block all newsgroups**: When this box is checked, the chosen screen name has no access to newsgroups. Young Teen and Kids Only screen names

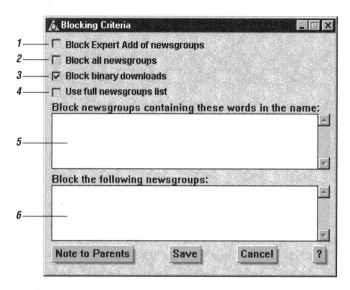

Figure 28-7: Blocking Criteria for newsgroups

are blocked from newsgroups by default; uncheck the box to allow access to newsgroups. Mature Teen and 18+ screen names aren't blocked from newsgroups by default.

3. **Block binary downloads**: When this box is checked, the chosen screen name can't view binary downloads attached to newsgroup posts. All screen names (even 18+) are blocked by default from viewing binaries. Uncheck the box to allow the viewing of binaries.

4. **Use full newsgroups list**: By default, when you click `Add News-groups` or `Search All Newsgroups`, AOL allows you to see only a subset of the complete listing. We suppose that this is to protect sensitive eyes from viewing the number of newsgroups—and their names—that contain sexually explicit material. However, the holder of the Master Account can choose to allow any screen name to view the entire list. Even if you can't view the entire list, knowledgeable users can use Expert Add to subscribe to newsgroups not on the list (that is, unless the accounts have be blocked from using Expert Add by the master screen name, see the **Block Expert Add of newsgroups** entry above).

5. **Block newsgroups containing these words in the name**: Use this feature to keep the chosen screen name from signing up for groups with any given words in the title. For instance, if you want to give your kids access to newsgroups, but don't want to give access to groups containing the words "death" or "taxes," enter the words `death` and `taxes` in the box. Beware when you use this feature, since you block all instances of the string of letters. For instance, blocking "cat" also blocks out all *.*education*.* groups. Clearly, this feature is probably aimed at parents who want to block access to groups

that focus on sex. If you're trying to block pornographic images, you're best bet is to Block binary downloads (which is the default anyway).

6. Block the following newsgroups: You must know the exact Internet name of the group you want blocked, then enter the exact name (e.g., *alt.swedish.chef.bork.bork.bork*) in the box.

When you are done customizing your screen names' newsgroup controls, click OK.

Web

To adjust web controls (for AOL's browser only; see the next section for controls using other browsers):

Keyword: Parental Controls → Fine Tune with Custom Controls → Web → Web Controls

We have our doubts about the screening process for kid-safe and teen-safe sites. Our company's utterly smut-free web site (*http://www.songline.com*) was blocked, as were many other innocuous sites. That's just because sites are blocked by default until Microsystems, Inc., a screening company, approves them.

You can use the Report a Site button to put innocuous sites up for approval, but we think you're better off websurfing *with* your kids; or, depending on their age and maturity, letting them explore the Web themselves.

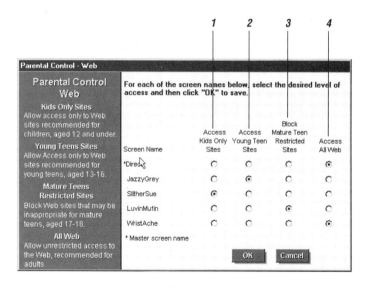

Figure 28-8: Parental Controls Web customization screen

The numbers below correspond to the numbers in Figure 28-8:

1. Access Kids Only Sites: Allows access to web sites that Microsystems, Inc. has deemed appropriate for the 6- to 12-year-old age group.

2. Access Young Teen Sites: Allows access to web sites that Microsystems, Inc. has deemed appropriate for the 13- to 16-year-old age group.

3. **Block Mature Teen Restricted Sites**: Allows access to all web sites, except for those that that Microsystems, Inc. has deemed inappropriate for the 17- to 18-year-old age group.

4. **Access All Web**: Gives you free reign over the Web and is the default for all 18+ accounts.

When you are done customizing your screen names' web controls, click OK.

Standalone Web Browsers

AOL's custom web controls (explained above in the "Web" section) work only for AOL's integrated browser. If you use a standalone browser over your AOL connection, you'll have to customize those browsers themselves, since you can't rely on AOL's controls; by default, AOL isn't filtering web sites viewed with standalone browsers. Remember that, when you set up your children's screen names as Kids Only or Young Teen or Mature Teen, they are automatically prohibited from viewing certain sites if they use AOL's integrated, default browser, running inside AOL. With any other browser, whether you install it or your kids install it, things aren't so easy to control.

It's possible that your kids will be savvy enough to want to use a browser running on top of AOL, rather than the built-in version. They, and you, might want to do this since the standalone version of MSIE and Netscape Navigator have richer menu and bookmarking features compared to the more slimmed-down version of MSIE that's standard with AOL 4.0 (we cover these browsers and their features in Chapter 16, *The Web*). We prefer using external web browsers over our AOL connection, mainly because of the increased number of features. In the following sections, we show you our best advice on how to make the external browsers behave just like AOL's integrated one, Parental Controls and all.

Since AOL won't be filtering web sites, you have to set it up manually in every standalone browser you use. Don't worry; it's not tough if you follow the instructions below. But first some rather big standalone browser caveats:

- Savvy children can undo AOL proxy filtering just by going into the browser's preferences and removing the proxy information we're about to show you how to add. They can then go in and replace it when they're done browsing. You won't even know they ever changed a thing.

- Using MSIE's own filtering, part of the Recreational Software Advisory Council (RSAC) rating standard, gives parents password-protected filtering. But this doesn't prevent a child from downloading and installing another browser, as we describe next.

- Internet-savvy kids can download, install, use, and then remove a standalone web browser without parental knowledge. Granted, downloading a browser takes hours, but they also come on CD-ROMs and be installed in minutes. No matter what other method of filtering you apply to your other browsers, your kids, if they're old enough to know how to install software, can circumvent all the browser-filtering methods we cover in this book. There's no way around this.

Given these important warnings, you can put in place some pretty strong filtering, and just hope your kids don't figure out how to undo it. If they do, however, you should probably look on the bright side: they're intelligent, curious kids who love computers enough to learn all there is to know about them, including thwarting their parents. We imagine, when they grow up, such kids will lead happy, successful lives in some highly technical field. Who knows.

If you decide to filter your kids' content, you have one very low-tech solution and two more high-tech (but still rather simple) solutions, all of which are presented next.

The Low-Tech Method

Remove all other browsers from your PC, so that the AOL integrated browser is the only browser available to your children. With this option, they can get to sites only through AOL's web filter. By default, Mature Teen screen names are blocked from certain sites deemed inappropriate for 17- to 18-year-olds; Young Teen screen names can go only to sites approved for 13- to 16-year olds; Kids Only screen names can go only to sites approved for 6- to 12-year-olds. You can over-ride these defaults (see "Web" in this chapter). If you choose this method, kids can still install a browser, use it, then uninstall it—all without your knowledge.

Higher-Tech Method #1 (Our Personal Recommendation)

Configure all other browsers on your PC to use AOL's Kids Only and Teen filters. You can do this by telling your browser to ask another computer for information and directions. All of your browser's traffic will be directed through what's called a proxy server. This means that when you try to go to a web site, your request is sent to AOL's proxy server; the browser sends information about who's browsing (a child or an 18+ account?) and picks up some vital information about the web site you want to go to. The proxy will say, in effect, whether the site is on a blocked sites list, and then either load the web page, or return a message saying the site is blocked from that particular user.

While signed on with a Kids Only or Teen screen name, the external browser that has been properly configured to use a proxy behaves in the same way as the AOL internal browser, restricting sites based on the child or teen's level of access. On the other hand, if your child logs on using an 18+ account (like yours!) he or she will have full access. This is why each child needs his or her own account, and why your account needs a password to prevent kids from signing on as 18+ if you're trying to restrict their web access.

Benefits to using AOL's proxy servers for filtering

- When signed on with their own screen names, your kids' web experience is filtered exactly the same whether they're using the integrated AOL browser or a standalone browser. If you've set up special exceptions for your kids in AOL web Parental Controls, these are in effect with all browsers configured with the AOL proxy.

- As AOL modifies the list of blocked and open access sites, that is updated in the proxy. This means you get only the latest filtering from all browsers that use the AOL proxy.

Drawbacks

- You have to modify, by hand, every browser on your system.

- If kids know what they're doing, they can go in to the browser's preferences, and remove the proxy configuration, thereby annulling your filtering.

To use AOL filters for Netscape 4.0

These instructions assume that you have already downloaded Netscape or another browser. If you haven't, see "Using Alternate Browsers" in Chapter 16, *The Web*.

Sign on to AOL, start Netscape, and follow this path from within Netscape:

> Edit menu → Preferences → Advanced (click the + to see the nested options) → Proxies → Manual Proxy Configuration → View button → type ie3.proxy.aol.com in the HTTP Address of proxy server to use field → type 80 in the Port box → OK → OK

Note that you use "ie3," not "ie4," in the proxy server address whether you're using MSIE5.0, Netscape3.0, Opera, or another browser. This is simply because AOL has created a proxy address that incorporates the name of the latest version of AOL's integrated browser, which is "ie3." Perhaps "ie4" will be used in the future, so try that if "ie3" doesn't appear to work. Figure 28-9 shows the Manual Proxy Configuration screen where you'll insert your new proxy server address.

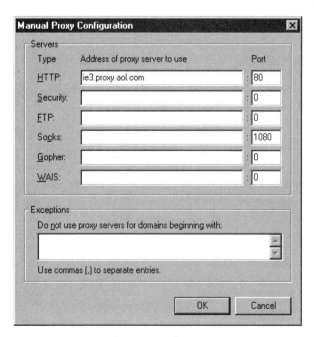

Figure 28-9: Manual Proxy Configuration in Netscape Navigator 4.0

To use AOL filters for an external version of Internet Explorer 4.0

Download and install the browser. If you haven't done this, see "Using Alternate Browsers" in Chapter 16, *The Web*.

Sign on to AOL, start MSIE (typically the desktop shortcut `The Internet`), and follow this path from within MSIE (this is for MSIE 4.0, but MSIE 3.0 is similar):

> View menu → `Internet Options...` → `Connection` tab → check the box next to `Access the Internet using a proxy server` → click the `Advanced` button → type `ie3.proxy.aol.com` in the `HTTP Address of Proxy to use` field → type 80 in the `Port` box → `OK` → `OK`

Figure 28-10 shows the `Proxy Settings` window where you'll enter the proxy server address in the standalone version of MSIE.

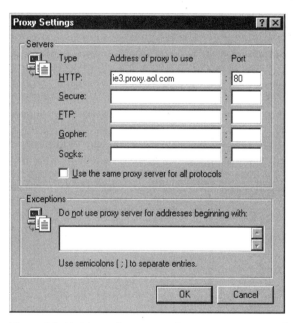

Figure 28-10: Manual Proxy Configuration in Microsoft Internet Explorer 4.0

Higher-Tech Method #2

In MSIE, there are special settings from the Recreational Software Advisory Council (RSAC) that can help you set your browser to filter out objectionable content. Parents can adjust actual browser settings to use the RSAC ratings for sex, nudity, violence, and offensive language, both vulgar and hate-motivated (see Figure 28-11). To set up the RSAC content advisor in Internet Explorer 4.0 (Version 3.0 has a similar path):

> View menu → `Internet Options...` → `Content` tab → `Enable` → type a password of your choice (just remember it!) → `OK` → highlight each of the ratings you want to customize → when you're all done customizing all four ratings, click `OK`

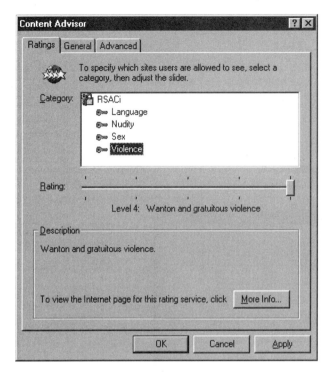

Figure 28-11: RSAC configuration in the MS Internet Explorer 4.0

If you click on each of the four content areas, language, nudity, sex, and violence have four levels of tolerance. We won't detail each level of tolerance, since what each restricts is plainly visible as you slide the ratings bar.

Potential problems and annoyances with the current RSAC implementation

RSAC sounds at first like a great solution to monitoring what your kids see; however, all isn't rosy. At this time, each web site must add the RSAC ratings to its site, and so far, there's no indication that a majority of web sites use RSAC. Currently RSAC is completely voluntary and at this time, the majority of sites don't rate their content according to RSAC.

To get around the problem of sites not using RSAC, you have the option of blocking all sites that aren't rated. Clearing the Users can see sites which have no rating box is probably the best way to block access to children. Of course, the downside to this is that they won't be able to see perfectly innocuous sites that haven't used the RSAC rating.

If you don't uncheck the Users can see sites which have no rating box, your children can see any site not using the RSAC ratings—which really means the great majority of sites.

Benefit of using RSAC in MSIE

- Parents can customize all the settings to their own liking, and use a password.

Drawbacks

- Every user of the browser, including adults, views the Web through RSAC. The way around this annoyance is to manually disable RSAC for the session (you have to have the password). But then, you must enable it again, before your kids use the browser.

- If you don't disable it, you have to type the supervisor password for each blocked site you want to access. That can get extremely annoying. What's worse, sites with frames require you to repeatedly type in your supervisor password in order to view each frame.

CHAPTER 29

Preferences

The settings found at MY AOL toolbar icon → Preferences are your preferences. (We think they should be at Keyword: Preferences, but alas, that keyword takes you to the beginners' tutorials at MY AOL). Many people don't know that AOL gives you some control over how your online sessions look, feel, sound, and act. Preferences help seasoned AOL members stay sane, because they allow you to "have it your way." Of course, you can't have it your way all the time, but these preferences are more helpful than you might think.

We've organized this chapter alphabetically, using the titles of the buttons you see at MY AOL → Preferences. The main Preferences screen and its 14 buttons are shown in Figure 29-1. Note that email is called Mail; Web is called WWW. We want you to be able to easily use this chapter as your guide while you're online tweaking your preferences, so we've used AOL's terms in this chapter.

For every preference, we've noted the default settings and told you what happens if you change them. An important thing to know is that when you change preferences (with the exception of password preferences), you change them for all screen names on your account. If you share your account with other people, you might want to ask them before you set any preferences. To understand the concept of multiple (master and secondary) screen names, see also "Master Versus Additional Screen Names" in Chapter 3, *Screen Names, Passwords, and Signing On*.

AOL 3.0 users, your preferences are located here: Members menu → Preferences. Many of these preferences are available in 3.0—we note which preferences are AOL 4.0-specific—but all paths and figures will be of AOL 4.0 for Windows 95/98. Also, AOL 3.0's Multimedia Preferences, which allowed members to turn off some graphics and all sound, have been removed from 4.0. You can disable sound in 4.0 with General preferences.

To explore preferences not listed on the main AOL preferences screen, see the "Preferences" sections in Chapter 9, *Instant Messages and Buddy Lists*, Chapter 11, *Message Boards*, and Chapter 13, *Newsgroups*.

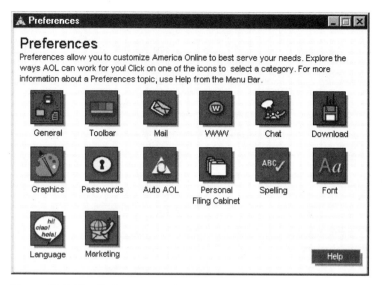

Figure 29-1: The Preferences main screen

Preferences Essentials

- Get rid of the Channels screen that appears every time you sign on. See "General."

- Clear your History Trail (the list of AOL areas and web sites you've visited), so other screen names on your account can't see where you've been. See "Toolbar."

- Eliminate the `Your mail has been sent` confirmation box that makes you click OK every time you send a piece of email. See "Mail."

- Save each piece of email you read and/or send in your Personal Filing Cabinet. See "Mail."

- Use "Internet-style" quoting in email replies and forwarded messages. We're not usually conformists, but this option helps your email look like the rest of the Internet's. See "Mail."

- Instead of *http://www.aol.com*, we like to have AOL's browser open to a blank page or the page of our choice. See "WWW."

- Alter the maximum space AOL can use for online art: we've made it small for machines with small hard drives and big for slow machines that take forever to load images. (If you have a small hard drive *and* a slow machine, good luck using AOL; we speak from experience.) See "Graphics."

- Eliminate deletion confirmation messages. See "Personal Filing Cabinet."

- We love all the marketing preferences, and you will too. See "Marketing."

Auto AOL

The options on the Automatic AOL preferences screen are not all, strictly speaking, preferences. The four icons on the left perform specific tasks, which we describe below. The list of checkboxed items are Automatic AOL settings, which we'll also explain. To set your Automatic AOL preferences:

MY AOL toolbar icon → `Preferences` → `Auto AOL`

In AOL 3.0, you can find similar settings at:

`Mail` menu → `Set up FlashSession`

The `Automatic AOL` front screen is shown in Figure 29-2.

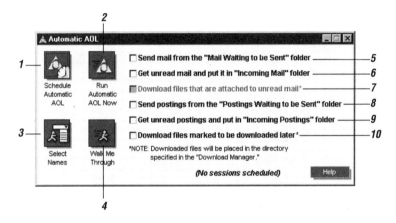

Figure 29-2: Automatic AOL preferences

The following numbers correspond to the numbers in Figure 29-2:

1. `Schedule Automatic AOL` icon: Check the boxes next to the days of the week you want to run Automatic AOL. Then check the `Enable Scheduler` box, select a starting time, select `How Often` (from every half hour to once each day) from the drop-down menu, and click OK.

2. `Run Automatic AOL Now` icon: The `Continue` button takes you through the Automatic AOL setup process step by step. If you do this, you won't need any of the preferences below (such as `Send mail from the "Mail Waiting to be Sent" folder`).

   The `Expert Setup` button takes you back to first Auto AOL preferences screen

3. `Select Names` icon: Check the checkbox next to the screen name you want to select for your next Automatic AOL session. If you have only one screen name, you have to do this just once. To schedule Automatic AOL for another time, you must enter your password in the `Password` box.

4. Walk Me Through icon: Goes to the same screen as the Run Automatic AOL Now icon. The checkboxes allow you to select the tasks that are performed during your next Automatic AOL session. You don't need to bother with these if you've selected Run Automatic AOL Now or Walk Me Through. You only have to revisit this setting if you change your mind about what tasks you want Automatic AOL to perform.

5. Send mail from the "Mail Waiting to be Sent" folder: The default is to have this preference disabled. Enabling this preference ensures that the email you write offline is sent during your next Automatic AOL session.

6. Get unread mail and put it in "Incoming Mail" folder: The default is to have this preference disabled. Enabling this preference ensures that your new, incoming email is received during your next Automatic AOL session.

7. Download files that are attached to unread mail: The default is to have this preference disabled. Enabling it ensures that Automatic AOL downloads files that are attached to incoming email. Downloading email attachments is the only way you can get a virus via email, so we really can't recommend it. (See also *viruses* and *Trojan horses* in Chapter 8, *Email.*)

8. Send postings from the "Postings Waiting to be Sent" folder: The default is to have this preference disabled. Enabling it ensures that Automatic AOL sends outgoing newsgroup and message board posts during your next Automatic AOL session.

9. Get unread postings and put in "Incoming Postings" folder: The default is to have this preference disabled. Enabling it ensures that Automatic AOL retrieves new, incoming newsgroup and message board posts during your next Automatic AOL session.

10. Download files marked to be downloaded later: The default is to have this preference disabled. Enabling it ensures that Automatic AOL downloads files you've marked to "download later" and places them in your default download directory.

Chat

Chat preferences affect what you see and hear in chat rooms. To adjust chat preferences:

MY AOL toolbar icon → Preferences → Chat

The Chat Preferences screen is shown in Figure 29-3.

1. Notify me when members arrive: The default is to have this option disabled. If you enable it, whenever someone enters the room, a line like this will appear amidst your usual chat room conversation:

OnlineHost: Screen_Name has entered the room.

2. Notify me when members leave: The default is to have this option disabled. Whenever someone leaves the room, a line like this appears amidst your usual chat room conversation:

OnlineHost: Screen_Name has left the room.

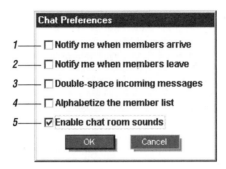

Figure 29-3: The Chat Preferences screen

3. **Double-space incoming messages**: The default is to have this option disabled, resulting in single-spaced chat. If you enable it, the text is double-spaced, which might make it easier on the eyes. In fast-paced chat rooms, however, it makes it harder to follow conversations.

4. **Alphabetize the member list**: The default is not to alphabetize chat room member lists. As a result, screen names are displayed in random order. Enabling this option alphabetizes the member list, which makes it easier to locate people. You must reenter the chat room or switch rooms to have this take effect.

5. **Enable chat room sounds**: The default is to have chat room sounds enabled. "Chat room sounds" refers only to *.wav* files played by chat room participants.

Download

Downloading may seem like a simple business, but AOL's Download Manager comes with plenty of bells and whistles. All these preferences are available in AOL 3.0 except #6. To adjust your download preferences:

> **MY AOL** toolbar icon → **Preferences** → **Download**

or:

> **My Files** toolbar icon → **Download Manager** → **Download Preferences**

The **Download Preferences** screen is shown in Figure 29-4.

1. **Display Image Files on Download**: The default is to automatically display graphic files (*.art*, *.avi*, *.bmp*, *.gif*, and *.jpg*) as they're downloading. The alternative is to disable this option and use a separate graphics viewer after you sign off.

2. **Automatically decompress files at sign-off**: When you download compressed (zipped) files, the default is for AOL to automatically decompress them when you sign off. The decompressed files are placed in

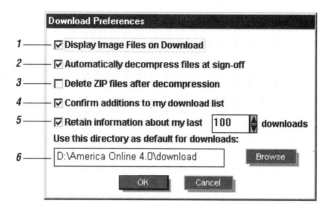

1 — ☑ Display Image Files on Download
2 — ☑ Automatically decompress files at sign-off
3 — ☐ Delete ZIP files after decompression
4 — ☑ Confirm additions to my download list
5 — ☑ Retain information about my last [1 0 0] downloads
Use this directory as default for downloads:
6 — [D:\America Online 4.0\download] Browse
OK   Cancel

Figure 29-4: The Download Preferences screen

the *aolxx/download* folder. If you disable this option, you have to decompress the files manually, either with the download manager's `Decompress` button or with a separate decompression utility such as PKunzip.

3. `Delete ZIP files after decompression`: The default is to have this option disabled: AOL leaves your *.zip* files alone after you decompress them. If you enable it, AOL deletes your *.zip* files after decompression, which saves hard drive space but makes it impossible to ever reinstall the software contained in the *.zip* file.

4. `Confirm additions to my download list`: The default is to give you a long, annoying confirmation screen whenever you add anything to your Download Manager queue. Disabling this option means you won't see that confirmation screen anymore.

5. `Retain information about my last [number] downloads`: The default is to retain information about your last 100 downloads. This refers to the number of files stored in the Download Manager's `Files You've Down-loaded` folder. To view the information, use the Download Manager's `Show Files Downloaded` button.

6. `Use this directory as default for downloads`: The default directory for downloads is *C:\America Online 4.0\download*. To change the default directory, use the `Browse` button to navigate to the directory of your choice, then click `Save`.

Font

Font preferences set the default font for all your outgoing email, Instant Messages, chat room conversation, and text documents—basically, anything you type. You can always change the current font within any of these individual applications (email, IMs, chat rooms, and text documents). The ability to globally change your default font is new in 4.0, though 3.0 users can change font styles for individual email messages by using the toolbar in the `Compose Mail` window.

To adjust your font preferences:

> MY AOL toolbar icon → Preferences → Font

The Font Preferences screen is shown in Figure 29-5.

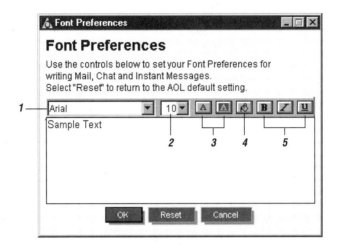

Figure 29-5: The Font Preferences screen

1. The default font is Arial. You have 27 other options, at last count.

2. The default font size is 10. Your other options are 8, 12, 14, 16, 18, 20, 22, 24, 26, 28, 36, 48, and 72.

3. The default text foreground color is black. The default text and page background colors are white. If you want to change any of these, you have a whole palette of colors to choose from. For each option, click the icon and choose from the palette.

4. The default page background color, which is white (but not text background color—that's covered in #3 above).

5. The default is plain text, but you can also select bold, italic, and underline.

The Reset button returns your text to the default settings.

General

The word "general" doesn't do justice to these useful settings. All these preferences except #8 are available in AOL 3.0. To adjust your general preferences:

> MY AOL toolbar icon → Preferences → General

The General Preferences screen is shown in Figure 29-6.

1. Display Channels at Sign On: The default is to display the Channels screen every time you sign on. Disabling this option means you only see the

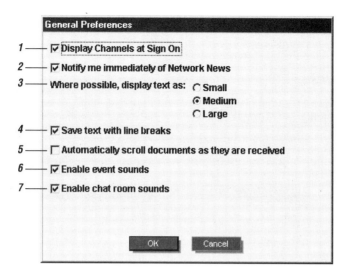

Figure 29-6: The General Preferences screen

Welcome screen. This is one of our favorite preferences, since most people don't use the Channels screen after they've been around the AOL block a few times.

2. **Notify me immediately of Network News**: The default is to let you see systemwide announcements from AOL. They're bound to be at least a little bit relevant when they happen, so you might as well leave this enabled. For instance, if AOL needs to shut down the chat system, you'll get a message telling you about it. If you have this preference disabled, you'll get disconnected from the chat room without knowing why.

3. **Where possible, display text as**: The default text size is **Medium**. To fit more text on your screen (and scroll less), select **Small**. If you're having trouble reading the text, select **Large**. This preference applies mostly to email and text articles. It won't change the size of the text in your Buddy List, on the Welcome screen, or in many AOL content areas.

4. **Save text with line breaks**: The default is to save text with automatic line breaks (hard returns) based on the size of the window you're typing in. Unless you use AOL's text editor, this preference doesn't matter much, and you should leave it as the default. If you are using AOL's text editor, however, you shouldn't save text with line breaks, as it interferes with your formatting.

5. **Automatically scroll documents as they are received**: The default is not to do this. Unless you're using a 2400-baud modem, you might as well leave the default alone. Otherwise, documents scroll to the bottom before you get a chance to read the text at the top.

6. **Enable event sounds**: The default is to have event sounds enabled. Event sounds include: Welcome, You've Got Mail, File's Done, Goodbye, the IM chimes, Buddy List sounds (You've Got Company and Later), and the Favorite Place noise.

7. **Enable chat room sounds**: The default is to have chat room sounds enabled. Chat room sounds refer only to *.wav* files played by chat room participants.

Graphics

AOL is nothing if not graphical, so these are important settings. All of these preferences except #3 are available in AOL 3.0. To adjust your graphics preferences:

MY AOL toolbar icon → **Preferences** → **Graphics**

The **Graphics Viewing Preferences** screen is shown in Figure 29-7.

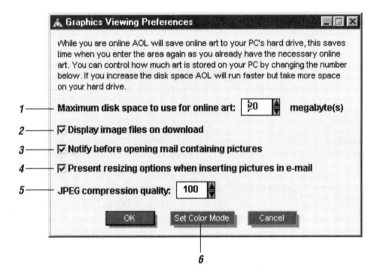

Figure 29-7: The Graphics Viewing Preferences screen

1. **Maximum disk space to use for online art**: The default is to allot 20 MB of hard disk space for online art, though you can change it to any amount you want. When choosing how much disk space to use for online art, decide whether you'd rather save online time (by allotting more space) or save disk space (by allotting less space). The artwork file, by the way, is the file in your *C:\America Online 4.0* folder, called *MAIN.IDX*.

2. **Display image files on download**: The default is to automatically display graphic files (*.art*, *.avi*, *.bmp*, *.gif*, and *.jpg*) as they're downloading. The alternative is to disable this option and use a separate graphics viewer after you sign off.

3. **Notify before opening mail containing pictures**: The default is to notify you before you read email containing embedded images. You get a screen asking if you know the person that sent the email and warning you that the email contains a picture that you might find objectionable. See also *images* in Chapter 8, *Email*.

4. Present resizing options when inserting pictures in e-mail: This option is enabled by default. When you embed a picture in the body of an outgoing email message, if the image is wider or longer than your email window, you'll be asked if you want to resize it. Shrinking the image can make it look better or worse, depending on the situation. We suggest you leave this option enabled and experiment with each image you insert in email.

5. JPEG compression quality: The default JPEG compression quality is 100, though you can lower it. Lowering the compression quality makes the images look a bit worse, but it makes the images load faster. 100% compression quality is unnecessary, but also beware of setting the quality too low; AOL is so graphics-based that very poor graphics quality might make navigation harder. 50 is a good compromise.

6. Set Color Mode button: "Color mode" refers to how many colors your computer can display. The default is Detect Automatically, which lets AOL figure out your computer's video configuration on its own. The default is fine for almost everyone. If you need to change your video configuration (for a game you're playing on the Internet that recommends 256 colors, for instance), you can manually set your color mode to 256 colors or More than 256 colors.

Language

When you add languages to your Languages Preferences, you'll see certain international AOL areas in those languages. Language preferences are new in AOL 4.0. To add or remove a language (i.e., adjust language preferences):

MY AOL toolbar icon → Preferences → Language

The Language Preferences screen is shown in Figure 29-8.

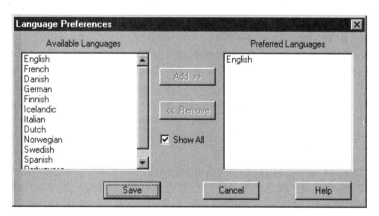

Figure 29-8: The Language Preferences screen

Click **Add** to add a highlighted language to your list. The default language is English only. You can add French, Danish, German, Finnish, Icelandic, Italian, Dutch, Norweigan, Swedish, Spanish, and Portuguese.

Click **Remove** to take a highlighted language out of your list.

Mail

These preferences are crucial if you send and receive a lot of email, especially keeping your old email in your Personal Filing Cabinet. Preferences #3, 6, 7, 8, and 9 are new to AOL 4.0. To adjust your email preferences:

MY AOL toolbar icon → Preferences → Mail

The Mail Preferences screen is shown in Figure 29-9.

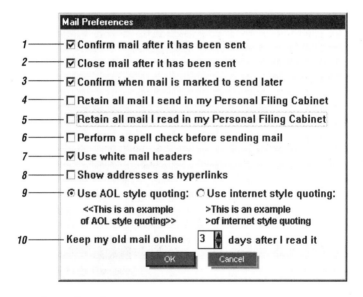

Figure 29-9: The Mail Preferences screen

1. **Confirm mail after it has been sent**: The default is to have this option enabled. Disable it if you're tired of the **Your mail has been sent** confirmation box, and/or are tired of clicking **OK** whenever the box comes up.

2. **Close mail after it has been sent**: The default is for an email message to close after the email has been sent, but some people prefer to keep the email open on the desktop after sending.

3. **Confirm when mail is marked to send later**: The default is to have this option enabled. The **Send Later** confirmation box says: **Your mail has been placed in the "Mail Waiting to be Sent" folder of your Personal Filing Cabinet. To see your outgoing mail,**

click Mail Waiting to be Sent. To send your outgoing mail later, click Auto AOL. It's probably not a bad idea to keep confirmation around the first few times you use Automatic AOL, but after that, you might find it easier to ditch it (see also Chapter 21, *Automatic AOL*).

4. Retain all mail I send in my Personal Filing Cabinet: The default is not to save mail you've sent in your PFC, which means sent mail remains in your Sent Mail mailbox for about three days. If you enable this option, all the mail you send is saved in the Mail You've Sent folder of your PFC until you manually delete it.

5. Retain all mail I read in my Personal Filing Cabinet: The default is not to save mail you've read in your PFC, which means read mail remains in your Old Mail mailbox for about three days. If you enable this option, all the mail you receive is saved in the Incoming/Saved Mail folder of your PFC until you manually delete it.

6. Perform a spell check before sending mail: The default is not to automatically spellcheck outgoing email. Enable this option to have your spelling (and grammar) automatically checked before you send out any email.

7. Use white mail headers: The default is to use white headers in email messages. The alternative to white headers is a headache-inducing landscape of tiny gray dots, so we recommend you leave this one alone.

8. Show addresses as hyperlinks: The default is to have this option disabled. Enabling it makes screen names in the headers of incoming mail appear as hyperlinks, so that clicking a name starts an email message to that screen name. We're not sure why you'd want to do this, since it's just as easy to use the Reply or Reply to All button.

9. Use AOL style quoting or Use Internet style quoting: The default is to use AOL-style quoting. See *quoting* in Chapter 8, *Email*, for examples of each.

10. Keep my old mail online [number] days after I read it: The default is to keep old mail online for three days, though you can keep it for one to seven days.

Marketing

If you think AOL tries too hard to sell you things—who doesn't?—there's something you can do to cut it down a bit. To adjust your marketing preferences:

MY AOL toolbar icon → Preferences → Marketing

or (this method works in AOL 3.0 and 4.0):

Keyword: Marketing Prefs

The Marketing Preferences screen is shown in Figure 29-10.

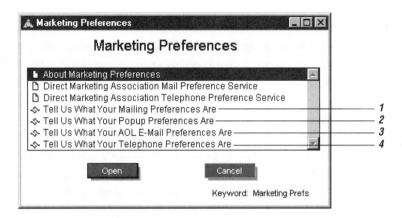

Figure 29-10: The Marketing Preferences screen

1. **Tell Us What Your Mailing Preferences Are**: "Mailing" refers to postal mail, not email.

   Option 1: Check the boxes corresponding to your interests so AOL can give your name to specific commercial mailing lists.

   Option 2: Enter an X in the box next to If you prefer not to receive any mailings from other companies, enter X here. That means AOL can't give your name to other companies, but they can send you mail themselves.

   Option 3: Enter an X in the box next to If you prefer not to receive any special member mailings from AOL, enter X here.

   Option 4: Enter an X in the boxes for both Option 2 and Option 3.

   When you're done, click Send.

2. **Tell Us What Your Popup Preferences Are**: "Popup preferences" refers to the ad splashscreens you see when you first sign on, and sometimes when entering AOL areas.

   Option 1: Check the boxes corresponding to your interests so you can get *more* popups.

   Option 2: Click the box next to If you prefer not to receive any special member benefit pop-up offers, click here. Another box pops up. Check the box next to I prefer not to receive special member pop-up offers from AOL. Click OK.

   Like it says, you'll still get the occasional popup about AOL itself, but you won't get any more "special member benefit" popups, i.e., ads.

   When you're done, click Send.

3. **Tell Us What Your AOL E-Mail Preferences Are**: At least AOL doesn't give your email address to junk mailers, though they imply that they spam you themselves.

Option 1: Check the boxes corresponding to your interests so AOL can send you "very special product and service offers;" you know what that means by now, don't you?

Option 2: Enter an X in the box next to If you prefer not to receive any special member benefits email offers, enter X here.

When you're done, click Send.

4. Tell Us What Your Telephone Preferences Are: Now this one's scary: "telephone preferences" refers to telemarketing.

Option 1: You know the drill. Tell AOL your interests; get targeted for advertising.

Option 2: Enter an X in the box next to If you prefer not to receive any special member benefits offers by telephone, enter X here.

When you're done, click Send.

Passwords

Password preferences refer only to storing or adding passwords, not changing them. These preferences are the only ones that don't apply to all screen names on your account; you must be signed on with a screen name in order to store its password. AOL 4.0 users can store your sign-on password so you don't have to type it every time you sign on, and put a password on your Personal Filing Cabinet. AOL 3.0 users can store their sign-on password.

To adjust your password preferences:

MY AOL toolbar icon → Preferences → Passwords

The Store Passwords (i.e., password preferences) screen is shown in Figure 29-11.

- Sign-On: When you first install AOL 4.0, the Sign On box is checked for all your passwords (the option is enabled). The next time you sign on with any screen name, AOL prompts you to store your password. If you don't, the Sign On box for that screen name is cleared (the option is disabled). However, AOL still periodically hassles you to store your password. We wish there was a preference to disable that, too.

  When this preference is disabled, you have to enter your password manually every time you sign on. If you enable it, the password you're currently using is stored in the system. You can sign on faster this way, but it's not always safe. If you store your password, you still have to enter a password when you switch screen names without signing off. See also Chapter 3, *Screen Names, Passwords, and Signing On.*

- Personal Filing Cabinet: The default is to have this preference disabled. If you enable it, you must choose a password (different from your sign-on password) and type it in the Password box. By putting a password on your PFC, you theoretically keep your saved email, newsgroup posts, and

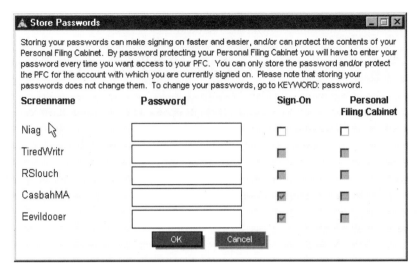

Store Passwords

Storing your passwords can make signing on faster and easier, and/or can protect the contents of your Personal Filing Cabinet. By password protecting your Personal Filing Cabinet you will have to enter your password every time you want access to your PFC. You can only store the password and/or protect the PFC for the account with which you are currently signed on. Please note that storing your passwords does not change them. To change your passwords, go to KEYWORD: password.

Screenname	Password	Sign-On	Personal Filing Cabinet
Niag		☐	☐
TiredWritr		☑	☑
RSlouch		☑	☑
CasbahMA		☑	☑
Eevildooer		☑	☑

OK   Cancel

Figure 29-11: The Store Passwords screen

download history from prying eyes. However, your PFC password can be disabled by anyone who signs on to your account (for example, using a stored sign-on password).

Personal Filing Cabinet

These preferences can keep your PFC from getting too big or too fragmented. This is also the place to turn off the annoying "Are you sure you want to delete that file?" confirmation popups.

MY AOL toolbar icon → Preferences → Personal Filing Cabinet

The Personal Filing Cabinet Preferences screen is shown in Figure 29-12.

1. Issue warning about the PFC if file size reaches [*number*] megabytes: By default, you get a warning that your PFC size is weighing in at 10 MB. If you don't care how much space you take up with your PFC, you can make the maximum size larger than 10 MB (on today's huge hard drives, who cares how big the file size is?). If you have a small hard drive and want to save space, you can make the maximum size smaller than 10 MB, but if you make it too small, you get the annoying PFC size warning all the time.

2. Issue warning about the PFC if free space reaches [*number*] percent: By default, you get a warning if your PFC free space reaches 35%. If you want to increase or decrease this amount, type in a new number. Compacting your PFC regularly saves hard drive space.

3. Confirm before deleting single items: By default, you get a warning before you delete items from your PFC (and from your online email box, and

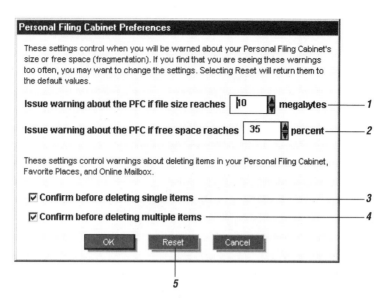

Figure 29-12: The Personal Filing Cabinet Preferences screen

your list of Favorite Places). Disabling this preference is a good idea if you know what you're doing and find the confirmations annoying.

4. **Confirm before deleting multiple items**: By default, you get a warning before you delete items from your PFC (and from your online email box, and your list of Favorite Places). Disabling this preference is a good idea if you know what you're doing and find the confirmations annoying.

5. **Reset** button: Restores the default PFC preference settings.

Spelling

The spellchecker is new with AOL 4.0, and we like it. We're not fond of how nitpicky the spellchecker gets, though. The default is to enable all its options, but we prefer to disable most of them. To set your spelling preferences:

MY AOL toolbar icon → **Preferences** → **General**

The **Spelling Preferences** front screen is shown in Figure 29-13.

1. **Capitalization of sentences and proper nouns**: A good one to disable if you write mostly casual email where capitalization doesn't matter much.

2. **Doubled words**: "The the" and other such errors.

3. **'A' vs. 'An'**: FYI, both "a historic event" and "an historic event" are accepted here.

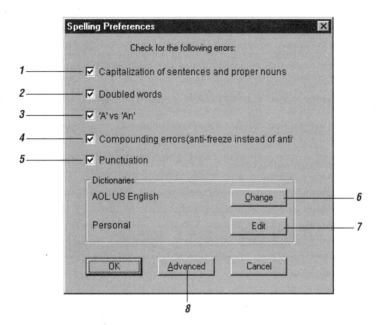

Figure 29-13: The Spelling Preferences screen

4. **Compounding errors**: You can probably safely disable this, unless you find unnecessary hyphens really offensive. This feature doesn't add hyphens when they're missing: anti-freeze becomes antifreeze, but "twenty two year old starving writer" goes by without comment.

5. **Punctuation**: Finds duplicated punctuation marks, corrects some comma errors, corrects punctuation within quotation marks and parentheses. Also forces you to put two spaces between sentences, which hasn't been considered correct since the days when everyone used typewriters.

6. **Change** button: "Change" is a misnomer since you can't actually change anything here. The default (and only) dictionary is AOL U.S. English.

7. **Edit** button: Allows you to view (or delete) the words you've added to the spellchecking dictionary. This is labeled **Personal Dictionary**.

8. Click the **Advanced** button to see all your options, listed below:

   – **A vs. an**: see #3.

   – **Capitalization errors**: see #1.

   – **Compounding errors**: see #4.

   – **Doubled words**: see #2.

   – **Formatting errors**: Corrects errors relating to numbers, dates, times, currency, and other symbols. For instance, when you spellcheck "If I had

100000$," you are reminded that you should put commas in numbers and hyphens in phone numbers, and that the dollar sign goes in front of the number.

- **Hyphenation errors**: Corrects you when you incorrectly split a word at the end of a line. However, you shouldn't ever need to split a word at the end of a line, unless you're using full justification (see also *justification* in Chapter 8, *Email*).

- **Inappropriate prepositions**: Corrects you when you use the wrong preposition within a phrase. You probably don't need this unless you're in the habit of saying things like "I wouldn't settle on less." Besides, that phrase went through without comment, which means this feature isn't very comprehensive anyway.

- **Misspelled expressions**: Like "inappropriate prepositions" above, checks for errors within phrases. You can probably disable this and never notice.

- **Open vs. closed spelling**: Corrects spacing errors. It looks like it puts words together (like turning "none the less" into "nonetheless") but doesn't take words apart ("eachother" comes up as a spelling error, not a spacing error). This isn't the annoying option that forces you to put two spaces between sentences; punctuation is (see also #5).

- **Punctuation errors**: see #5.

- **Spelling errors**: Isn't that what spellchecking is for? Anyway, this option finds words that aren't in the dictionary. Of course, you can add words to the dictionary. Some words that are already in the dictionary: Microsoft, Netscape, CompuServe, and many proper names, even O'Reilly.

- **Ungrammatical expressions**: Ain't passes the test, but irregardless doesn't. It's not really grammar that's covered but poor word use.

Toolbar

Toolbar preferences are new to AOL 4.0 and a welcome improvement. Control how your toolbar looks, where it is, and the information it stores. For more about your toolbar, see also Chapter 4, *Getting Around AOL: Toolbars and Menus*.

To adjust your toolbar preferences:

MY AOL toolbar icon → Preferences → Toolbar

The Toolbar Preferences screen is shown in Figure 29-14.

1. **Appearance: Icons and Text/Text Only**: The default is to use toolbar icons with text and pictures. Changing to text only makes the buttons take up less vertical space but slightly more horizontal space on your monitor.

2. **Location: Move to Top/Move to Bottom**: The default toolbar location is the top of your screen, but you can move it to the bottom.

Figure 29-14: The Toolbar Preferences screen

3. **Navigation: Use Previous and Next navigation arrows to track open windows only:** The arrow icons on the toolbar let you navigate backwards and forwards through your History Trail (the record of the last 25 AOL areas or web sites you've visited). The default is to have this option disabled, so you can use the arrows to navigate to windows you've closed. If you enable this option by checking the box, you can use the arrows only to navigate within open windows (though you can revisit closed windows with the History Trail drop-down menu).

4. **History Trail: Clear History Trail after each Sign Off or Switch Screen Name:** The History Trail is located in the drop-down toolbar menu between the Keyword button and the Go button. It lists the last 25 places you've been on AOL or the Web. The default is to keep the last 25 places at all times, but by enabling this preference, you clear the history trail every time you sign off or switch screen names. This is a good way to keep other screen names on your account from seeing where you've been.

5. **Clear History Now** button: This button clears the history trail, but you'll have to enable the **Clear History Trail After Each Sign Off or Switch Screen Name** preference to have it cleared regularly and by default.

WWW

Web preferences are more complicated than other AOL preferences, because they're based on the settings for Microsoft's Internet Explorer. Because AOL members use a slightly scaled-down, integrated version of MSIE, the preferences aren't as extensive (or complicated) as they are in the standalone version of MSIE. In some cases, you see options you can't change; we've indicated those.

There are five tabbed sections to the WWW preferences, each of which has subsections. We've given each tab its own section, with its entries under it. If you've installed a standalone version of Internet Explorer 4.0 or later, your preferences might look different than these. However, since the vast majority of AOL users use the web browser AOL gives them, we've covered the default Internet Explorer 3.0 preferences.

Depending on how your computer is configured, when you change the preferences of your AOL integrated browser you may also change the settings in the standalone version of Internet Explorer that came bundled with Windows.

To adjust your web preferences within AOL:

MY AOL toolbar icon → **Preferences** → **WWW**

The front **AOL Internet Properties** (i.e., web preferences) screen is shown in Figure 29-15.

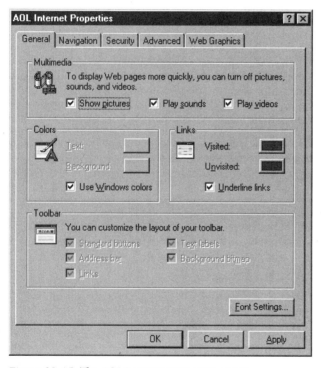

Figure 29-15: The AOL Internet Properties screen

We've included all web preferences in this section. However, we have a feeling that only the very curious will want to read through all of them. Here's our list of the ones that apply to the most people:

- General Tab → Multimedia
- Navigation Tab → Customize

- Security Tab → Content Advisor
- Web Graphics tab

General Tab

Multimedia (Show pictures, Play sounds, and Play videos)

By default, all these options are enabled. You can disable any multimedia option by clearing the checkbox next to it. If you've got a modem slower than 28.8, you might want to disable sounds and videos, and even pictures, which helps load your pages faster. When disabled, you can still see multimedia, but you have to double-click on the image outline to load it.

Colors (Use Windows colors)

The default text color for web documents is black; the default background color is white. If you clear the box next to Use Windows colors, you can choose a different default text and background color by clicking the black or gray rectangles. This option is irrelevant, by the way, if the creator of a web site you're viewing has coded the site to display specific colors. Most web site designers code their sites this way.

Links

These preferences affect how web links look, not where they go.

- The default is for visited links to be purple and unvisited links to be blue. Click the purple or blue rectangles to open up a palette, where you can select a color to replace the default.

- Underline links: The default is to underline hyperlinks, but you can change the default by clearing this checkbox.

Toolbar

Because you're using an AOL-integrated browser, you use AOL's toolbar. Therefore, you can't change these toolbar options.

Font Settings button

When you click this button, you open another window full of settings.

- The default language and character set is Western (i.e., English). In AOL's browser, you can't add any others.

- The Proportional Font and Fixed-Width Font defaults are, for the sake of viewing web site design, better left alone.

- The default MIME encoding version is Windows-1252. You can't change the MIME encoding version, but that's not because you're using the AOL-integrated browser. Other Internet Explorer users can't change it either. (For a short explanation of MIME encoding, see *MIME* in Chapter 8, *Email.*)

Navigation Tab

Customize

Your default start page (the one that pops up as soon as you launch your browser from the Internet toolbar icon) is *http://www.aol.com.* You can

---

change that to any web page, or leave it blank. The other options in the drop-down `Page` menu don't apply to AOL's browser, only standalone Internet Explorer.

History

These preferences correspond to an ever-changing list of all the web sites you've visited with AOL's browser lately.

- The default is to keep a record of all the web sites you've visited in the last 20 days. You can change the number of days from 20 to whatever you want.

- `View History` button: Shows you every web site you've visited in the last 20 (or whatever number you select) days. Double-clicking a site launches the browser and displays it. To look for a specific site, sort by clicking the `Title` or `Internet Address` bar.

- `Clear History` button: Deletes all the web sites in your `History` folder.

Security Tab

Content Advisor

In the bundled MSIE, there are special settings from the Recreational Software Advisory Council (RSAC) that can help you set your browser to filter out objectionable material.

- The `Enable Settings` button turns on the RSAC filter.

- The `Settings` button allows you, after you've enabled the filter, to adjust settings for sex, nudity, violence, and offensive language, both vulgar and hate-motivated.

To set up the Content Advisor:

Within `Settings`, click the `General` tab for more options: you can change the default setting and enable users to see sites that have no rating (the majority); you can also change the default setting, which allows the Supervisor (master account-holder who sets the preferences) to type a password to allow others to view restricted pages. Click the `Change Password` button to change the Supervisor password. Within `Settings`, clicking `Advanced` allows you to add other Ratings Bureaus to filter content, but you'll have to find them and add them to your system yourself. As far as we're concerned, RSAC is the big one, and you might as well use it if you choose any content filters.

Certificates

Certificates are statements that establish the identity of a person or the security of a web site. Most casual web users will never need to think twice (or even once) about certificates. We've covered them briefly just for the sake of completeness, but if you're interested in the details, see this web page: *http://www.microsoft.com/ie/ie40/features/sec-certificates.htm*, or search *http://www.microsoft.com/Search/Default.htm* for the word "certificates."

- `Personal`: Personal certificates contain information (such as your user-name and password), and enable encryption/decryption of documents you send and receive over the Internet. It's for people who are serious about protecting the integrity of their information from possible snoops. Most users, including us, aren't. You can purchase such a "digital ID" from companies such as Verisign, at *http://www.Verisign.com/*.

– Sites: By clicking the boxes here, you can check to see which site certificates you'll accept, and which publishers you'll always accept certificates from. If you have reason to be worried about a certificate (say, you've downloaded something or visited a web page with a certificate, and you later found major problems with the download or with what happened when you accessed the site; perhaps you got a bad ActiveX control), you can delete it. Such problems are rare.

– Publishers: Here, you are supposed to be able to specify software publishers you trust, so that Windows can automatically download and install software from these publishers without asking you for confirmation. As far as we can tell, this is mainly something for Microsoft Developers to play with; we don't know anyone who's ever used it. On the other hand, if some site passes you corrupt or pernicious code, you can block them from future downloads.

– You can check a box marked Consider all commercial software publishers trustworthy, so that Windows can automatically download and install software from just about anywhere without asking for confirmation. We prefer the default of asking for your permission every time.

Active Content

These preferences decide what software your web browser can download and run.

– The default is to allow the following web features: downloading of active content, ActiveX controls and plug-ins, ActiveX scripts, Java scripts. Clear any of the checkboxes to disable those features. All of these are just small programs that run on your computer, and we think, for the most part, they're pretty harmless, especially when this content comes from major, professional web sites. For an alternate view of active content's possible security risks, see this web site: *http://www.users.zetnet.co.uk/hopwood/ papers/compsec97.html.*

– Safety Level button: determines the level of warning you get about potentially unsafe active web content. The default is medium, and you should probably stick with it (despite its designation for "expert users and developers," we think it's fine for most people).

Advanced Tab

Warnings

Warnings are dialog boxes that pop up telling you something about the web page you're visiting. You can click OK to proceed or Cancel to stop what you're doing. We find the Warnings preferences irrelevant to most web surfers. We choose to leave the defaults as they are.

- **Warn before sending over an open connection**: Check this box to receive a warning when you send data to a web site that isn't secure. If you check the box, you can then choose "only when I'm sending more than one line of text" or "always." The "always" setting always warns you before sending out short, confidential data like you fill in on forms, including passwords and credit card numbers.

- **Warn if changing between secure and unsecure mode**: When this box is checked (the default), you're warned when going from a secure web site to an unsecure web site. For instance, you might want to know when making a web purchase that you're sending credit card information securely, but that you're browsing in unsecure mode.

- **Warn about invalid site certificates**: "Invalid" here means that the site certificate contains an incorrect URL. The default is to have this warning enabled.

- **Warn before accepting cookies**: The default is no warnings. If you're really worried about cookies (see also "Cookies" in Chapter 30, *Privacy*), enable it. But most people just find it annoying to be clicking away the warnings at every web site that has cookies, as most web sites do these days.

Temporary Internet Files

Temporary Internet Files, a record of where you've been on the Web, can be useful. It goes further back than your AOL History Trail (see also "Toolbar"), which only records the last 25 places you've been. If the Web is running slowly for you, try emptying the folder containing the files (that's the Settings button, below).

- **View Files** button: Allows you to view your cache, including images, HTML files, and cookies.

- **Settings** button: This button lets you decide how often you want to check for newer versions of stored web pages (every time you visit the page, every time you start Internet Explorer, or never). It lets you determine how much space to allow for your temporary Internet files (default is 3% of your drive). In addition, you can choose to move the cache files to another location on your hard drive; view the files; or empty the folder containing the files.

Other

- **Show friendly URLs**: A "friendly URL" is the web address (such as *http://www.oreilly.com*) that shows up on the bottom of your browser when you move your mouse over a hyperlink. This is so you can see where a link takes you before you follow it. The default is to have this enabled.

- **Highlight links when clicked**: This is enabled by default. Links change color as they're clicked.

- **Use smooth scrolling**: This setting (enabled by default) simply affects the way your scrollbar looks. Smooth scrolling is more aesthetically pleasing, but it really doesn't matter either way.

- Use style sheets: Style sheets are enabled by default. They are basically HTML templates used by web designers to make their pages look good. They're not hurting anyone, and can make web pages look better, so you might as well leave this option enabled.

- Enable Java JIT compilers: Just In Time (JIT) compilers are enabled by default. They are another way to bring web pages programmed in Java to your computer. They can make certain web pages load faster, so you might as well leave the default alone.

- Enable Java logging: "Java logging" creates a file (*C:\WINDOWS\JAVA\javalog.txt*) that logs Java applet activity. You only really need this if you're a Java whiz who wants to examine the log when you encounter an error. This is disabled by default.

- Automatic Configuration button: Doesn't apply to ISPs or AOL. These settings are configured by a systems administrator and put in a file for companies and institutions using MSIE systemwide.

- Cryptography Settings button: Lets you specify your cryptography protocol. The default is to allow several standard secure connection types—SSL2, SSL3, and PCT—and not to save secure web pages to your hard drive. We suggest you leave those options enabled and not worry about web security. If you want to learn more about cryptography, like the technical differences between SSL and PCT, see this web page: *http://www.rsa.com/rsalabs/newfaq/*.

Web Graphics Tab

Use compressed graphics

Compressed graphics are the default. That means that when you use AOL's integrated browser, graphics from the Web are compressed by AOL so they can load faster. Compressed images may be of slightly lower quality than a web site's native images, but most people won't notice. Clear the checkbox to use the default, slower-loading graphics.

CHAPTER 30

Privacy

Concern for privacy is on the rise among nearly everyone online. Is credit-card fraud really a major concern? Why do we need powerful encryption to protect online transactions? You're constantly told not to give out your password or credit card information anywhere on AOL, unless you're making a purchase that's guaranteed secure. Are we justified to worry about our personal information online? What can other people find out about you?

Like most everything, privacy online has two sides: the good news is that others will know only what you tell them. The bad news is that unsuspecting or overly trusting individuals give out too much information online, and are sorry later. Our tips below help you avoid the feeling that you've revealed too much.

Basically, it is all a matter of choice. Some people feel comfortable telling others what their hobbies are, or even what their measurements are, online. You have to decide when and where you want your information to appear.

We're big proponents of the "Use alternate screen names" school of thought. If you screw up with one and start getting bombed by junk email or crazy fans you've been chatting with, you can always delete it and create a new one. Decide for yourself what you want others to know, then we'll show you where to go to either protect or diminish your privacy.

Another privacy issue is that some people don't trust AOL to keep their secrets. You might be worried that AOL will reveal your identity if an important enough agency (such as the U.S. military) asks. Yes, AOL told the Navy who the man behind a certain screen name was, but the backlash was so great that we doubt it will ever happen again. We don't think it's worth getting paranoid about AOL divulging your identity, but since some people no longer trust AOL, we suggest non-AOL privacy alternatives in the "Discussion Groups" and "Email" sections of this chapter.

Buddy Lists

We love Buddy Lists and we like keeping them enabled for all our screen names, but some people find that the interruption from some of their friends and possible foes can get in the way of whatever else they're trying to do on AOL. Thankfully, you can block certain members from adding you to their Buddy Lists, thereby cutting them off from seeing that you're online. Use this path:

Keyword: Buddy → Privacy Preferences → Block only those people whose screen names I list

The Buddy List `Privacy Preferences` screen is shown in Figure 30-1.

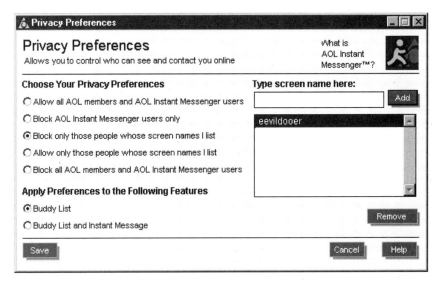

Figure 30-1: Buddy List Privacy Preferences screen

When you use this option, most people can add you to their Buddy Lists. Type in the screen names of particularly annoying members, or anyone you're hiding from. Once you block them, they won't be able to see that you're online, and they can't locate you if you're in a chat room—maybe you don't want them to know what you're talking about (see also "People in Chat Rooms" in Chapter 10, *Chatting*).

To block these same people from sending Instant Messages at the same time you block them from adding you to their Buddy Lists, click `Buddy List and Instant Messages`.

Benefits

- Stalkers/former friends/surly chat room participants can't find you online, even if you are online.

- New members and friends are allowed to add you to their list.

Drawback

- Stalkers/former friends/surly chat room participants can use other, non-blocked screen names to find you.

For more radical ways to protect your privacy using buddy lists, see "Privacy" in Chapter 9, *Instant Messages and Buddy Lists.*

Cookies

A cookie is something web sites use to know when you've visited their site before, or to track where you've been while visiting their site. A cookie is a little piece of text that gets sent back and forth between your browser and the web server.

Lot's of people will tell you that cookies are dangerous, that they can corrupt your system files, and that your personal privacy is compromised. For the most part, such claims are outright fallacies. Your browser saves small *cookie.txt* files onto your hard drive, but *txt* files can't do any damage to your system.

As for your personal information, that's guarded to the extent that you protect it. If you tell a site who you are and give it a password, the site may use a cookie to remember your name or login alias (and your password) each time you go to it with your browser. We think this is extremely convenient, by the way, since you don't have to keep remembering your login name and password.

Cookies are designed so that only the site that sent the cookie to your browser can read it. The only way a cookie, and by extension, a web site can know who you are, where you live, or your phone number is if you personally give that information to a site, and it sends it back to you as a cookie. Cookies can't share information about your local files.

Discussion Groups

Discussion groups include Usenet newsgroups, Internet mailing lists, AOL message boards, and any discussion areas or message boards on web sites. The Internet is a great place for open communication, but it is also a place where what you say can be accessed any time, anywhere—a benefit and a drawback.

Assume that anyone, at any time now, or in the future, can read what you've posted. Archives can and have been used before by job recruiters to investigate what your interests are, your grammar, and your way of conducting yourself in public.

Another major problem is with unwanted email. Spammers use robots, or automatic programs, that scan newsgroup headers and signatures, pulling any text that resembles an email address. Once you've posted to a newsgroup, your email address is prey to spammers. After collection, your email address is resold to other spammers, and the mail barrage will begin.

Our suggestions:

- Use alternate screen names to post anything you don't want a spammer, a current or prospective employer, your mom, or a journalist to know. Never forget that the searchable Usenet archives at *www.dejanews.com* know all and so do the spammers! We suggest you have one screen name for friends, one for business, and one for posting to Usenet.

- Better yet, post to Usenet via DejaNews' special interface, currently at *http://www.postnews.dejanews.com*. You'll have to use an email address, but it can be an address that forwards mail to your real email account, or a free email account, such as one you can get at *http://www.hotmail.com* (see the next section).

Email

Email can be a not-so-private business. Your system administrator at school or at work could read any piece of email you send, if he or she wanted to. Some companies really do monitor their employees' email, so, on company time, it's safest to write only what you'd want your boss to read.

The good news is that no one you know can watch your AOL account. But remember: if you email it, it's in writing, and you can't take it back. Don't write anything that you need to keep confidential, because there are many ways the recipient of your "private" email can take it public. He could forward it, print it, or save it to use against you later. And if you use your email address to post to newsgroups or mailing lists, people can use your member profile to find out who the person behind the screen name is (but only if you've included your real name).

We like the idea of using anonymous, secondary AOL screen names—with no member profiles!—for confidential correspondence, like posting to a mailing list you'd never want Mom or your boss to know you read. Your real name won't be on the email, and if someone hops on AOL to profile that screen name, they'll come up empty-handed. The only time anyone would ever know about your secret screen name is if they were using your computer and saw the screen name on your Sign On screen.

If you distrust AOL for some reason, your alternative is to look into free email services and decide if one of them better suits your privacy needs. Register with one of these, don't provide your real name, and keep your username a secret from most people. Then you can send messages to any kind of mailing list or person you want, and no one (except the people who receive the email) will ever know. Be warned: it looks like any email provider will reveal your identity if they're asked to for legal reasons, so anything you write in email could someday be held against you in court.

Here are a few web pages to investigate if you're interested in obtaining a new email account:

Juno (http://www.juno.com)
    This is what the Juno web site has to say about privacy:

    We don't read the email messages Juno members send and receive (and don't intend to, barring extraordinary circumstances, such as being required to do otherwise by law).

Hotmail (http://www.hotmail.com)

This is what the Hotmail web site says about privacy:

> Hotmail realizes that Email is private correspondence between the sender and the recipient. It is Hotmail's policy to respect the privacy of its Members. Therefore, Hotmail will not monitor, edit, or disclose the contents of a Member's private communications unless required to do so by law or in the good faith belief that such action is necessary to: (1) conform to the edicts of the law or comply with legal process served on Hotmail; (2) protect and defend the rights or property of Hotmail; or (3) act under exigent circumstances to protect the personal safety of its members or the public.

In addition, there are many other free email services out there. Feel free to explore for yourself at Yahoo's list of free email providers: *http://www.yahoo.com/ Business_and_Economy/Companies/Internet_Services/Email_Providers/Free_Email/*.

History Trail

The History Trail is located in the drop-down toolbar menu between the `Keyword` button and the `Go` button. It lists the last 25 places you've been on AOL or the Web (with AOL's browser). In its default state, your history trail is visible to other screen names on your account after you sign off or switch screen names. To change that:

> My AOL toolbar icon → `Preferences` → `Toolbar` → `Clear History Trail after each Sign Off or Switch Screen Name`

By enabling this preference, you clear the history trail every time you sign off or switch screen names. This is a good way to keep other screen names on your account from seeing where you've been.

To clear the History Trail immediately:

> My AOL toolbar icon → `Preferences` → `Toolbar` → `Clear History Now`

This button clears the History Trail, but you'll have to enable the `Clear History Trail After Each Sign Off or Switch Screen Name` preference to have it cleared regularly and by default.

Instant Messages

Below we have several quick tips on how to maintain your sanity in the face of IMs you don't want. For more about other features of Instant Messages, see Chapter 9.

To Permanently Block All Incoming IMs

> Keyword: `Parental Controls` → `Fine Tune with Custom Controls` → `Instant Messages` → `IM Controls` → check the `Block Instant Message` box

You must be signed on with the Master Account to use any custom control (if you don't know what a master account is, see "Master Versus Additional Screen Names" in Chapter 3, *Screen Names, Passwords, and Signing On*). Once signed on with the Master Account, you can block IMs for any screen name on your account. Once you block using this feature, there's typically a delay before the blocking takes effect.

As an alternative, you can also apply your Buddy List preferences to Instant Messages:

Keyword: Buddy → Privacy Preferences → click Buddy List and Instant Messages in the section labeled Apply Preferences to the Following Features

When you use this feature, anyone you block in Buddy Lists is also blocked from sending you IMs. Only those members whom you allow to add you to their Buddy List can send you IMs.

To Temporarily Block All Incoming IMs

Use the instructions below to block Instant Messages for the current session only. Members attempting to send Instant Message greetings to you also receive a message that you can't receive IMs.

Use CTRL-i to bring up an IM window. Type $im_off into the To: box, type at least one character into the Message field, and click Send (see Figure 30-2). You will receive the confirmation You are now ignoring Instant Messages.

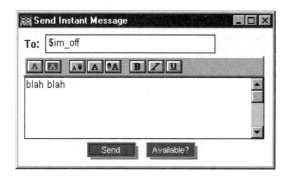

Figure 30-2: Turning off Instant Messages

Ignoring messages endures for your current online session. The next time you log on, IMs are enabled. If you want to reenable your IMs before you sign off from the current session, see the next entry.

To Reenable All IMs

CTRL-i

or

People toolbar icon → Instant Message

By default, you can receive Instant Messages when you log on. If you've disabled them, you can enable them again by typing $im_on into the To: box and at least one character into the Message field, then clicking Send.

Member Profile

All members have access to AOL's searchable database of its members' profiles located at **Keyword: Member Directory**. Everyone who's created a profile is listed there. You can browse the directory using search phrases, such as hobbies or cities of residence. You can even find out if someone's online or not (a red arrow next to the screen name means that member is currently online).

It used to be that each screen name had a profile automatically, but now, you have to go to **My AOL** toolbar icon → **My Member Profile** to create and modify yours. Until you create a profile, no member can find you by searching the Member Directory. Essentially, you've got ultimate privacy from the very first moment you start using a new screen name.

But then, maybe you don't want too much privacy. We like having profiles since long-lost friends can look us up. On the other hand, we dislike them since spammers can skim our names out of the listings and send us annoying email.

AOL makes it easy to modify or even delete your profile in the Member Directory, so that you've got one tailored to your privacy needs. To create or edit your profile:

> My AOL toolbar icon → **My Member Profile**

or:

> **Keyword: Member Directory** → **My Profile**

A sample profile is shown being edited in Figure 30-3.

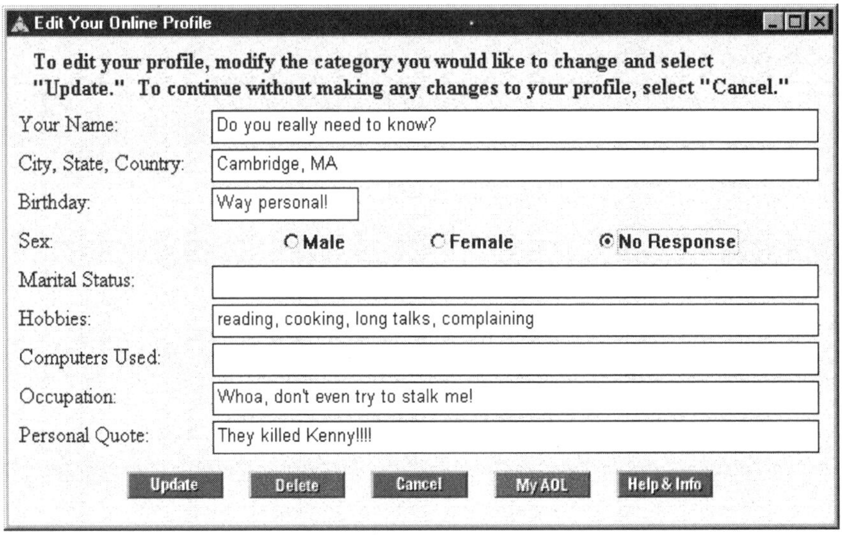

Edit Your Online Profile	

To edit your profile, modify the category you would like to change and select "Update." To continue without making any changes to your profile, select "Cancel."

Your Name:	Do you really need to know?
City, State, Country:	Cambridge, MA
Birthday:	Way personal!
Sex:	○ Male ○ Female ◉ No Response
Marital Status:	
Hobbies:	reading, cooking, long talks, complaining
Computers Used:	
Occupation:	Whoa, don't even try to stalk me!
Personal Quote:	They killed Kenny!!!!

Update   Delete   Cancel   My AOL   Help & Info

Figure 30-3: Modifying your member profile

Our hints for a profile that guards your privacy:

- Never put telephone numbers in your member profile, unless you want a lot of strange calls.

- Check your kids' profiles regularly to make sure they're not saying anything you don't want them to say (like where you live!).

- Put in only what you want anyone else on AOL to know about you. If you use your screen name to post to newsgroups or mailing lists, assume anyone in the world can see it. It's better to be safe than sorry; assume that information in your profile isn't even close to private.

For more on your AOL profile, see Chapter 3.

Personal Filing Cabinet

Theoretically, putting a password on your PFC is a way to keep your saved email, newsgroup posts, and download history from prying eyes. But we've found that it can easily be breached by anyone who signs on to your account. Figure 30-4 shows a password being saved for the PFC only; this is the right way to protect your Personal Filing Cabinet. Don't click the box under Sign-On, or anyone who can turn on your computer can sign on with your screen name and gain access to your PFC.

Note that you must be signed on with the account whose PFC, you're trying to password protect. Follow the path below to get to the Store Passwords screen.

My AOL toolbar icon → Preferences → Passwords → check the box that corresponds to the screen name whose PFC you want to password protect.

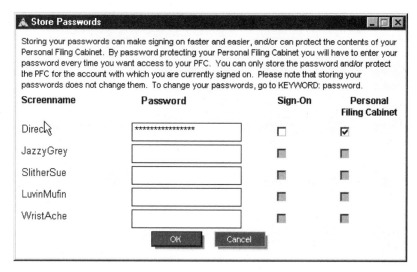

Figure 30-4: Protecting a screen name's PFC with a password

Drawback

- Anyone who signs on to your account with your computer (where your PFC files are located) can still gain access by signing on in your name and turning off passwording by clearing the Personal Filing Cabinet box.

CHAPTER 31

Canceling and Suspending Service

Despite having a good AOL reference book in your hands, perhaps you've decided that AOL isn't for you. Maybe you're going to be away for your computer for a year, or you need to sever your ties to AOL for financial reasons. This chapter has three parts:

*   "Canceling": How to cancel and how you'll be billed for your last month on AOL.

*   "Suspending Your AOL Account (Temporarily)": How to put your account on hold, or cancel it temporarily, if you intend to return to AOL someday.

*   "Uninstalling the AOL Software": How to remove the AOL application and all the associated icons from your computer.

Canceling

You've decided to pack your bags and leave AOL. This should be much easier than leaving a bad relationship, but AOL makes it almost as hard. For instance, you can't cancel online, which we find ironic for an *online* service. You have three cancellation options: phone, fax, or snail mail.

*   Telephone: Toll free at 1-800-827-6364 or 1-888-265-8008

    AOL representatives are waiting to convince you not to cancel. It's their duty to get you to stay on AOL. They will offer you free months of online time, and may ask you what your hobbies are so they can tailor future mailings to your individual interests. Be strong if you want to cancel. To make the process a bit quicker and less painful, be ready to give your name, address, day

461

and evening phone numbers, and payment method (credit card or checking account debit). Alternatives to the dreaded phone reps are:

- Fax: 801-622-7969

  Include in the fax your full name, address, phone number, and master account screen name.

- Mail:

  America Online
  P.O. Box 1600
  Ogden, UT 84401

Whether you mail or fax, be sure to include your full name, address, phone number, and master screen name. If you mail it in, give it some time to arrive, since you don't want to be charged for an extra month because you sent it in the day before a new billing period.

No matter how you cancel, you'll be billed through the end of the current billing month, and you can't get the month prorated. If you cancel within the last 72 hours of a billing month, you might still get charged for the next month. Call customer service (1-800-827-6364) and complain loudly.

You can avoid this distress by finding out when your current billing month ends:

Keyword: Billing → Display Your Billing Terms → Your next billing date

About ten days after you cancel, you'll get a snail-mail confirmation letter that your account has been killed. You might want to try signing on with your old account to make sure it's really gone.

After you cancel and are sure your account is gone, the cancellation process isn't over. You will probably receive periodic letters from AOL, asking you to rejoin and offering you free online time.

Suspending Your AOL Account (Temporarily)

Let's say you're going on a Luddite retreat for a few months, and you have no intention of touching your computer while you're there. You know, however, that your technology-addicted brain is going to want AOL again when you get back. You have several options:

- If you're going to be gone for less than six months, you can cancel your account. See the previous section. Your screen names will not be released for six months after you cancel. When you get back, you have to call AOL customer service at 1-800-827-3338 and tell them you want to rejoin. This is a bit of a pain, but you won't pay a dime for AOL while you're gone.

- Whether you'll be gone for a month or a year, you might be interested in AOL's "hold" plan. Under this plan, you pay $2.95 per month to keep your account active for as many months as you want. If you can't control yourself and sign on to AOL anyway during this time, you'll be charged $2.50 per hour for access. So if you sign on and check your email for five minutes, it will only cost you about a quarter. You can sign up for the "hold" plan by calling AOL's Billing customer service at 1-888-265-8003.

- If you know in advance that you're not going to be able to stay offline entirely, maybe you shouldn't cancel your account or put it on hold. You can opt for the Light Usage Plan, which costs $4.95 per month for the first three hours and $2.50 for each additional hour.

Uninstalling the AOL Software

If you're quitting AOL, it's time to remove that huge AOL application—and its abundance of associated icons—from your hard drive. Windows 3.x users can delete the AOL directory from File Manager. Mac people, delete the AOL folder and delete your AOL preferences from the System folder. The standard way to uninstall any Windows 95/98 software is through Windows' Add/Remove Programs feature:

Windows Start menu → Settings → Control Panel → Add/Remove Programs → highlight America Online → Add/Remove

This takes you to the AOL uninstaller (both AOL 3.0 and 4.0 have them, but we'll only go into details about the 4.0 version), which allows you to choose which copies of the AOL software you want to uninstall (if you have multiple versions) and gives you the option of saving your downloaded files (see Figure 31-1).

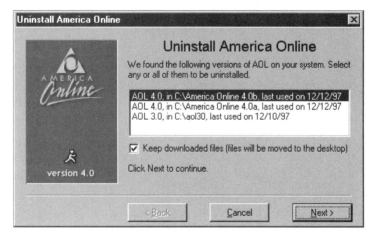

Figure 31-1: Uninstalling your AOL software

You'll also find a shortcut to the uninstaller, a file simply called *uninstall,* in your *C:\America Online 4.0* directory. (The actual uninstaller, called *aolunins.exe,* is located in your *C:\Windows* directory.) Double-clicking either of these items opens the same uninstaller as the Windows control panel method.

The uninstaller searches for all copies of AOL on your system and asks you to click the ones you want to uninstall. (Even if you think you may rejoin AOL someday, you might as well preserve your hard-drive space and uninstall all the versions. Just hold onto the next free AOL disc you get in the mail.) You'll also be asked if you want to keep your downloaded files. If you leave the box checked, the files are moved to a folder on your desktop called AOL Downloaded Files. Note this saves only files you've actually downloaded, not files you've saved to or moved to your C:\America Online 4.0\download folder.

You'll be asked if you're sure you want to do this. Click Next. AOL is uninstalled before your eyes.

Uninstalling AOL this way, thankfully, also removes all the AOL icons from your desktop, tray, Start menu, and MS Office toolbar (if applicable).

PART VII

Appendixes

It may be esoterica, but it is important esoterica. Be the first on your block to know *all*.

Appendix A, *AOL as an ISP*: How does AOL compare to other Internet service providers?

Appendix B, *File Extensions*: You come across many kinds of files on the Internet. Find out what to do with them.

Appendix C, *Top-Level Domain Names*: Decipher web and email addresses: *.com, .edu, .gov,* and all the rest.

Appendix D, *Terms of Service*: AOL's official rules of conduct.

APPENDIX A

AOL as an ISP

AOL has always been an online service: a company that offers proprietary content and communication. Since AOL began giving its members access to the Web and the rest of the Internet, it can be considered an Internet service provider as well as an online service. The question is, how good an ISP is it?

The answer depends on your needs. If you're new to the online world, AOL is an ideal choice. AOL may not suit your needs as well if you're an experienced, more technologically adept Internet user who spends most of your online time reading newsgroups or browsing the Web. The purpose of this chapter is to show you how AOL stacks up as an ISP. Overall, we think AOL is a pretty average ISP, but that "average" rating can turn into "stellar" or "heinous" depending on which criteria are most important to you. Use this chapter to help put it all into perspective.

We'd suggest using the following as a reference to compare alternate ISPs to AOL in the event you'd like to switch or want to see if you can get better modem connections, lower rates, more reliable access, more web server space, or a better newsreader. AOL compares favorably in some areas, poorly in others.

For each feature, we tell you whether AOL's capabilities are average, above average, or below average compared to most other ISPs. Please note that the ratings are not scientifically based, but rather general feelings we've gained through using alternate access services, testing other software, and our own knowledge gained from assessments of recent news reports comparing AOL to other ISPs.

Costs

Start-up fee (cheaper than average)
    None. Some ISPs have a startup fee of up to $25.

30-day free trial period (average)

Many ISPs have a 30-day trial period, but on AOL it's usually 50 free hours.

Monthly fee for basic access and hours included (average)

$9.95 for 5 hours ($2.95 for each additional hour), or $4.95 for three hours ($2.50 for each additional hour).

Monthly fee for unlimited access through local access numbers (slightly above average)

$21.95.

Hourly charge for 800/888 toll-free access (average)

$6.

Connectivity

Setup (easier than average)

As long as you have a setup disc or CD, installation and setup is typically the easiest of any ISP. If you must download the software yourself, the long download time can try one's patience.

Fastest modem speed available (average)

AOL has numerous 56K (x2 and K56flex) modem numbers in many cities and available through surcharged 800/888 numbers. Until the 56K modem standard is widely used, you have to use the access numbers that correspond to your modem type. 33.6 modem connections should be available everywhere. You can also use a cable modem if you have one, but you'll have to configure AOL to connect via TCP/IP. For more on connecting via TCP/IP, see Chapter 27, *Connecting.*

ISDN support (average)

At the time of this writing, AOL doesn't support direct ISDN connections. You can connect to AOL with ISDN only if you're using the Bring Your Own Access billing plan (see also Chapter 27, *Connecting* and Chapter 22, *Billing*), and the ISP you use to TCP/IP to AOL supports ISDN.

Points of Presence (POPs) (more than average)

Basically, POPs represent the number of local access numbers you have to choose from. Of course, it depends on where you live, but you're bound to have more than a few near you, throughout the U.S., and there are significant numbers of local international access numbers, too; AOL is omnipresent.

Ease of connectivity (average)

Again, this depends on where you live. Our strategically placed friends around the U.S. haven't had any problems connecting since the big busy-signal hoopla of late 1996 and early 1997. But some independent research groups continue to report that AOL users encounter a greater than average number of busy signals.

Features

Web space available (average)
2 MB for each screen name. If you use all five screen names, you can have 10 MB total.

Number of mailboxes (more than average)
Five for each account. This, in our opinion, is one of the major reasons to choose AOL over other ISPs. Just think: a household of five can get online for $4.40 each per month, unlimited hours. Other ISPs offer only one account, or charge extra for multiple accounts.

Email software (below average)
Until AOL starts letting its members use any MAPI-compliant email program, such as Eudora, MS Outlook Express, or Netscape's email client (implementation of any or all of these is promised for the future), you're stuck with their simplistic, proprietary email system. The biggest problem with AOL's current email system is that it doesn't support any other clients. On the other hand, AOL's email has a few of its own perks no other mail client has. See also Chapter 8, *Email.*

Browser software (average)
An integrated version of Microsoft's Internet Explorer 3.0, which is a vast improvement over AOL's older proprietary browser. If you prefer Netscape or the standalone version of MSIE, you can launch those separately and use one of them instead.

Internet access (average)
AOL isn't so proprietary anymore: you can FTP, telnet, and access the Web via any clients you choose. For newsreading, you're stuck with their anemic, built-in client. All told, their tools (especially the newsreader) may not be the most feature-rich out there, but they're easy to use, and AOL does give you the entire Internet if you want it.

Content (above average)
We may not like all of AOL's proprietary content, but you have to admit they have a ton of it, and that some of it is very good. AOL's aggregation of content makes it easy for the not-so-web-savvy to find interesting items online.

Interface (average)
The graphical interface is easy for anyone to navigate, but veteran Net users who just want a browser will probably hate it.

Community (above average)
11 million members—and always growing—makes it the single largest online access provider in the world. Among some online veterans, AOL members have a bad reputation, and there are certainly some cretins *@aol.com.* However, among the membership, there are bound to be a few whom you'll want to befriend.

Communication (above average)

Between email, IMs, and Buddy Lists, you have a lot of opportunity to talk with other AOL members and Internet users (with the invention of AOL's stan-dalone Instant Messenger). As you probably know, AOL chat rooms are extremely popular. You can also page someone through AOL (People toolbar icon → Send Message to Pager).

Downloading capabilities (above average)

Conveniently, AOL's Download Manager allows you to stop a download in the middle and resume at a later time. With most other services, you'd have to start a download from the beginning if you lose your connection or stop a download part way through. Also, AOL's Keyword: File Search and Keyword: Download Software make it easy for members to find files. The files aren't always as recent as they could be, so if you know exactly what you're looking for, you might be better off searching the Web. See also Chapter 20, *Downloading*.

Support (average)

AOL's phone tech support is acceptable, but it's busy. Your best bet is to try to get help online first, from AOL's copious and easy-to-understand tutorials and searchable help files. See also Chapter 6, *Help from AOL*.

System Requirements

System requirements might not immediately factor into your ISP decision, but let's face it: you need a pretty good computer to run AOL with any sort of speed. If you have an ancient 486 with 8 MB of RAM and a 2400-baud modem, like one of us does at home, either prepare to upgrade or use another (preferably text-based) ISP. We explain AOL 4.0's hardware needs in detail in Chapter 26, *System Requirements*.

APPENDIX B

File Extensions

Throughout this book, we've warned you of the potential evils of downloading and running *.exe* (executable or self-extracting compressed) files from people you don't know (if you've missed it so far: it's because they may contain viruses). These cryptic suffixes, like *.exe*, are called *file extensions*. A file extension is a suffix at the end of a filename that lets you (and your computer) know what kind of file you're dealing with.

This appendix is a quick reference to some of the most common file extensions you may come across in your online travels. We tell you what each one means and whether AOL can handle them. If you feel the need to know every file format in existence—we sure don't, but you might!—this web page can fill you in: What Is...Every File Format in the World? at *http://www.whatis.com/ff.htm.*

Common File Extensions and the Files They Indicate

.aiif (or .aif or .aifc): AIIF format sound
     AOL can play these.

.arc: A compressed file
     AOL for Windows can automatically decompress *.arc* files, so don't worry about them.

.art: AOL image file
     AOL shows *.art* files, obviously. Most other image viewers won't be able to handle *.art* files.

.au: AU format sound
     AOL plays *.au* files.

.avi: Windows video clip
     AOL for Windows plays *.avi* files.

.bfc: Windows briefcase

AOL can't open these files, but Windows 95/98 can.

.bmp: bitmap image

AOL shows *.bmp* files.

.cda: CD audio track

A CD-ROM drive and software to use the drive are required to play .cda files.

.com: MS-DOS executable program

AOL can't open these programs, but PCs with MS-DOS can.

.dic: Text document

AOL or any word processor can open these.

.doc: Microsoft Word document

For the best results, open *.doc* files with Word. You can open a *.doc* file as a text-only document in AOL, but it will include a lot of computer-generated garbage characters.

.dot: Microsoft Word template

AOL can't open these; use Microsoft Word.

.exc: Text document

AOL or any word processor can open these.

.exe: Executable program, usually for Windows.

Double-click the *.exe* file to run it, or: Windows Start menu → Run.

.gif: GIF image

AOL can show *.gif* files.

.html or .htm: Hypertext document

AOL's web browser or any other browser can open these files.

.jpg (or .jpeg or .jpe or .jfif): JPEG image

AOL can show *.jpg* files.

.log: An AOL log file.

Clearly, AOL can open these. Since they're nothing but text files, any other word processor can open them, too. To learn how to create log files, see also Chapter 8, *Email*.

.mid: MIDI audio sequence

AOL can play *.mid* files.

.mme: MIME file

To learn all about MIME files, see "MIME" in Chapter 8 and Chapter 20, *Downloading*.

.mov: QuickTime movie

AOL can't play these; you need to download QuickTime Movie Player at *http://www.apple.com/quicktime/*.

.pct, .pic, or .pict: Macintosh image

AOL for Macs shows these files.

.pdf: Adobe Acrobat document (could be almost anything!)

AOL can't read these. You'll need Adobe Acrobat reader, available at *http://www.adobe.com/supportservice/custsupport/download.html*.

.pfc: AOL Personal Filing Cabinet
AOL, and only AOL, can open a Personal Filing Cabinet.

.ra or .ram: RealAudio sound file
AOL can play these, or download a Real Audio player from *http:// www.real.com*.

.rmi: MIDI audio sequence
AOL can play these.

.rtf: Rich Text Format document
AOL can convert *.rtf* files to text-only and open them, but with the usual computer-generated garbage characters added. You might prefer to open .rtf files with Microsoft Word or any word processor.

.scr: Windows screen saver
AOL can't help you here; you have to put *.scr* files in your *C:\Windows* directory. To change screen savers: Windows `Start` menu → `Settings` → `Control Panel` → `Desktop` → `Display` → `Screensaver`

.sea: Macintosh self-extracting archive (i.e., one compressed files that contains several smaller files)
Run these on your Mac, not necessarily through AOL.

.shtml: Hypertext document
AOL's and any other web browser can show *.shtml* files.

.sit: Mac Stuffit compressed file
Both Mac and Windows users can use Stuffit to decompress *.sit* files, though they may not always translate correctly for Windows users. Download Stuffit at *http://www.aladdinsys.com*.

.snd: Macintosh sound
AOL for Macs plays *.snd* files.

.txt: Text document
AOL can open *.txt* files. If a *.txt* file is too big for AOL to open (larger than 31k), use Notepad, SimpleText, Word, Write, or any other word processor.

.wav: Windows sound file
AOL for Windows plays *.wav* files.

.wri: Windows 3.x Write document
AOL can convert this to a text file, but it adds some computer-generated garbage characters to the document. You can also open *.wri* files in Wordpad or any word processor.

.xls (or .xlb): Microsoft Excel worksheet
AOL can't display these files; use Microsoft Excel.

.zip: Windows compessed file.
Use PKZIP or Winzip to decompress these, or let AOL do it automatically (see also **decompressing** in Chapter 20, *Downloading*).

APPENDIX C

Top-Level Domain Names

Top-level domain names are the suffixes at the end of email addresses and web sites. They can tell you what country a newsgroup poster is from, or whether a certain web page is for a nonprofit company or a commercial company. They can, however, be a bit cryptic. You might already know what *.com* and *.edu* signify, but maybe domains like *.de* and *.fj* have you puzzled. This appendix provides all the top-level domain names you need to know, and many more that you don't.

Basic Names

Here are some domain names you probably already know, and some information about them:

.com
> Originally intended for commercial enterprises, but now used for both commercial and individual purposes. Internationally used.

.edu
> For educational institutions, preferably 4-year ones that one can get a degree from. Other schools, such as community colleges and K–12 schools, are usually found under country domains.

.gov
> For U.S. federal government civilian agencies.

.mil
> For U.S. military agencies.

.net
> Intended for Internet service providers, though other people and organizations have registered domain names under the *.net* top-level domain with few repercussions. Internationally used.

.org
> Intended for nonprofit organizations. Internationally used.

New Names

Seven additional top-level domain names have been created, and by the time you pick up this book, they may be in use.

.arts
> For cultural and entertainment organizations

.firm
> For businesses and firms

.info
> For organizations that provide information services

.nom
> For individual people

.rec
> For recreational and entertainment organizations

.store
> For retail businesses

.web
> For web-related organizations

There are some other "alternative" top-level domains you can register, such as *.law* and *.sex*, but there is no rule saying they have to be supported. In other words, a browser that can easily negotiate a *.com* address might have trouble figuring out a *.law* address. For that reason, and because the seven official new top-level domain names will alleviate the shortage of catchy domain names, alternative top-level domain names are not in wide use.

Countries

Every country has its own top-level domain name. If you're looking for a site in Spain, for example, use the *www.domain_name.es* address, in much the same way that you might use *www.domain_name.com* in the U.S. The top-level domains *.com*, *.net*, and *.org* are used internationally, however, so there are no hard-and-fast rules for tracking down international web pages.

The *.us* domain in particular is intended for regional, state, and local U.S. agencies. Each state has a domain name under the *.us* top-level domain, and each state domain name has additional subdomains. For instance, *k12.ma.us* is for Massachusetts schools, and *ci.boston.ma.us* means the city of Boston, Massachusetts in the U.S.

Table 3-1 is a list of all countries' top-level domain names, alphabetically by domain name.

Table 3-1: Countries' Top-Level Domain Names

Domain Name	Country	Domain Name	Country
AD	Andorra	CG	Congo
AE	United Arab Emirates	CH	Switzerland
AF	Afghanistan	CI	Cote D'Ivoire (Ivory Coast)
AG	Antigua and Barbuda	CK	Cook Islands
AI	Anguilla	CL	Chile
AL	Albania	CM	Cameroon
AM	Armenia	CN	China
AN	Netherlands Antilles	CO	Colombia
AO	Angola	CR	Costa Rica
AQ	Antarctica	CS	the former Czechoslovakia
AR	Argentina	CU	Cuba
AS	American Samoa	CV	Cape Vertde
AT	Austria	CX	Christmas Island
AU	Australia	CY	Cyprus
AW	Aruba	CZ	Czech Republic
AZ	Azerbaijan	DE	Germany
BA	Bosnia and Herzegovina	DJ	Djibouti
BB	Barbados	DK	Denmark
BD	Bangladesh	DM	Dominica
BE	Belgium	DO	Dominican Republic
BF	Burkina Faso	DZ	Algeria
BG	Bulgaria	EC	Ecuador
BH	Bahrain	EE	Estonia
BI	Burundi	EG	Egypt
BJ	Benin	EH	Western Sahara
BM	Bermuda	ER	Eritrea
BN	Brunei Darussalam	ES	Spain
BO	Bolivia	ET	Ethiopia
BR	Brazil	FI	Finland
BS	Bahamas	FJ	Fiji
BT	Bhutan	FK	Falkland Islands (Malvinas)
BV	Bouvet Island	FM	Micronesia
BW	Botswana	FO	Faroe Islands
BY	Belarus	FR	France
BZ	Belize	FX	metropolitan France
CA	Canada	GA	Gabon
CC	Cocos (Keeling Islands)	GB	Great Britain

Table 3-1: Countries' Top-Level Domain Names (continued)

Domain Name	Country	Domain Name	Country
CF	Central African Republic	KG	Kyrgyzstan
GD	Grenada	KH	Cambodia
GE	Georgia	KI	Kiribati
GF	French Guiana	KM	Comoros
GH	Ghana	KN	Saint Kitts and Nevis
GI	Gibraltar	KP	North Korea
GL	Greenland	KR	South Korea
GM	Gambia	KW	Kuwait
GN	Guinea	KY	Cayman Islands
GP	Guadeloupe	KZ	Kazakhstan
GQ	Equatorial Guinea	LA	Laos
GR	Greece	LB	Lebanon
GSS	Georgia and South Sandwich Islands	LC	Saint Lucia
GT	Guatemala	LI	Liechtenstein
GU	Guam	LK	Sri Lanka
GW	Guinea-Bissau	LR	Liberia
GY	Guyana	LS	Lesotho
HK	Hong Kong	LT	Lithuania
HM	Heard and McDonald Islands	LU	Luxembourg
HN	Honduras	LV	Latvia
HR	Croatia (Hrvatska)	LY	Libya
HT	Haiti	MA	Morocco
HU	Hungary	MC	Monaco
ID	Indonesia	MD	Moldova
IE	Ireland	MG	Madagascar
IL	Israel	MH	Marshall Islands
IN	India	MK	Macedonia
IO	British Indian Ocean Territory	ML	Mali
IQ	Iraq	MM	Myanmar
IR	Iran	MN	Mongolia
IS	Iceland	MO	Macau
IT	Italy	MP	Northern Mariana Islands
JM	Jamaica	MQ	Martinique
JO	Jordan	MR	Mauritania
JP	Japan	MS	Montserrat
KE	Kenya	MT	Malta

Top-Level Domains

Table 3-1: Countries' Top-Level Domain Names (continued)

Domain Name	Country	Domain Name	Country
MU	Mauritius	SA	Saudi Arabia
MV	Maldives	SB	Solomon Islands
MW	Malawi	SC	Seychelles
MX	Mexico	SD	Sudan
MY	Malaysia	SE	Sweden
MZ	Mozambique	SG	Singapore
NA	Namibia	SH	St. Helena
NC	New Caledonia	SI	Slovenia
NE	Niger	SJ	Svalbard and Jan Mayan Islands
NF	Norfolk Island	SK	Slovak Republic
NG	Nigeria	SL	Sierra Leonne
NI	Nicaragua	SM	San Marino
NL	Netherlands	SN	Senegal
NO	Norway	SO	Somalia
NP	Nepal	SR	Suriname
NR	Nauru	ST	Sao Tome and Principe
NT	Neutral Zone	SU	USSR (former)
NU	Niue	SV	El Salvador
NZ	New Zealand (Aotearoa)	SY	Syria
OM	Oman	SZ	Swaziland
PA	Panama	TC	Turks and Caicos Islands
PE	Peru	TD	Chad
PF	French Polynesia	TF	French Southern Territories
PG	Papua New Guinea	TG	Togo
PH	Philippines	TH	Thailand
PK	Pakistan	TJ	Tajikistan
PL	Poland	TK	Tokelau
PM	St. Pierre and Miquelon	TM	Turkmenistan
PN	Pitcairn	TN	Tunisia
PR	Puerto Rico	TO	Tonga
PT	Portugal	TP	East Timor
PW	Palau	TR	Turkey
PY	Paraguay	TT	Trinidad and Tobago
QA	Qatar RE Reunion	TV	Tuvalu
RO	Romania	TW	Taiwan
RU	Russian Federation	TZ	Tanzania
RW	Rwanda	UA	Ukraine

Table 3-1: Countries' Top-Level Domain Names (continued)

Domain Name	Country	Domain Name	Country
UG	Uganda	VN	Vietnam
UK	United Kingdom	VU	Vanuatu
UM	US Minor Outlying Islands	WF	Wallis and Futuna Islands
US	United States	WS	Samoa
UY	Uruguay	YE	Yemen
UZ	Uzbekistan	YT	Mayotte
VA	Vatican City State (Holy See)	YU	Yugoslavia
VC	Saint Vincent and the Grenadines	ZA	South Africa
VE	Venezuela	ZM	Zambia
VG	Virgin Islands (British)	ZR	Zaire
VI	Virgin Islands (U.S.)	ZW	Zimbabwe

Top-Level Domains

APPENDIX D

Terms of Service

The Terms of Service (TOS) are the official, and often very technical, rules that govern what you are legally allowed to do and say while using AOL. TOS is a lot of legalese, but it's important legalese. TOS tells you what's OK to do and say on AOL and what will get you kicked out. The most basic thing to know about AOL is that doing anything that would be illegal offline is also illegal online. So if you think that your pyramid moneymaking scheme is any less reprehensible in the eyes of the law just because you used email instead of the U.S. postal service, you're in for a big surprise.

TOS is one huge set of rules, and, online, it takes up several screens of text. If you're curious about all the niggling details, by all means go to `Keyword: TOS` to read more. But if you're confident that you're a pretty regular person, we've provided you with the quick reference below that hits on the major points in the TOS. Follow these, and we don't imagine you'll have too many problems with the Community Action Team, the group who takes care of TOS violations.

The Terms of Service in Brief

Account Information

- The master account holder is at least 18 years old.

- You can't choose a screen name that is the real name of another person, unless it's also your real name. You can't violate copyrights with your screen names, and AOL may remove screen names it deems offensive.

- The master account holder is entirely responsible for all subaccounts, even if they are held by other people (like spouses, children, etc.).

- If your membership has been terminated, you need AOL's express written permission to once again access AOL. The primary account holder agrees not to allow use of subaccounts to users whom AOL has prohibited access.

Billing

Get current rates and surcharges for using AOL by calling Customer Service at 1-800-827-6364 or by selecting "Billing" under "Member Services" (or Keyword: Billing).

You must pay your bill. If you do not pay within 30 days of the invoice date, AOL can charge 1.5% interest per month.

AOL reserves the right to change its fees effective 30 days after a notification at Keyword: Billing. If you don't say you want to discontinue AOL before the rate change occurs, your continued use signals that you accept the new charges.

You are responsible for your telephone charges. You should be aware that you may not have an access number that is a local call. You are responsible for checking with your local phone company to ensure that you are making a local phone call. AOL adds a fee to your bill if you use certain numbers to access AOL (typically the 1-800 surcharged numbers).

Rights and Responsibilities

You bear the responsibility for assessing the accuracy of the content of the service (content includes all the writing, graphics, sounds, and software on AOL). In other words, let the buyer beware.

You can upload only files that aren't covered under any other copyrights, trademarks, and other intellectual and proprietary rights. By uploading, you acknowledge you are not violating any of these rights.

Anything you post to any public area of AOL (such as message boards, forums, and the member directory) grants AOL the:

> royalty-free, perpetual, irrevocable, nonexclusive right (including any moral rights) and license to use, reproduce, modify, adapt, publish, translate, create derivative works from, distribute, communicate to the public, perform and display the Content (in whole or in part) worldwide and/or to incorporate it in other works in any form, media or technology now known or later developed, for the full term of any rights that may exist in such Content.

Basically, if you post it, they can use it for any purpose, now and until said rights legally expire.

Conduct and Communication

- You acknowledge that AOL may contain content that is inappropriate for minors.
- AOL can't screen or monitor all of the activity that occurs on its service, but may monitor some of it.
- You agree to use AOL only for lawful purposes.
- You can't "post, transmit, or promote any unlawful, harmful, threatening, abusive, harassing, defamatory, vulgar, obscene, hateful, racially, ethnically or otherwise objectionable Content."

Terms of Service

- Do not "harass, threaten, embarrass, or cause distress, unwanted attention or discomfort upon another" AOL user.

- You can't "post, transmit, promote, link, or facilitate the distribution of sexually explicit or other Content."

- You can't disrupt normal discussion in a chat room or message board.

- You can't "impersonate any person or entity" on AOL or off, including employees.

- You can't impersonate a minor.

- You can't post pyramid letters or promulgate such schemes.

- You can't post any "unsolicited advertising, promotional materials, or other forms of solicitation to other Members, individuals or entities, except in those areas that are expressly designated for such a purpose (e.g., the classified areas)."

- You can't "collect or harvest screen names of other Members, without permission".

- You can't post or transmit in any form any password or other account information.

- You can't "intentionally or unintentionally violate any applicable local, state, national, international or foreign law, including, but not limited to, any rules or regulations having the force of law."

AOL is a private service that allows access to the Internet, but is not the Internet, even if the Internet appears seamlessly integrated into AOL.

AOL may make some of your member mailing addresses available to third parties. Go to **Keyword: Marketing Prefs** → **Tell Us What Your Mailing Preferences Are** to limit the dispersal of your mailing information.

AOL won't disclose identity information to third parties that would link a Member's screen name to a Member's actual name, unless required to do so by law or legal process.

Navigation and Transaction

AOL can keep track of where you go on the service, what choices you make, and what merchandise you select.

Private Communications

The AOL computer system doesn't record or retain chat room communications, Instant Messages, records of with whom you chat or IM, or any oral conversations you may have (when that technology is available). Read email is housed on the system for only 3 days, by default. Unread email is deleted from the system after approximately 25 days.

AOL doesn't access or disclose the contents of private communications (such as email, Instant Messages, member-created private chat rooms, and oral online communications). There are a few circumstances under which AOL will release this information: (1) It must do so to comply with applicable law or valid legal process (such as a warrant or court order); (2) to protect AOL's rights; and (3) in emergencies when AOL, Inc. believes that physical safety is at risk.

AOL denounces any responsibility or liability for any conduct, content, goods, and services available on or through the Internet.

Termination

AOL or you can terminate your relationship at any time.

If AOL terminates your account, you won't receive credits or refunds for remaining online time, online time earned, or free hours.

How to Report a Violation

Notify AOL if someone is violating the TOS, and you don't like it (or if you do like it, you needn't do anything; just sit back and enjoy the show):

    Keyword: Notify AOL

Report password phishers, people wanting your credit card number, or bothersome or inappropriate IMs or chat. See the section "Scams and How to Avoid Them."

Do the Terms of Service Apply to the Internet?

For the most part, AOL's Terms of Service don't apply to the Internet, its content, or what you do and say while connected to the Internet via AOL. Web sites are not part of AOL and are not controlled by its rules (the exceptions are web sites owned by AOL, such as *www.AOL.com*). There are a couple of exceptions, which we try to clarify below.

AOL gives somewhat contradictory information regarding whether their TOS apply to newsgroups and mailing lists, and more specifically, what you post to these groups.

Newsgroups

AOL claims that its Terms of Service apply to what its members post to newsgroups. However, there is no official terms of service for newsgroups. We recommend you understand netiquette and how it applies to newsgroups (see the section "Posting to a Group" in Chapter 13, *Newsgroups*).

AOL can, will, and has suspended members' access to newsgroups for repeated violations of the following sort:

- Sending chain letters. Other members can actually report this violation to AOL, which results in a warning to your account.

- Sending commercial articles that "market, advertise, or sell products or services."

- Sending "inappropriate posts," which seems to include posting unrelated topics and points of discussion to a newsgroup.

Clearly, each of these violations must be reported to AOL by someone on the Internet or another AOL member, probably a reader or recipient of your bad posts; AOL doesn't go looking for (minor) violators.

Mailing Lists

AOL claims not to have jurisdiction over mailing lists, as they are part of the Internet (why they don't say the same thing about newsgroups is unknown to us).

However, if AOL is notified that you have abused your privileges on a mailing list, they consider it a violation of your agreement with AOL. You may receive a TOS warning or have your account terminated. Basically, don't join a list and then really annoy its members or the list owner, since they can report you to AOL.

Scams and How to Avoid Them

It is an obvious violation of TOS to attempt to get another member's password or any other account information, whether directly from the member (as in asking in an IM) or by using small programs that install themselves on the member's computer and relay account information to the perpetrator.

Take a close look at the items below; just a few minutes familiarizing yourself with the scams you or family members might be exposed to could save you headaches later. We've listed the most common ways ruthless individuals will attempt to acquire personal information or do damage to your computer system. You needn't worry about scams if you know how to protect yourself. Typically, you must be an active, if unsavvy, participant in their schemes: your ignorance leaves you open to the scams.

If you follow two simple rules, you'll protect yourself from the overwhelming majority of all scams: (1) Don't give your password to anyone, ever. (2) Don't download attachments unless you know the sender. In addition, the only place you should be giving out your credit card information is at Keyword: Billing, and only then in AOL's special forms.

Password and Credit Card Phishers

Always remember: AOL never asks you for your password in an IM, email, or over the phone! Ever!

The only time you give AOL your credit card number is when you sign up for the service or when you call to cancel. Never give out this information in an IM or email to someone claiming to represent AOL.

Evildoers will try to trick you into thinking they're AOL staff members who need your password or credit card number to correct an online problem or to verify the validity of your account. Or they may say that you've won something, and they need information about your account in order to give you the prize.

How to avoid trouble: if you get solicited, don't give out your password or other personal information.

How to report violations: you must send the offending material to AOL. So, leave the offending window open (whether the solicitation came in email, chat, or an IM) and go to Keyword: Notify AOL, where you'll find further instructions depending on what sort of violation you've encountered.

Trojan Horses (Downloadable Software)

Trojan horses are executable programs that can invade your system and corrupt other programs, send your password to evildoers, erase data from your hard drive, and other schemes we can't even imagine now, but will inevitably be thought up by nefarious hackers.

How to avoid trouble: think twice before downloading attachments that come from screen names or email addresses you don't recognize, even when accompanied by a chummy "remember me?" message or a "Re: Your Request" subject header. The most dangerous attachments will be executables, with the .exe file extension.

Don't automatically download email attachments if you're using Automatic AOL (see "Email" in Chapter 21, *Automatic AOL*).

How to report violations: follow the directions at Keyword: Notify AOL → Attached File Violations with Email.

Pyramid Schemes

These are schemes that tell you how to make money fast by mailing five dollars to a certain place. They are against U.S. law, whether in print or online.

How to report violations: forward the offending email according to the instructions at Keyword: Notify AOL.

Terms of Service

Index

C

cable modems, 408

call waiting, disabling, 18, 75, 400

canceling
  downloads in progress, 332
  member accounts (AOL service), 64, 349, 461–462
  newsgroup postings, 223
  scheduled Automatic AOL sessions, 339

capacity, modem (see modems, speed of)

capitalization, 91, 443

Capture Picture (Edit menu), 40

carbon copies, 84–85, 90–91

cars conference room, 178

cartoons conference room, 178

Cascade (Window menu), 40

case sensitivity, 91

Case, Steve, 3

CCs (see carbon copies)

CD-ROM, AOL on, 13

celebrity chats (see auditorium chats)

certificates, preferences for, 449

CGI (Common Gateway Interface), 359

chain letters, 91

"Change the order in which your AOL access phone numbers are dialed" option, 391

channels
  AOL Channels icon (Welcome), 6
  Channels screen, 7
  displaying at sign-on, 434
  list of (reference), 240–270

Channels toolbar icon, 49

charters, newsgroup, 213

Chat Now (People icon), 50

chats, 149–184
  adding to Favorite Places, 160
  audio in, 163, 432, 436
  auditorium chats, 151, 172–175
  blocking, 415
  with buddies, 141–143
  Buddy Chats, 151, 168–170
  conference rooms, 151, 175–184
  creating, 168, 170
  CRoom tool, 381
  double-spacing messages, 432
  entering (see entering chat rooms)

exiting (see exiting chat rooms)

Favorite Places, sharing via, 289

finding, 152, 237

finding people in, 142, 154–157

harassment in, responding to, 73–74

how they work, 152–154

hyperlinks in comments, 163–165, 415

Internet Relay Chat (IRC), 377

joining (see joining chats)

leaving (see leaving chats)

logging, 159–160

member profiles and, 156–157

notification of arrivals/departures, 155, 431

online shorthand, 57–62

parental control over, 150, 415–416

People Connection lobbies, 151, 165, 166

People Here window, 29

preferences for, 161–162, 431–432

private, 151, 167–172

public, 151, 165–167

public (featured and member), 151, 165–167

responding to bothersome members, 157–159

rich text in, 162

spam, avoiding, 150

types of, 151

children (see kids)

Christian community conference room, 178

cities online (see Digital City)

Clear History Now button, 446

Clear History Now option (AOL Toolbar preferences), 54

clicking, 4

clients, 91

Close (System menu), 37

Close All Except Front (Window menu), 40

"Close mail after it has been sent", 92, 438

collectors, conference room for, 178

colors
  background, 89–90
  Color Mode button, 437
  fonts (see fonts; text)

cursor, hand icon for, 4
custom modem setup, 17
Customize preferences (web
    navigation), 448
customizing keyboard shortcuts,
    313–314
Cut (Edit menu), 39

D

decoding files (see encoded binary
    files, decoding)
decompressing files, 124, 319–320
default
    download directory, 321, 330, 433
    email color scheme, 90
    fonts, 433–434
        for email, 95
    web browser start page, 448
DejaNews site, 216
delays (see performance)
deleting
    Address Book entries, 84
    AOL toolbar icons, 56
    confirming before, 442
    dial-in locations, 396
    from Download Manager's queue,
        322
    downloaded files, 320
    email messages, 71, 93–94, 439
    Favorite Places, 288
    files/directories in server space, 366
    message board posts, 190
    message boards from My Boards, 193
    from Personal Filing Cabinet, 298,
        300
    screen names, 27, 302
    toolbar icons, 56
    uninstalling AOL software, 463–464
    .zip files after decompression, 320,
        330, 433
descriptions of downloadable files, 331
descriptive titles for newsgroups, 229
desktop, Favorite Places on, 292
detaching file attachments, 87
devices, options for modems, 404–405
"Dial *70..." option, 75, 400
"Dial 9..." box, 400

dialing into AOL (see connecting to
    AOL)
dictation, software for, 94
dictionary, 239
Dictionary (Edit menu), 39
Digital City (area), 259
directories (see folders/directories)
disabling call waiting, 18, 75, 400
discussion groups
    on AOL (see message boards)
    on AOL (see mailing lists)
    on AOL (see newsgroups)
    privacy and, 455
    on the Web, 280
disk space
    available server space, 359
    installing AOL and, 16
    JPEG compression quality and, 437
    maximum for online art, 436
    for Personal Filing Cabinet, 300, 442
"Display Channels at Sign On" option,
    434
displaying images during downloads,
    325, 330, 432, 436
distribution lists (see mailing lists)
domain name
    for AOL, 25
    registering new, 360
    top level, 474–479
doubled words, correcting, 443
double-spacing chat messages, 432
Download Article button, 225
Download File button, 225
Download Later button, 318, 322
Download Manager, 45, 321–323
Download Now button, 323
downloading, 316–333
    AOL software from Internet, 13
    AOL upgrades and, 15
    Automatic AOL and, 318, 340
    binary files, 224–226, 327–328
    destination for downloaded files, 321,
        327, 330, 433
    email message attachments, 86–88,
        123–124, 323–324
        blocking, 419
    finding downloadable files, 326–327
    images, 325, 330, 432, 436

email addresses, 24–25, 85–86
Address Book, 82–85
administrative, for mailing lists, 200, 203
blocking email from, 419
displaying as hyperlinks, 439
top-level domain names, 474–479
embedding graphics (see images)
emoticons, 58–59, 106
employment channel (WorkPlace), 269–270
"Enable chat room sounds" option, 432
"Enable Java JIT compilers" option, 452
"Enable Java logging" option, 452
Enable Scheduler checkbox, 339
enclosures, email (see attachments to email messages)
encoded binary files, 225, 316, 328
decoding, 316
entering chat rooms
auditorium chats, 173
Buddy Chats, 170
People Connection Lobby, 166
private chat rooms, 171
entertainment
conference rooms for, 179, 181, 183
arts, 177
sports (see sports)
women's magazines, 184
Entertainment Channel, 243–246
web sites for, 282
error messages, 124
General Protection Faults, 65
"host unknown" error message, 98
"That mail is no longer available..." message, 124
"unrecoverable error" message, 125
user unknown, 126
Escape key to stop incoming data, 75
etiquette online (see netiquette)
event sounds, 435
.exe files, 123
Exit (File menu), 38
exiting chat rooms, 167
auditorium chats, 173
private chats, 172
Expert Add (modems or access numbers), 396

expiring
email messages, 71, 439
message board posts, 189
extensions, filename, 471–473

F

Failed response (AOLPress), 367
family
conference rooms for, 179
Families Channel, 246–247, 412
kids' safety tips, 409–410
Parental Controls (see Parental Controls)
teenagers conference rooms, 183
FAQs
for mailing lists, 202
for newsgroups, 213, 218
fashion conference room, 179
Favorite Places, 73, 285–292
adding, in general, 287
chat rooms as, 160
email messages as, 114
message boards and, 191–192
newsgroups as, 231
organizing, 287–288
sharing with others
via chat, 289
via email hyperlinks, 99, 289
via Instant Messages, 133, 291
(see also preferences)
Favorite Places (Favorites icon), 47
Favorites menu, 285–286
Favorites toolbar icon, 47–48, 286
faxes via AOL, 95
featured chat rooms, 151, 165–167
56K modems, 388
file attachments (see attachments)
File menu, 38
File Transfer Protocol (see FTP)
files
in AOL server space, 364–367
attaching to email messages, 86–88, 323–324
blocking attachments, 419
Trojan horses, 123–124, 485
binary (see binary files)

compressing/decompressing,
318–320
downloading (see downloading)
encoded (see encoded binary files)
.exe files, 123
filename extensions, list of, 471–473
inserting in email messages, 122
saving Instant Messages as, 135
.sig (see signature files)
signature files, 117–118
uploading to server space, 363–370
.zip files, 123
film, conference rooms on, 181
(see also entertainment)
filtering
email messages, 298
newsgroup content, 230
web content, 423–425
finance
conference rooms for, 179
Personal Finance Channel, 261–262,
326
taxes conference room, 183
web sites on, 281
Find a Chat (People icon), 50
Find icon (Channels screen), 8
Find icon (navigation bar), 53
Find in Top Window feature, 39, 239
Find it on the Web (Find icon), 53
Find on AOL (Find icon), 53
finding, 53, 235–239
areas by content, 236
auditorium chat row members, 174
chat room members, 154–157
chats, 152, 237
downloadable files, 326–327
mailing lists, 201–202, 237
in Member Directory, 30
members, 237
message board posts, 193
message boards, 187–188
newsgroup posts, 232
newsgroups, 211, 215–218, 238
people in chats, 142
people/places on the Web, 279
Personal Filing Cabinet contents, 238,
299
randomly, 238

software, 238
street addresses, 236
on Web (see NetFind web site)
word definitions, 239
Finish Later button, 324
fishing conference rooms, 179
flames and flame wars, 213
Flashsessions (see Automatic AOL)
folders/directories
AOL server space, 358, 364–367
choosing for AOL software, 16
for downloaded files, 321, 327, 330,
433
for Favorite Places, 287
in Personal Filing Cabinet, 297–298
fonts
for email, 95
in Instant Messages, 135
preferences for, 433–434, 448
size of, 435
football conference room, 179
foreign language conference rooms,
179
Forget Window Size and Position
(Window menu), 40
forgotten passwords, 32
forwarding email messages, 96
chain letters, 91
quoting style, 111, 439
free disk space (see disk space)
free games, 248
freeware, 238, 316
Frequently Asked Questions (see FAQs)
frozen screen, responding to, 70
FTP (File Transfer Protocol), 324,
356–357, 361–362, 370
blocking downloads, 329, 416
FTP (Internet icon), 49
FTP addresses, 25
full justification, 103

G

games
conference rooms for, 179
Games Channel, 247–249
gardening conference rooms, 180
gay community conference rooms, 179

mail extras, 105–107
Mail Extras (Mail Center icon), 44
mail flags, broken, 107
Mail Preferences (Mail Center icon), 44
Mailbase commands, 208
Mailbox icon (Welcome screen), 6
mailing addresses, finding, 236
Mailing List Directory, 201
mailing lists, 197–209
    administrative address for, 200, 203
    finding, 201–202, 237
    list address for, 203
    netiquette, 200
    one-way vs. two-way, 197
    posting to, 205
    programs for running (listservs), 202
        commands for, list of, 206–209
        reactive lists, 197
    reading messages from, 204–205
    subscribing to, 202–204
    too much email, 199, 204
    unsubscribing from, 205–206
    (see also newsgroups)
Mailserv commands, 208
Majordomo commands, 208
manually copying PFC, 303–305
Mark All Read button (message
        boards), 194
Mark Read button (message boards),
        194
Mark Unread button (message boards),
        195
marketing preferences, 21, 439–441
marking
    files for later download, 322
    message board posts, 194–195
    newsgroups as read, 220
martial arts conference room, 181
master screen names, 23
    (see also screen names)
Match Your Interests system, 68
Maximize (System menu), 37
"Maximum disk space to use for online
        art" option, 436
maximum unread email messages, 107
Meg (tips for using AOL), 68
member accounts
    adding to particular computer, 15
    billing (see billing)

canceling/suspending, 64, 349,
        461–463
    creating new, 20–21
    help on, 64
    on multiple computers, 28
    online information about, 352–354
    pricing plans for, 350–353
    transferring PFCs to, 302–305
member chat rooms, 151, 165–167
    blocking, 415
Member Directory, 29–30
member profiles, 30–31, 459
    auditorium chat row members, 175
    chats and, 156–157
Member Service Online Help, 66
Member Services icon (Welcome
        screen), 7
Member Services Online Help (Help
        menu), 42
members
    billing (see billing)
    in chat rooms, 154–157
        bothersome, responding to,
            157–159
        (see also chats)
    conduct of, 481
    contacting (see chats; email; IMs)
    contacting non-members, 145–148
    finding, 237
    new, 20–21
        chat information, 150–151
        email information for, 80–82
        help for, 67
        joining AOL as, 14
        mailing list information, 198, 212
        message board information,
            186–187
        Personal Filing Cabinets, 293
        setting up Automatic AOL, 335
        (see also tips for using AOL)
    URLs for, 358
    "user unknown" message, 126
Members Helping Members (area), 67
membership conditions, 20
memory
    disk space (see disk space; saving)
    RAM required for AOL, 386
mental health conference rooms, 181
menus, 8–9, 37–42

resources for further reading
  books on AOL, 21
  for first-time users, 11
  web publishing, 362–363, 371
Restore (System menu), 37
restoring deleted screen names, 27
restoring PFC for old screen names, 302
restricting access (see access; Parental
    Controls)
"Retain information about my last X
    downloads" option, 324, 330,
    433
retaining (see saving)
rich text
  in chats, 162
  in Instant Messages, 135
rich text in email messages, 113
right arrow (navigation bar), 52
right-aligning (see justification)
romance conference rooms, 182
rooms (see chat rooms)
rows in auditorium chats, 174–175
RSAC (Recreational Software Advisory
    Council), 449
RSAC settings, 425–427
Run Automatic AOL Now (Mail Center
    icon), 44
runners conference room, 181

S

Save (File menu), 38
Save As (File menu), 38
Save to Personal Filing Cabinet (File
    menu), 38
Save to Personal Filing Cabinet (My
    Files icon), 45
saving
  chats and chat rooms, 159–161
  download information, 324, 330, 433
  email messages in PFC, 38, 72, 114,
    115, 295–296
  Favorite Places (see Favorite Places)
  Instant Messages, 135
  Instant Messages IMs (Instant
    Messages)
    logging, 135
  message board posts, 191
  passwords, 32, 338, 441–442

temporarily (see expiring)
text with line breaks, 435
scams, how to avoid, 484–485
scheduling Automatic AOL sessions,
    338
schools conference rooms, 182
sci. newsgroups, 215
science conference rooms, 182
science newsgroups, 215
screen names, 22–31
  Automatic AOL and, 337–338
  in Buddy Lists, adding/removing,
    138–139
  canceled member accounts and, 349
  checking for new email, 116
  for children, 410, 413–414
  choosing, 20
  creating and managing, 25–27
  hyperlinking in email messages, 99
  mailing lists and, 205
  master screen name, 23
  multiple, 69, 150
  obtaining for spam, 69
  privacy and, 29–31
  registering with Instant Messenger,
    147
  restoring deleted, 302
  signing on as guest, 24
  switching between, 27
  updating, 28
  (see also preferences)
Screen Names (My AOL icon), 46
screen, frozen, 70
scrolling documents automatically, 435
Search All Newsgroups tool, 215
Search AOL Member Directory (People
    icon), 51
search engines, 279
searching (see finding)
security
  bothersome chat room members,
    157–159
  harassment, responding to, 73–74
  kids' safety tips, 409–410
  password solicitations (phishers), 33,
    109, 131, 484
  passwords (see passwords)
  PFC, passwords for, 301
  scams, how to avoid, 484–485

Temporary Internet Files, 451
Terminator utility, 381
Terms of Service (see TOS)
test messages (newsgroups), 222
text
    background color for, 89
    capitalization, 91
    color of, in email, 95
    fonts (see fonts)
    justifying in email messages, 103
    language preferences, 437
    newsgroup attachments for, 224
    rich text (see rich text)
    saving with line breaks, 435
    text files (see files)
text files (see files)
"That mail is no longer available...", 124
theater conference rooms, 183
    (see also entertainment)
Thesaurus (Edit menu), 40
third-party add-ons for AOL, 379–382
third-party web publishing tools, 368
"This phone has touch-tone service"
    option, 401
threads, newsgroup, 187, 214, 219
    posting and, 222
    starting new, 189
thumbnails of images, 87
Tile (Window menu), 40
time spent online, 354
tips for using AOL, 69–75
    avoiding scams, 484–485
    chain letters, 91
    chats, 150–151
    creating keyboard shortcuts, 313–314
    kids' safety tips, 409–410
    Meg, at AOL Insider, 68
    netiquette (see netiquette)
    signature files, 117
    too much mailing list mail, 199, 204
    troubleshooting modem, 405
toll-free access numbers, 393, 397–398
toolbar icons, 8–9
toolbar, AOL, 35–53
    icons on, 42–51, 55–56
    keyboard shortcuts vs., 53
    preferences for, 53–54, 445–446

Top News Story icon (Welcome
    screen), 6
top-level domain names, 474–479
TOS (Terms of Service), 480–485
    Internet and, 483
    mailing lists and, 199, 484
    newsgroups and, 231, 483
    reporting violations of, 159
touch-tone dialing, 401
TransAOL utility, 382
transcripts of auditorium chats, 173
transferring PFCs, 302–305
travel
    conference rooms, 183
    Travel Channel, 267–268
    web sites for, 282
Tray icon, 74
Trojan horses, 123–124, 485
troubleshooting
    broken mail flags, 107
    chain letters, 91
    frozen screen, 70
    interrupted downloads, 72, 325–326
    modem problems, 405
    too much mailing list mail, 199, 204
    (see also tips for using AOL)
two-way lists (see interactive mailing
    lists)
"Type Keyword or Web Address here"
    box, 52

U

unavailable email messages, 124
unblocking (see blocking)
Undo (Edit menu), 39
uninstalling AOL software, 463–464
"unknown host" error message, 98
unlimited pricing plan, 350
unmoderated vs. moderated, 212
unread email messages
    checking for, by screen name, 116
    expiring, 71, 439
    maximum allowable, 107
unread newsgroup articles, 219
"unrecoverable error" message, 125
unsending email messages, 125

About the Authors

Curt Degenhart is a writer and editor at Songline Studios' East Coast office in Cambridge, MA. Besides separating the wheat from the chaff of his AOL projects, he writes advice to the lovelorn at mix 'n match (*www.mixnmatch.com*), manages databases, hunts down the best of broadband, and daydreams. Curt's foggy about how his life evolved from concentrating in psychology at Vassar to writing about what's online, but he knows there must be a really good explanation.

Jen Muehlbauer is a writer and editor at Songline Studios, an affiliate of O'Reilly & Associates. When not knee-deep in AOL, she writes about geeky topics such as broadband web sites and happy couples who met on the Net. Before moving to Boston and settling into 9-to-5 life, Jen was a coffee-chugging English major at Wesleyan University.

Colophon

The animal featured on the cover of *AOL in a Nutshell* is a lion, a large, carnivorous cat inhabiting western India and Africa south of the Sahara. The most sociable of cats, lions live in prides consisting of one to four males and a collection of up to 30 females and cubs. However, the members of a pride are seldom all together at one time, instead moving about their territory as individuals or small groups. A pride's territory may be anywhere from 15 to 150 square miles, depending on the abundance of food, and is marked by scent and roaring.

Lions eat both fresh kill and carrion—dead animals or the kill of other animals. When they do kill, they show a preference for large prey such as zebra or wildebeest, which will feed the entire pride. Females do the majority of the hunting, frequently working cooperatively to encircle or bring down large game. During the hunt, lions are careful to move under cover of darkness or foliage, but tend to disregard the wind direction and thus frequently give themselves away.

Edie Freedman designed the cover of this book. The illustration is by Lorrie LeJeune. The cover layout was produced with Quark XPress 3.3 using the ITC Garamond font. Whenever possible, our books use RepKover™, a durable and flexible lay-flat binding. If the page count exceeds RepKover's limit, perfect binding is used.

The inside layout was designed by Nancy Priest and implemented in FrameMaker by Mike Sierra. The text and heading fonts are ITC Garamond Light and Garamond Book. The screenshots that appear in the book were created in Adobe Photoshop 4.0 by Robert Romano. This colophon was written by Michael Kalantarian.

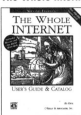

All the Facts. Not the Frills.

Director in a Nutshell

By Bruce A. Epstein
1st Edition September 1998 (est.)
450 pages (est.), ISBN 1-56592-382-0

Director in a Nutshell is the most concise and complete guide available for Director®. The reader gets both the nitty-gritty details and the bigger context in which to use the multiple facets of Director. It is a high-end handbook, at a low-end price—an indispensable desktop reference for every Director user.

Java Examples in a Nutshell

By David Flanagan
1st Edition September 1997
414 pages, ISBN 1-56592-371-5

From the author of Java in a Nutshell, this companion book is chock full of practical real-world programming examples to help novice Java programmers and experts alike explore what's possible with Java 1.1. If you learn best by example, this is the book for you.

Windows NT in a Nutshell

By Eric Pearce
1st Edition June 1997
364 pages, ISBN 1-56592-251-4

Anyone who installs Windows NT, creates a user, or adds a printer is an NT system administrator (whether they realize it or not). This book features a new tagged callout approach to documenting the 4.0 GUI as well as real-life examples of command usage and strategies for problem solving, with an emphasis on networking. Windows NT in a Nutshell will be as useful to the single-system home user as it will be to the administrator of a 1,000-node corporate network.

Java in a Nutshell, Second Edition

By David Flanagan
2nd Edition May 1997
628 pages, ISBN 1-56592-262-X

This second edition of the bestselling Java book describes all the classes in the Java 1.1 API, with the exception of the still-evolving Enterprise APIs. And it still has all the great features that have made this the Java book most often recommended on the Internet: practical real-world examples and compact reference information. It's the only quick reference you'll need.

Lingo in a Nutshell

By Bruce Epstein
1st Edition September 1998 (est.)
656 pages (est.), ISBN 1-56592-493-2

This companion book to Director in a Nutshell covers all aspects of Lingo, Director's powerful scripting language, and is the book for which both Director users and power Lingo programmers have been yearning. Detailed chapters describe messages, events, scripts, handlers, variables, lists, file I/O, Behaviors, child objects, Xtras, browser scripting, media control, performance optimization, and more.

Linux in a Nutshell

By Jessica P. Hekman &
the Staff of O'Reilly & Associates
1st Edition January 1997
438 pages, ISBN 1-56592-167-4

Linux in a Nutshell covers the core commands available on common Linux distributions. This isn't a scaled-down quick reference of common commands, but a complete reference containing all user, programming, administration, and networking commands. Also documents a wide range of GNU tools.

All the Facts. Not the Frills.

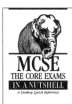

All the Facts. Not the Frills.

WebMaster in a Nutshell

*By Stephen Spainhour &
Valerie Quercia
1st Edition October 1996
374 pages, ISBN 1-56592-229-8*

Web content providers and administrators have many sources for information, both in print and online. WebMaster in a Nutshell puts it all together in one slim volume for easy desktop access. This quick reference covers HTML, CGI, JavaScript, Perl, HTTP, and server configuration.

Windows 95 in a Nutshell

*By Tim O'Reilly &
Troy Mott
1st Edition June 1998 (est.)
528 pages (est.), ISBN 1-56592-316-2*

This book systematically unveils the Windows 95 operating system and allows the user to modify any aspect of it, using the Command Line from the DOS or Run prompt, the Explorer, the Registry, the Control Panel, or any other tool or application that exists in Windows 95.

Web Programming

Frontier: The Definitive Guide

*By Matt Neuburg
1st Edition February 1998
618 pages, 1-56592-383-9*

This definitive guide is the first book devoted exclusively to teaching and documenting Userland Frontier, a powerful scripting environment for web site management and system level scripting. Packed with examples, advice, tricks, and tips, *Frontier: The Definitive Guide* teaches you Frontier from the ground up. Learn how to automate repetitive processes, control remote computers across a network, beef up your web site by generating hundreds of related web pages automatically, and more. Covers Frontier 4.2.3 for the Macintosh.

Web Programming

WebMaster in a Nutshell, Deluxe Edition

*By O'Reilly & Associates, Inc.
1st Edition September 1997
374 pages, includes CD-ROM & book
ISBN 1-56592-305-7*

The Deluxe Edition of *WebMaster in a Nutshell* is a complete library for web programmers. It features the Web Developer's Library, a CD-ROM containing the electronic text of five popular O'Reilly titles: *HTML: The Definitive Guide*, 2nd Edition; *JavaScript: The Definitive Guide*, 2nd Edition; *CGI Programming on the World Wide Web*; *Programming Perl*, 2nd Edition—the classic "camel book"; and WebMaster in a Nutshell, which is also included in a companion desktop edition.

HTML: The Definitive Guide, 2nd Edition

*By Chuck Musciano & Bill Kennedy
2nd Edition May 1997
552 pages, ISBN 1-56592-235-2*

This complete guide is chock full of examples, sample code, and practical, hands-on advice to help you create truly effective web pages and master advanced features. Learn how to insert images and other multimedia elements, create useful links and searchable documents, use Netscape extensions, design great forms, and lots more. The second edition covers the most up-to-date version of the HTML standard (HTML version 3.2), Netscape 4.0 and Internet Explorer 3.0, plus all the common extensions.

Dynamic HTML: The Definitive Reference

*By Danny Goodman
1st Edition July 1998 (est.)
1128 pages (est.), ISBN 1-56592-494-0*

Dynamic HTML: The Definitive Reference is an indispensable compendium for Web content developers. It contains complete reference material for all of the HTML tags, CSS style attributes, browser document objects, and JavaScript objects supported by the various standards and the latest versions of Netscape Navigator and Microsoft Internet Explorer.

Web Programming

CGI Programming on the World Wide Web

By Shishir Gundavaram
1st Edition March 1996
450 pages, ISBN 1-56592-168-2

This book offers a comprehensive explanation of CGI and related techniques for people who hold on to the dream of providing their own information servers on the Web. It starts at the beginning, explaining the value of CGI and how it works, then moves swiftly into the subtle details of programming.

JavaScript: The Definitive Guide, 3rd Edition

By David Flanagan & Dan Shafer
3rd Edition June 1998 (est.)
794 pages (est.), ISBN 1-56592-392-8

This third edition of the definitive reference to JavaScript covers the latest version of the language, JavaScript 1.2, as supported by Netscape Navigator 4.0. JavaScript, which is being standardized under the name ECMAScript, is a scripting language that can be embedded directly in HTML to give web pages programming-language capabilities.

Learning VBScript

By Paul Lomax
1st Edition July 1997
616 pages, includes CD-ROM
ISBN 1-56592-247-6

This definitive guide shows web developers how to take full advantage of client-side scripting with the VBScript language. In addition to basic language features, it covers the Internet Explorer object model and discusses techniques for client-side scripting, like adding ActiveX controls to a web page or validating data before sending it to the server. Includes CD-ROM with over 170 code samples.

Web Client Programming with Perl

By Clinton Wong
1st Edition March 1997
228 pages, ISBN 1-56592-214-X

Web Client Programming with Perl shows you how to extend scripting skills to the Web. This book teaches you the basics of how browsers communicate with servers and how to write your own customized web clients to automate common tasks. It is intended for those who are motivated to develop software that offers a more flexible and dynamic response than a standard web browser.

Information Architecture for the World Wide Web

By Louis Rosenfeld & Peter Morville
1st Edition January 1998
226 pages, ISBN 1-56592-282-4

Learn how to merge aesthetics and echanics to design web sites that "work." This book shows how to apply principles of architecture and library science to design cohesive web sites and intranets that are easy to use, manage, and expand. Covers building complex sites, hierarchy design and organization, and techniques to make your site easier to search. For webmasters, designers, and administrators.

How to stay in touch with O'Reilly

1. Visit Our Award-Winning Site

http://www.oreilly.com/

★ "Top 100 Sites on the Web" —*PC Magazine*
★ "Top 5% Web sites" —*Point Communications*
★ "3-Star site" —*The McKinley Group*

Our web site contains a library of comprehensive product information (including book excerpts and tables of contents), downloadable software, background articles, interviews with technology leaders, links to relevant sites, book cover art, and more. File us in your Bookmarks or Hotlist!

2. Join Our Email Mailing Lists

New Product Releases

To receive automatic email with brief descriptions of all new O'Reilly products as they are released, send email to:
listproc@online.oreilly.com
Put the following information in the first line of your message (*not* in the Subject field):
subscribe oreilly-news

O'Reilly Events

If you'd also like us to send information about trade show events, special promotions, and other O'Reilly events, send email to:
listproc@online.oreilly.com
Put the following information in the first line of your message (*not* in the Subject field):
subscribe oreilly-events

3. Get Examples from Our Books via FTP

There are two ways to access an archive of example files from our books:

Regular FTP

* ftp to:
  ftp.oreilly.com
  (login: anonymous
  password: your email address)
* Point your web browser to:
  ftp://ftp.oreilly.com/

FTPMAIL

* Send an email message to:
  ftpmail@online.oreilly.com
  (Write "help" in the message body)

4. Contact Us via Email

order@oreilly.com
To place a book or software order online. Good for North American and international customers.

subscriptions@oreilly.com
To place an order for any of our newsletters or periodicals.

books@oreilly.com
General questions about any of our books.

software@oreilly.com
For general questions and product information about our software. Check out O'Reilly Software Online at **http://software.oreilly.com/** for software and technical support information. Registered O'Reilly software users send your questions to:
website-support@oreilly.com

cs@oreilly.com
For answers to problems regarding your order or our products.

booktech@oreilly.com
For book content technical questions or corrections.

proposals@oreilly.com
To submit new book or software proposals to our editors and product managers.

international@oreilly.com
For information about our international distributors or translation queries. For a list of our distributors outside of North America check out:
http://www.oreilly.com/www/order/country.html

O'Reilly & Associates, Inc.
101 Morris Street, Sebastopol, CA 95472 USA
TEL   707-829-0515 or 800-998-9938
       (6am to 5pm PST)
FAX   707-829-0104

Titles from O'Reilly

WEB PROGRAMMING

Advanced Perl Programming
Apache: The Definitive Guide
Building Your Own
  Web Conferences
Building Your Own Website™
CGI Programming for the
  World Wide Web
Designing for the Web
Dynamic HTML:
  The Complete Reference
Frontier: The Definitive Guide
HTML: The Definitive Guide,
  2nd Edition
Information Architecture for the
  World Wide Web
JavaScript: The Definitive Guide,
  2nd Edition
Learning Perl, 2nd Edition
Learning Perl for Win32 Systems
Mastering Regular Expressions
Netscape IFC in a Nutshell
Perl5 Desktop Reference
Perl Cookbook
Perl in a Nutshell
Perl Resource Kit—UNIX Edition
Perl Resource Kit—Win32 Edition
Programming Perl, 2nd Edition
WebMaster in a Nutshell
WebMaster in a Nutshell,
  Deluxe Edition
Web Security & Commerce
Web Client Programming with Perl

GRAPHIC DESIGN

Director in a Nutshell
Photoshop in a Nutshell
QuarkXPress in a Nutshell

JAVA SERIES

Database Programming with
  JDBC and Java
Developing Java Beans
Exploring Java, 2nd Edition
Java AWT Reference
Java Cryptography
Java Distributed Computing
Java Examples in a Nutshell
Java Fundamental Classes
  Reference
Java in a Nutshell, 2nd Edition
Java in a Nutshell, Deluxe Edition
Java Language Reference,
  2nd Edition
Java Native Methods
Java Network Programming
Java Security
Java Threads
Java Virtual Machine

SONGLINE GUIDES

NetLaw   NetResearch
NetLearning NetSuccess
NetLessons   NetTravel

SYSTEM ADMINISTRATION

Building Internet Firewalls
Computer Crime:
  A Crimefighter's Handbook
Computer Security Basics
DNS and BIND, 2nd Edition
Essential System Administration,
  2nd Edition
Essential WindowsNT
  System Administration
Getting Connected:
  The Internet at 56K and Up
Linux Network
  Administrator's Guide
Managing Internet Information
  Services, 2nd Edition
Managing IP Networks
  with Cisco Routers
Managing Mailing Lists
Managing NFS and NIS
Managing the WinNT Registry
Managing Usenet
MCSE: The Core Exams in a Nutshell
MCSE: The Electives in a Nutshell
Networking Personal Computers
  with TCP/IP
Palm Pilot: The Ultimate Guide
Practical UNIX & Internet Security,
  2nd Edition
PGP: Pretty Good Privacy
Protecting Networks with SATAN
sendmail, 2nd Edition
sendmail Desktop Reference
System Performance Tuning
TCP/IP Network Administration,
  2nd Edition
termcap & terminfo
Using & Managing PPP
Using & Managing UUCP
Virtual Private Networks
Volume 8: X Window System
  Administrator's Guide
Web Security & Commerce
WindowsNT Backup & Restore
WindowsNT Desktop Reference
WindowsNT in a Nutshell
WindowsNT Server 4.0 for
  Netware Administrators
WindowsNT SNMP
WindowsNT User Administration

WEB REVIEW STUDIO SERIES

Designing Sound for the Web
Designing with Animation
Designing with JavaScript
Gif Animation Studio
Photoshop for the Web
Shockwave Studio
Web Navigation:
  Designing the User Experience

UNIX

Exploring Expect
Learning VBScript
Learning GNU Emacs, 2nd Edition
Learning the bash Shell,
  2nd Edition
Learning the Korn Shell
Learning the UNIX Operating
  System, 4th Edition
Learning the vi Editor, 5th Edition
Linux Device Drivers
Linux in a Nutshell
Linux Multimedia Guide
Running Linux, 2nd Edition
SCO UNIX in a Nutshell
sed & awk, 2nd Edition
Tcl/Tk Tools
UNIX in a Nutshell, Deluxe Edition
UNIX in a Nutshell,
  System V Edition
UNIX Power Tools, 2nd Edition
Using csh & tsch
What You Need To Know:
  When You Can't Find Your UNIX
  System Administrator
Writing GNU Emacs Extensions

WINDOWS

Access Database Design
  and Programming
Developing Windows
  Error Messages
Excel97 Annoyances
Inside the Windows 95
  File System
Inside the Windows 95 Registry
Office97 Annoyances
VB/VBA in a Nutshell:
  The Languages
Win32 Multithreaded
  Programming
Windows95 in a Nutshell
Windows97 Annoyances
Windows NT File System Internals
Windows NT in a Nutshell
Word97 Annoyances

USING THE INTERNET

AOL in a Nutshell
Bandits on the Information
  Superhighway
Internet in a Nutshell
Smileys
The Whole Internet
  for Windows95
The Whole Internet:
  The Next Generation
The Whole Internet
  User's Guide & Catalog

PROGRAMMING

Advanced Oracle PL/SQL
  Programming with Packages
Applying RCS and SCCS
BE Developer's Guide
BE Advanced Topics
C++: The Core Language
Checking C Programs with lint
Encyclopedia of Graphics File
  Formats, 2nd Edition
Guide to Writing DCE Applications
lex & yacc, 2nd Edition
Managing Projects with make
Mastering Oracle Power Objects
Oracle8 Design Tips
Oracle Built-in Packages
Oracle Design
Oracle Performance Tuning,
  2nd Edition
Oracle PL/SQL Programming,
  2nd Edition
Oracle Scripts
Porting UNIX Software
POSIX Programmer's Guide
POSIX.4: Programming
  for the Real World
Power Programming with RPC
Practical C Programming,
  3rd Edition
Practical C++ Programming
Programming Python
Programming with curses
Programming with GNU Software
Pthreads Programming
Software Portability with imake,
  2nd Edition
Understanding DCE
UNIX Systems Programming
  for SVR4

X PROGRAMMING

Vol. 0: X Protocol Reference
  Manual
Vol. 1: Xlib Programming Manual
Vol. 2: Xlib Reference Manual
Vol. 3M: X Window System User's
  Guide, Motif Edition
Vol. 4M: X Toolkit Intrinsics
  Programming Manual,
  Motif Edition
Vol. 5: X Toolkit Intrinsics
  Reference Manual
Vol. 6A: Motif Programming
  Manual
Vol. 6B: Motif Reference Manual
Vol. 8 : X Window System
  Administrator's Guide

SOFTWARE

Building Your Own WebSite™
Building Your Own Web Conference
WebBoard™ 3.0
WebSite Professional™ 2.0
PolyForm™

O'REILLY™

TO ORDER: **800-998-9938** • **order@oreilly.com** • **http://www.oreilly.com/**

OUR PRODUCTS ARE AVAILABLE AT A BOOKSTORE OR SOFTWARE STORE NEAR YOU.

FOR INFORMATION: **800-998-9938** • **707-829-0515** • **info@oreilly.com**

International Distributors

UK, EUROPE, MIDDLE EAST AND NORTHERN AFRICA (except
France, Germany, Switzerland, & Austria)

INQUIRIES
International Thomson Publishing Europe
Berkshire House
168-173 High Holborn
London WC1V 7AA, UK
Telephone: 44-171-497-1422
Fax: 44-171-497-1426
Email: itpint@itps.co.uk

ORDERS
International Thomson Publishing Services, Ltd.
Cheriton House, North Way
Andover, Hampshire SP10 5BE,
United Kingdom
Telephone: 44-264-342-832 (UK)
Telephone: 44-264-342-806 (outside UK)
Fax: 44-264-364418 (UK)
Fax: 44-264-342761 (outside UK)
UK & Eire orders: itpuk@itps.co.uk
International orders: itpint@itps.co.uk

FRANCE
Editions Eyrolles
61 bd Saint-Germain
75240 Paris Cedex 05
France
Fax: 33-01-44-41-11-44

FRENCH LANGUAGE BOOKS
All countries except Canada
Telephone: 33-01-44-41-46-16
Email: geodif@eyrolles.com

ENGLISH LANGUAGE BOOKS
Telephone: 33-01-44-41-11-87
Email: distribution@eyrolles.com

GERMANY, SWITZERLAND, AND AUSTRIA

INQUIRIES
O'Reilly Verlag
Balthasarstr. 81
D-50670 Köln
Germany
Telephone: 49-221-97-31-60-0
Fax: 49-221-97-31-60-8
Email: anfragen@oreilly.de

ORDERS
International Thomson Publishing
Königswinterer Straße 418
53227 Bonn, Germany
Telephone: 49-228-97024 0
Fax: 49-228-441342
Email: order@oreilly.de

JAPAN
O'Reilly Japan, Inc.
Kiyoshige Building 2F
12-Banchi, Sanei-cho
Shinjuku-ku
Tokyo 160 Japan
Tel: 81-3-3356-5227
Fax: 81-3-3356-5261
Email: kenji@oreilly.com

INDIA
Computer Bookshop (India) PVT. Ltd.
190 Dr. D.N. Road, Fort
Bombay 400 001 India
Tel: 91-22-207-0989
Fax: 91-22-262-3551
Email: cbsbom@giasbm01.vsnl.net.in

HONG KONG
City Discount Subscription Service Ltd.
Unit D, 3rd Floor, Yan's Tower
27 Wong Chuk Hang Road
Aberdeen, Hong Kong
Telephone: 852-2580-3539
Fax: 852-2580-6463
Email: citydis@ppn.com.hk

KOREA
Hanbit Publishing, Inc.
Sonyoung Bldg. 202
Yeksam-dong 736-36
Kangnam-ku
Seoul, Korea
Telephone: 822-554-9610
Fax: 822-556-0363
Email: hant93@chollian.dacom.co.kr

TAIWAN
ImageArt Publishing, Inc.
4/fl. No. 65 Shinyi Road Sec. 4
Taipei, Taiwan, R.O.C.
Telephone: 886-2708-5770
Fax: 886-2705-6690
Email: marie@ms1.hinet.net

SINGAPORE, MALAYSIA, AND THAILAND
Longman Singapore
25 First Lok Yan Road
Singapore 2262
Telephone: 65-268-2666
Fax: 65-268-7023
Email: daniel@longman.com.sg

PHILIPPINES
Mutual Books, Inc.
429-D Shaw Boulevard
Mandaluyong City, Metro
Manila, Philippines
Telephone: 632-725-7538
Fax: 632-721-3056
Email: mbikikog@mnl.sequel.net

CHINA
Ron's DataCom Co., Ltd.
79 Dongwu Avenue
Dongxihu District
Wuhan 430040
China
Telephone: 86-27-83892568
Fax: 86-27-83222108
Email: hongfeng@public.wh.hb.cn

AUSTRALIA
WoodsLane Pty. Ltd.
7/5 Vuko Place, Warriewood NSW 2102
P.O. Box 935,
Mona Vale NSW 2103
Australia
Telephone: 61-2-9970-5111
Fax: 61-2-9970-5002
Email: info@woodslane.com.au

ALL OTHER ASIA COUNTRIES
O'Reilly & Associates, Inc.
101 Morris Street
Sebastopol, CA 95472 USA
Telephone: 707-829-0515
Fax: 707-829-0104
Email: order@oreilly.com

THE AMERICAS
McGraw-Hill Interamericana Editores,
S.A. de C.V.
Cedro No. 512
Col. Atlampa 06450
Mexico, D.F.
Telephone: 52-5-541-3155
Fax: 52-5-541-4913
Email: mcgraw-hill@infosel.net.mx

SOUTHERN AFRICA
International Thomson Publishing Southern Africa
Building 18, Constantia Park
138 Sixteenth Road
P.O. Box 2459
Halfway House, 1685 South Africa
Tel: 27-11-805-4819
Fax: 27-11-805-3648

O'REILLY™

TO ORDER: **800-998-9938** • **order@oreilly.com** • **http://www.oreilly.com/**
OUR PRODUCTS ARE AVAILABLE AT A BOOKSTORE OR SOFTWARE STORE NEAR YOU.
FOR INFORMATION: **800-998-9938** • **707-829-0515** • **info@oreilly.com**